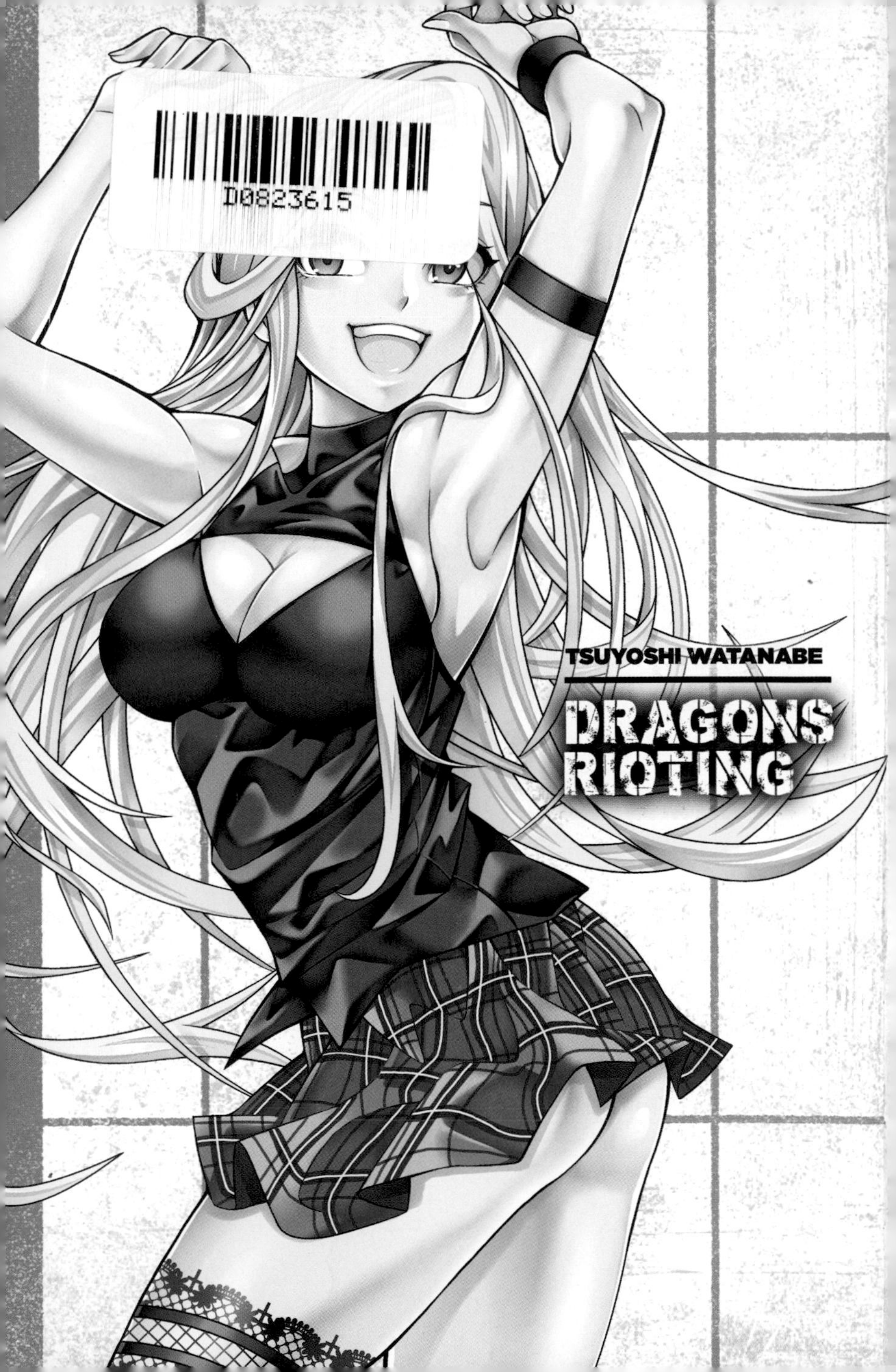
TSUYOSHI WATANABE
DRAGONS
RIOTING

男獄煉

⟨NAN-GOKUREN HIGH SCHOOL.⟩

⟨NUMBER ONE⟩ STRONGEST SCHOOL IN ⟨JAPAN...⟩

ZA (ZSH)

KIRA (TWINKLE)

MUCHI (SNUG)

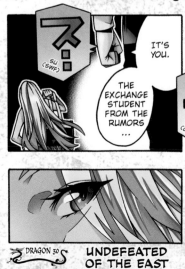

ス... SU (SWF)

IT'S YOU.

THE EXCHANGE STUDENT FROM THE RUMORS...

二 NI (GRIND)

KIRA KIRA KIRA KIRA KIRA

DRAGON 30

UNDEFEATED OF THE EAST

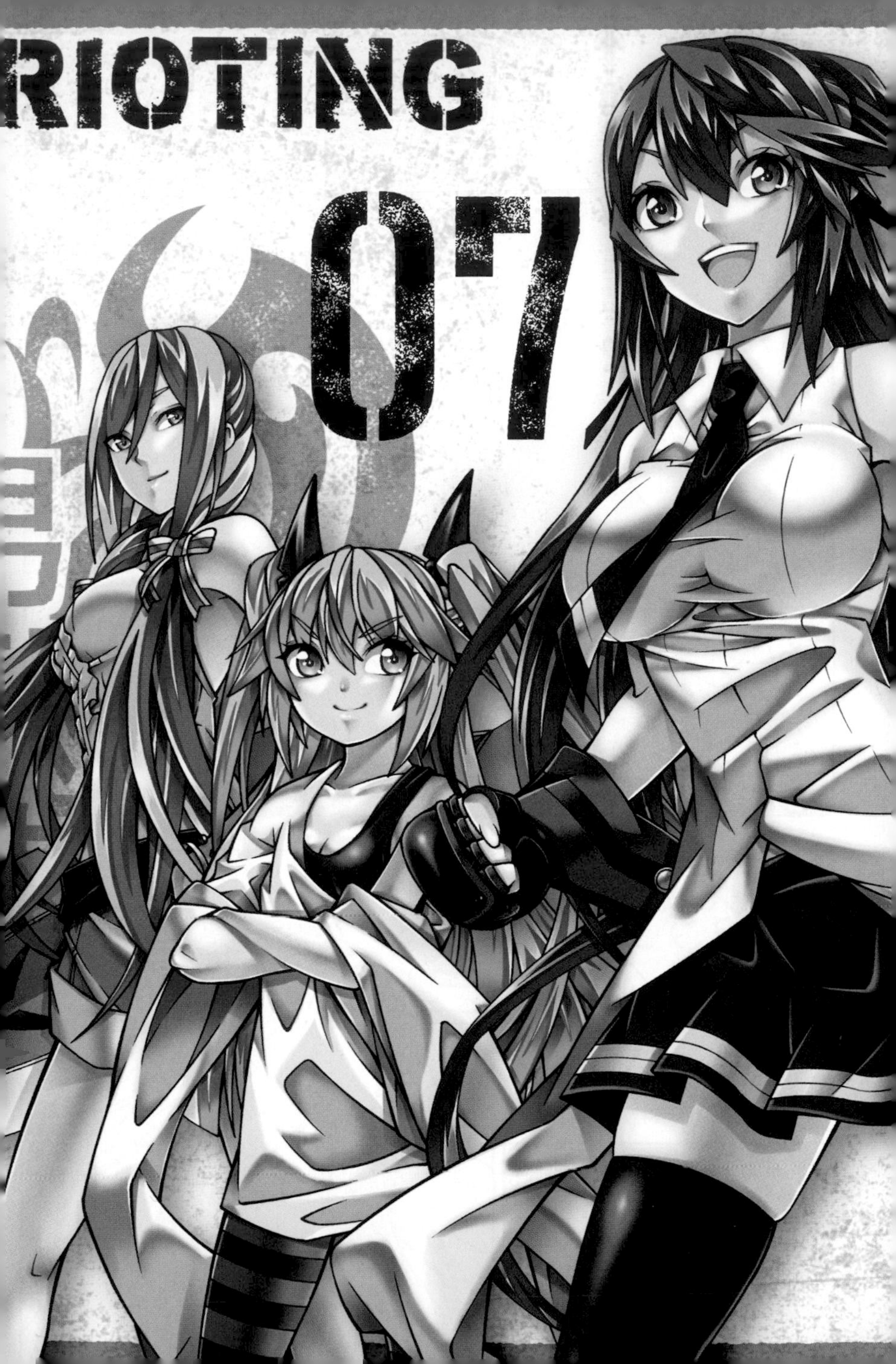
RIOTING
07

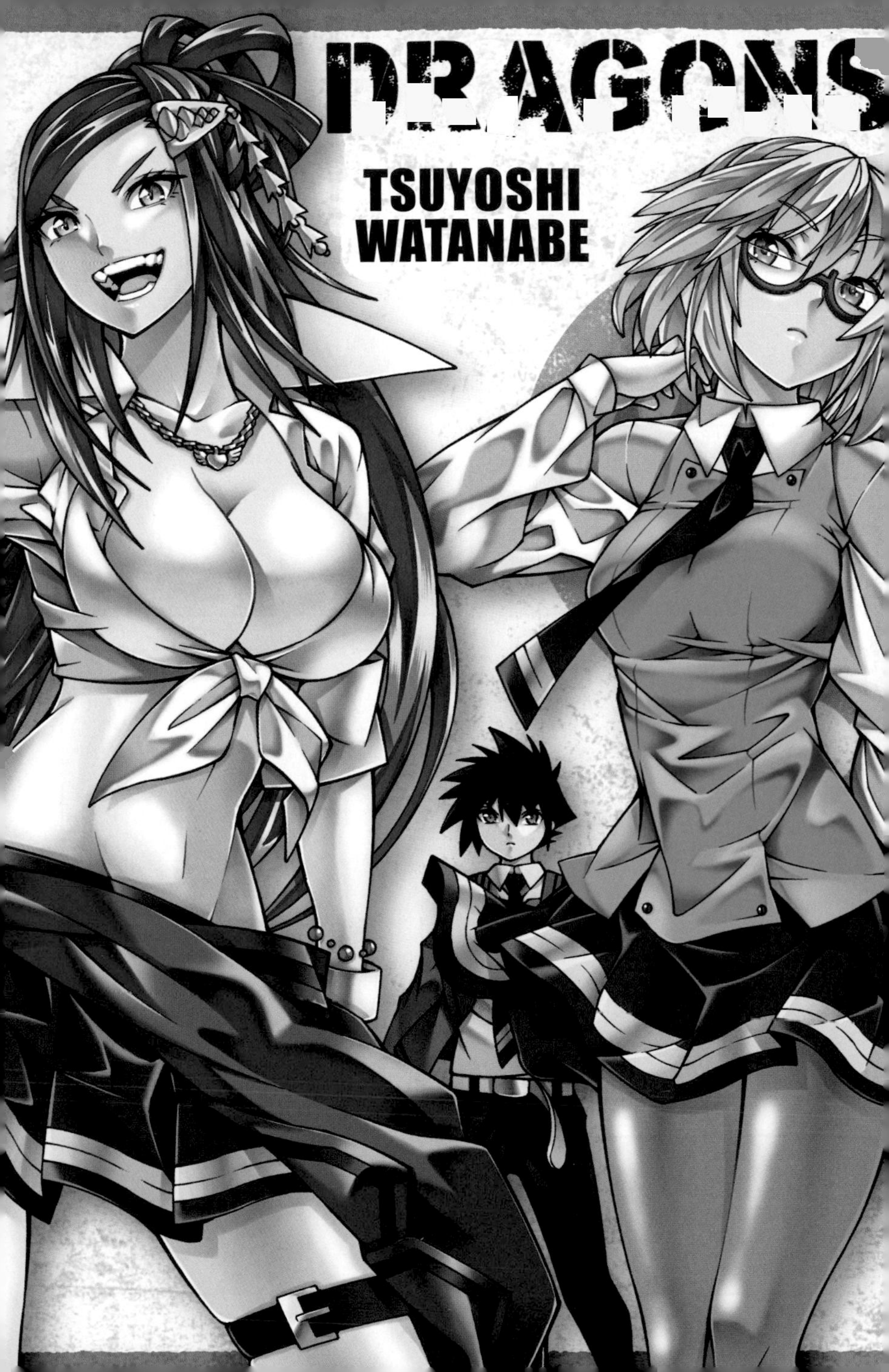
DRAGONS
TSUYOSHI
WATANABE

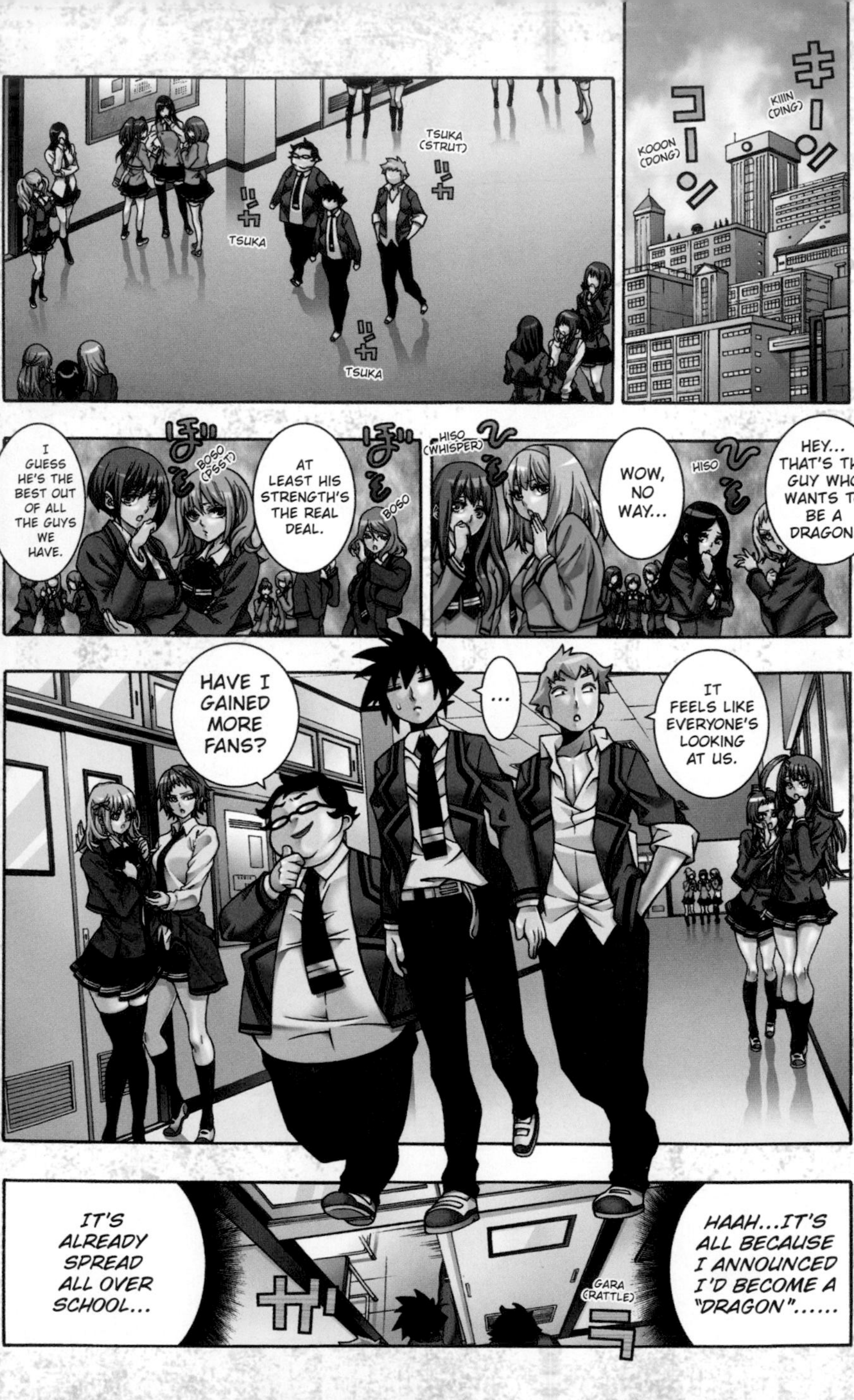
KIIIN (DING)
KOOON (DONG)
TSUKA (STRUT)
TSUKA
TSUKA
HEY... THAT'S THE GUY WHO WANTS TO BE A DRAGON.
HISO
WOW, NO WAY...
HISO (WHISPER)
AT LEAST HIS STRENGTH'S THE REAL DEAL.
BOGO
BOGO (PSST)
I GUESS HE'S THE BEST OUT OF ALL THE GUYS WE HAVE.
IT FEELS LIKE EVERYONE'S LOOKING AT US.
...
HAVE I GAINED MORE FANS?
HAAH...IT'S ALL BECAUSE I ANNOUNCED I'D BECOME A "DRAGON"......
GARA (RATTLE)
IT'S ALREADY SPREAD ALL OVER SCHOOL...

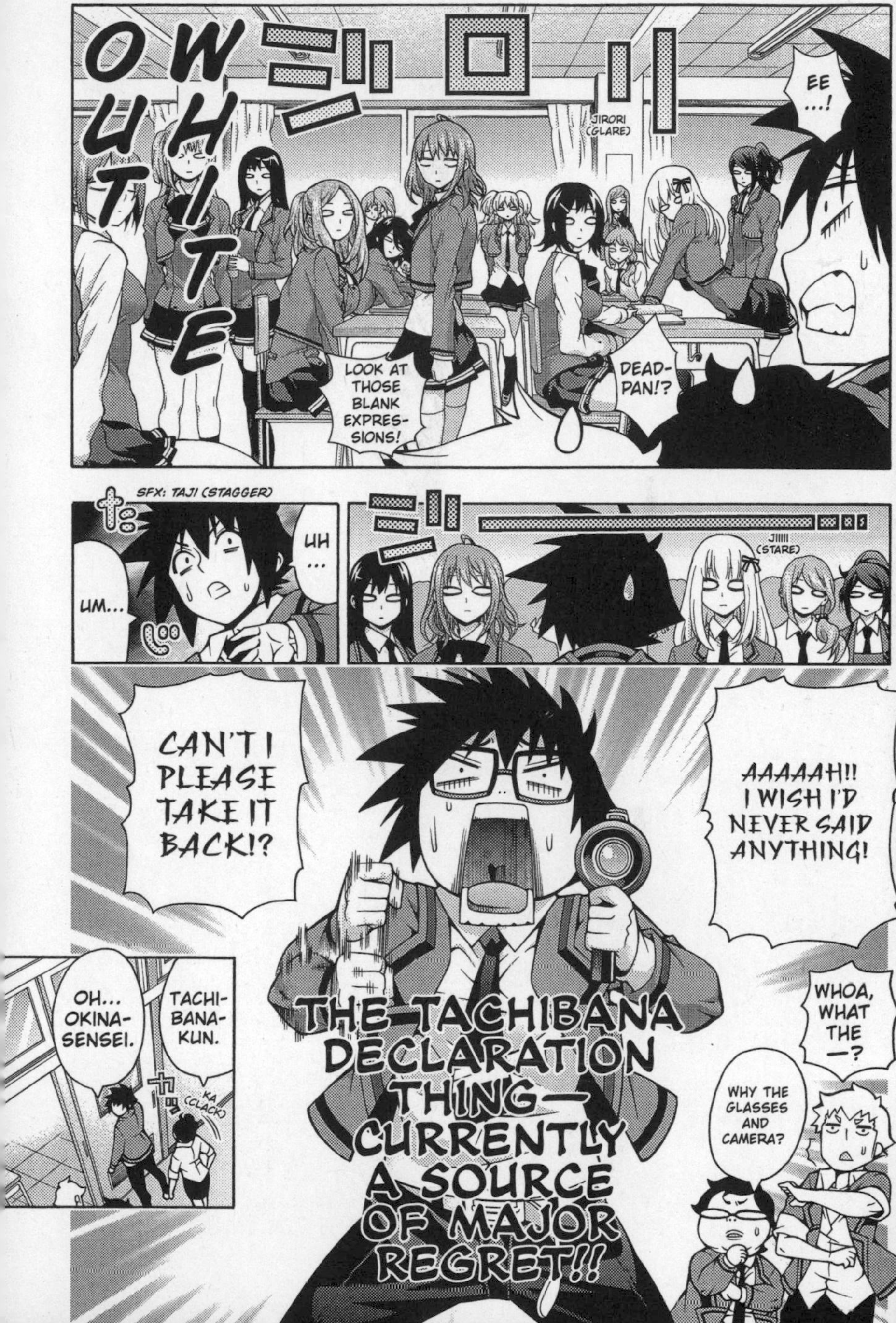
EE ...!
JIRORI (GLARE)
DEAD-PAN!?
LOOK AT THOSE BLANK EXPRESSIONS!
WHITE OUT
JIIII (STARE)
SFX: TAJI (STAGGER)
UH ...
UM...
AAAAAH!! I WISH I'D NEVER SAID ANYTHING!
CAN'T I PLEASE TAKE IT BACK!?
WHOA, WHAT THE—?
WHY THE GLASSES AND CAMERA?
THE TACHIBANA DECLARATION THING—CURRENTLY A SOURCE OF MAJOR REGRET!!
TACHI-BANA-KUN.
OH... OKINA-SENSEI.
KA (CLACK)

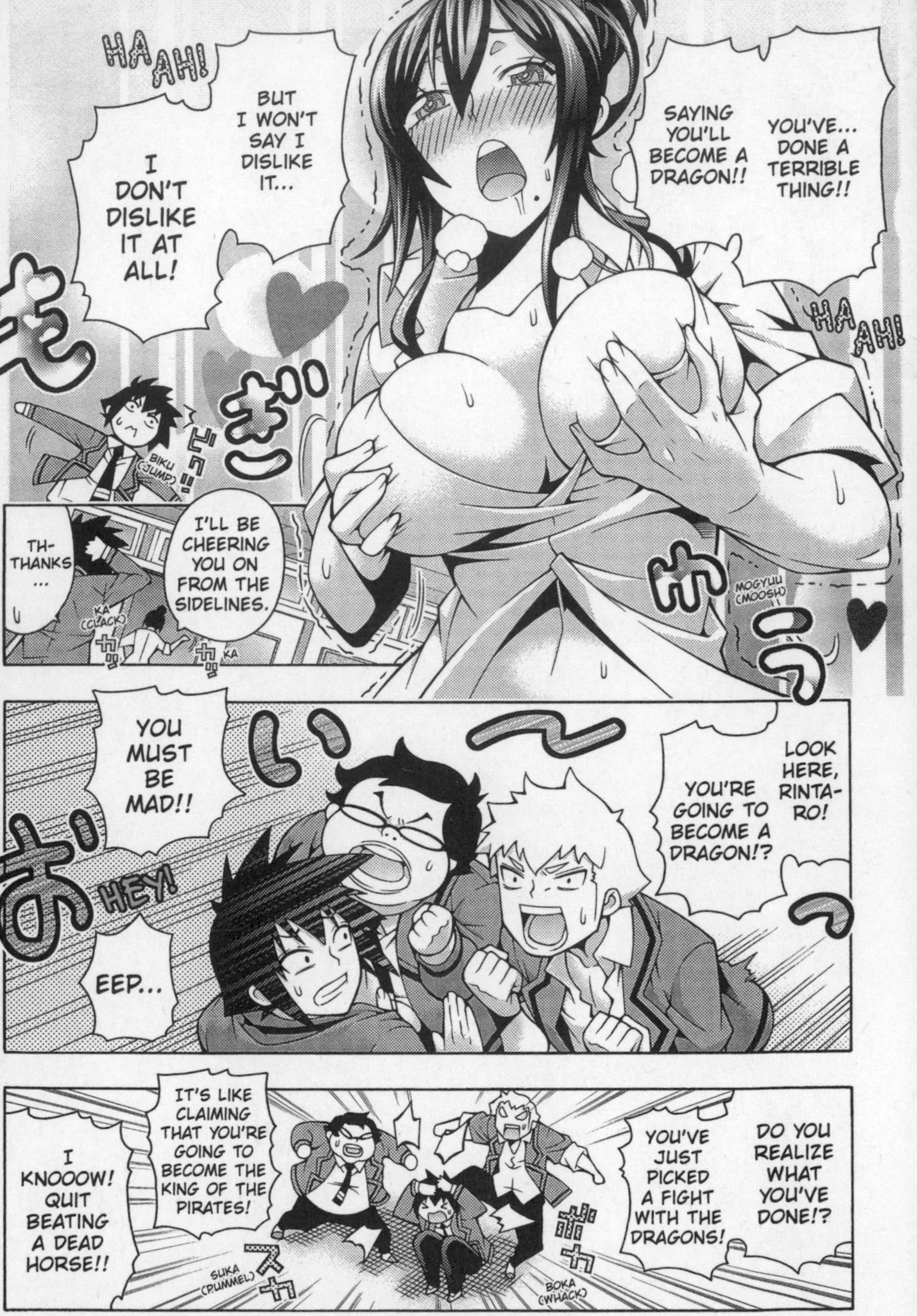

YOU'VE... DONE A TERRIBLE THING!!
SAYING YOU'LL BECOME A DRAGON!!
HAAH!
BUT I WON'T SAY I DISLIKE IT...
I DON'T DISLIKE IT AT ALL!
HAAH!
MOGYUU (MOOSH)
BIKU (JUMP)
I'LL BE CHEERING YOU ON FROM THE SIDELINES.
TH-THANKS...
KA (CLACK)
KA
LOOK HERE, RINTARO!
YOU'RE GOING TO BECOME A DRAGON!?
YOU MUST BE MAD!!
HEY!
EEP...
DO YOU REALIZE WHAT YOU'VE DONE!?
YOU'VE JUST PICKED A FIGHT WITH THE DRAGONS!
BOKA (WHACK)
IT'S LIKE CLAIMING THAT YOU'RE GOING TO BECOME THE KING OF THE PIRATES!
I KNOOOW! QUIT BEATING A DEAD HORSE!!
SUKA (PUMMEL)

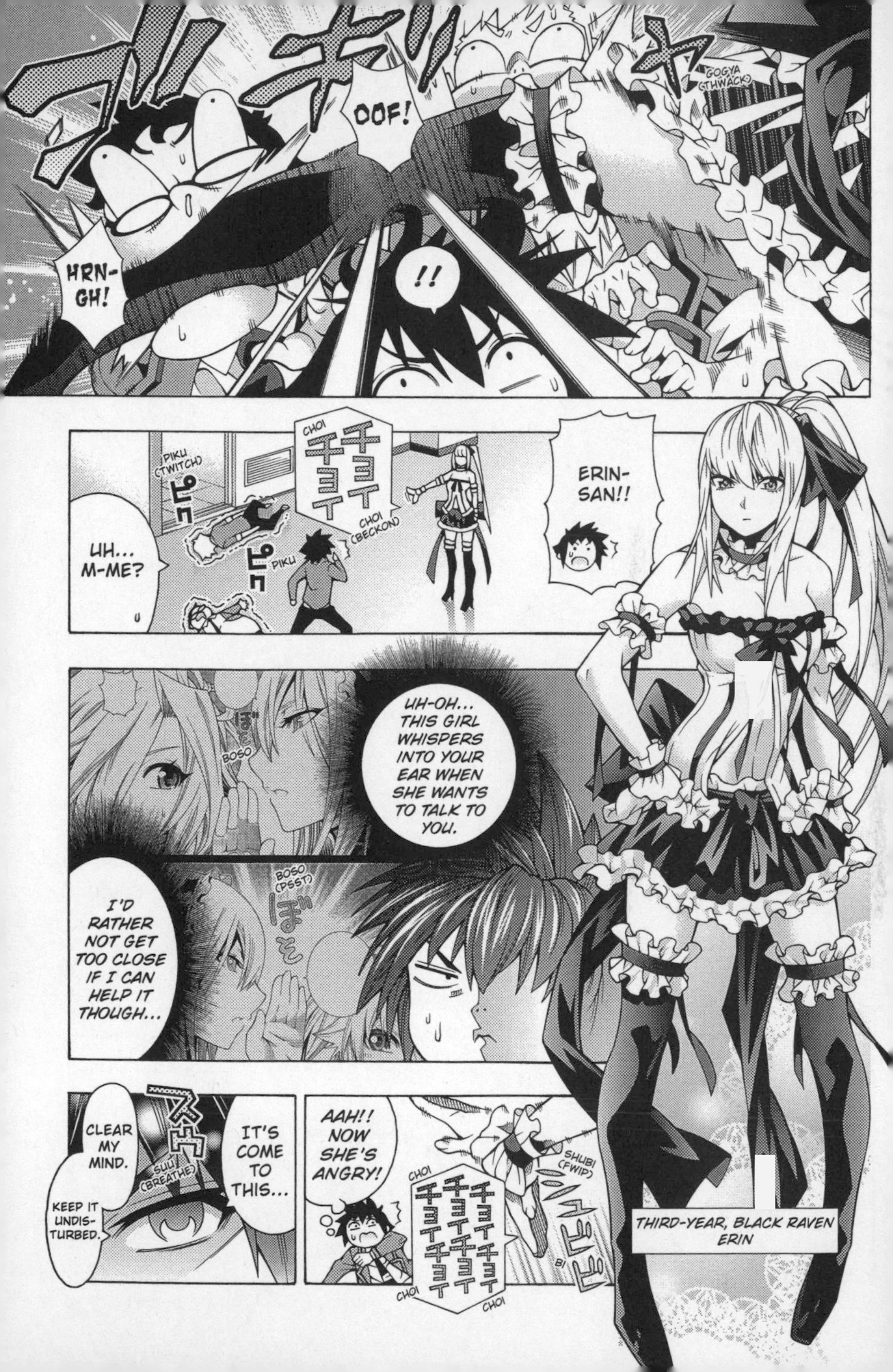
GOGYA (THWACK)
OOF!
!!
HRN-GH!
THIRD-YEAR, BLACK RAVEN ERIN
ERIN-SAN!!
CHOI
CHOI (BECKON)
PIKU (TWITCH)
PIKU
UH... M-ME?
UH-OH... THIS GIRL WHISPERS INTO YOUR EAR WHEN SHE WANTS TO TALK TO YOU.
BOSO
BOSO (PSST)
I'D RATHER NOT GET TOO CLOSE IF I CAN HELP IT THOUGH...
SHUBI (FWIP)
BI
CHOI
CHOI
CHOI
AAH!! NOW SHE'S ANGRY!
IT'S COME TO THIS...
CLEAR MY MIND.
SUU (BREATHE)
KEEP IT UNDISTURBED.

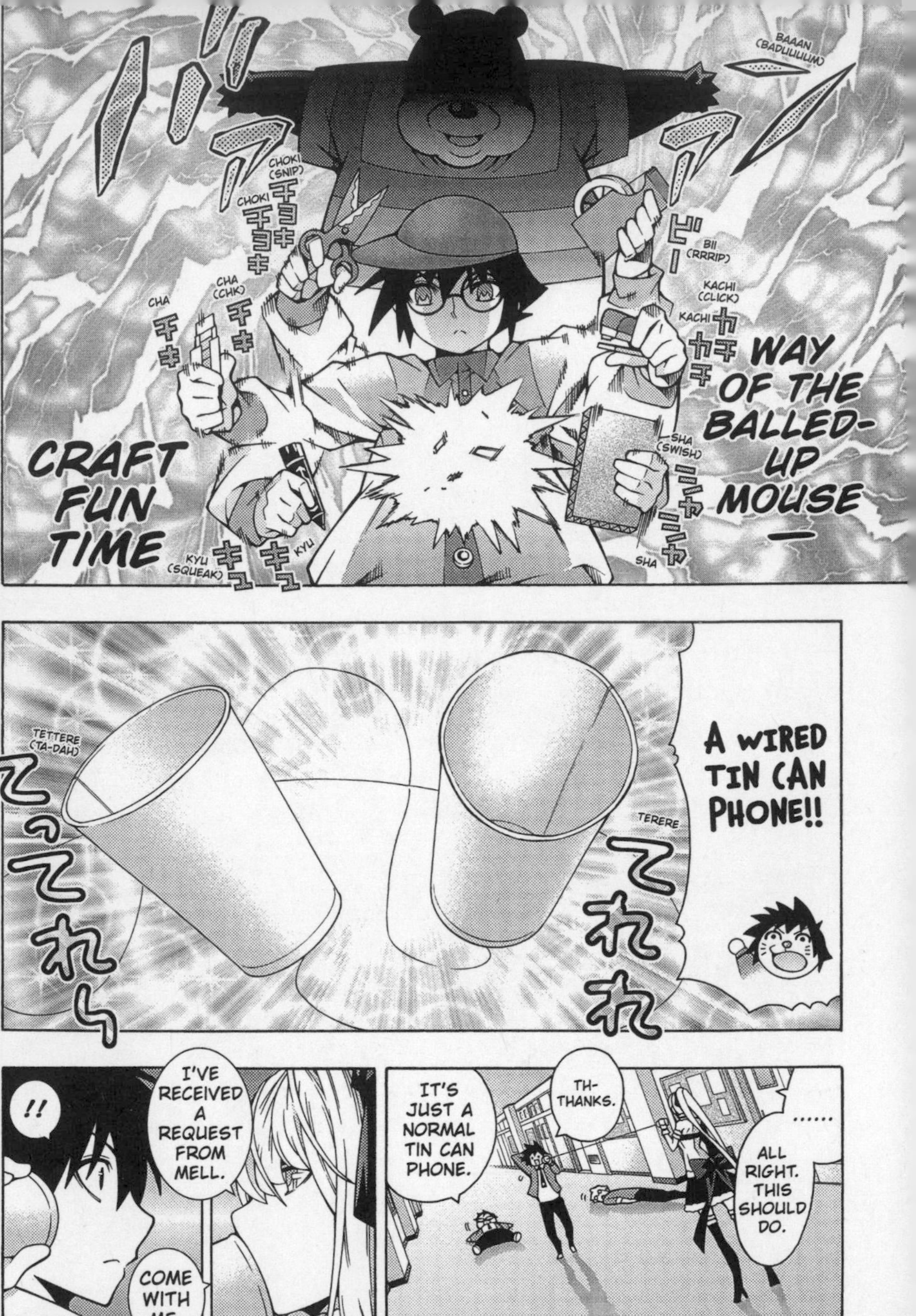
BAAAN (BADUUUUM)
BII (RRRIP)
KACHI (CLICK) KACHI
WAY OF THE BALLED-UP MOUSE —
SHA (SWISH) SHA
CHOKI (SNIP) CHOKI
CHA (CHK) CHA
CRAFT FUN TIME
KYU (SQUEAK) KYU
A WIRED TIN CAN PHONE!!
TERERE
TETTERE (TA-DAH)
......
ALL RIGHT. THIS SHOULD DO.
TH-THANKS.
IT'S JUST A NORMAL TIN CAN PHONE.
I'VE RECEIVED A REQUEST FROM MELL.
!!
COME WITH ME.

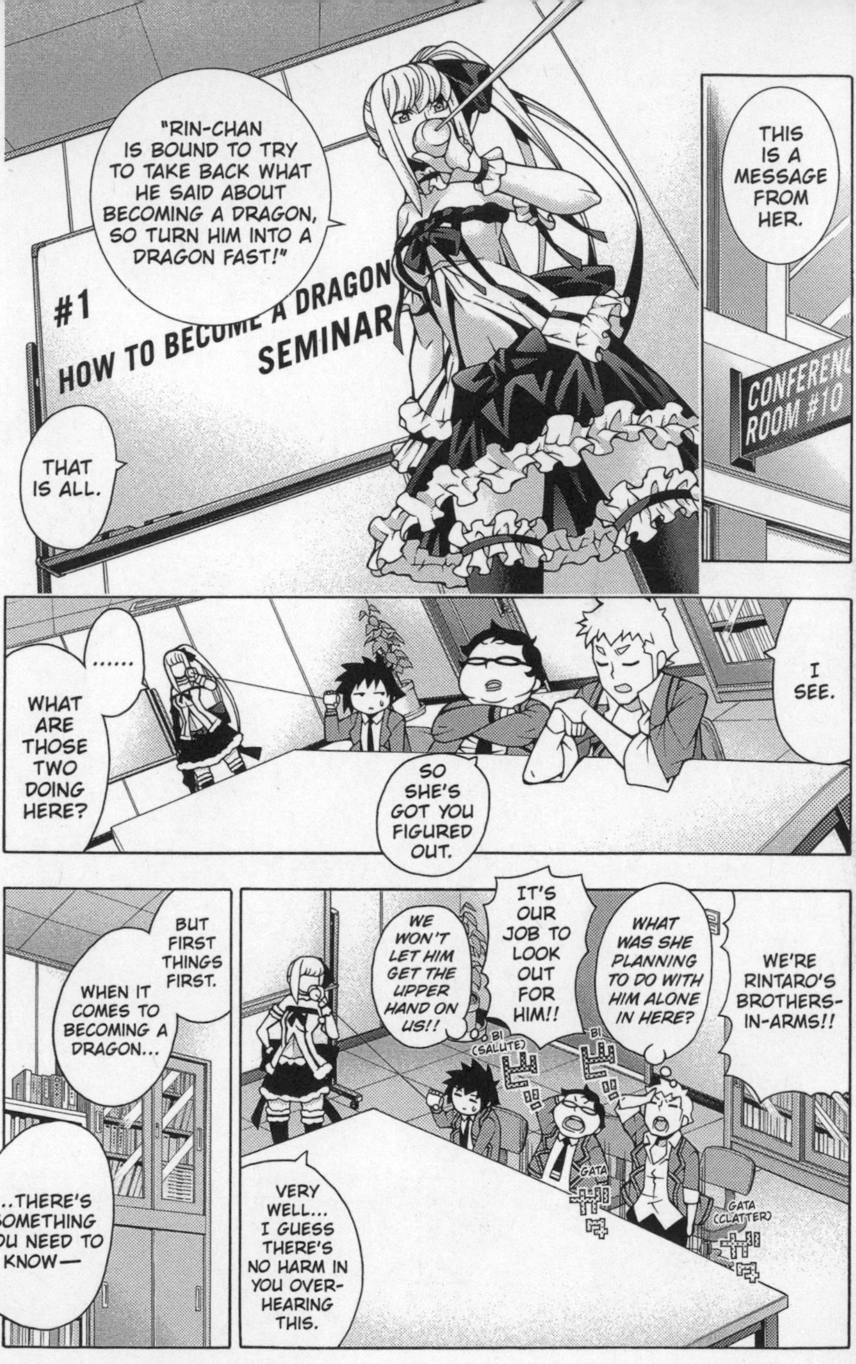
THIS IS A MESSAGE FROM HER.
CONFERENCE ROOM #10
"RIN-CHAN IS BOUND TO TRY TO TAKE BACK WHAT HE SAID ABOUT BECOMING A DRAGON, SO TURN HIM INTO A DRAGON FAST!"
#1
HOW TO BECOME A DRAGON SEMINAR
THAT IS ALL.
I SEE.
SO SHE'S GOT YOU FIGURED OUT.
......
WHAT ARE THOSE TWO DOING HERE?
WE'RE RINTARO'S BROTHERS-IN-ARMS!!
WHAT WAS SHE PLANNING TO DO WITH HIM ALONE IN HERE?
IT'S OUR JOB TO LOOK OUT FOR HIM!!
WE WON'T LET HIM GET THE UPPER HAND ON US!!
BI (SALUTE)
BI
GATA
GATA (CLATTER)
VERY WELL... I GUESS THERE'S NO HARM IN YOU OVER-HEARING THIS.
BUT FIRST THINGS FIRST.
WHEN IT COMES TO BECOMING A DRAGON...
...THERE'S SOMETHING YOU NEED TO KNOW—

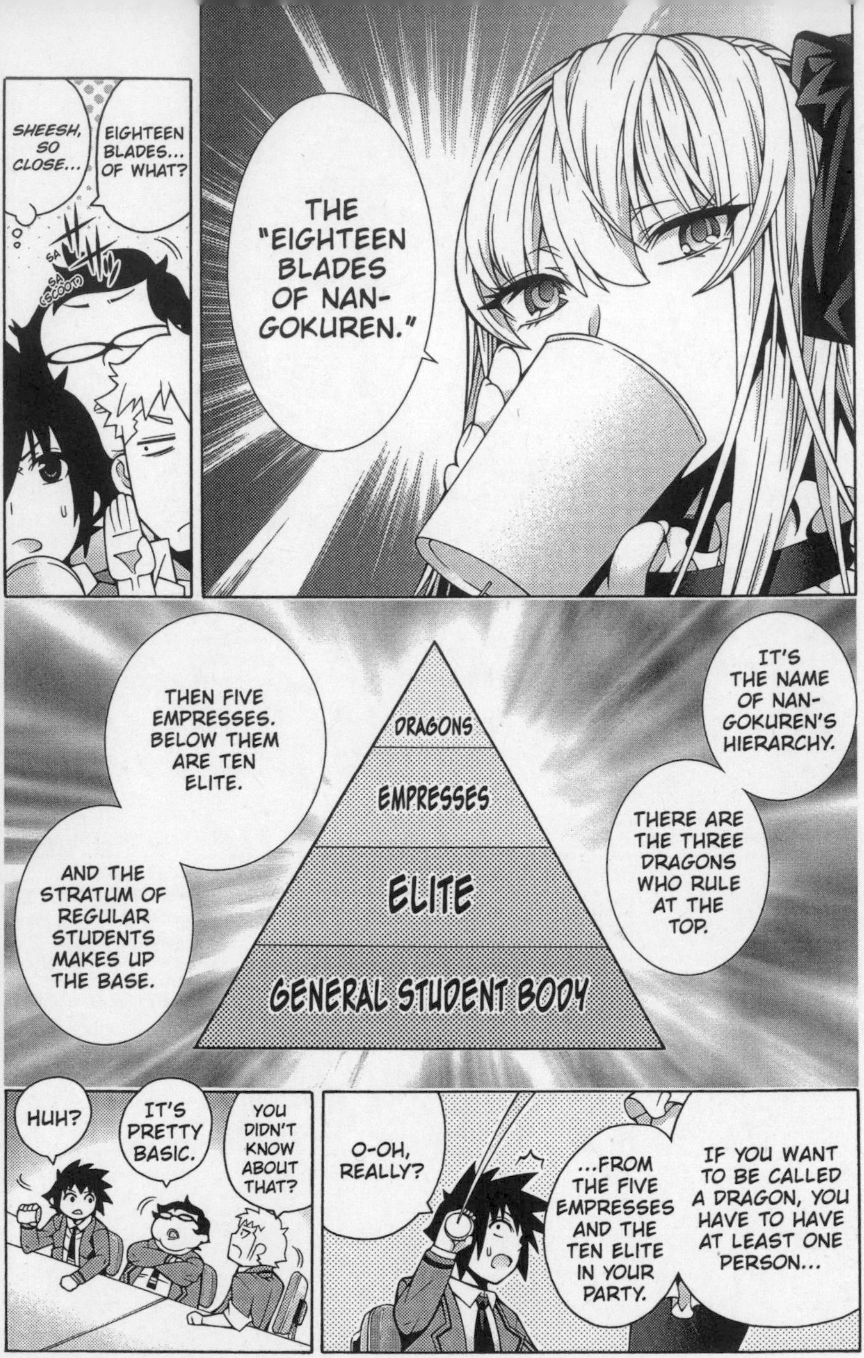
THE "EIGHTEEN BLADES OF NAN-GOKUREN."
EIGHTEEN BLADES... OF WHAT?
SHEESH, SO CLOSE...
SA SA (SCOOT)
IT'S THE NAME OF NAN-GOKUREN'S HIERARCHY.
THERE ARE THE THREE DRAGONS WHO RULE AT THE TOP.
DRAGONS
EMPRESSES
ELITE
GENERAL STUDENT BODY
THEN FIVE EMPRESSES. BELOW THEM ARE TEN ELITE.
AND THE STRATUM OF REGULAR STUDENTS MAKES UP THE BASE.
IF YOU WANT TO BE CALLED A DRAGON, YOU HAVE TO HAVE AT LEAST ONE PERSON...
...FROM THE FIVE EMPRESSES AND THE TEN ELITE IN YOUR PARTY.
O-OH, REALLY?
YOU DIDN'T KNOW ABOUT THAT?
IT'S PRETTY BASIC.
HUH?

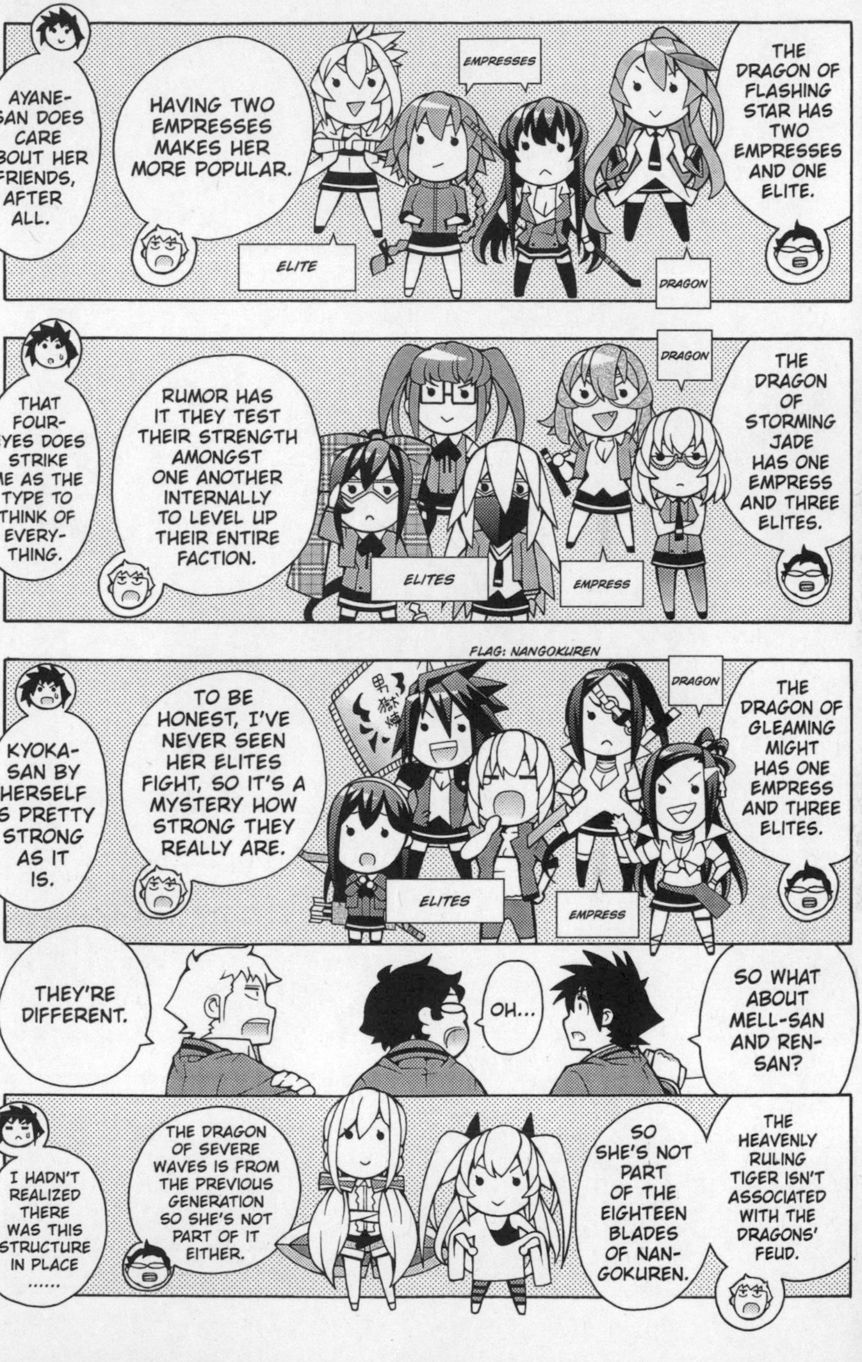
THE DRAGON OF FLASHING STAR HAS TWO EMPRESSES AND ONE ELITE.
EMPRESSES
DRAGON
HAVING TWO EMPRESSES MAKES HER MORE POPULAR.
ELITE
AYANE-SAN DOES CARE ABOUT HER FRIENDS, AFTER ALL.
THE DRAGON OF STORMING JADE HAS ONE EMPRESS AND THREE ELITES.
DRAGON
EMPRESS
RUMOR HAS IT THEY TEST THEIR STRENGTH AMONGST ONE ANOTHER INTERNALLY TO LEVEL UP THEIR ENTIRE FACTION.
ELITES
THAT FOUR-EYES DOES STRIKE ME AS THE TYPE TO THINK OF EVERY-THING.
FLAG: NANGOKUREN
THE DRAGON OF GLEAMING MIGHT HAS ONE EMPRESS AND THREE ELITES.
DRAGON
EMPRESS
TO BE HONEST, I'VE NEVER SEEN HER ELITES FIGHT, SO IT'S A MYSTERY HOW STRONG THEY REALLY ARE.
ELITES
KYOKA-SAN BY HERSELF IS PRETTY STRONG AS IT IS.
SO WHAT ABOUT MELL-SAN AND REN-SAN?
OH...
THEY'RE DIFFERENT.
THE HEAVENLY RULING TIGER ISN'T ASSOCIATED WITH THE DRAGONS' FEUD.
SO SHE'S NOT PART OF THE EIGHTEEN BLADES OF NAN-GOKUREN.
THE DRAGON OF SEVERE WAVES IS FROM THE PREVIOUS GENERATION SO SHE'S NOT PART OF IT EITHER.
I HADN'T REALIZED THERE WAS THIS STRUCTURE IN PLACE ......

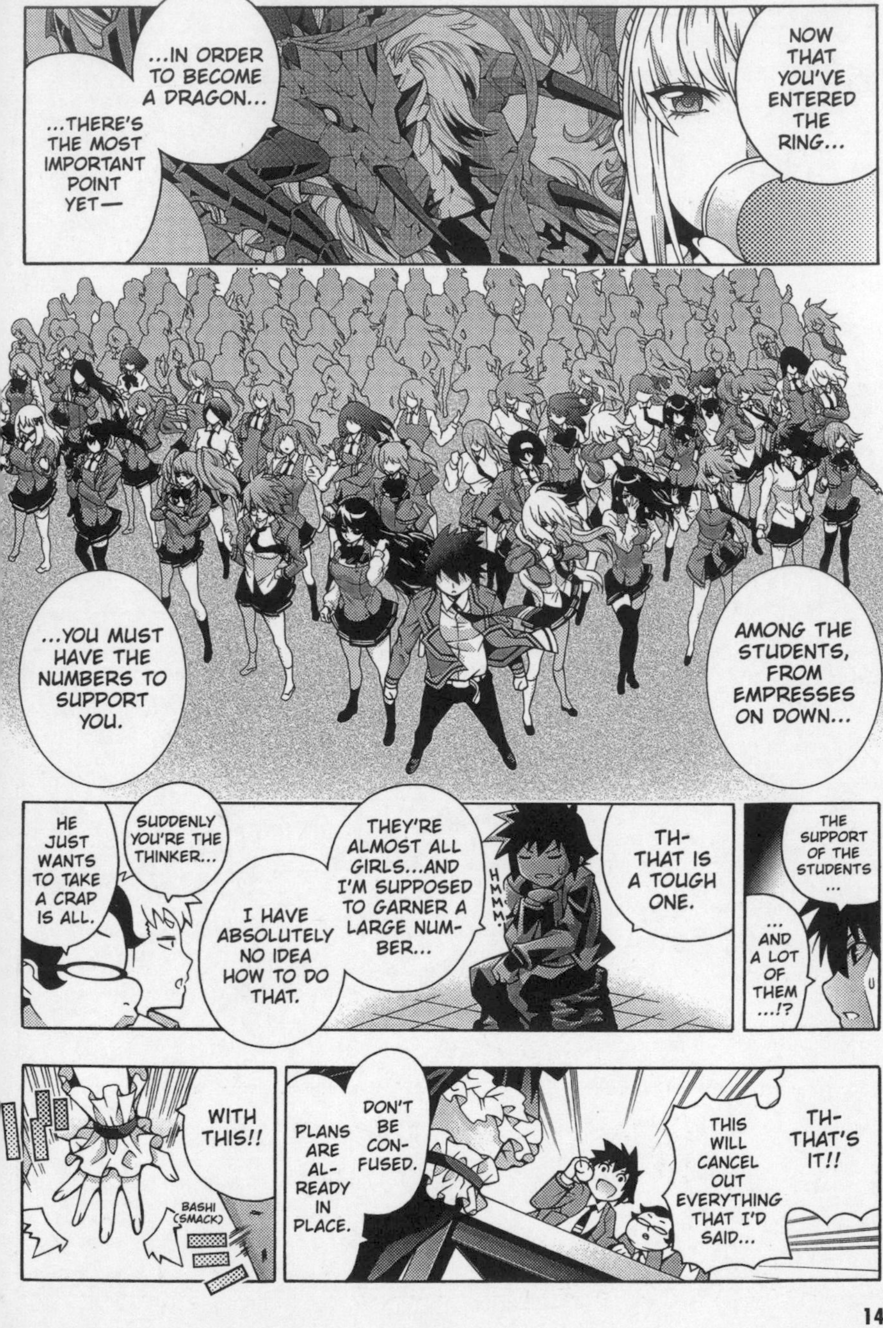
NOW THAT YOU'VE ENTERED THE RING...
...IN ORDER TO BECOME A DRAGON...
...THERE'S THE MOST IMPORTANT POINT YET—
AMONG THE STUDENTS, FROM EMPRESSES ON DOWN...
...YOU MUST HAVE THE NUMBERS TO SUPPORT YOU.
THE SUPPORT OF THE STUDENTS...
...AND A LOT OF THEM...!?
TH- THAT IS A TOUGH ONE.
HMMM...
THEY'RE ALMOST ALL GIRLS...AND I'M SUPPOSED TO GARNER A LARGE NUMBER...
I HAVE ABSOLUTELY NO IDEA HOW TO DO THAT.
SUDDENLY YOU'RE THE THINKER...
HE JUST WANTS TO TAKE A CRAP IS ALL.
TH- THAT'S IT!!
THIS WILL CANCEL OUT EVERYTHING THAT I'D SAID...
DON'T BE CONFUSED.
PLANS ARE ALREADY IN PLACE.
WITH THIS!!
BASHI (SMACK)

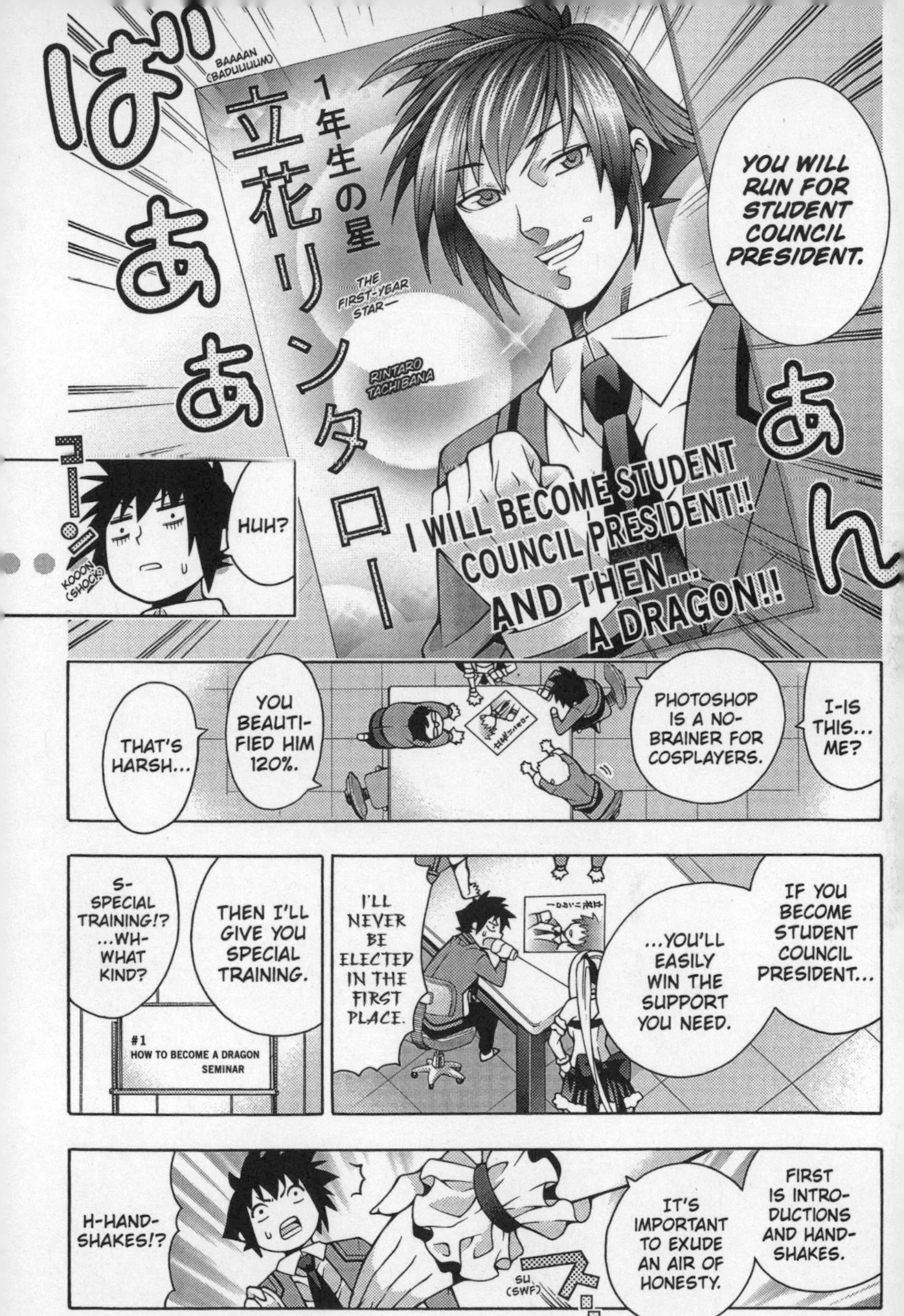
ばあああん
BAAAAN (BADUUUUUM)
1年生の星 立花リンタロー
THE FIRST-YEAR STAR—
RINTARO TACHIBANA
YOU WILL RUN FOR STUDENT COUNCIL PRESIDENT.
I WILL BECOME STUDENT COUNCIL PRESIDENT!! AND THEN... A DRAGON!!
KOOON (SHOCK)
HUH?
I-IS THIS... ME?
PHOTOSHOP IS A NO-BRAINER FOR COSPLAYERS.
YOU BEAUTIFIED HIM 120%.
THAT'S HARSH...
IF YOU BECOME STUDENT COUNCIL PRESIDENT...
...YOU'LL EASILY WIN THE SUPPORT YOU NEED.
I'LL NEVER BE ELECTED IN THE FIRST PLACE.
THEN I'LL GIVE YOU SPECIAL TRAINING.
S-SPECIAL TRAINING!? ...WH-WHAT KIND?
#1 HOW TO BECOME A DRAGON SEMINAR
FIRST IS INTRO-DUCTIONS AND HAND-SHAKES.
IT'S IMPORTANT TO EXUDE AN AIR OF HONESTY.
SU (SWF)
H-HAND-SHAKES!?

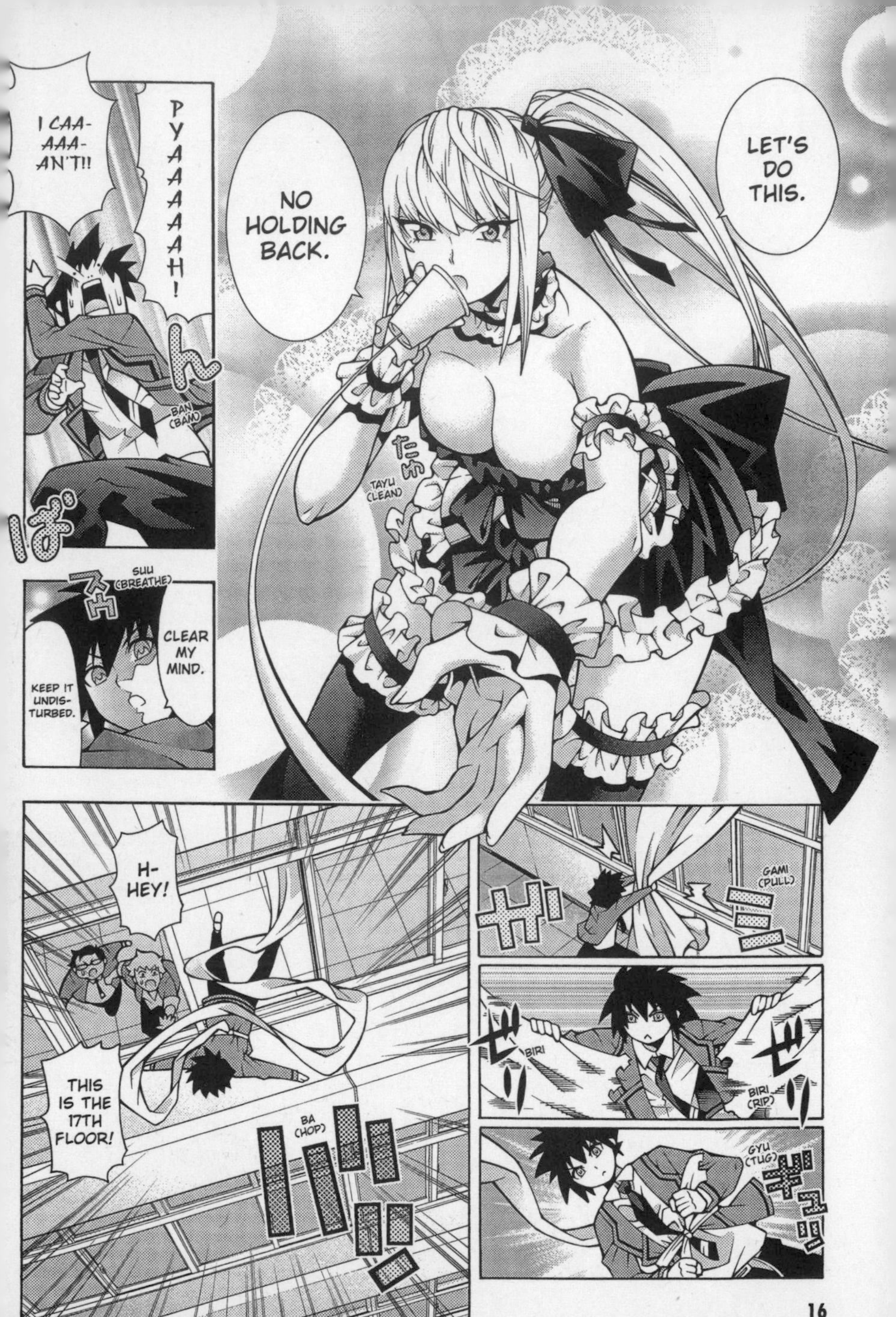
LET'S DO THIS.
NO HOLDING BACK.
TAYU (CLEAN)
PYAAAAAAAH!
I CAA-AAA-AN'T!!
BAN (BAN)
SUU (BREATHE)
CLEAR MY MIND.
KEEP IT UNDIS-TURBED.
GAMI (PULL)
BIRI
BIRI (RIP)
GYU (TUG)
H-HEY!
THIS IS THE 17TH FLOOR!
BA (HOP)

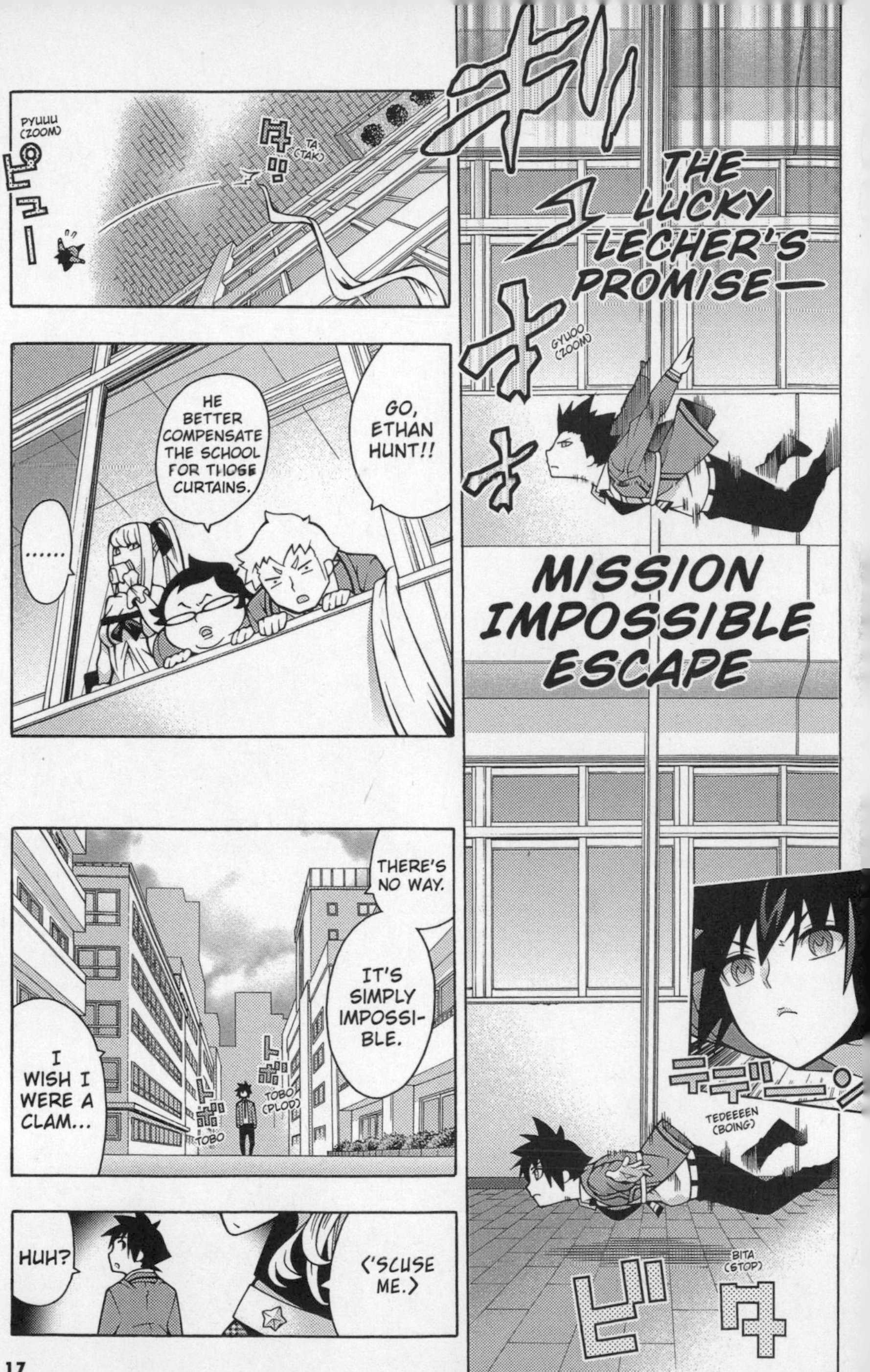
THE LUCKY LECHER'S PROMISE—
GYUOO (ZOOM)
MISSION IMPOSSIBLE ESCAPE
TEDEEEEN (BOING)
BITA (STOP)
PYUUU (ZOOM)
TA (TAK)
GO, ETHAN HUNT!!
HE BETTER COMPENSATE THE SCHOOL FOR THOSE CURTAINS.
......
THERE'S NO WAY.
IT'S SIMPLY IMPOSSIBLE.
TOBO (PLOD)
TOBO
I WISH I WERE A CLAM...
‹'SCUSE ME.›
HUH?

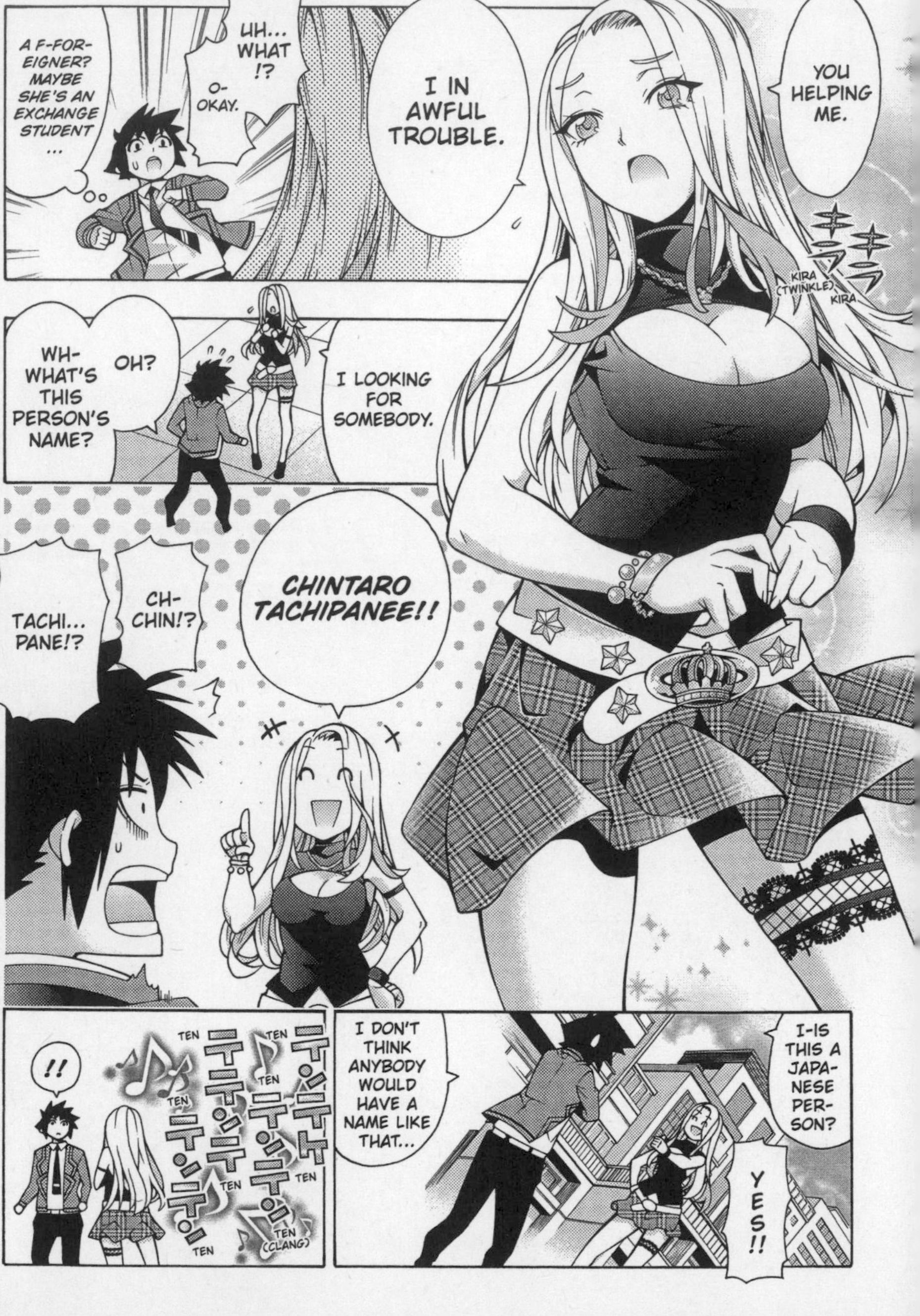
YOU HELPING ME.
KIRA (TWINKLE) KIRA
I IN AWFUL TROUBLE.
UH... WHAT!?
O-OKAY.
A F-FOREIGNER? MAYBE SHE'S AN EXCHANGE STUDENT...
I LOOKING FOR SOMEBODY.
OH?
WH-WHAT'S THIS PERSON'S NAME?
CHINTARO TACHIPANEE!!
CH-CHIN!?
TACHI... PANE!?
I-IS THIS A JAPANESE PERSON?
YES!!
I DON'T THINK ANYBODY WOULD HAVE A NAME LIKE THAT...
!!
TEN TEN TEN TEN TEN TEN TEN TEN (CLANG)

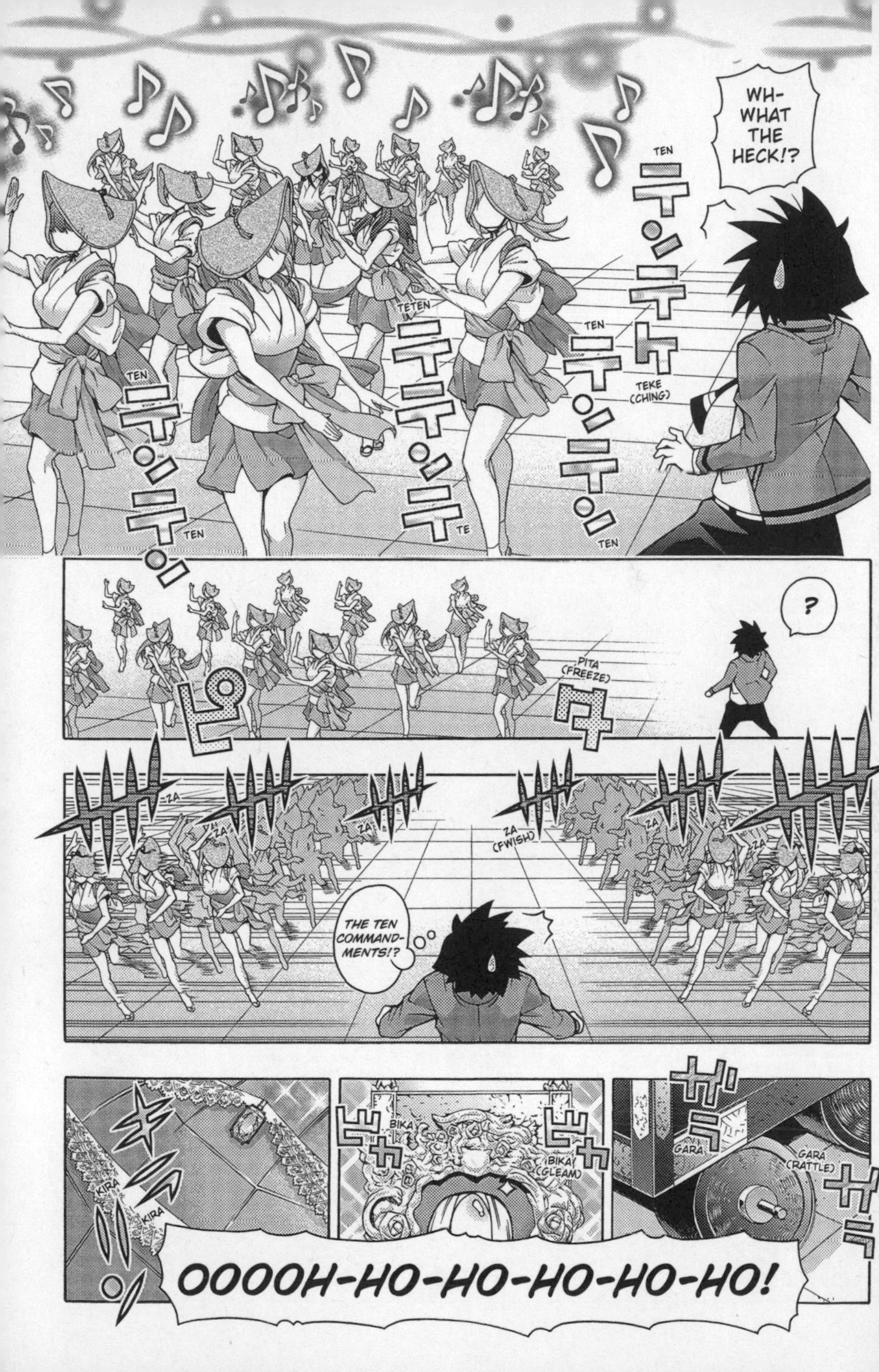
WH- WHAT THE HECK!?
TEN
TEKE (CHING)
TEN
TEN
TETEN
TE
TEN
TEN
?
PITA (FREEZE)
ZA
ZA (FWISH)
ZA
ZA
ZA
ZA
THE TEN COMMAND-MENTS!?
GARA
GARA (RATTLE)
BIKA
BIKA (GLEAM)
KIRA
KIRA
OOOOH-HO-HO-HO-HO-HO-HO!

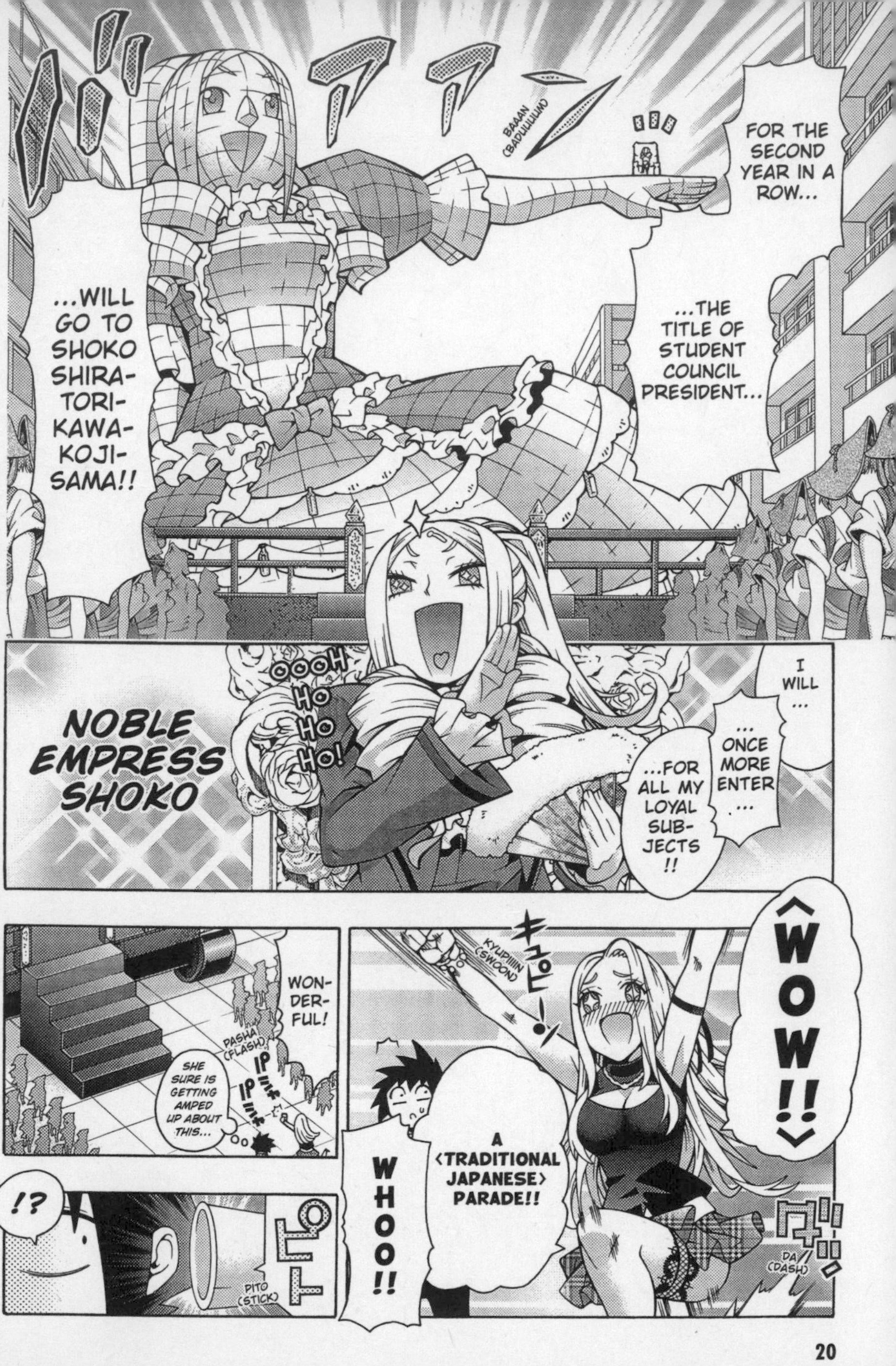
BAAAN (BADUUUUUN)
FOR THE SECOND YEAR IN A ROW...
...THE TITLE OF STUDENT COUNCIL PRESIDENT...
...WILL GO TO SHOKO SHIRATORI-KAWAKOJI-SAMA!!
I WILL...
...ONCE MORE ENTER...
...FOR ALL MY LOYAL SUBJECTS!!
OOOH HO HO HO!
NOBLE EMPRESS SHOKO
<WOW!!>
KYUPIIIN (SWOON)
A <TRADITIONAL JAPANESE> PARADE!!
WHOO!!
DA (DASH)
WON-DER-FUL!
PASHA (FLASH)
SHE SURE IS GETTING AMPED UP ABOUT THIS...
PITO (STICK)
!?

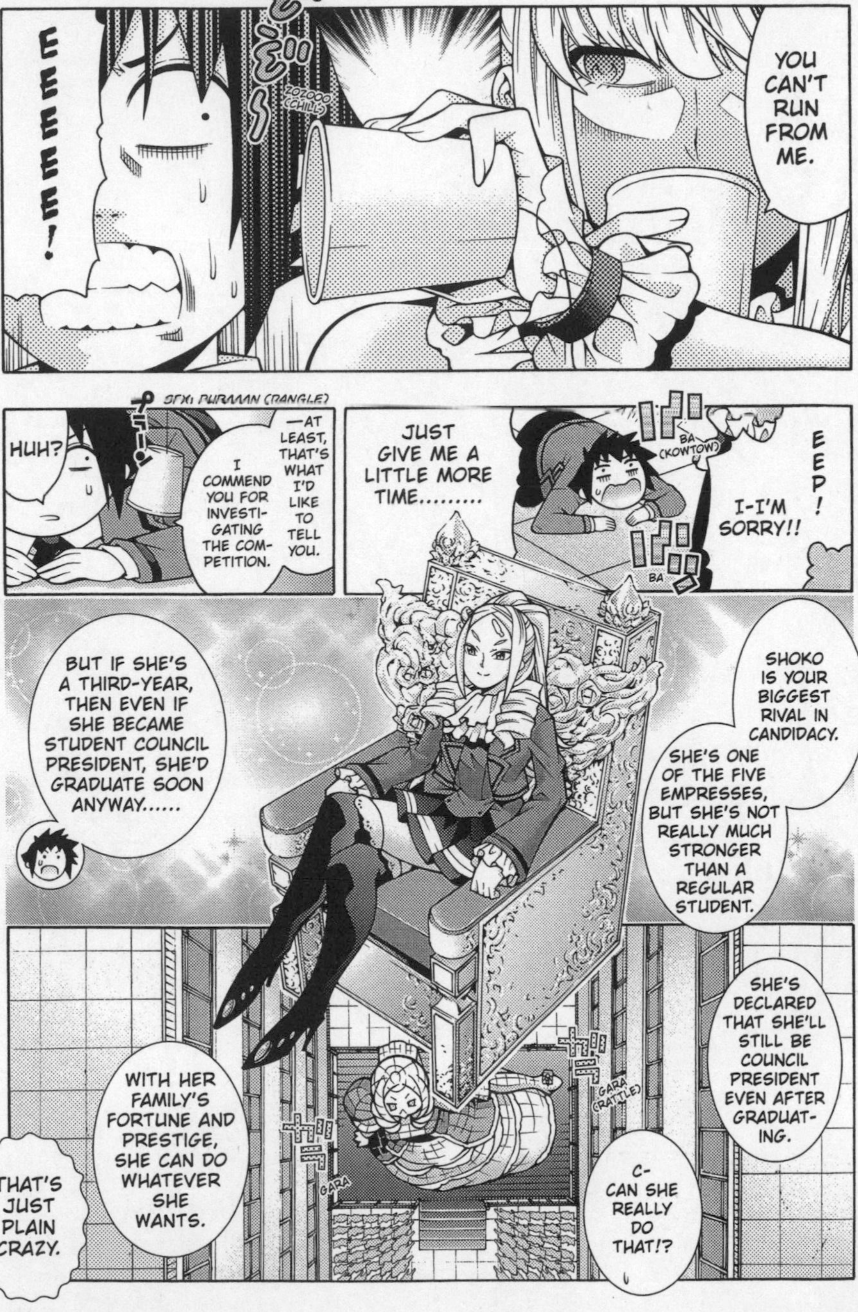
YOU CAN'T RUN FROM ME.
ZOZOOO (CHILL)
EEEEEEE!
EEP!
I-I'M SORRY!!
BA (KOWTOW)
BA
JUST GIVE ME A LITTLE MORE TIME.........
—AT LEAST, THAT'S WHAT I'D LIKE TO TELL YOU.
I COMMEND YOU FOR INVESTIGATING THE COMPETITION.
HUH?
SFX: PURAAAN (DANGLE)
SHOKO IS YOUR BIGGEST RIVAL IN CANDIDACY.
SHE'S ONE OF THE FIVE EMPRESSES, BUT SHE'S NOT REALLY MUCH STRONGER THAN A REGULAR STUDENT.
BUT IF SHE'S A THIRD-YEAR, THEN EVEN IF SHE BECAME STUDENT COUNCIL PRESIDENT, SHE'D GRADUATE SOON ANYWAY......
SHE'S DECLARED THAT SHE'LL STILL BE COUNCIL PRESIDENT EVEN AFTER GRADUATING.
C-CAN SHE REALLY DO THAT!?
GARA (RATTLE)
GARA
WITH HER FAMILY'S FORTUNE AND PRESTIGE, SHE CAN DO WHATEVER SHE WANTS.
THAT'S JUST PLAIN CRAZY.

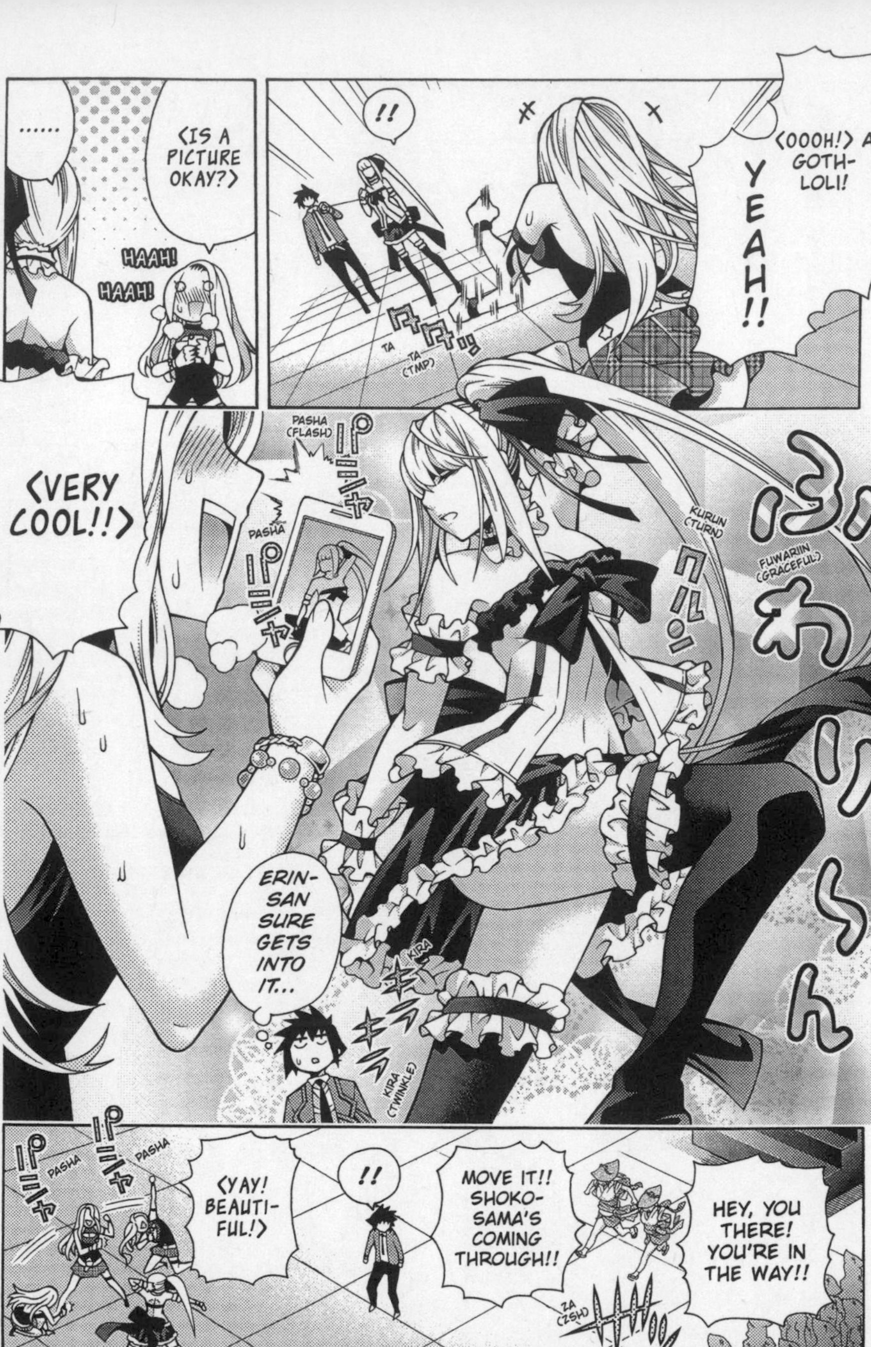
<OOOH!> A GOTH-LOLI!
YEAH!!
!!
TA TA (TMP)
<IS A PICTURE OKAY?>
......
HAAH! HAAH!
FUWARIIN (GRACEFUL)
KURUN (TURN)
PASHA (FLASH)
<VERY COOL!!>
PASHA
ERIN-SAN SURE GETS INTO IT...
KIRA KIRA (TWINKLE)
HEY, YOU THERE! YOU'RE IN THE WAY!!
ZA (ZSH)
MOVE IT!! SHOKO-SAMA'S COMING THROUGH!!
!!
<YAY! BEAUTI-FUL!>
PASHA PASHA

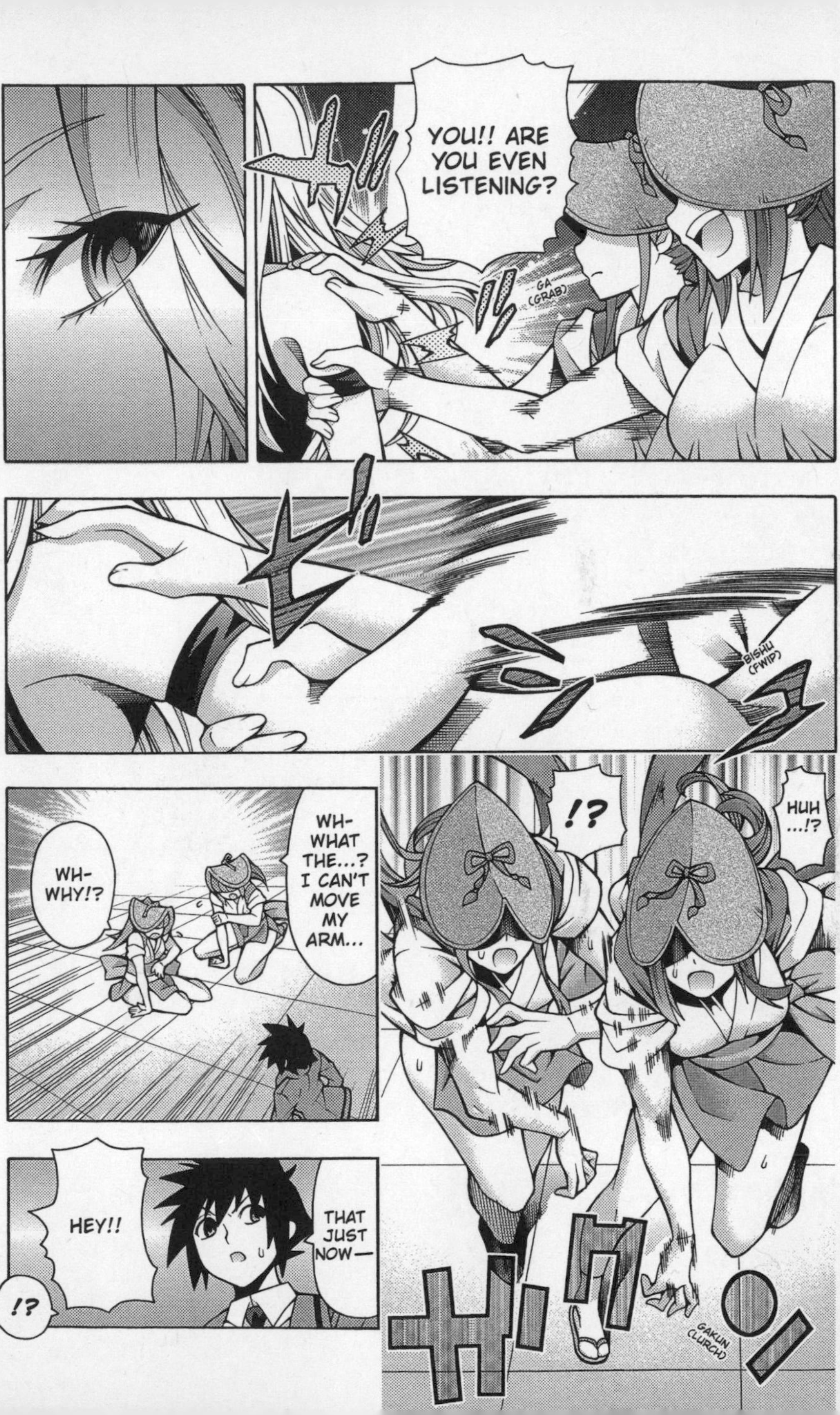
YOU!! ARE YOU EVEN LISTENING?
GA (GRAB)
BISHU (FWIP)
HUH ...!?
!?
GAKUN (LURCH)
WH-WHAT THE...? I CAN'T MOVE MY ARM...
WH-WHY!?
THAT JUST NOW—
HEY!!
!?

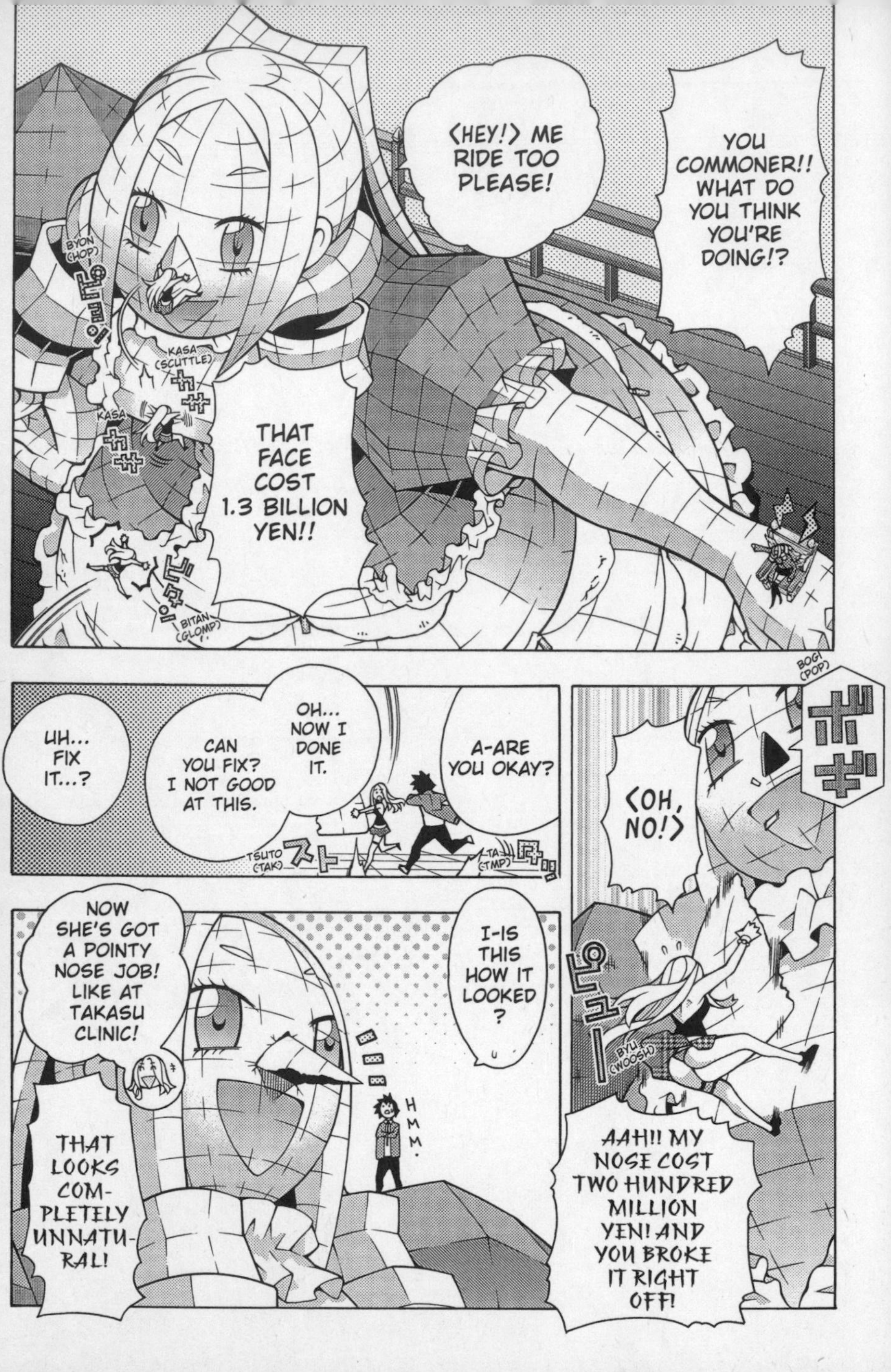
YOU COMMONER!! WHAT DO YOU THINK YOU'RE DOING!?
<HEY!> ME RIDE TOO PLEASE!
BYON (HOP)
KASA (SCUTTLE)
KASA
THAT FACE COST 1.3 BILLION YEN!!
BITAN (GLOMP)
BOGI (POP)
<OH, NO!>
BYU (WOOSH)
AAH!! MY NOSE COST TWO HUNDRED MILLION YEN! AND YOU BROKE IT RIGHT OFF!
A-ARE YOU OKAY?
OH... NOW I DONE IT.
CAN YOU FIX? I NOT GOOD AT THIS.
UH... FIX IT...?
TA (TMP)
TSUTO (TAK)
I-IS THIS HOW IT LOOKED?
NOW SHE'S GOT A POINTY NOSE JOB! LIKE AT TAKASU CLINIC!
THAT LOOKS COM-PLETELY UNNATU-RAL!
HMM.

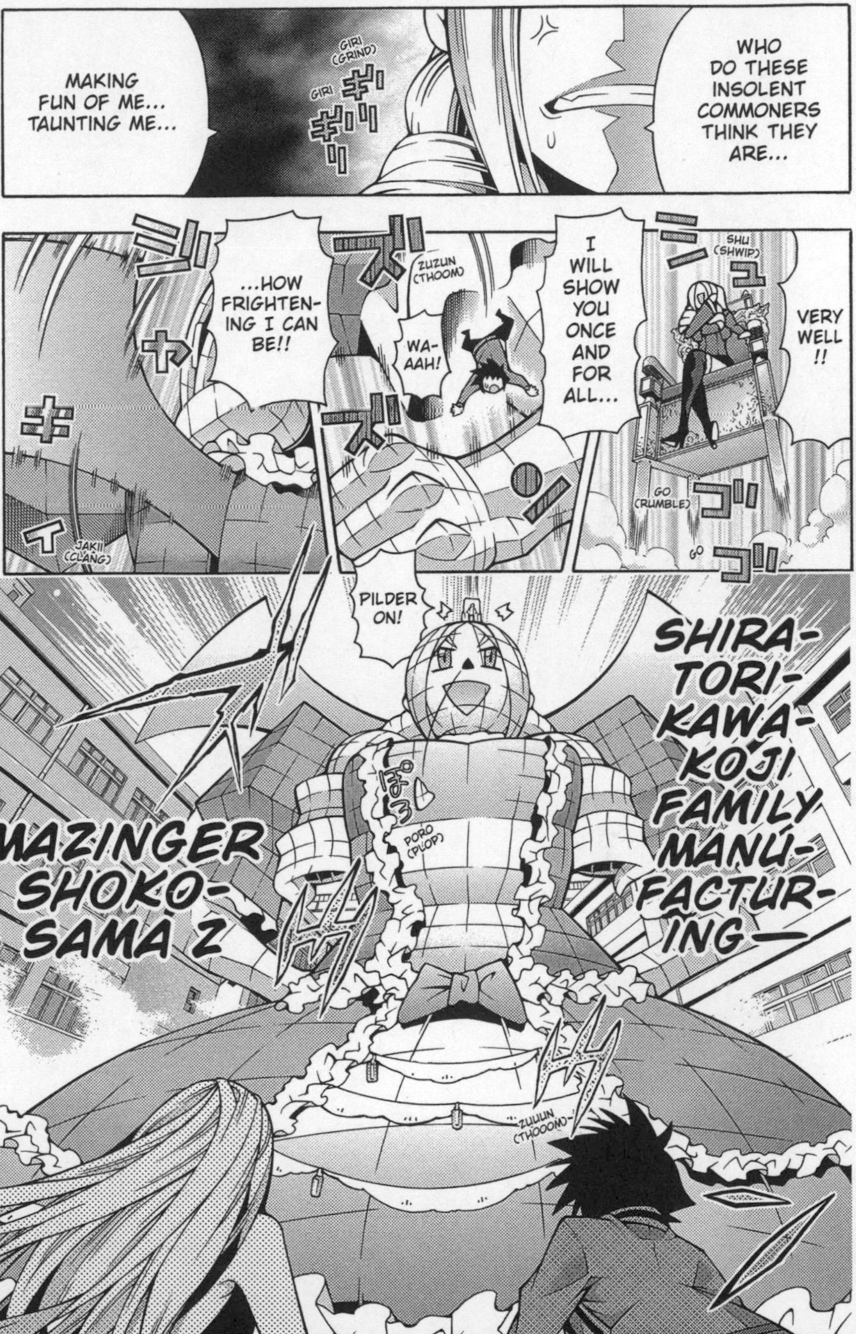
WHO DO THESE INSOLENT COMMONERS THINK THEY ARE...
GIRI (GRIND)
GIRI
MAKING FUN OF ME... TAUNTING ME...
SHU (SHWIP)
VERY WELL!!
GO (RUMBLE)
GO
I WILL SHOW YOU ONCE AND FOR ALL...
ZUZUN (THOOM)
WA-AAH!
...HOW FRIGHTEN-ING I CAN BE!!
JAKII (CLANG)
PILDER ON!
SHIRA-TORI-KAWA-KOJI FAMILY MANU-FACTUR-ING—
MAZINGER SHOKO-SAMA Z
PORO (PLOP)
ZUUUN (THOOOM)

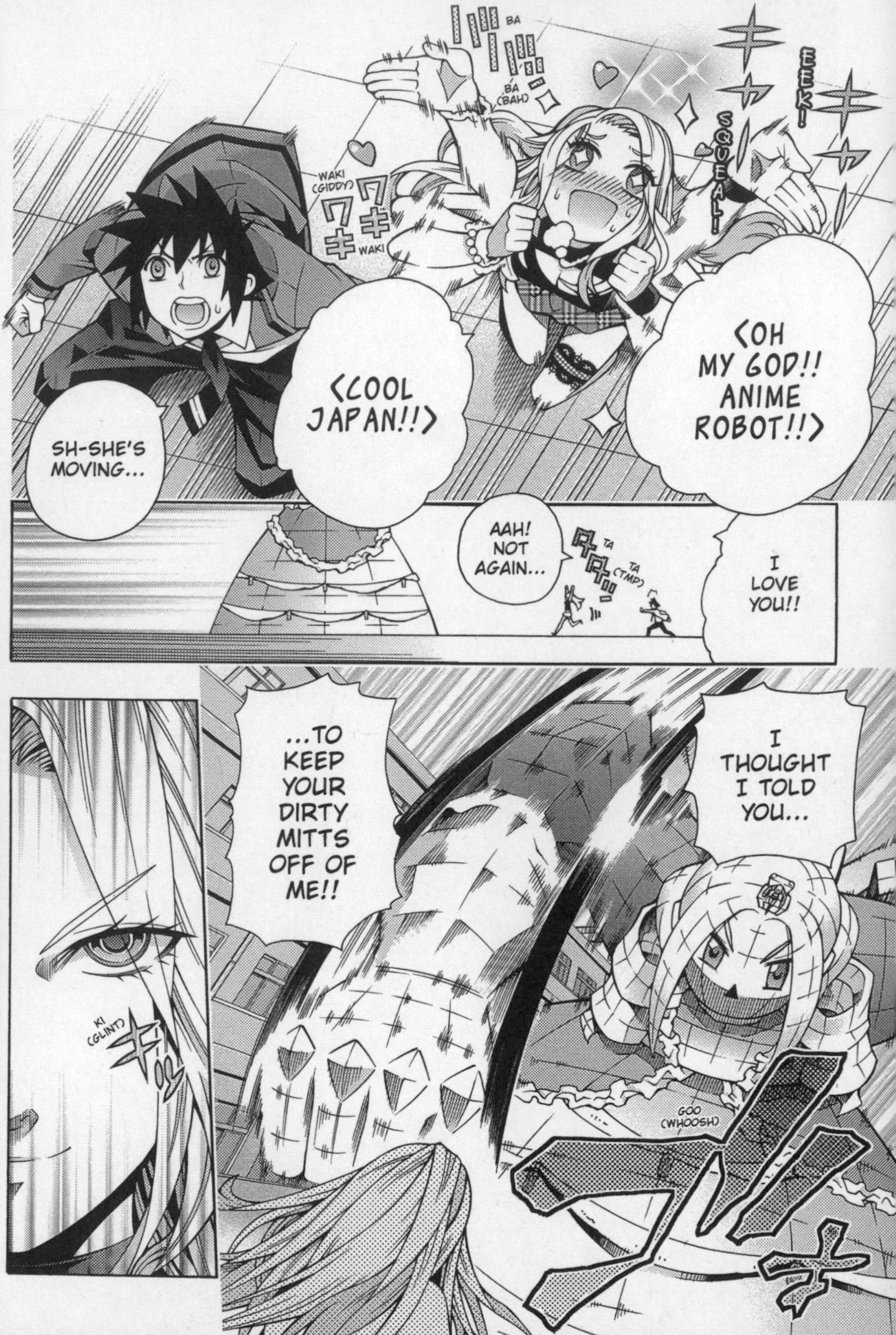
EEK!
SQUEAL!
<OH MY GOD!! ANIME ROBOT!!>
BA
BA (BAH)
WAKI (GIDDY)
WAKI
<COOL JAPAN!!>
SH-SHE'S MOVING...
I LOVE YOU!!
TA
TA (TMP)
AAH! NOT AGAIN...
I THOUGHT I TOLD YOU...
...TO KEEP YOUR DIRTY MITTS OFF OF ME!!
GOO (WHOOSH)
KI (GLINT)

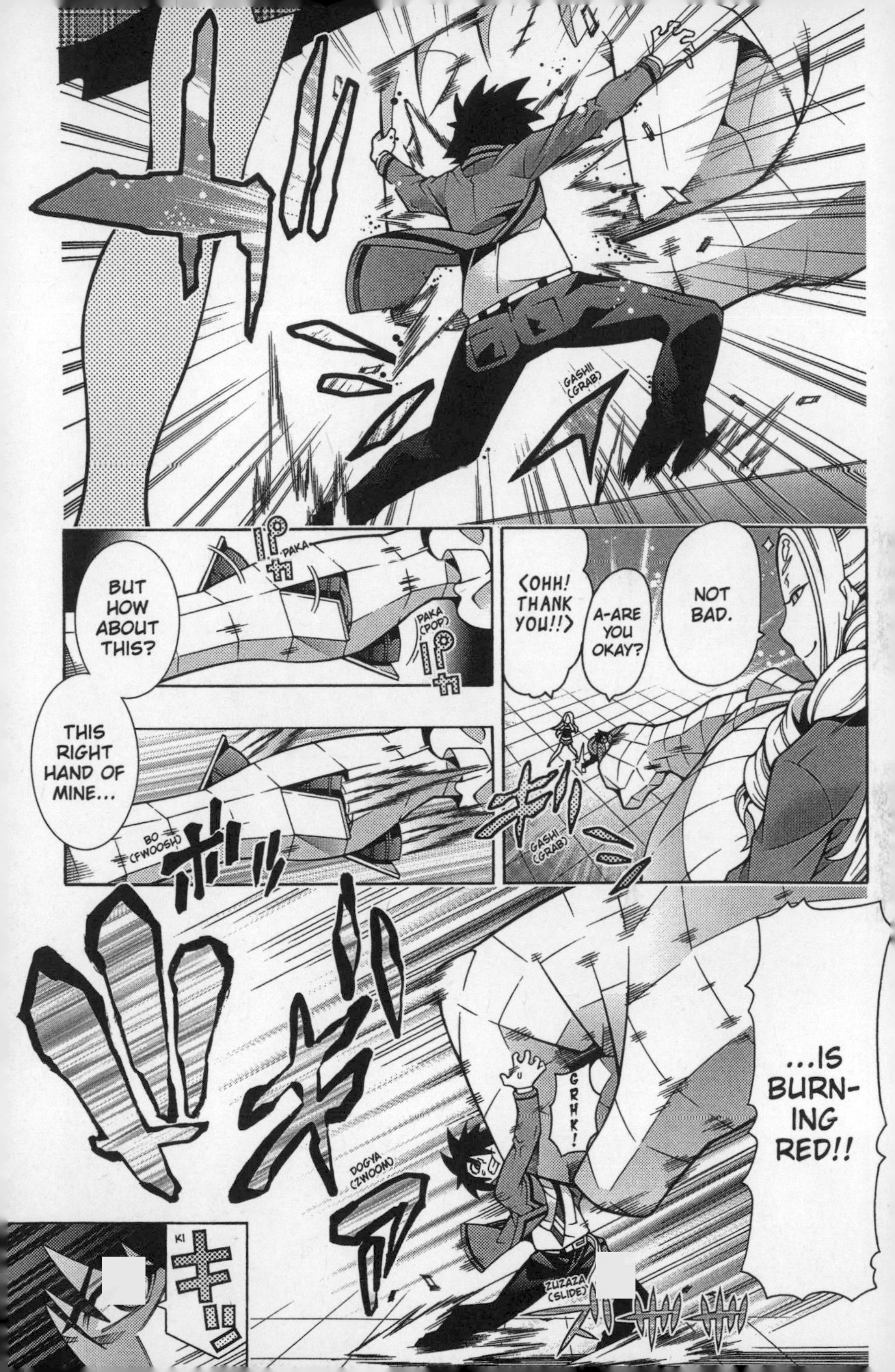
GASHI (GRAB)
NOT BAD.
A-ARE YOU OKAY?
<OHH! THANK YOU!!>
GASHI (GRAB)
PAKA
PAKA (POP)
BUT HOW ABOUT THIS?
THIS RIGHT HAND OF MINE...
BO (FWOOSH)
...IS BURNING-ING RED!!
GRHK!
DOGYA (ZWOOM)
ZUZAZA (SLIDE)
KI

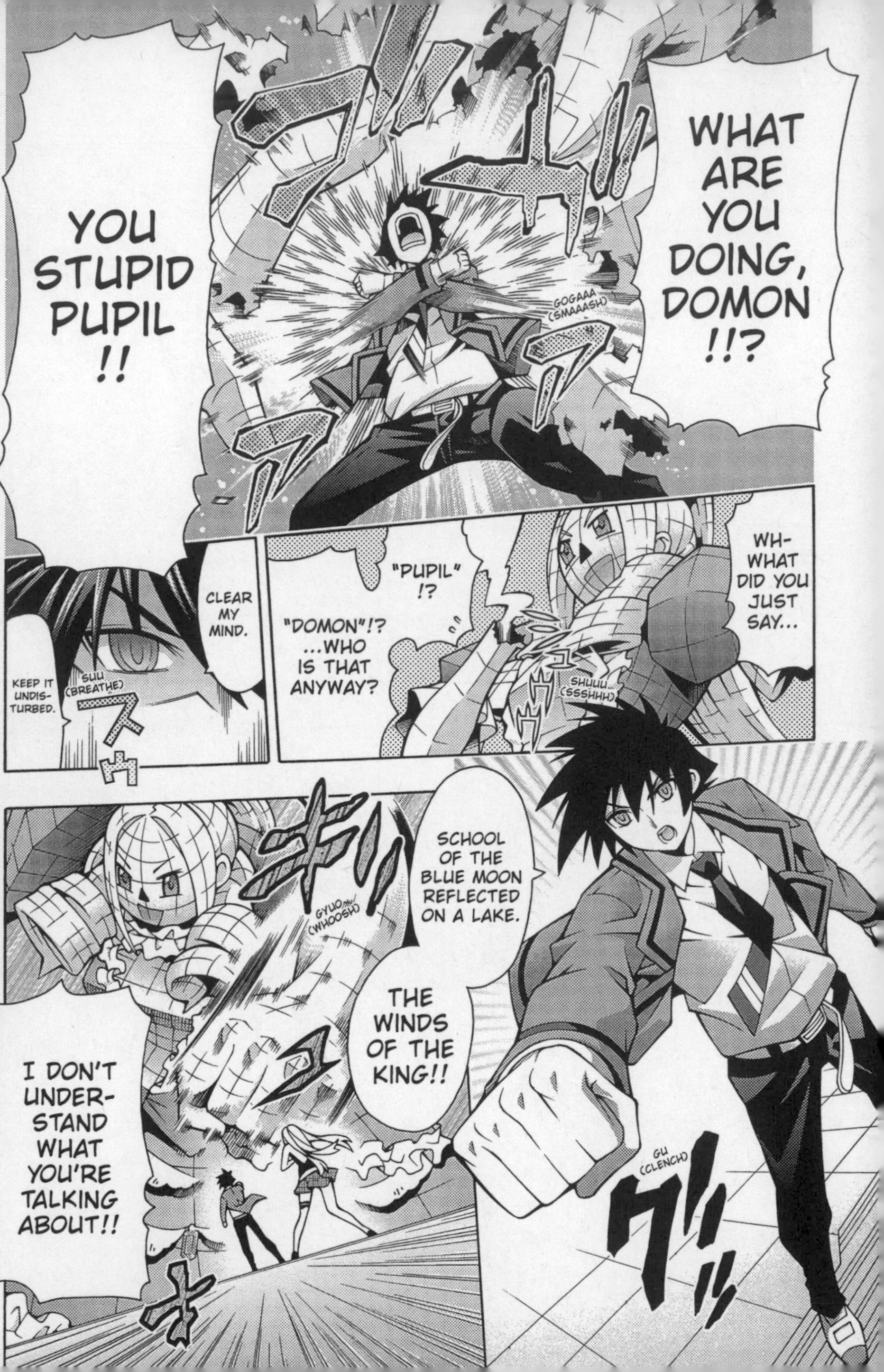
WHAT ARE YOU DOING, DOMON!!?
GOGAAA (SMAAASH)
YOU STUPID PUPIL!!
WH-WHAT DID YOU JUST SAY...
"PUPIL"!?
"DOMON"!? ...WHO IS THAT ANYWAY?
SHUUU (SSSHHH)
CLEAR MY MIND.
KEEP IT UNDISTURBED.
SUU (BREATHE)
SCHOOL OF THE BLUE MOON REFLECTED ON A LAKE.
THE WINDS OF THE KING!!
GYUO (WHOOSH)
GU (CLENCH)
I DON'T UNDERSTAND WHAT YOU'RE TALKING ABOUT!!

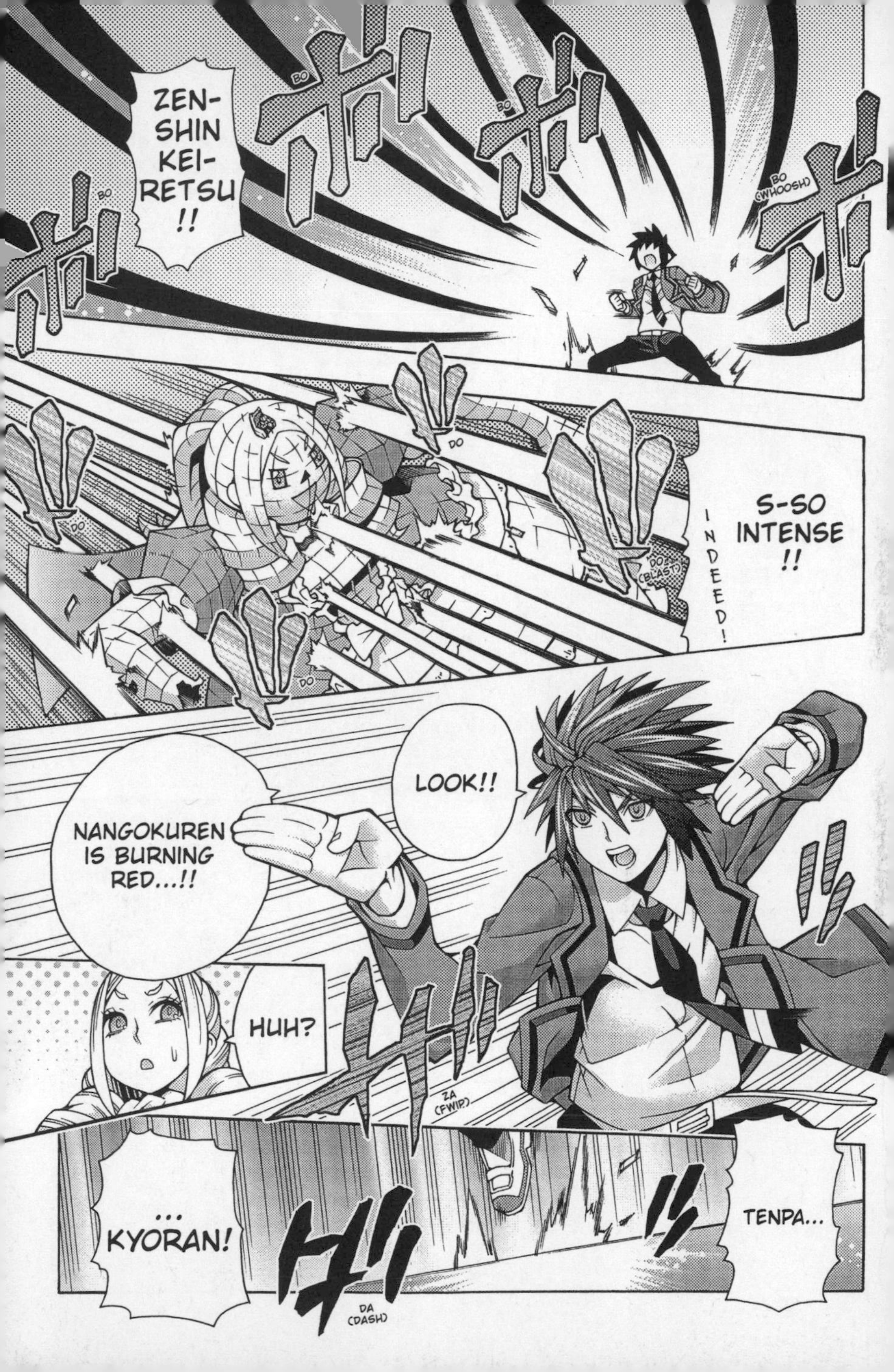
BO (WHOOSH)
BO
BO
ZEN-SHIN KEI-RETSU!!
BO
S-SO INTENSE!!
INDEED!
DO (BLAST)
DO
DO
DO
LOOK!!
NANGOKUREN IS BURNING RED...!!
HUH?
ZA (FWIP)
TENPA...
DA (DASH)
...KYORAN!

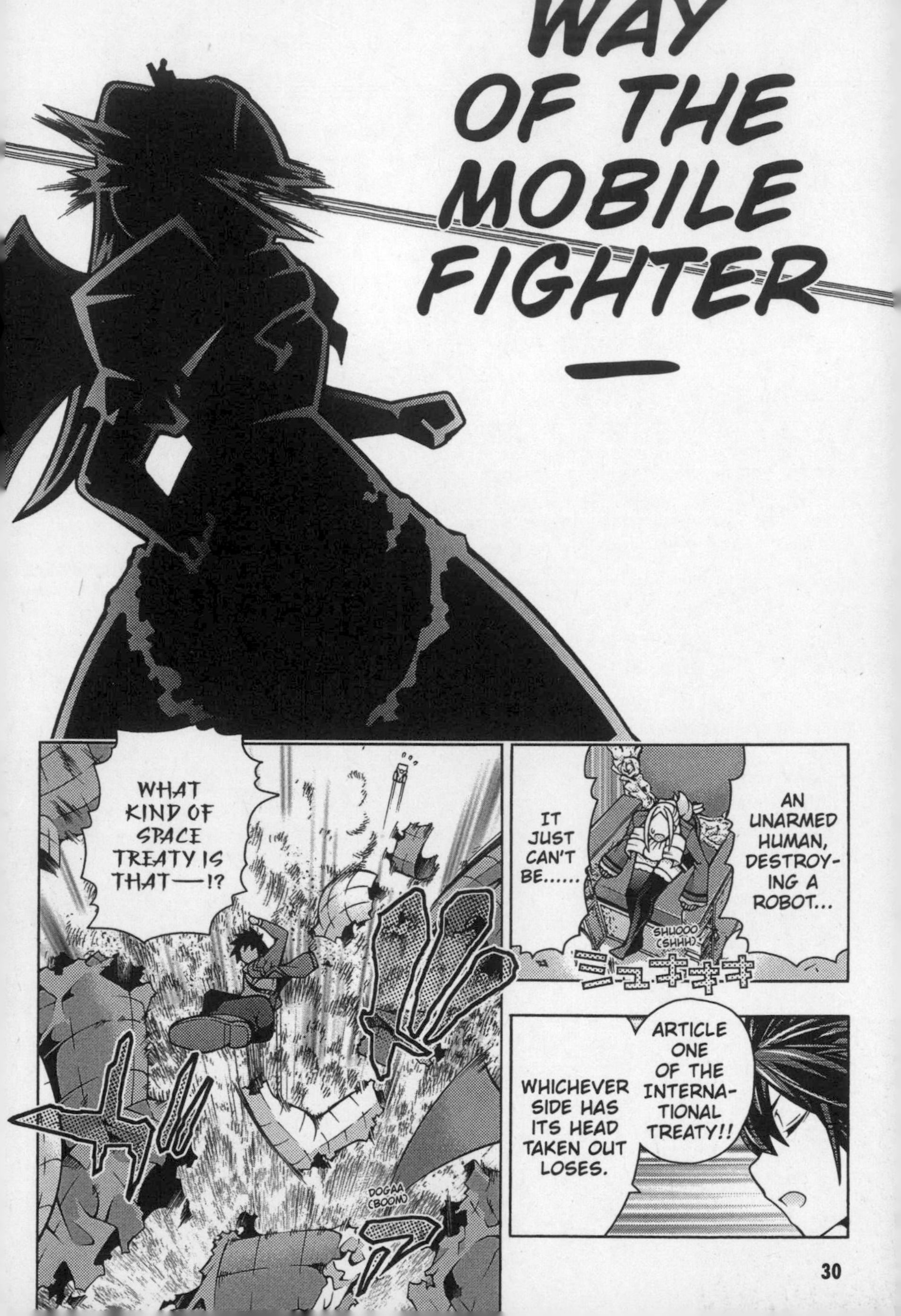
WAY OF THE MOBILE FIGHTER—
AN UNARMED HUMAN, DESTROYING A ROBOT...
IT JUST CAN'T BE......
SHUOOO (SHHH)
ARTICLE ONE OF THE INTERNATIONAL TREATY!!
WHICHEVER SIDE HAS ITS HEAD TAKEN OUT LOSES.
WHAT KIND OF SPACE TREATY IS THAT—!?
DOGAA (BOOM)

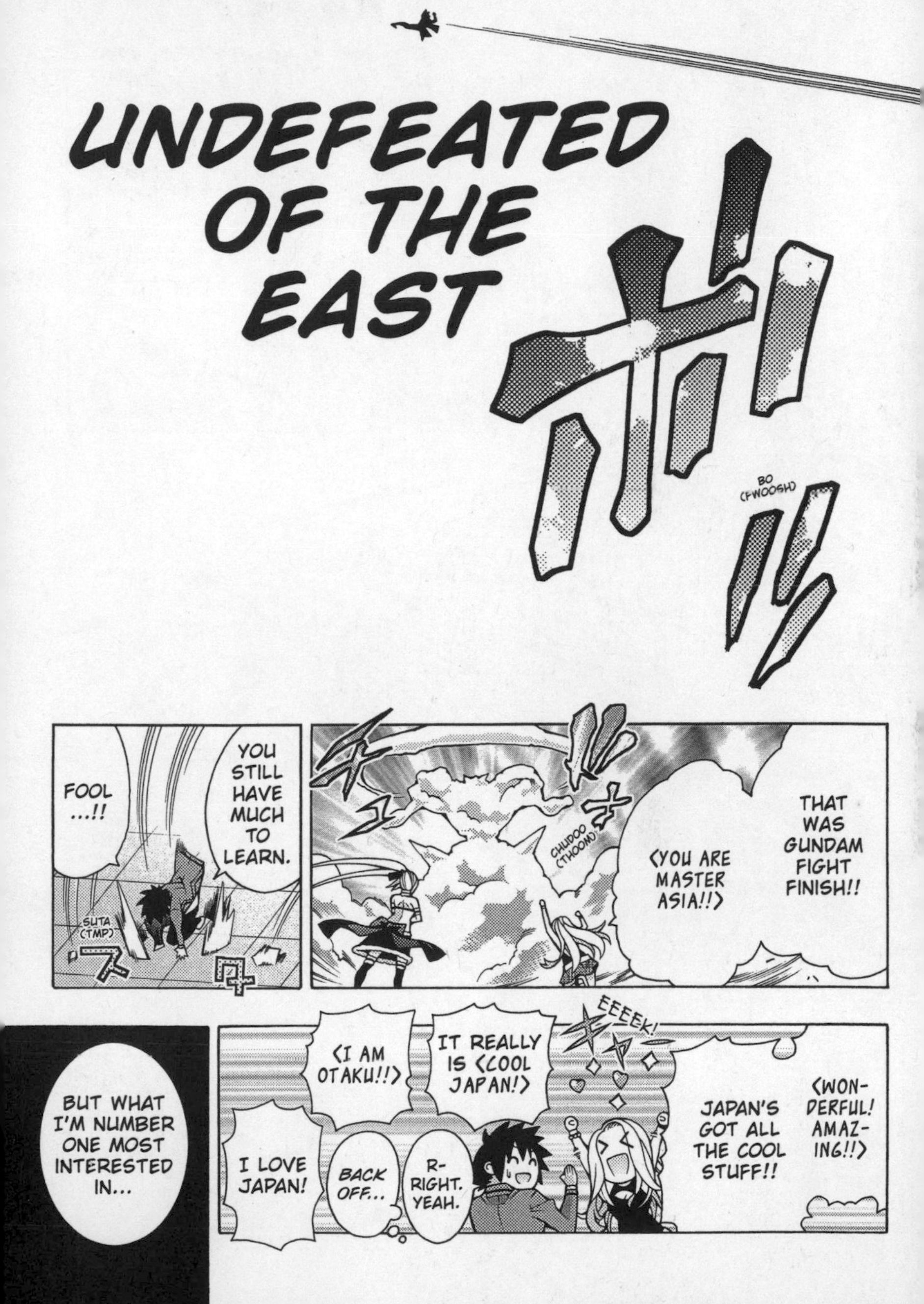
UNDEFEATED OF THE EAST
BO (FWOOSH)
THAT WAS GUNDAM FIGHT FINISH!!
<YOU ARE MASTER ASIA!!>
CHUDOO (THOOM)
YOU STILL HAVE MUCH TO LEARN.
FOOL ...!!
SUTA (TMP)
<WON-DERFUL! AMAZ-ING!!>
JAPAN'S GOT ALL THE COOL STUFF!!
EEEEK!
IT REALLY IS <COOL JAPAN!>
<I AM OTAKU!!>
R-RIGHT. YEAH.
BACK OFF...
I LOVE JAPAN!
BUT WHAT I'M NUMBER ONE MOST INTERESTED IN...

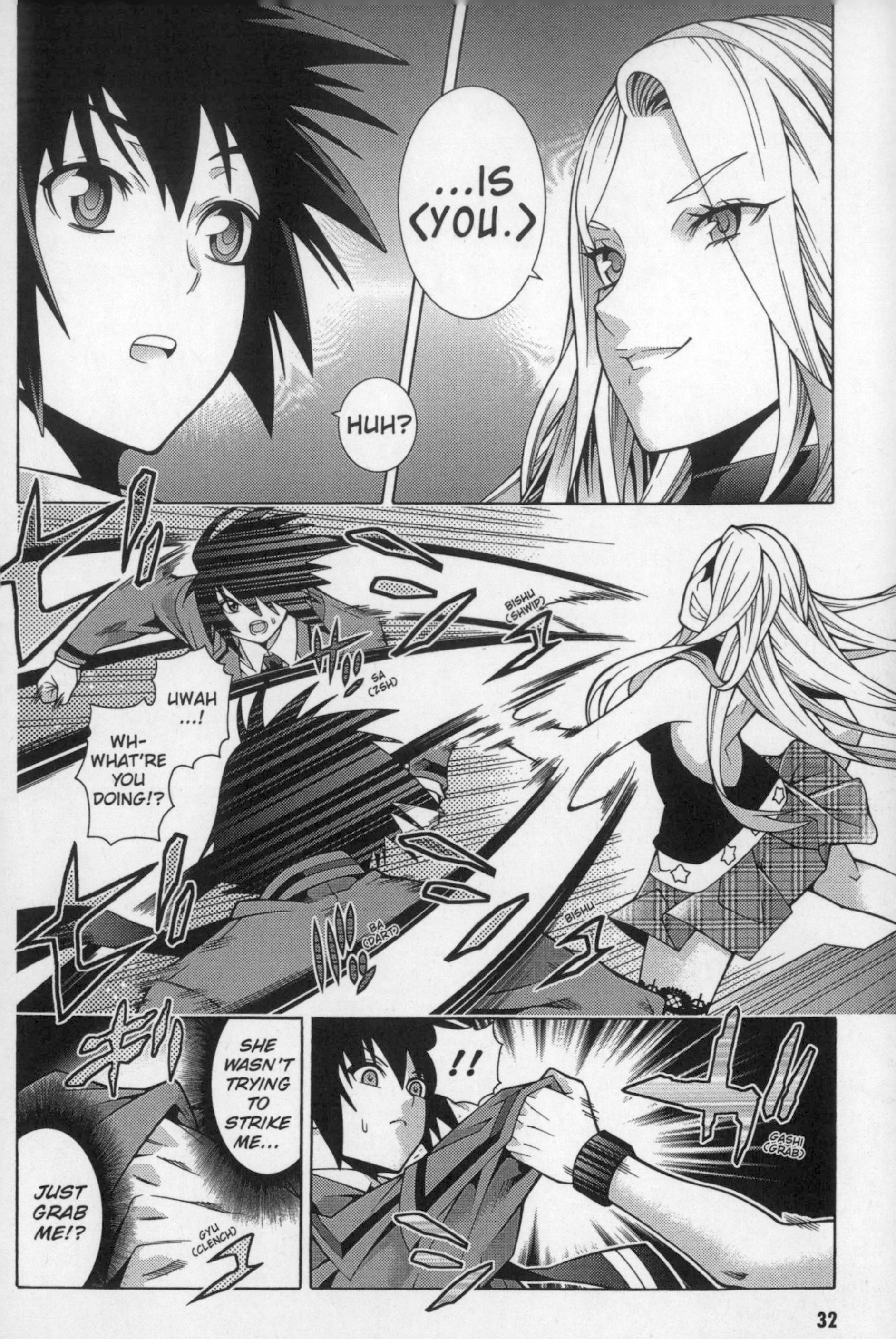
...IS <YOU.>
HUH?
BISHU (SHWIP)
SA (ZSH)
UWAH ...!
WH-WHAT'RE YOU DOING!?
BISHU
BA (DART)
GASHI (GRAB)
!!
SHE WASN'T TRYING TO STRIKE ME...
JUST GRAB ME!?
GYU (CLENCH)

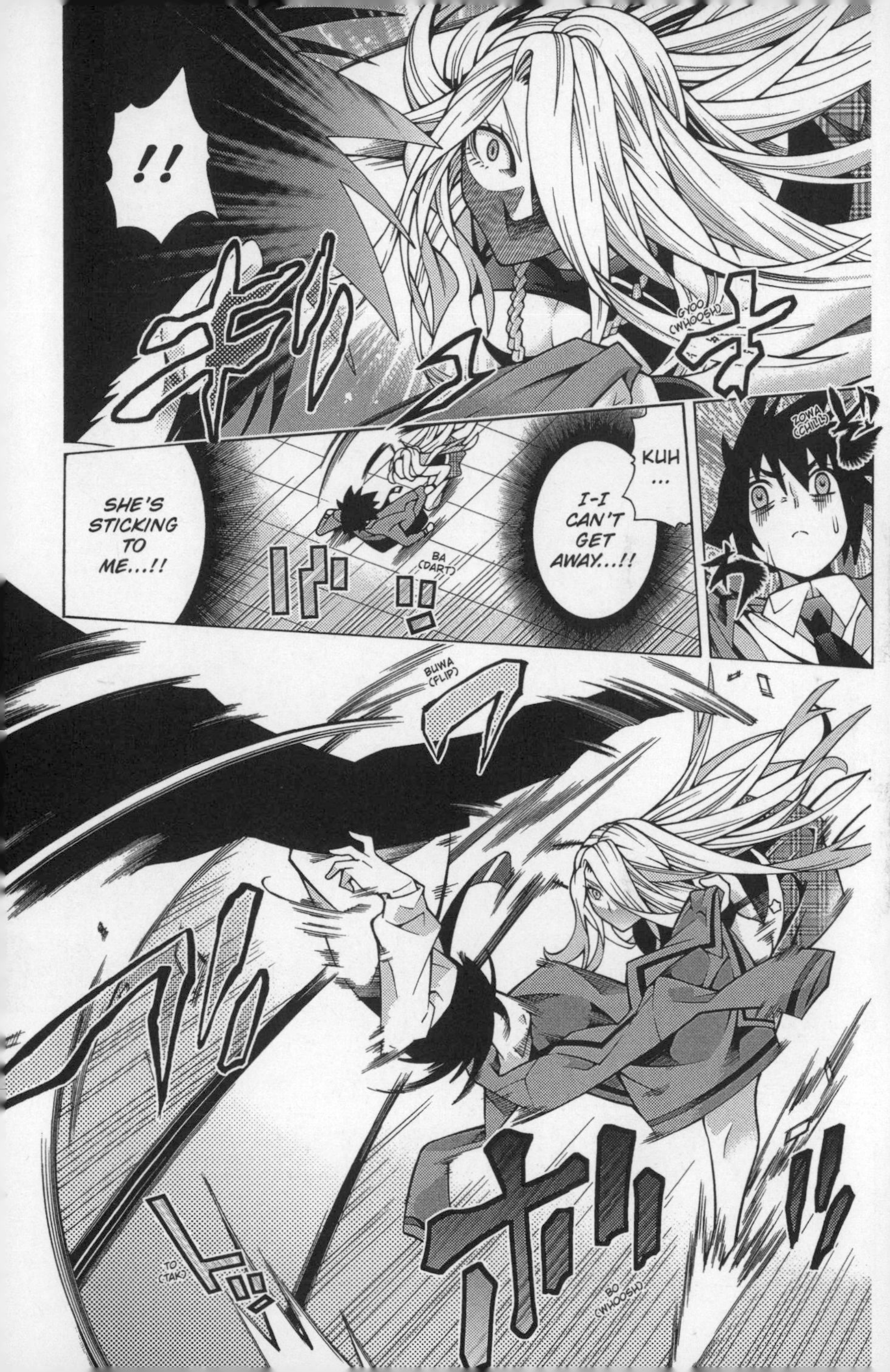
!!
GYOO (WHOOSH)
ZOWA (CHILL)
KUH ...
I-I CAN'T GET AWAY...!!
BA (DART)
SHE'S STICKING TO ME...!!
BUWA (FLIP)
BO (WHOOSH)
TO (TAK)

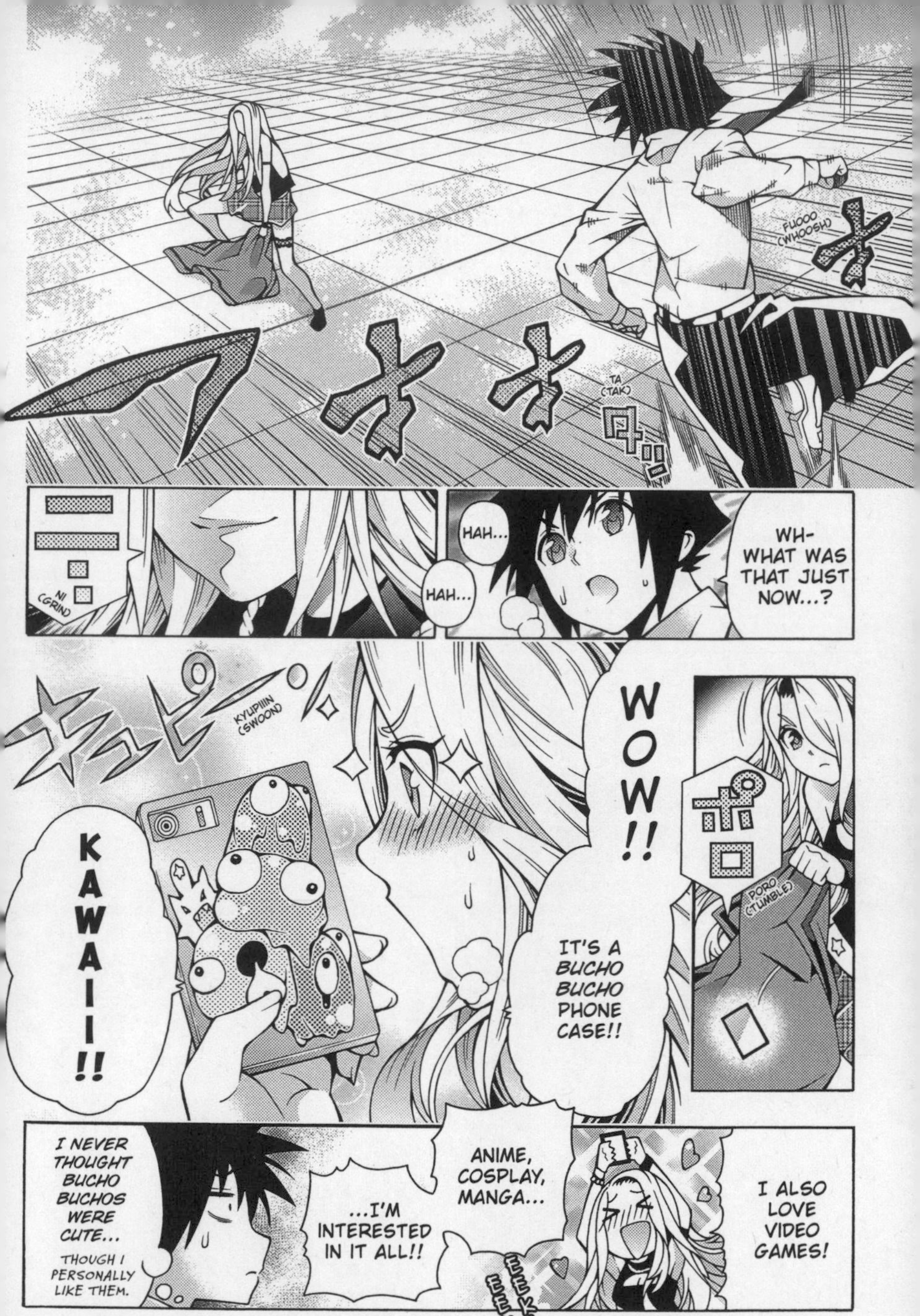
FUOOO (WHOOSH)
TA (TAK)
WH- WHAT WAS THAT JUST NOW...?
HAH...
HAH...
NI (GRIN)
PORO (TUMBLE)
WOW!!
IT'S A BUCHO BUCHO PHONE CASE!!
KYUPIIN (SWOON)
KAWAII!!
I ALSO LOVE VIDEO GAMES!
ANIME, COSPLAY, MANGA...
...I'M INTERESTED IN IT ALL!!
I NEVER THOUGHT BUCHO BUCHOS WERE CUTE...
THOUGH I PERSONALLY LIKE THEM.

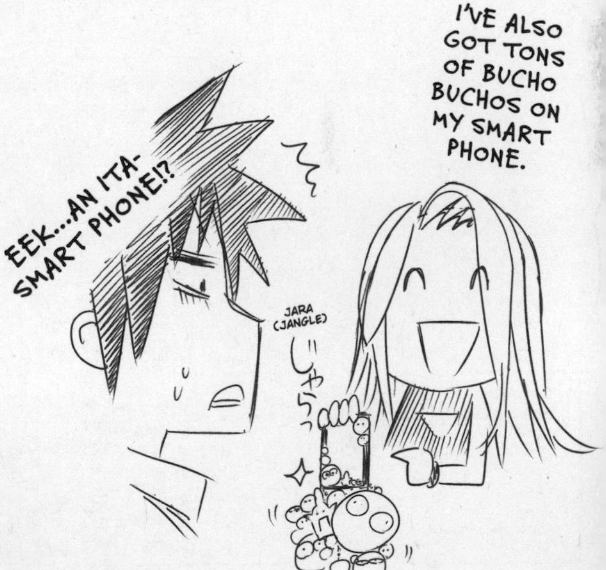
I'VE ALSO GOT TONS OF BUCHO BUCHOS ON MY SMART PHONE.
EEK...AN ITA-SMART PHONE!?
JARA (JANGLE)
じゃらっ

Dragons Rioting

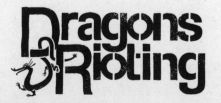

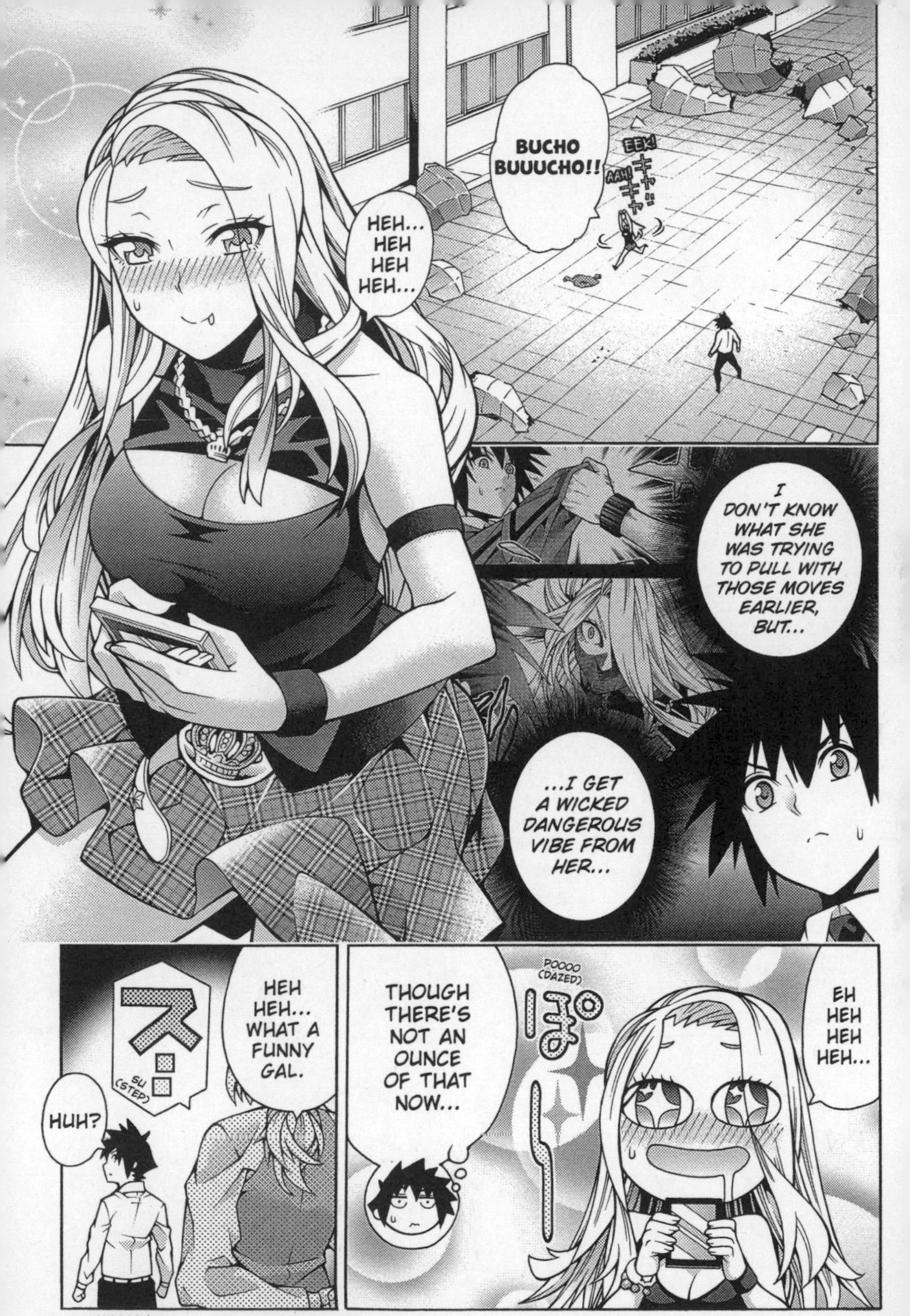

BUCHO BUUUCHO!!
EEK!
AAH!
I DON'T KNOW WHAT SHE WAS TRYING TO PULL WITH THOSE MOVES EARLIER, BUT...
...I GET A WICKED DANGEROUS VIBE FROM HER...
HEH... HEH HEH HEH...
EH HEH HEH HEH...
POOOO (DAZED)
THOUGH THERE'S NOT AN OUNCE OF THAT NOW...
HEH HEH... WHAT A FUNNY GAL.
SU (STEP)
HUH?

DRAGON 31 TRUE FRIENDS

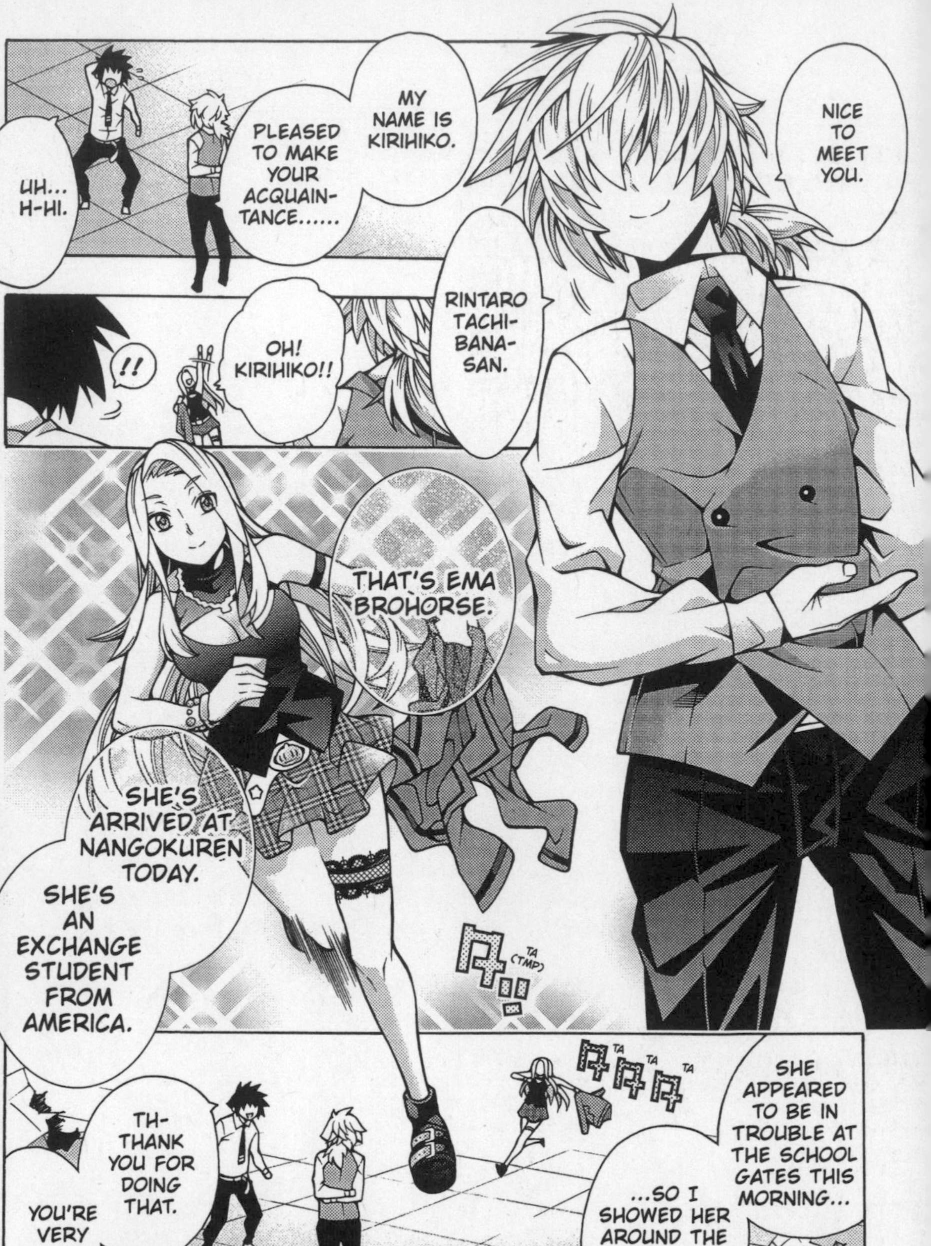
NICE TO MEET YOU.
RINTARO TACHIBANA-SAN.
MY NAME IS KIRIHIKO.
PLEASED TO MAKE YOUR ACQUAINTANCE......
UH... H-HI.
OH! KIRIHIKO!!
!!
THAT'S EMA BROHORSE.
SHE'S ARRIVED AT NANGOKUREN TODAY.
SHE'S AN EXCHANGE STUDENT FROM AMERICA.
TA (TMP)
TA TA TA
SHE APPEARED TO BE IN TROUBLE AT THE SCHOOL GATES THIS MORNING...
...SO I SHOWED HER AROUND THE GROUNDS.
TH-THANK YOU FOR DOING THAT.
YOU'RE VERY KIND.

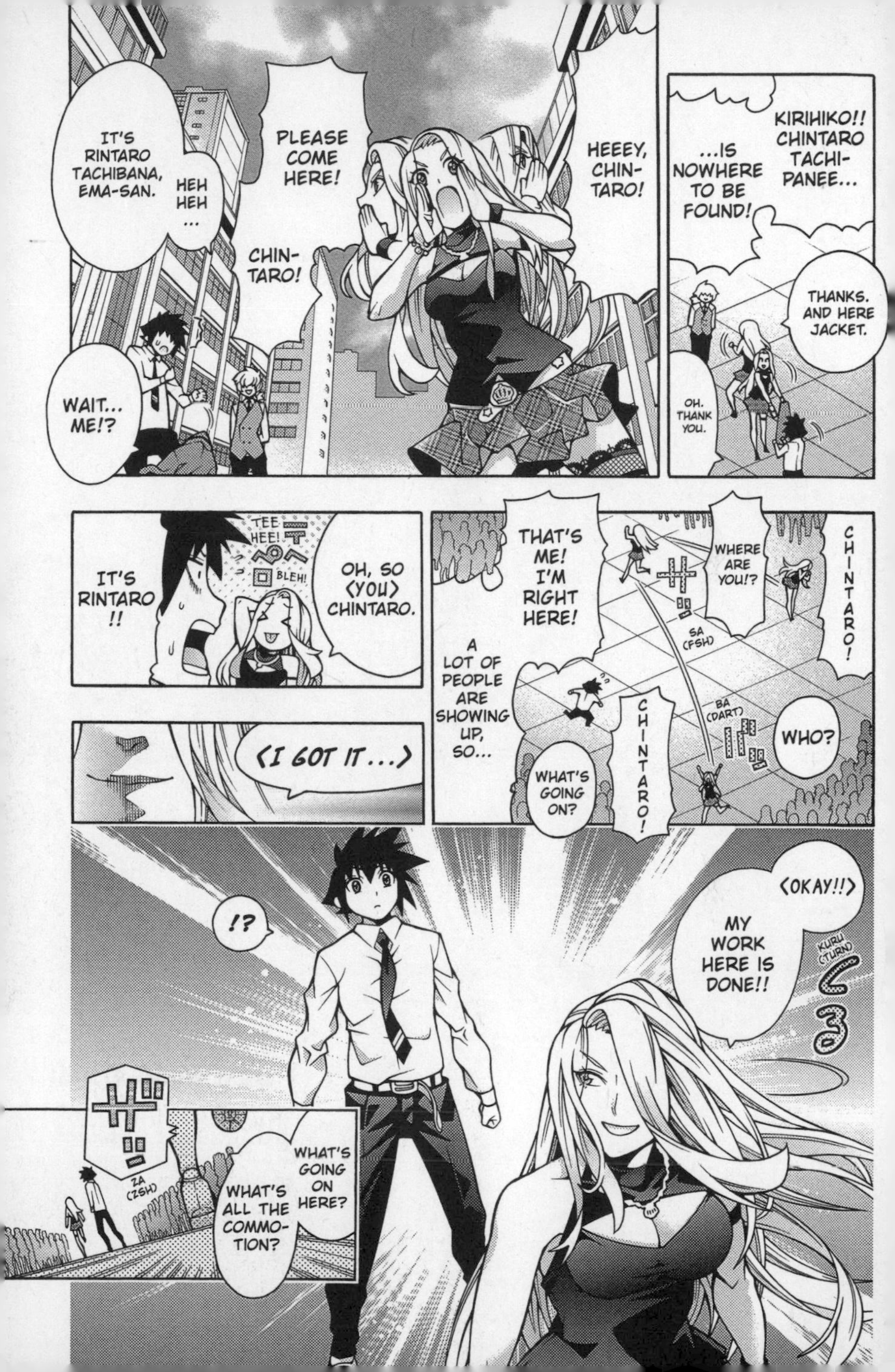
KIRIHIKO!! CHINTARO TACHI-PANEE...
...IS NOWHERE TO BE FOUND!
THANKS. AND HERE JACKET.
OH. THANK YOU.
HEEEY, CHIN-TARO!
PLEASE COME HERE!
CHIN-TARO!
IT'S RINTARO TACHIBANA, EMA-SAN.
HEH HEH ...
WAIT... ME!?
CHINTARO!
WHERE ARE YOU!?
THAT'S ME! I'M RIGHT HERE!
SA (FSH)
WHO?
BA (DART)
CHINTARO!
A LOT OF PEOPLE ARE SHOWING UP, SO...
WHAT'S GOING ON?
OH, SO 〈YOU〉 CHINTARO.
TEE HEE!
BLEH!
IT'S RINTARO !!
〈I GOT IT...〉
〈OKAY!!〉
MY WORK HERE IS DONE!!
KURU (TURN)
!?
WHAT'S GOING ON HERE?
WHAT'S ALL THE COMMOTION?
ZA (ZSH)

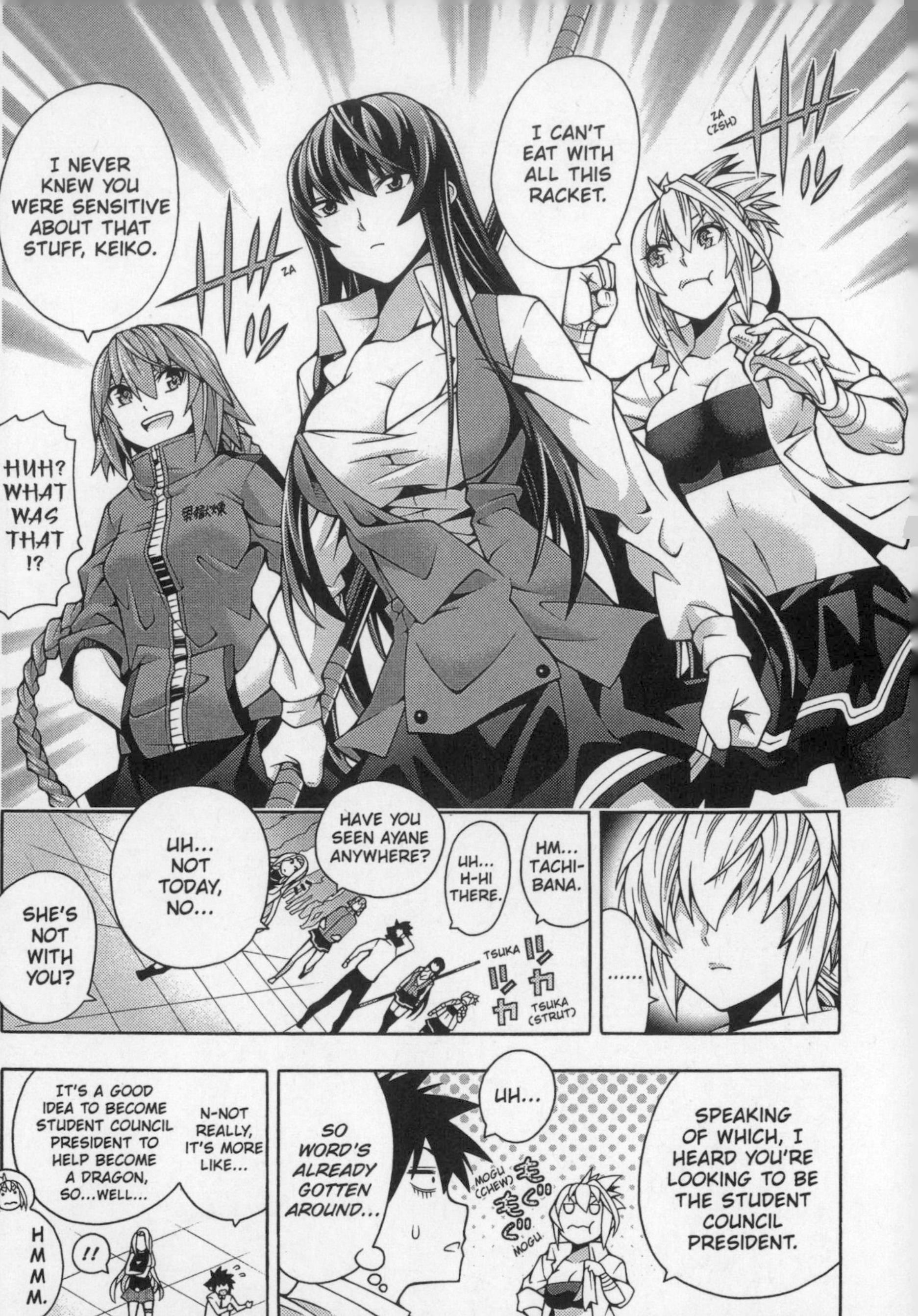
I CAN'T EAT WITH ALL THIS RACKET.
ZA (ZSH)
I NEVER KNEW YOU WERE SENSITIVE ABOUT THAT STUFF, KEIKO.
ZA
HUH? WHAT WAS THAT !?
......
HM... TACHIBANA.
UH... H-HI THERE.
HAVE YOU SEEN AYANE ANYWHERE?
UH... NOT TODAY, NO...
SHE'S NOT WITH YOU?
TSUKA
TSUKA (STRUT)
SPEAKING OF WHICH, I HEARD YOU'RE LOOKING TO BE THE STUDENT COUNCIL PRESIDENT.
UH...
MOGU (CHEW)
MOGU
SO WORD'S ALREADY GOTTEN AROUND...
IT'S A GOOD IDEA TO BECOME STUDENT COUNCIL PRESIDENT TO HELP BECOME A DRAGON, SO...WELL...
N-NOT REALLY, IT'S MORE LIKE...
!!
HMMMM.

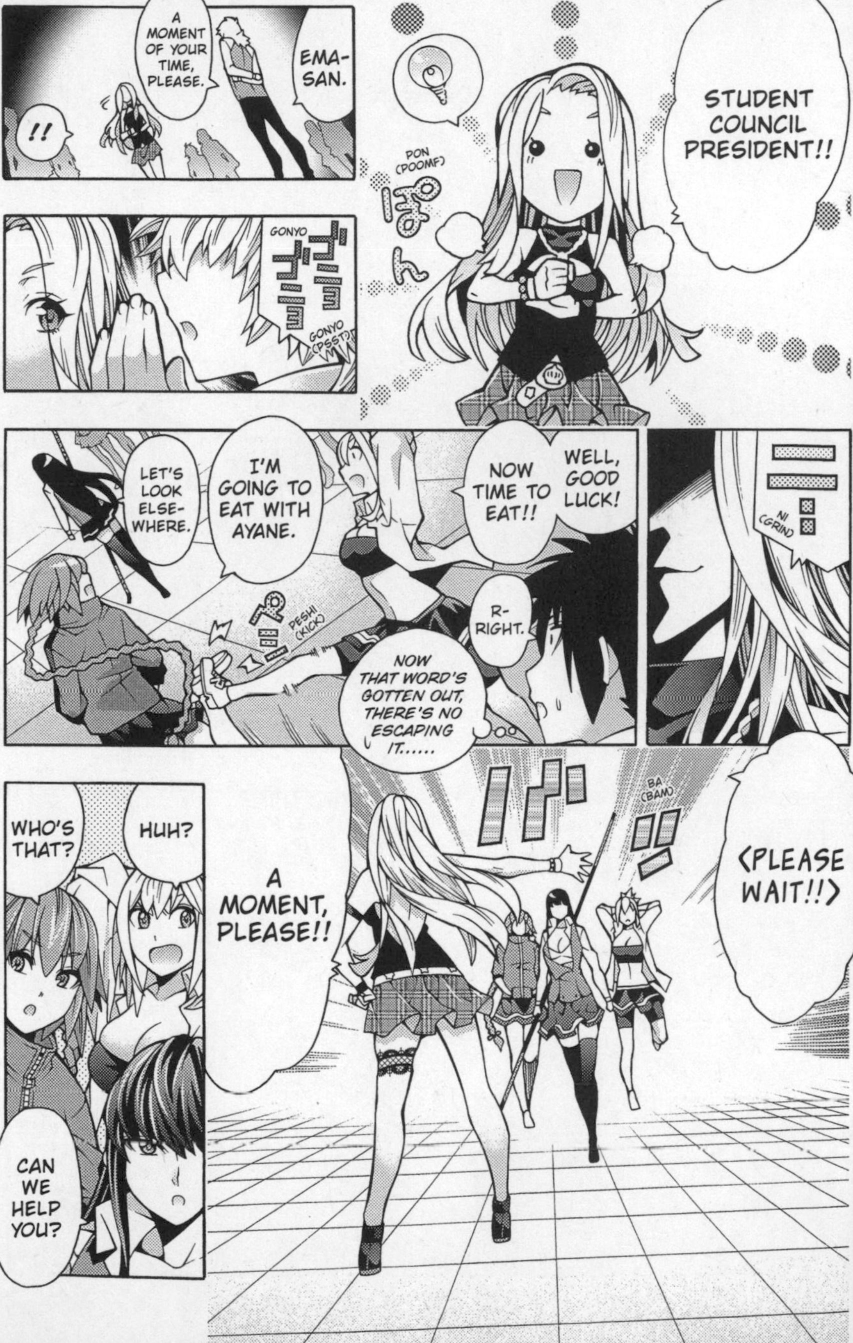
STUDENT COUNCIL PRESIDENT!!
PON (POOMF)
EMA-SAN.
A MOMENT OF YOUR TIME, PLEASE.
!!
GONYO
GONYO (PSST)
NI (GRIN)
WELL, GOOD LUCK!
NOW TIME TO EAT!!
R-RIGHT.
NOW THAT WORD'S GOTTEN OUT, THERE'S NO ESCAPING IT......
I'M GOING TO EAT WITH AYANE.
LET'S LOOK ELSE-WHERE.
PESHI (KICK)
<PLEASE WAIT!!>
BA (BAM)
A MOMENT, PLEASE!!
HUH?
WHO'S THAT?
CAN WE HELP YOU?

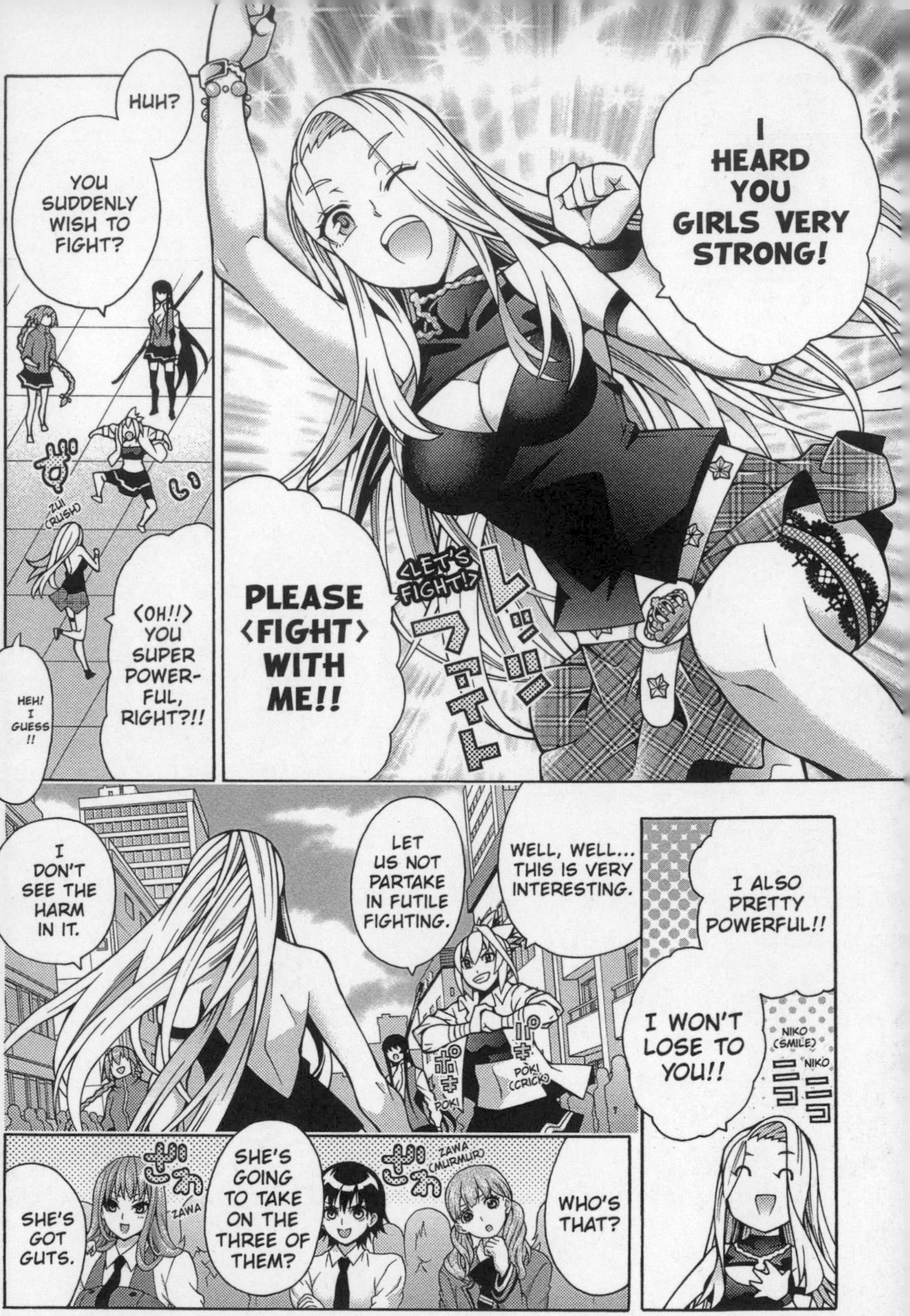
I HEARD YOU GIRLS VERY STRONG!
PLEASE ‹FIGHT› WITH ME!!
‹LET'S FIGHT!›
HUH?
YOU SUDDENLY WISH TO FIGHT?
ZUI (RUSH)
‹OH!!› YOU SUPER POWER-FUL, RIGHT?!!
HEH! I GUESS!!
I ALSO PRETTY POWERFUL!!
I WON'T LOSE TO YOU!!
NIKO (SMILE)
NIKO
WELL, WELL... THIS IS VERY INTERESTING.
LET US NOT PARTAKE IN FUTILE FIGHTING.
I DON'T SEE THE HARM IN IT.
POKI (CRICK)
POKI
WHO'S THAT?
ZAWA (MURMUR)
SHE'S GOING TO TAKE ON THE THREE OF THEM?
ZAWA
SHE'S GOT GUTS.

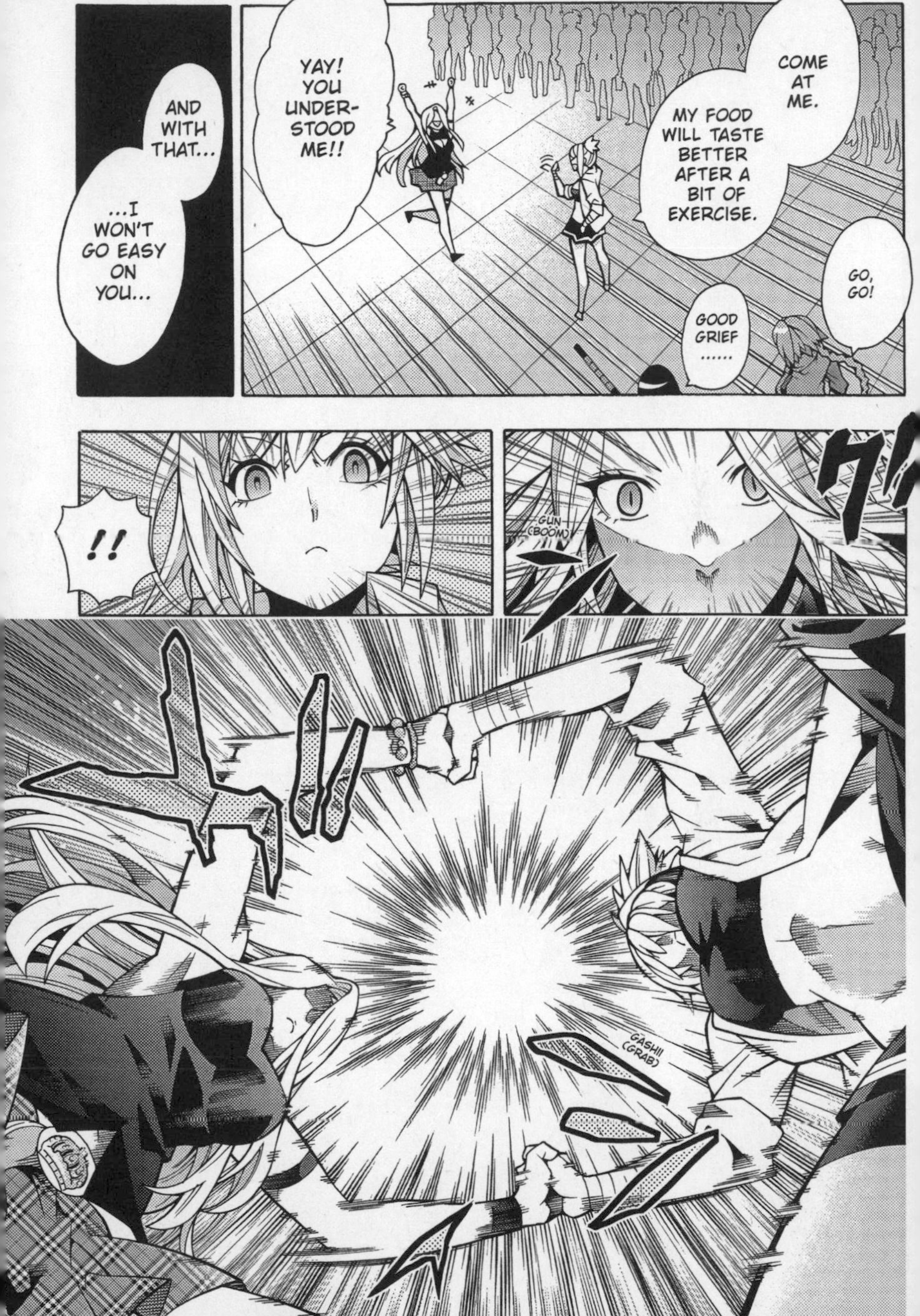
COME AT ME.
MY FOOD WILL TASTE BETTER AFTER A BIT OF EXERCISE.
GO, GO!
GOOD GRIEF ......
YAY! YOU UNDER-STOOD ME!!
AND WITH THAT...
...I WON'T GO EASY ON YOU...
GUN (BOOM)
!!
GASHII (GRAB)

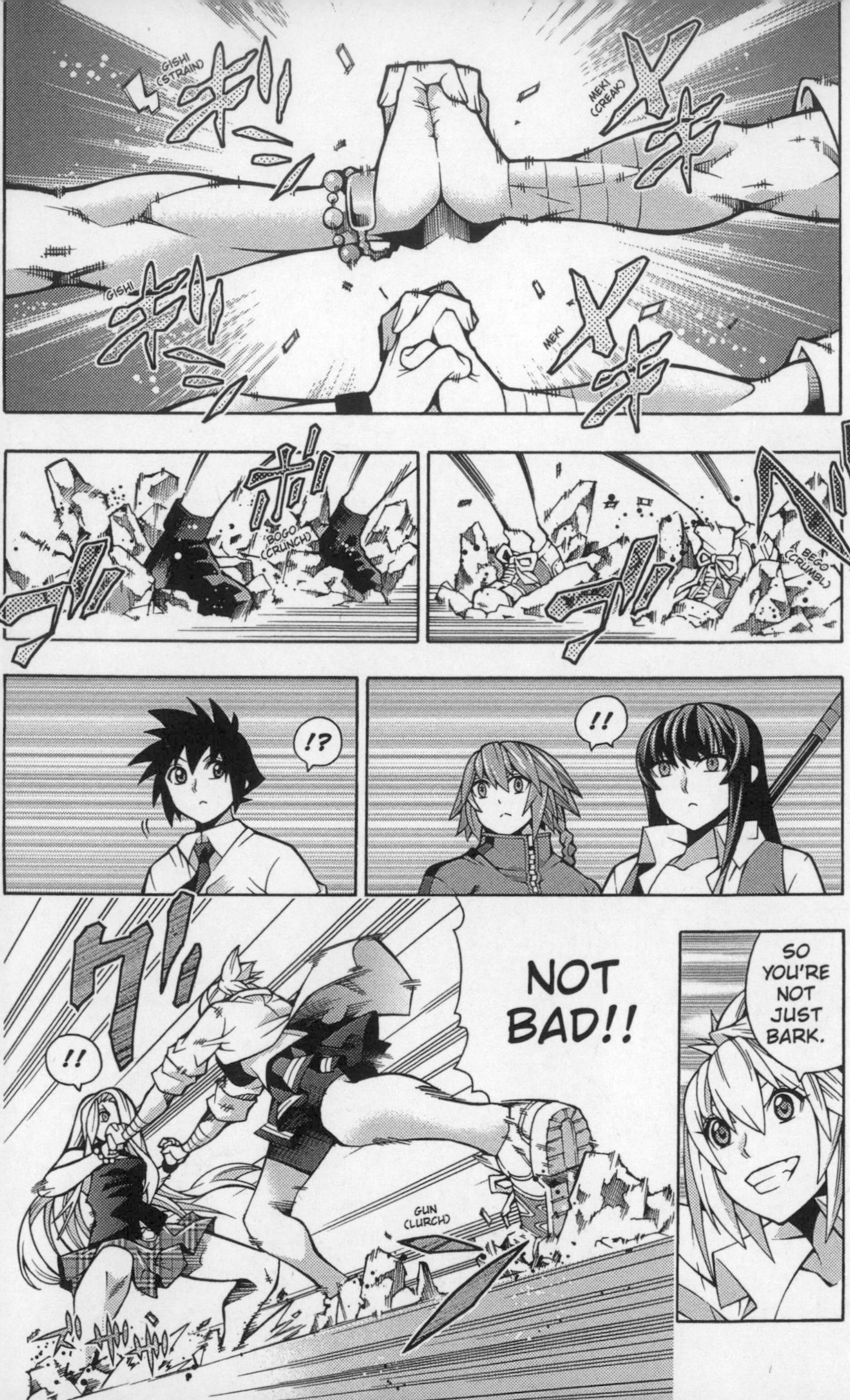
MEKI (CREAK)
GISHI (STRAIN)
MEKI
GISHI
A BEGO (CRUMBL)
BOGO (CRUNCH)
!!
!?
SO YOU'RE NOT JUST BARK.
NOT BAD!!
!!
GUN (LURCH)

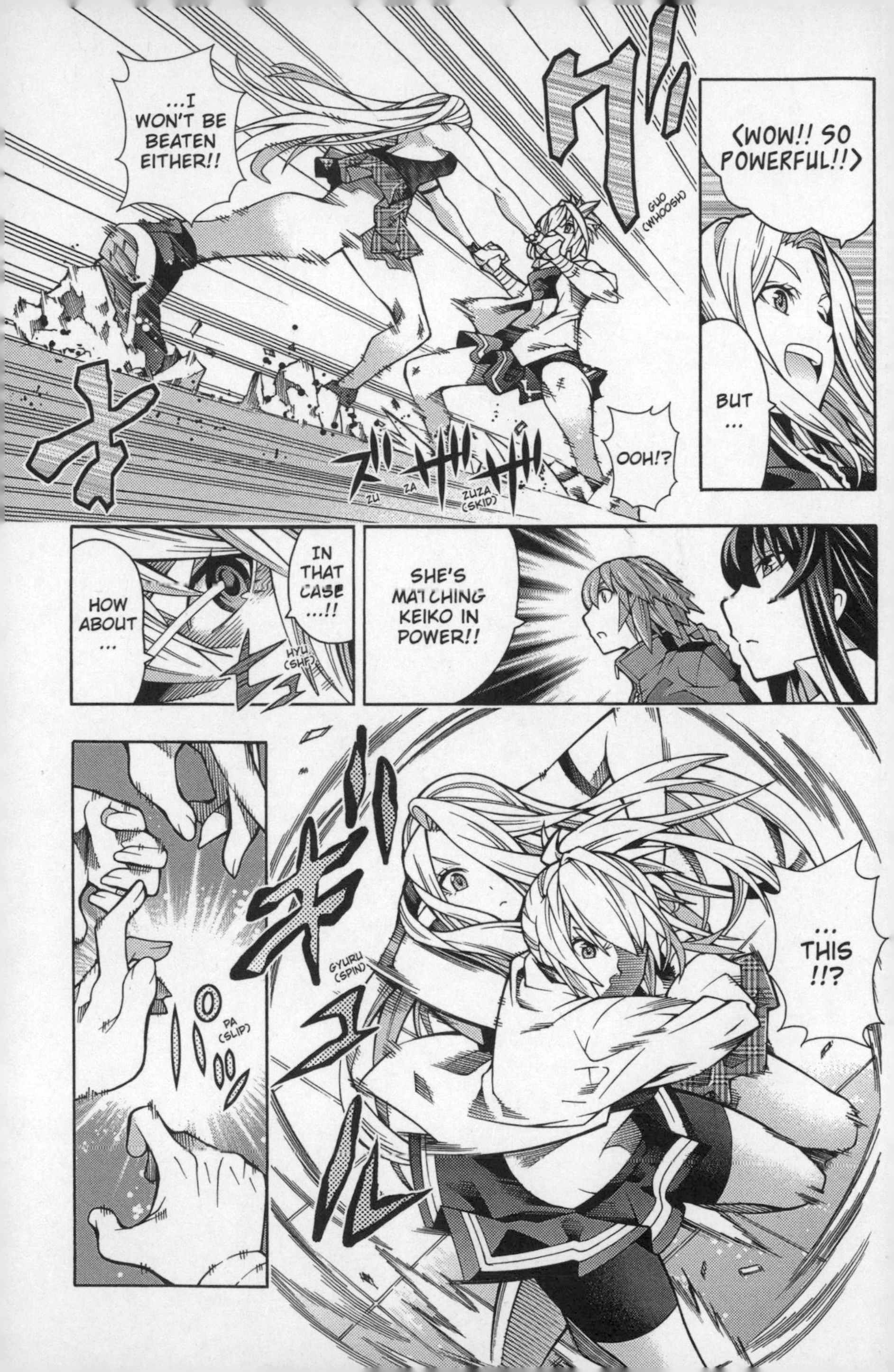
<WOW!! SO POWERFUL!!>
BUT ...
GUO (WHOOSH)
...I WON'T BE BEATEN EITHER!!
OOH!?
ZUZA (SKID)
ZA
ZU
SHE'S MATCHING KEIKO IN POWER!!
IN THAT CASE ...!!
HYU (SHF)
HOW ABOUT ...
... THIS !!?
GYURU (SPIN)
PA (SLIP)

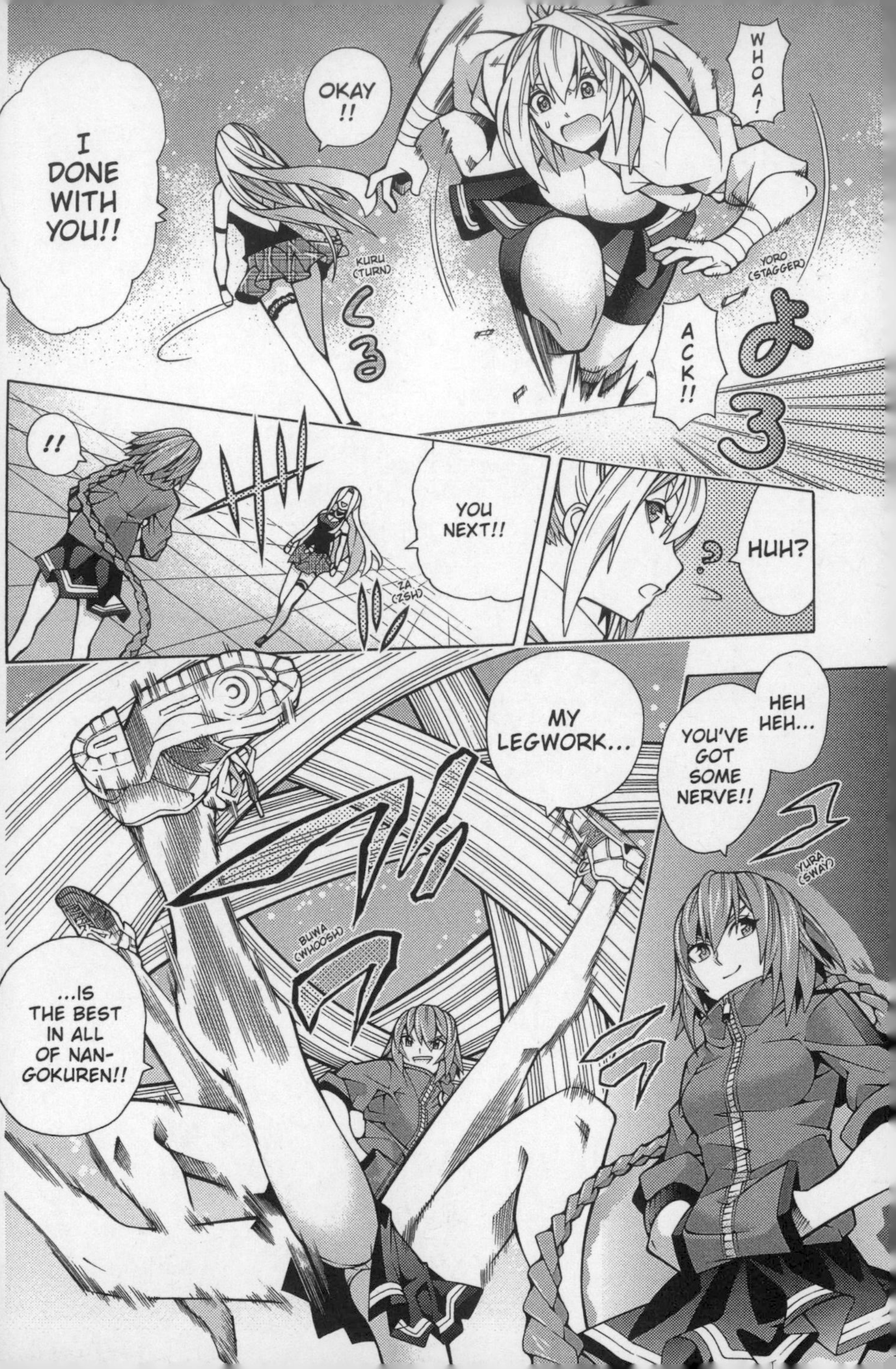
WHOA!
OKAY !!
I DONE WITH YOU!!
YORO (STAGGER)
よろ
ACK!!
KURU (TURN)
くる
HUH?
YOU NEXT!!
ZA (ZSH)
!!
HEH HEH...
YOU'VE GOT SOME NERVE!!
MY LEGWORK...
YURA (SWAY)
BUWA (WHOOSH)
...IS THE BEST IN ALL OF NAN-GOKUREN!!

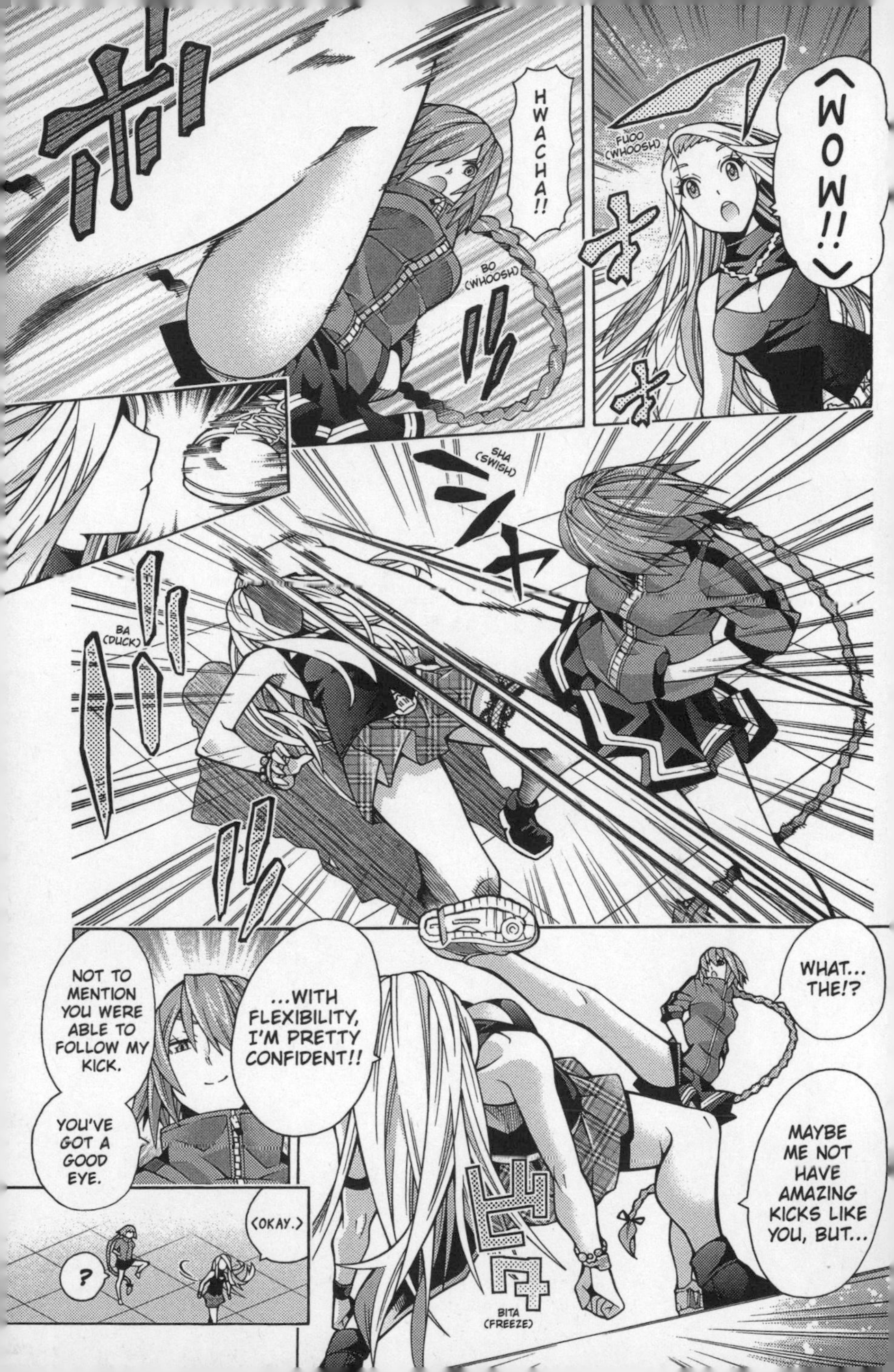
FUOO (WHOOSH)
<WOW!!>
HWACHA!!
BO (WHOOSH)
SHA (SWISH)
BA (DUCK)
WHAT... THE!?
MAYBE ME NOT HAVE AMAZING KICKS LIKE YOU, BUT...
...WITH FLEXIBILITY, I'M PRETTY CONFIDENT!!
BITA (FREEZE)
NOT TO MENTION YOU WERE ABLE TO FOLLOW MY KICK.
YOU'VE GOT A GOOD EYE.
<OKAY.>
?

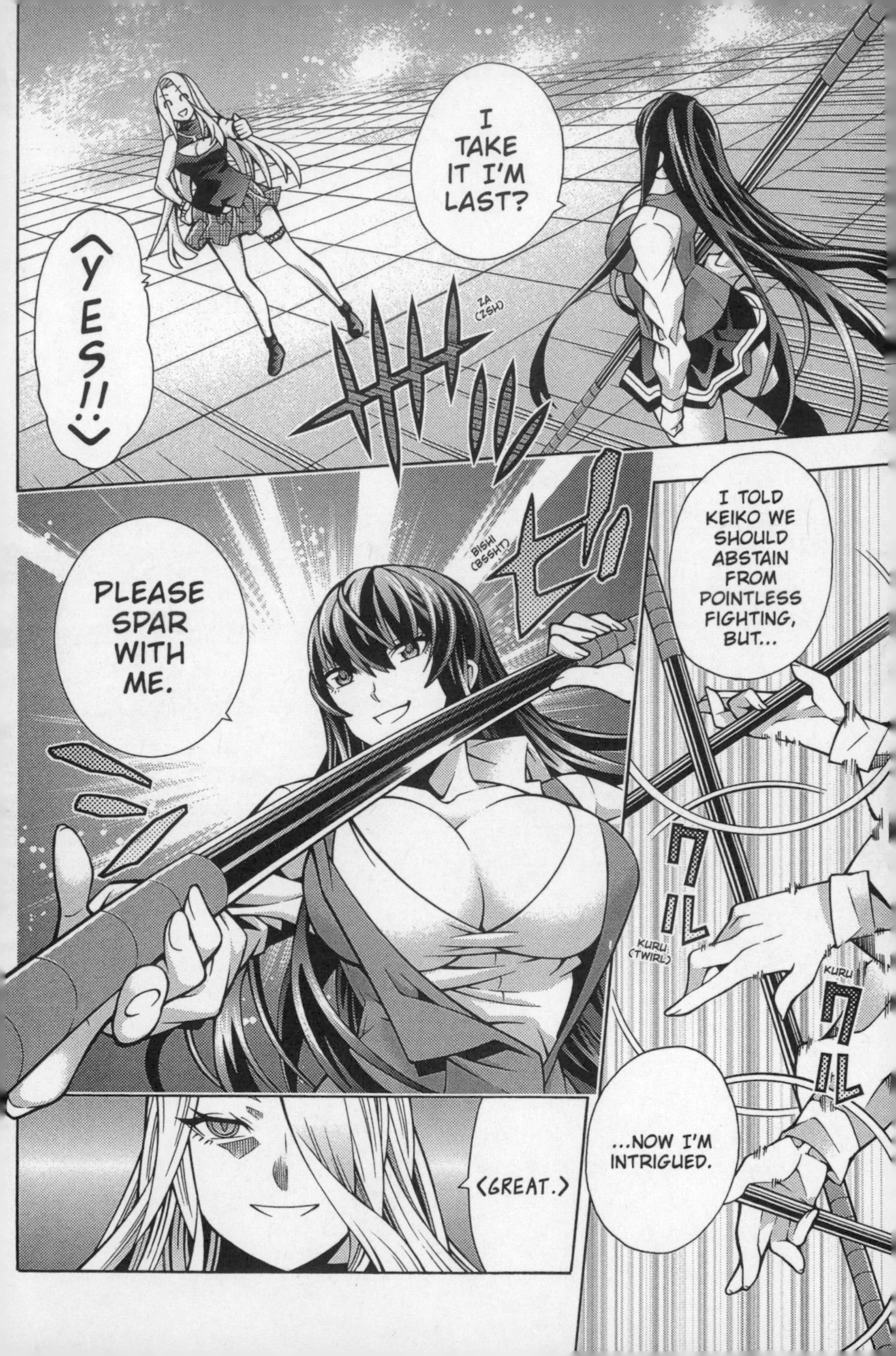
I TAKE IT I'M LAST?
ZA (ZSSH)
<YES!!>
I TOLD KEIKO WE SHOULD ABSTAIN FROM POINTLESS FIGHTING, BUT...
クル
KURU (TWIRL)
KURU
クル
...NOW I'M INTRIGUED.
BISHI (BSSHT)
PLEASE SPAR WITH ME.
<GREAT.>

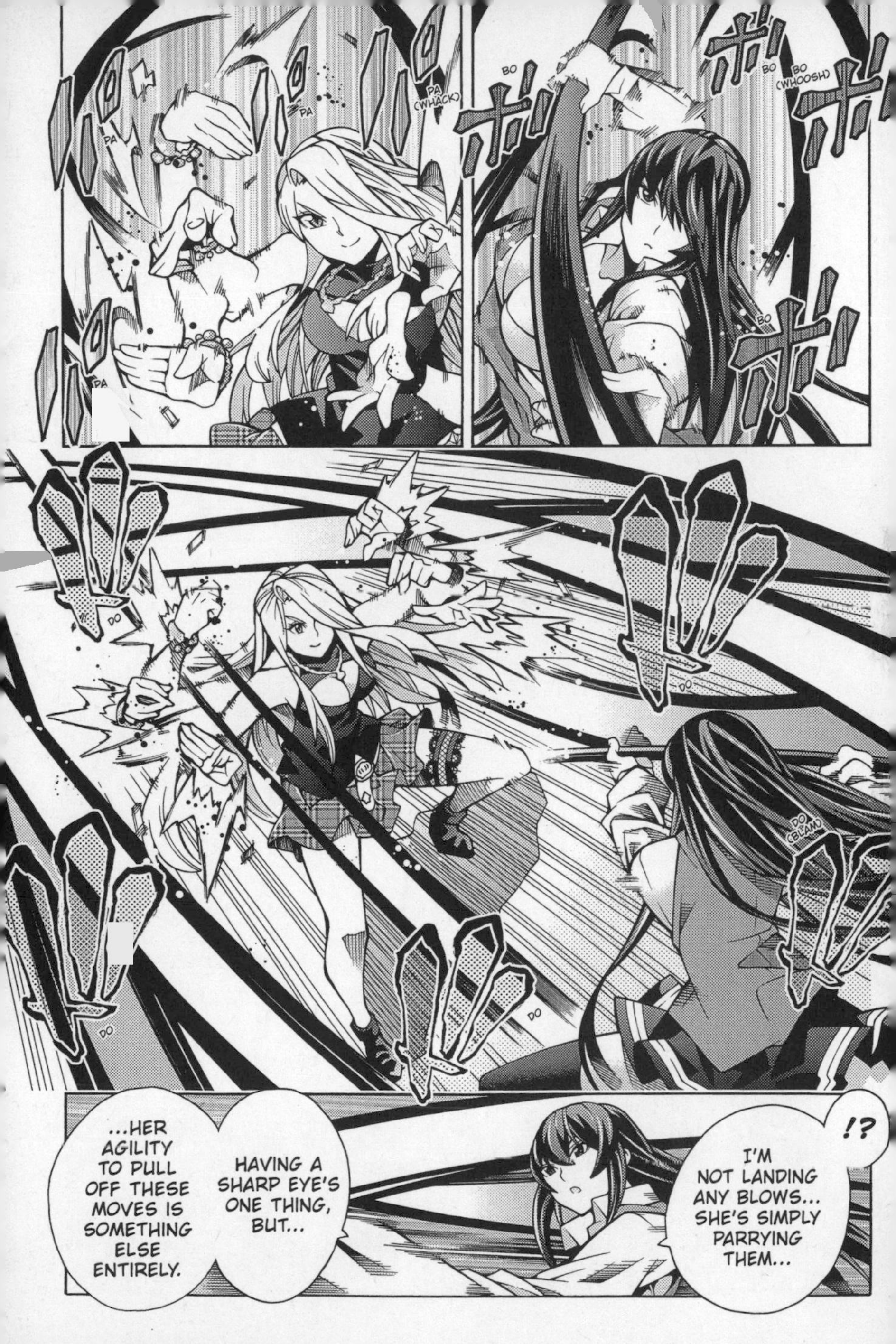
BO
BO
BO (WHOOSH)
BO
PA (WHACK)
PA
PA
PA
DO
DO (BLAM)
DO
DO
DO
!?
I'M NOT LANDING ANY BLOWS... SHE'S SIMPLY PARRYING THEM...
HAVING A SHARP EYE'S ONE THING, BUT...
...HER AGILITY TO PULL OFF THESE MOVES IS SOMETHING ELSE ENTIRELY.

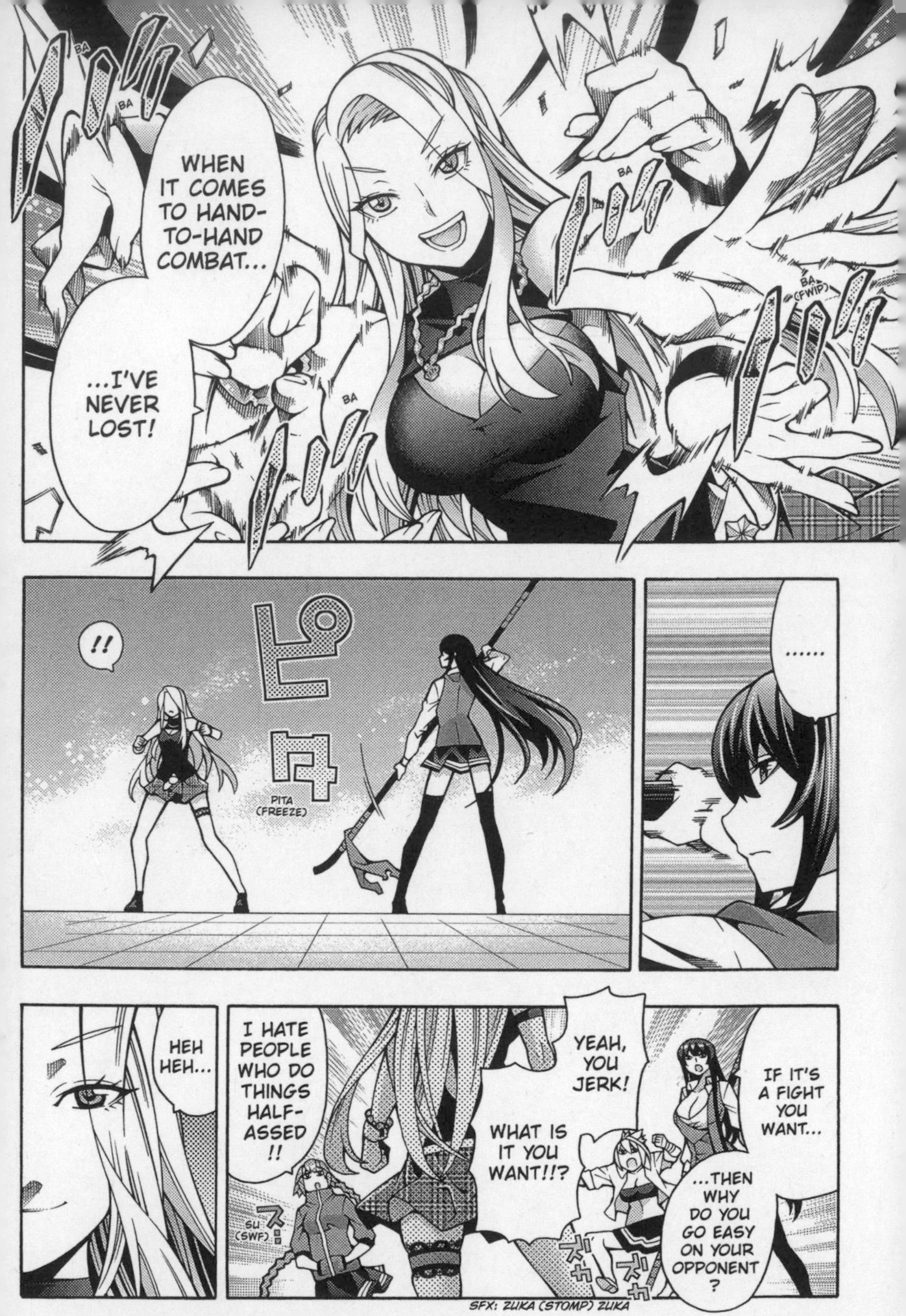
BA
BA (FWIP)
BA
BA
WHEN IT COMES TO HAND-TO-HAND COMBAT...
...I'VE NEVER LOST!
BA
......
!!
PITA (FREEZE)
IF IT'S A FIGHT YOU WANT...
YEAH, YOU JERK!
...THEN WHY DO YOU GO EASY ON YOUR OPPONENT?
WHAT IS IT YOU WANT!!?
I HATE PEOPLE WHO DO THINGS HALF-ASSED!!
SU (SWF)
HEH HEH...

SFX: ZUKA (STOMP) ZUKA

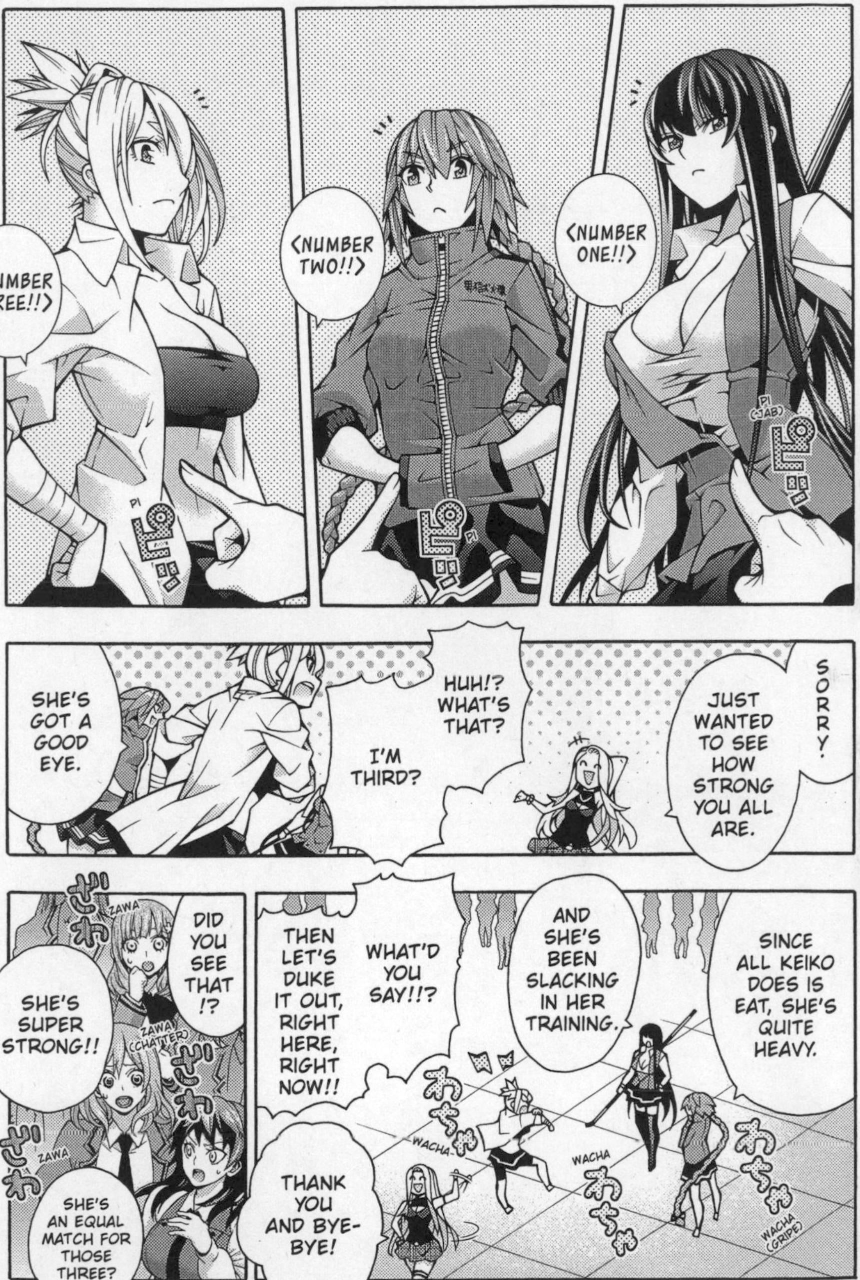
〈NUMBER ONE!!〉
PI (JAB)
〈NUMBER TWO!!〉
PI
〈NUMBER THREE!!〉
PI
SORRY.
JUST WANTED TO SEE HOW STRONG YOU ALL ARE.
HUH!? WHAT'S THAT?
I'M THIRD?
SHE'S GOT A GOOD EYE.
SINCE ALL KEIKO DOES IS EAT, SHE'S QUITE HEAVY.
AND SHE'S BEEN SLACKING IN HER TRAINING.
WHAT'D YOU SAY!!?
THEN LET'S DUKE IT OUT, RIGHT HERE, RIGHT NOW!!
WACHA (GRIPE)
WACHA
WACHA-
THANK YOU AND BYE-BYE!
DID YOU SEE THAT!?
ZAWA
ZAWA (CHATTER)
SHE'S SUPER STRONG!!
ZAWA
SHE'S AN EQUAL MATCH FOR THOSE THREE?

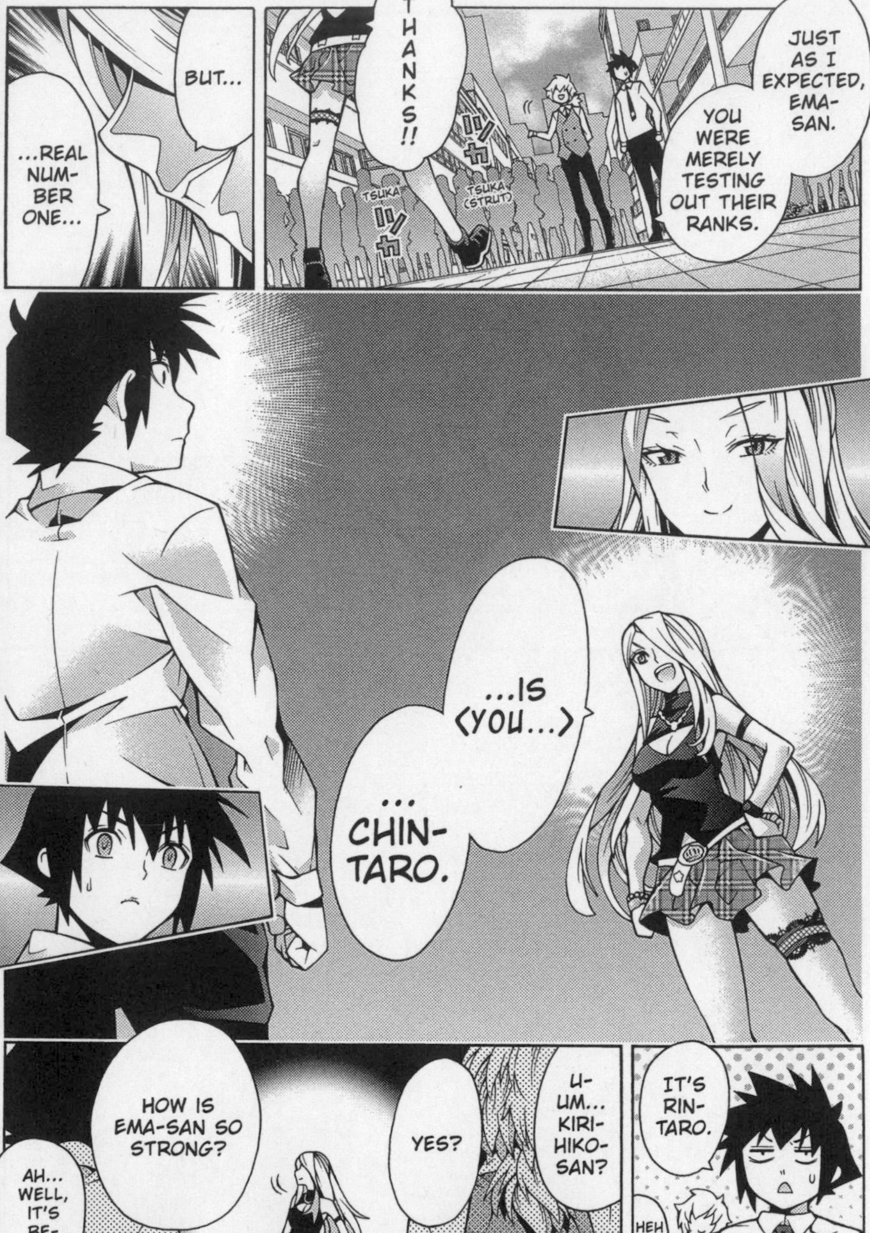
JUST AS I EXPECTED, EMA-SAN.
YOU WERE MERELY TESTING OUT THEIR RANKS.
THANKS!!
TSUKA (STRUT)
TSUKA
BUT...
...REAL NUMBER ONE...
...IS <YOU...>
...CHIN-TARO.
IT'S RIN-TARO.
HEH HEH ...
U-UM... KIRI-HIKO-SAN?
YES?
HOW IS EMA-SAN SO STRONG?
AH... WELL, IT'S BE-CAUSE ...

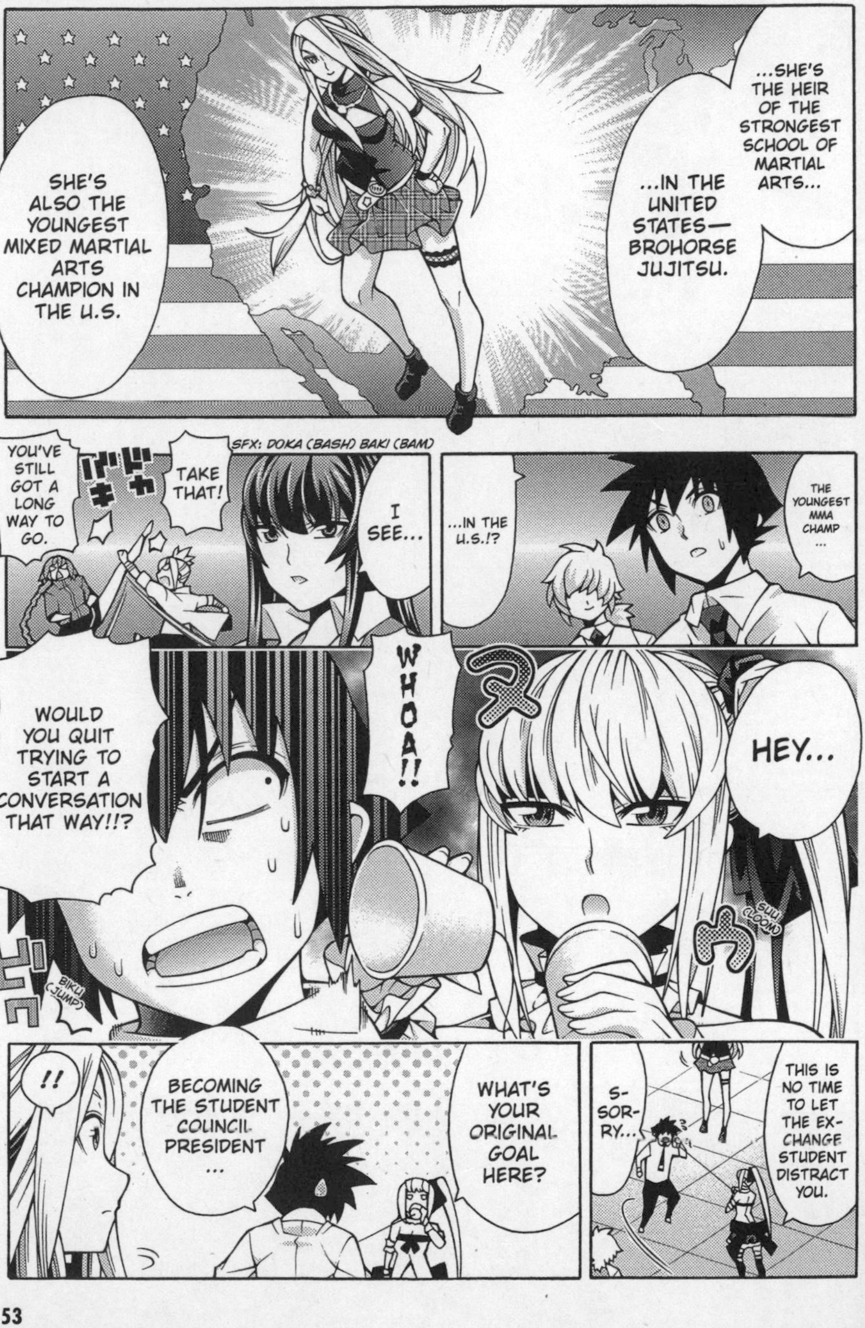
...SHE'S THE HEIR OF THE STRONGEST SCHOOL OF MARTIAL ARTS...
...IN THE UNITED STATES—BROHORSE JUJITSU.
SHE'S ALSO THE YOUNGEST MIXED MARTIAL ARTS CHAMPION IN THE U.S.
THE YOUNGEST MMA CHAMP ...
...IN THE U.S.!?
I SEE...
SFX: DOKA (BASH) BAKI (BAM)
TAKE THAT!
YOU'VE STILL GOT A LONG WAY TO GO.
HEY...
SUU (LOOM)
WHOA!!
WOULD YOU QUIT TRYING TO START A CONVERSATION THAT WAY!!?
BIKU (JUMP)
THIS IS NO TIME TO LET THE EX-CHANGE STUDENT DISTRACT YOU.
S-SOR-RY...
WHAT'S YOUR ORIGINAL GOAL HERE?
BECOMING THE STUDENT COUNCIL PRESIDENT ...
!!

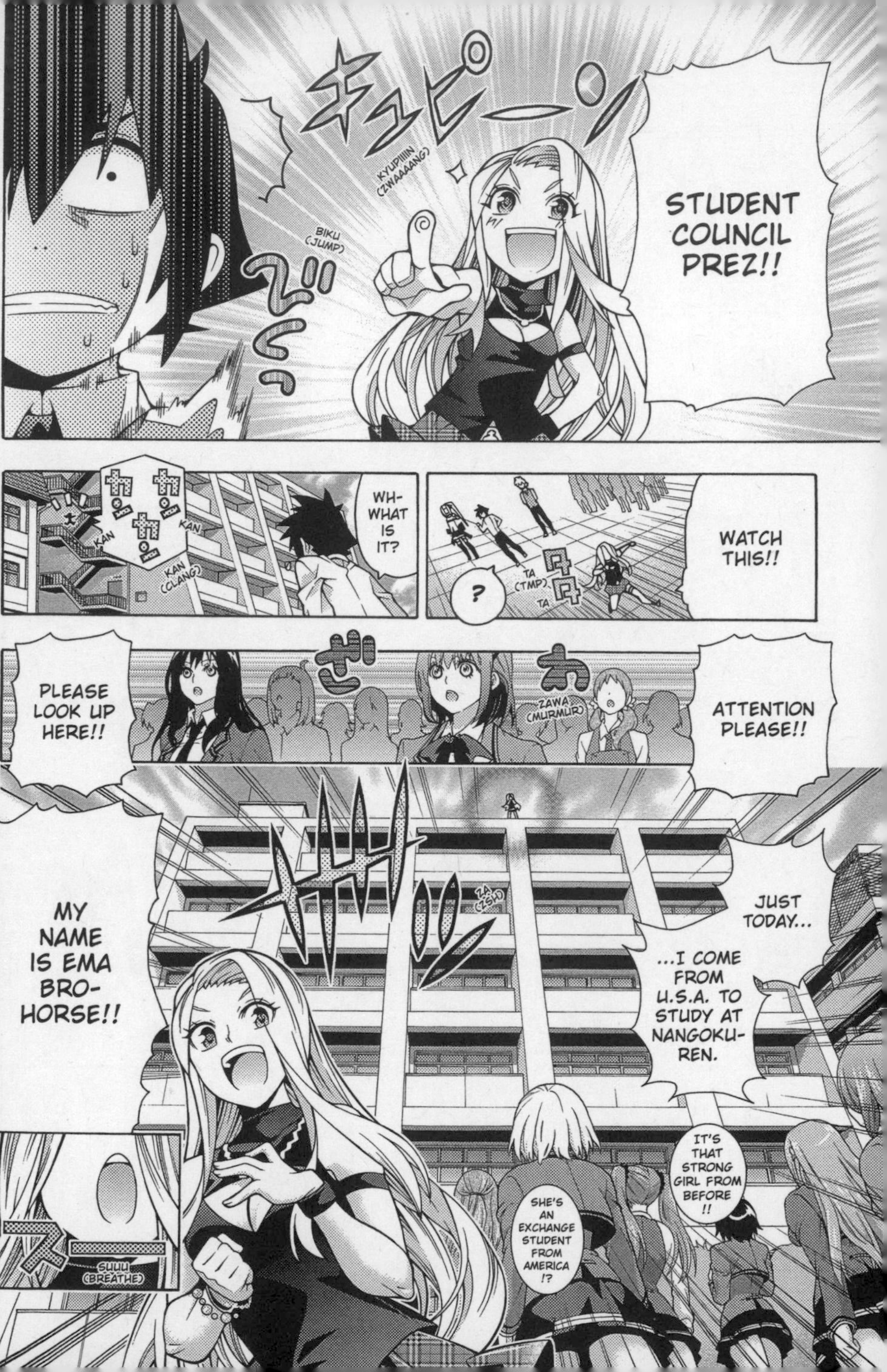
STUDENT COUNCIL PREZ!!
KYUPIIIIN (ZWAAAANG)
BIKU (JUMP)
WATCH THIS!!
?
TA (TMP)
TA
WH-WHAT IS IT?
KAN
KAN
KAN (CLANG)
ATTENTION PLEASE!!
ZAWA (MURMUR)
PLEASE LOOK UP HERE!!
ZA (ZSH)
JUST TODAY...
...I COME FROM U.S.A. TO STUDY AT NANGOKU-REN.
MY NAME IS EMA BRO-HORSE!!
IT'S THAT STRONG GIRL FROM BEFORE!!
SHE'S AN EXCHANGE STUDENT FROM AMERICA!?
SUUU (BREATHE)

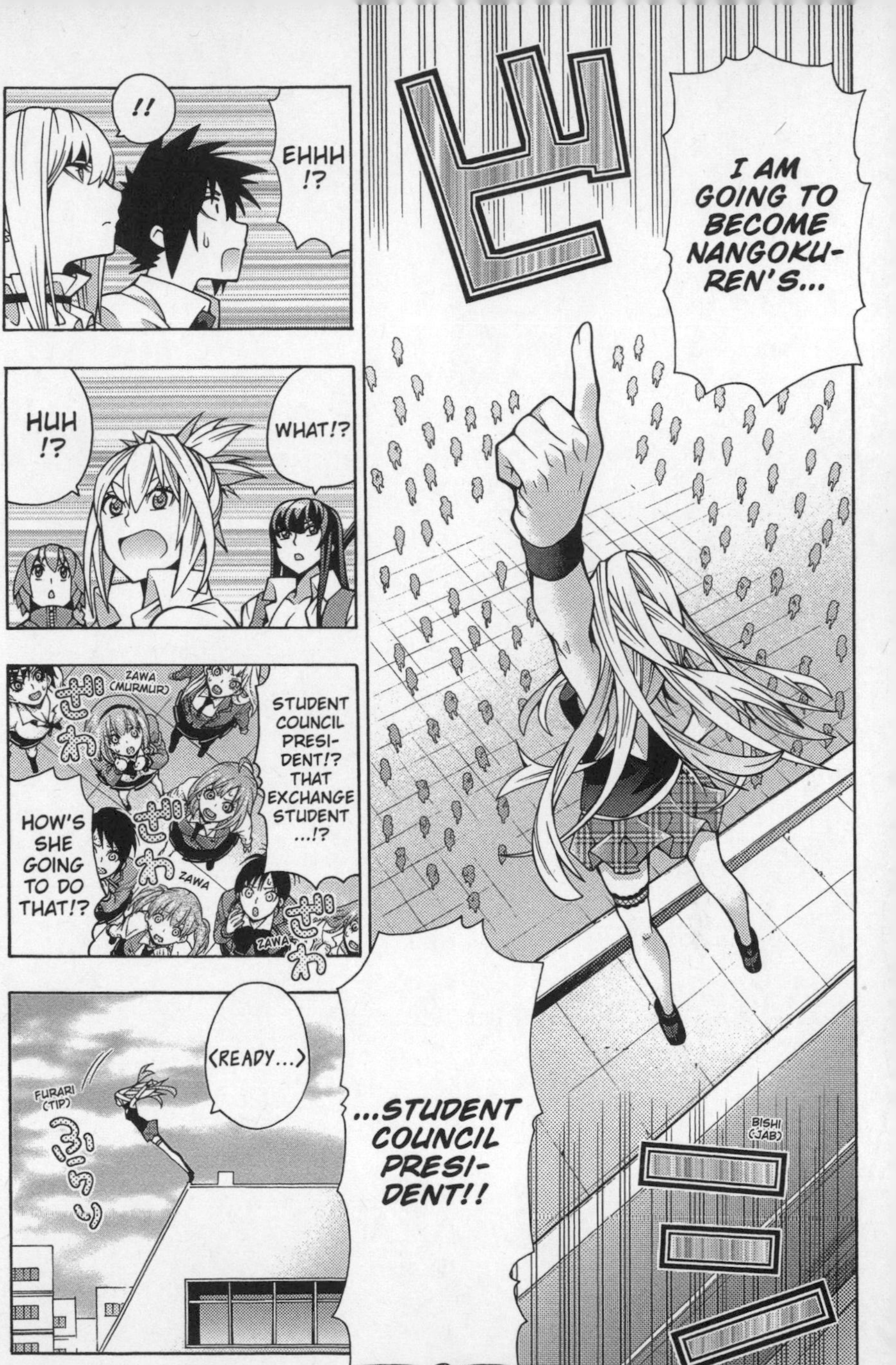

I AM GOING TO BECOME NANGOKU-REN'S...
BISHI (JAB)
...STUDENT COUNCIL PRESI-DENT!!
!!
EHHH !?
WHAT!?
HUH !?
STUDENT COUNCIL PRESI-DENT!? THAT EXCHANGE STUDENT ...!?
ZAWA (MURMUR)
HOW'S SHE GOING TO DO THAT!?
ZAWA
ZAWA
<READY...>
FURARI (TIP)

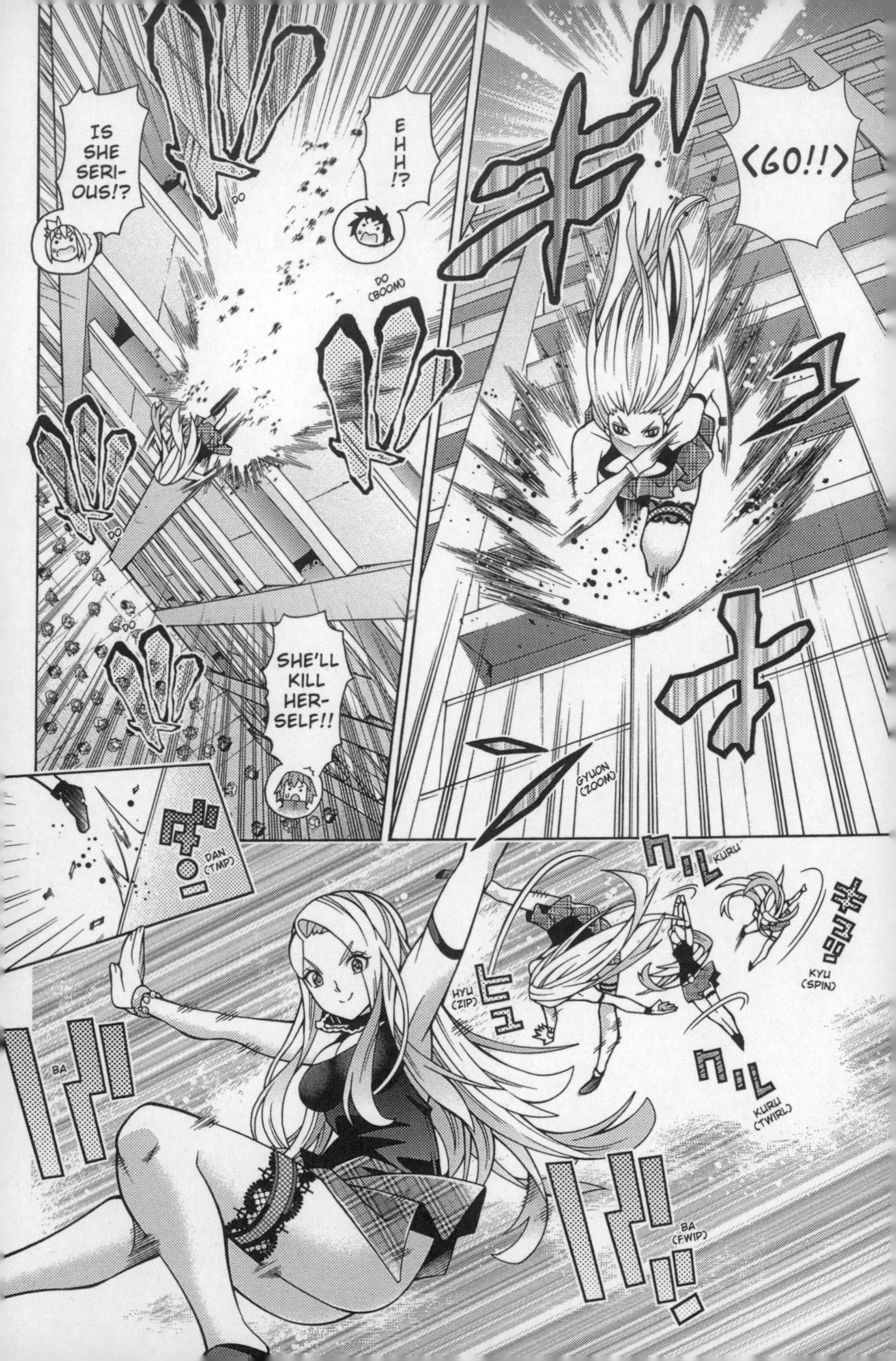
〈GO!!〉
GYUON (ZOOM)
EHH!?
IS SHE SERIOUS!?
DO
DO (BOOM)
DO
DO
SHE'LL KILL HERSELF!!
KURU
KYU (SPIN)
HYU (ZIP)
KURU (TWIRL)
DAN (TMP)
BA
BA (FWIP)

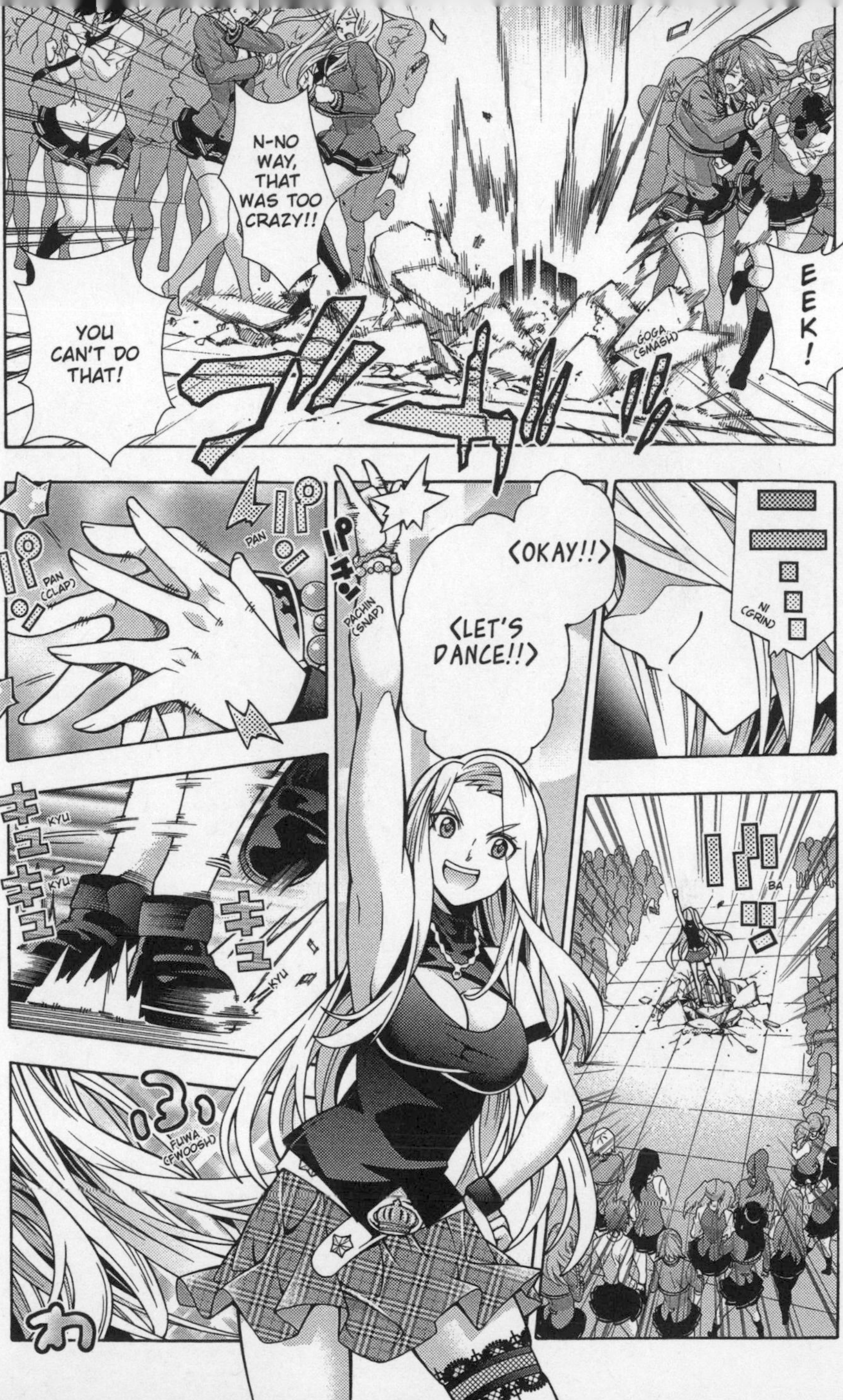

EEK!
GOGA (SMASH)
N-NO WAY, THAT WAS TOO CRAZY!!
YOU CAN'T DO THAT!
NI (GRIN)
BA
‹OKAY!!›
‹LET'S DANCE!!›
PACHIN (SNAP)
PAN
PAN (CLAP)
KYU
KYU
KYU
FUWA (FWOOSH)

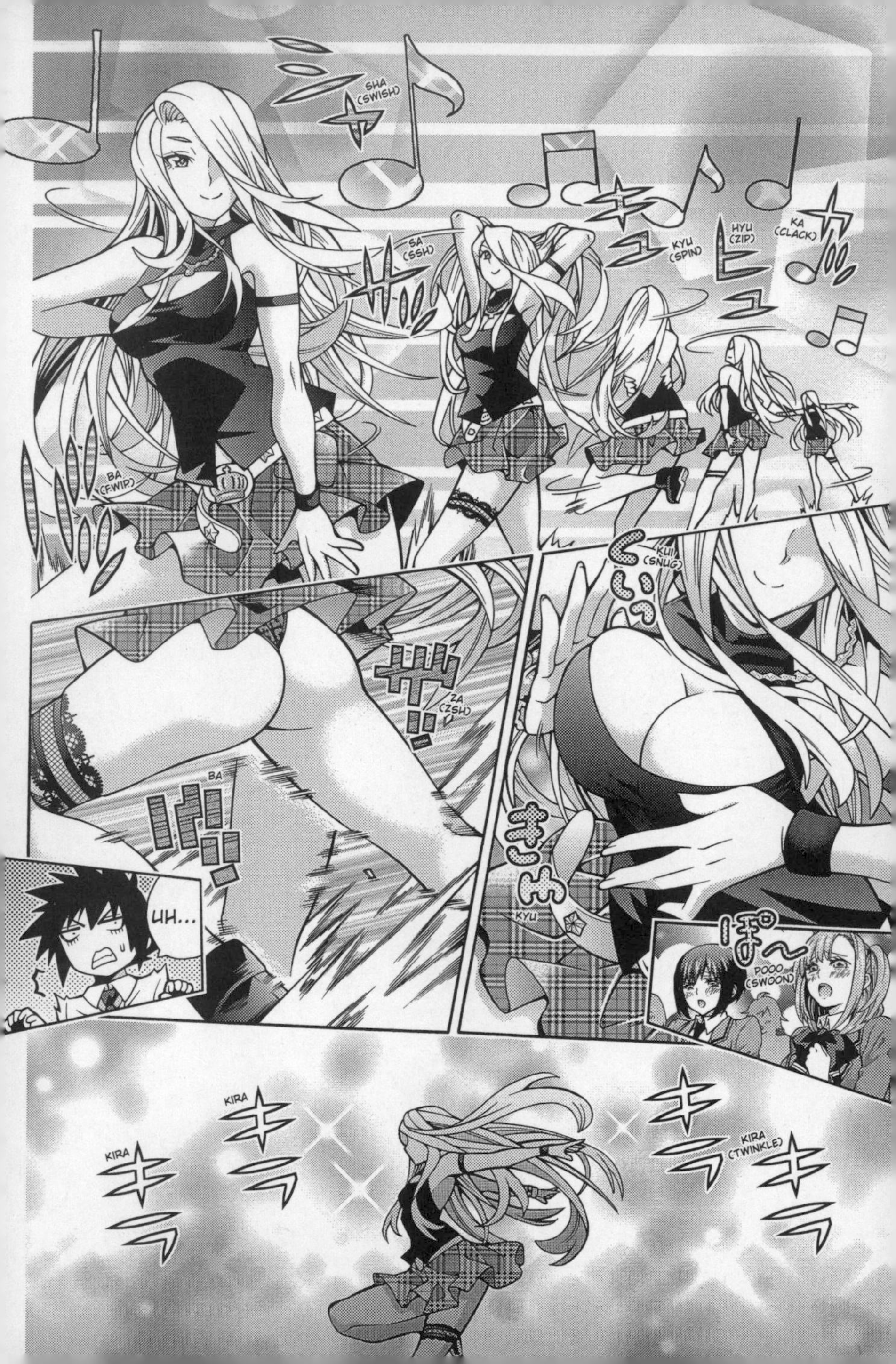
KA (CLACK)
HYU (ZIP)
KYU (SPIN)
SHA (SWISH)
SA (SSH)
BA (F.WIP)
KUI (SNUG)
KYU
POOO (SWOON)
ZA (ZSH)
BA
UH...
KIRA (TWINKLE)
KIRA
KIRA

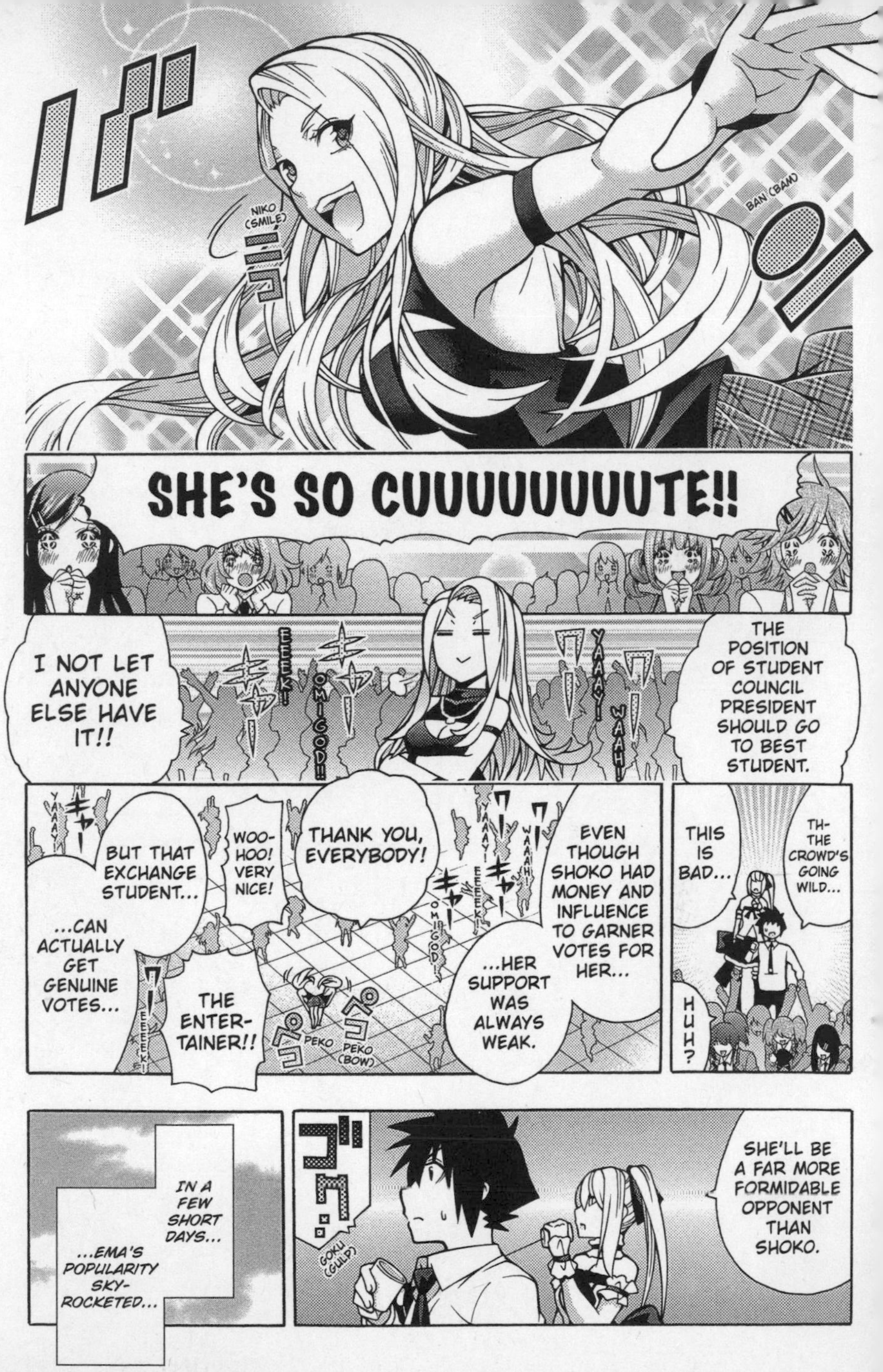
BAN (BAM)
NIKO (SMILE)
SHE'S SO CUUUUUUUUTE!!
THE POSITION OF STUDENT COUNCIL PRESIDENT SHOULD GO TO BEST STUDENT.
YAAAY!
WAAH!
EEEEK!
OMIGOD!!
I NOT LET ANYONE ELSE HAVE IT!!
TH-THE CROWD'S GOING WILD...
THIS IS BAD...
HUH?
EVEN THOUGH SHOKO HAD MONEY AND INFLUENCE TO GARNER VOTES FOR HER...
...HER SUPPORT WAS ALWAYS WEAK.
YAAAY!
WAAAH!
EEEEK!
OMIGOD!
THANK YOU, EVERYBODY!
PEKO (BOW)
PEKO
WOO-HOO! VERY NICE!
THE ENTER-TAINER!!
BUT THAT EXCHANGE STUDENT...
...CAN ACTUALLY GET GENUINE VOTES...
YAAAY
EEEEK!
SHE'LL BE A FAR MORE FORMIDABLE OPPONENT THAN SHOKO.
GOKU (GULP)
IN A FEW SHORT DAYS...
...EMA'S POPULARITY SKY-ROCKETED...

POSTER: I'M GOING TO BECOME STUDENT COUNCIL PRESIDENT
THE ANGEL OF THE FIRST-YEARS, EMA BROHORSE

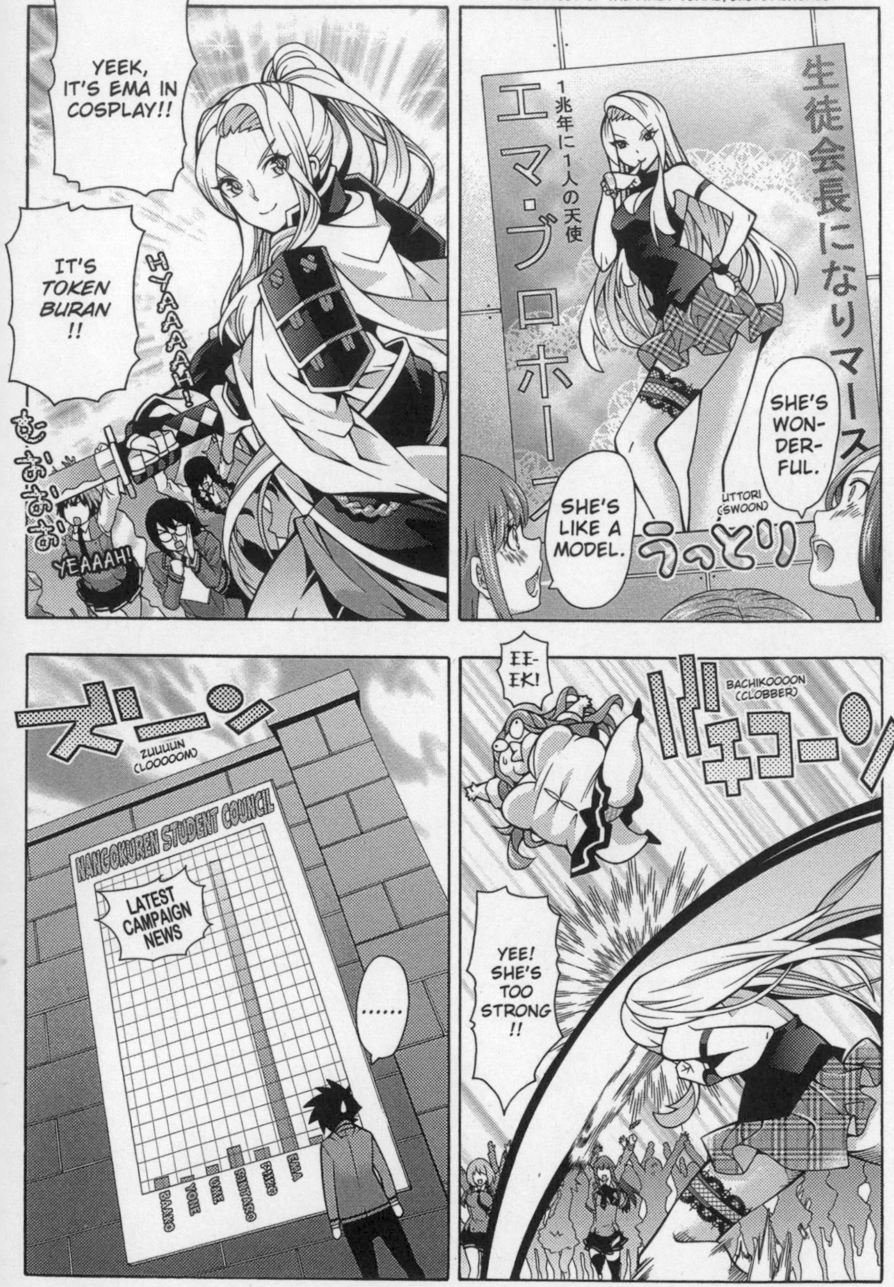

生徒会長になりマース
1兆年に1人の天使
エマ・ブロホース
SHE'S WONDER-FUL.
UTTORI (SWOON)
SHE'S LIKE A MODEL.
うっとり
YEEK, IT'S EMA IN COSPLAY!!
HYAAAAAAH!
IT'S TOKEN BURAN!!
YEAAAH!
EE-EK!
BACHIKOOOON (CLOBBER)
YEE! SHE'S TOO STRONG!!
ZUUUUUN (LOOOOOM)
NANGOKUREN STUDENT COUNCIL
LATEST CAMPAIGN NEWS
......
EMA
PIKO
KINTARO
UKE
YONE
BANJO

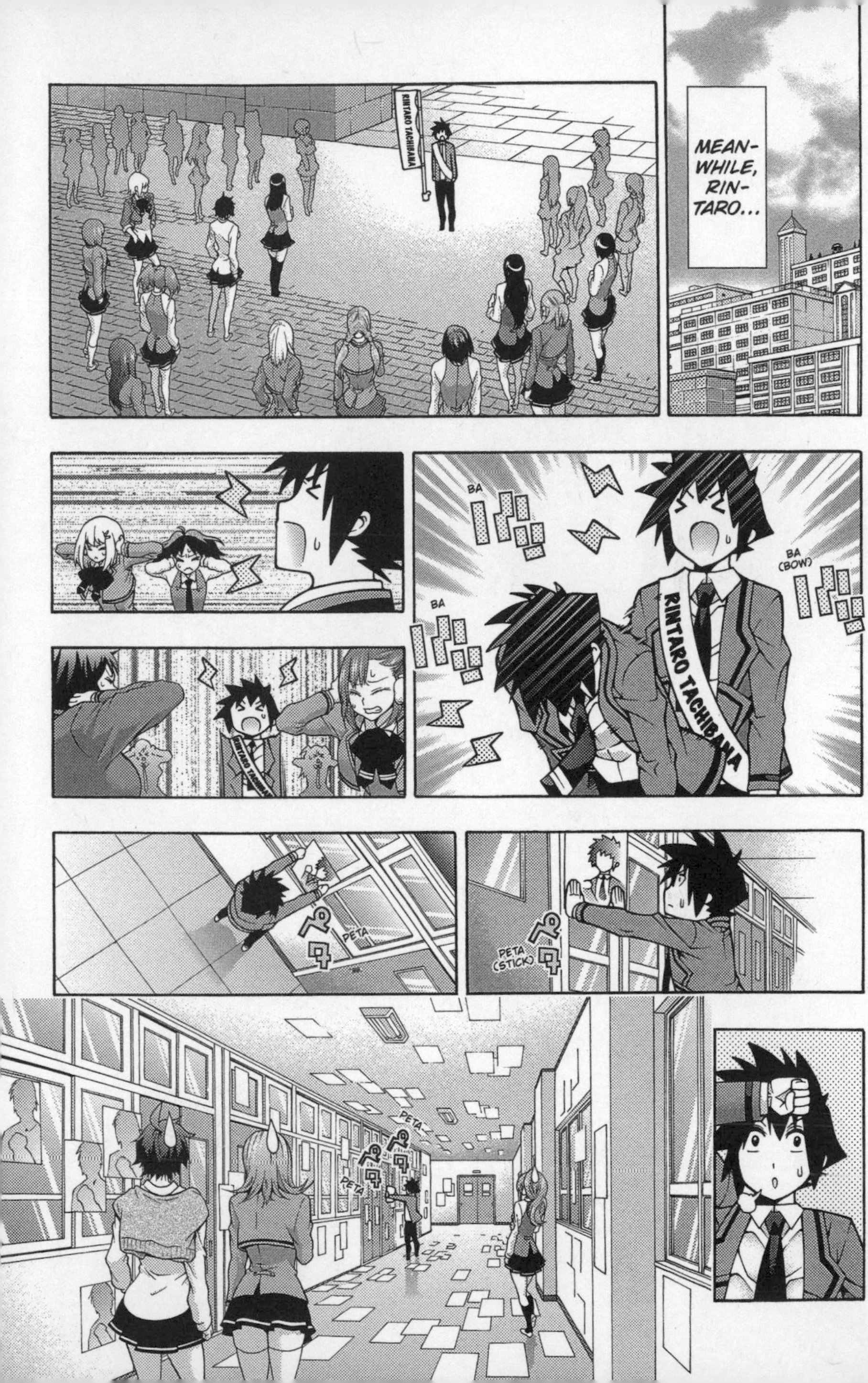
MEAN-WHILE, RIN-TARO...
RINTARO TACHIBANA
BA
BA (BOW)
BA
RINTARO TACHIBANA
RINTARO TACHIBANA
PETA (STICK)
PETA
PETA
PETA

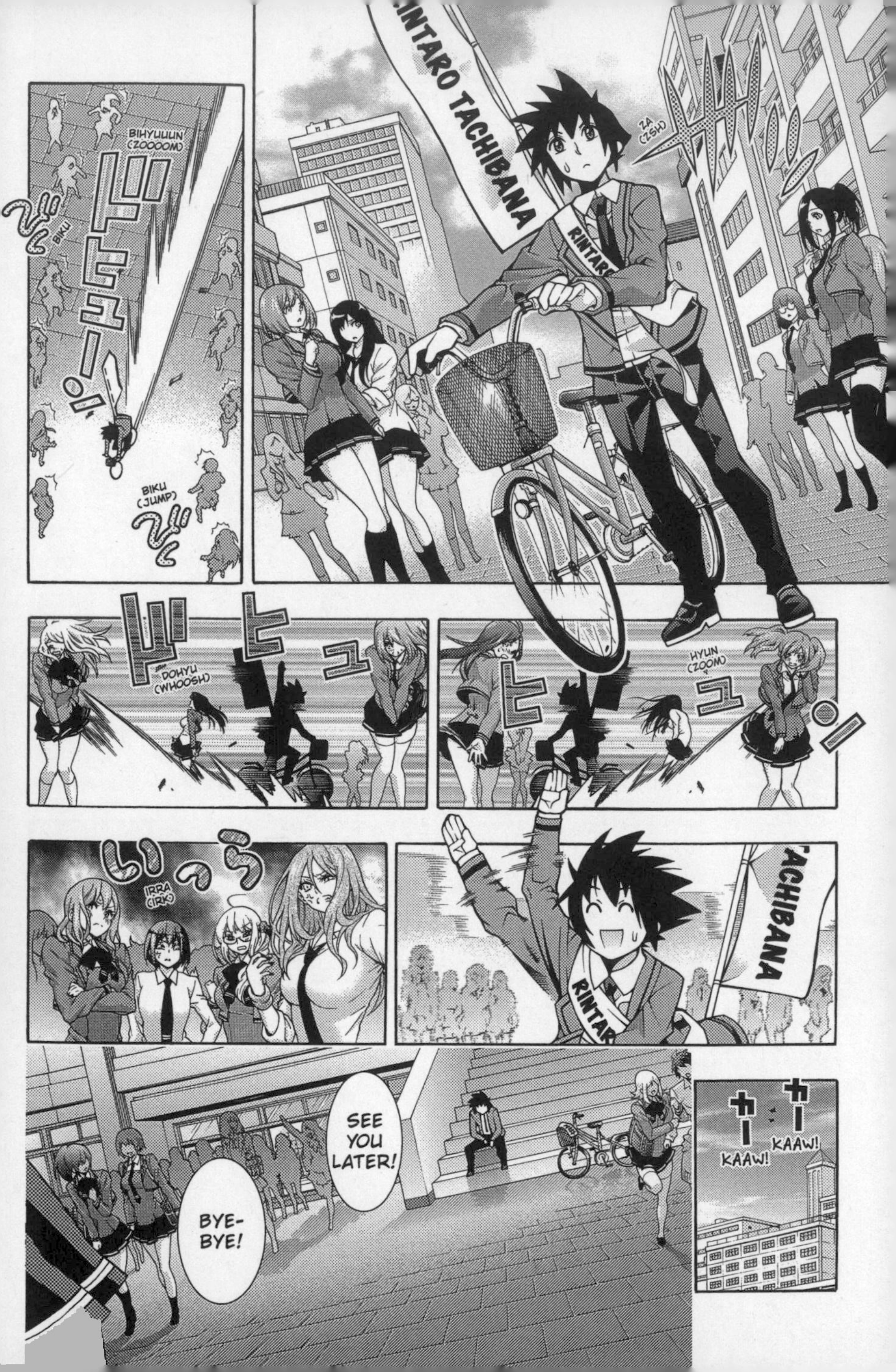
RINTARO TACHIBANA
ZA (ZSH)
BIHYUUUN (ZOOOOM)
BIKU
BIKU (JUMP)
HYUN (ZOOM)
DOHYU (WHOOSH)
TACHIBANA
IRRA (IRK)
KAAW!
KAAW!
SEE YOU LATER!
BYE-BYE!

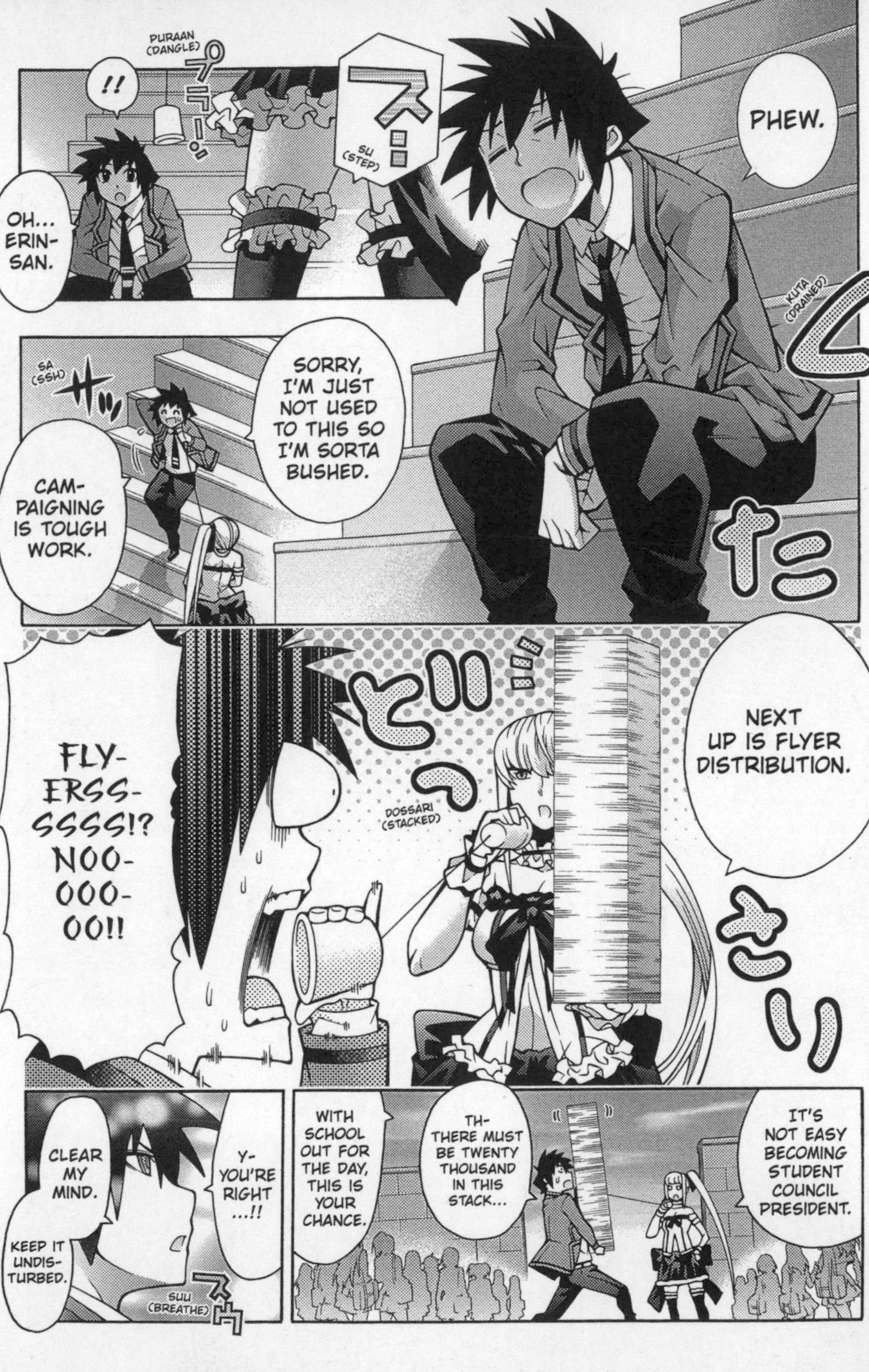
PHEW.
KUTA (DRAINED)
SU (STEP)
PURAAN (DANGLE)
!!
OH... ERIN-SAN.
SORRY, I'M JUST NOT USED TO THIS SO I'M SORTA BUSHED.
SA (SSH)
CAM-PAIGNING IS TOUGH WORK.
NEXT UP IS FLYER DISTRIBUTION.
DOSSARI (STACKED)
FLY-ERSS-SSSS!? NOO-OOO-OO!!
IT'S NOT EASY BECOMING STUDENT COUNCIL PRESIDENT.
TH- THERE MUST BE TWENTY THOUSAND IN THIS STACK...
WITH SCHOOL OUT FOR THE DAY, THIS IS YOUR CHANCE.
Y- YOU'RE RIGHT ...!!
CLEAR MY MIND.
KEEP IT UNDIS-TURBED.
SUU (BREATHE)

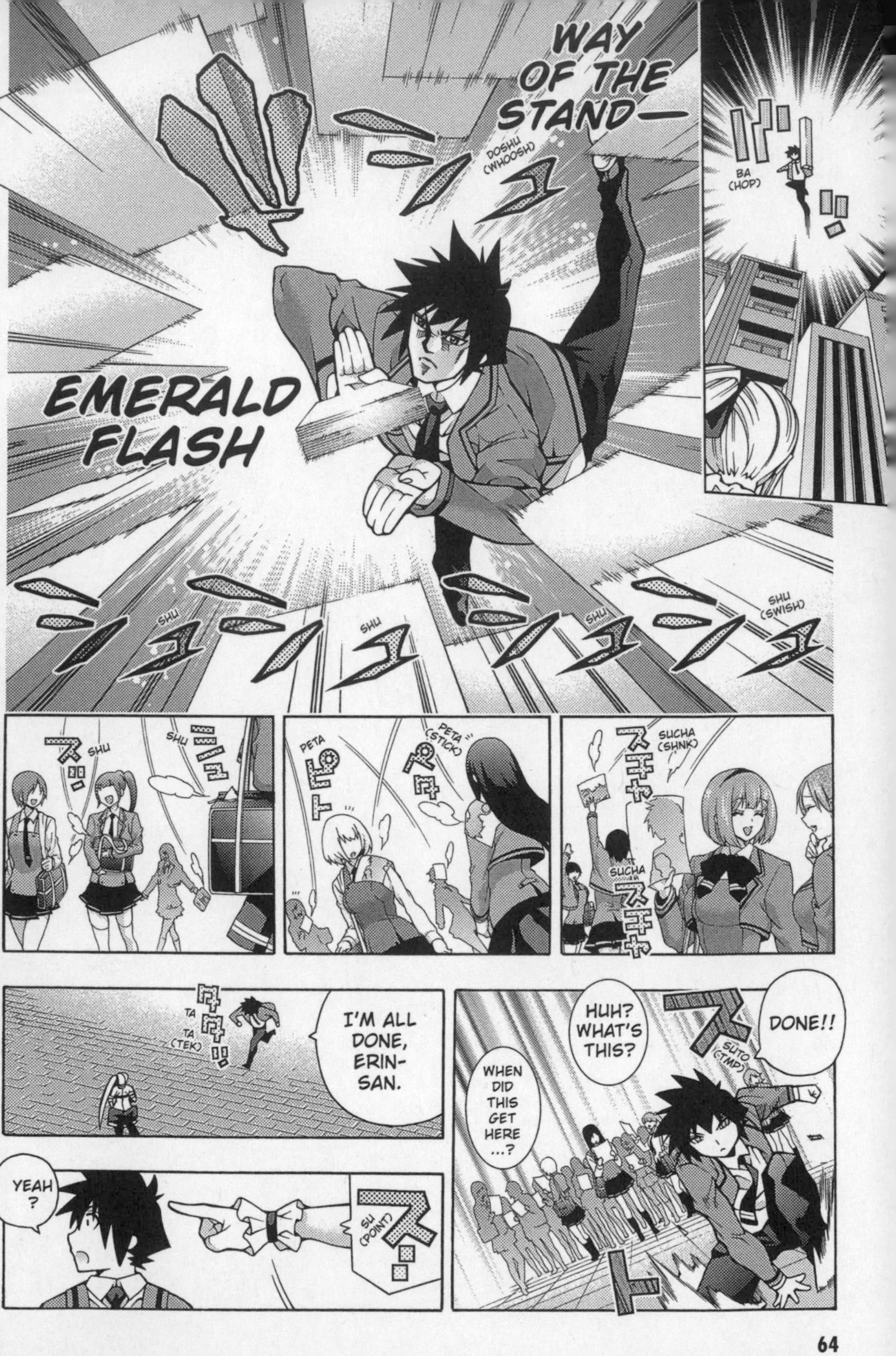
BA (HOP)
WAY OF THE STAND—
DOSHU (WHOOSH)
EMERALD FLASH
SHU (SWISH)
SHU
SHU
SHU
SUCHA (SHNK)
SUCHA
PETA (STICK)
PETA
SHU
SHU
DONE!!
SUTO (STMP)
HUH? WHAT'S THIS?
WHEN DID THIS GET HERE ...?
I'M ALL DONE, ERIN-SAN.
TA TA (TEK)
SU (POINT)
YEAH?

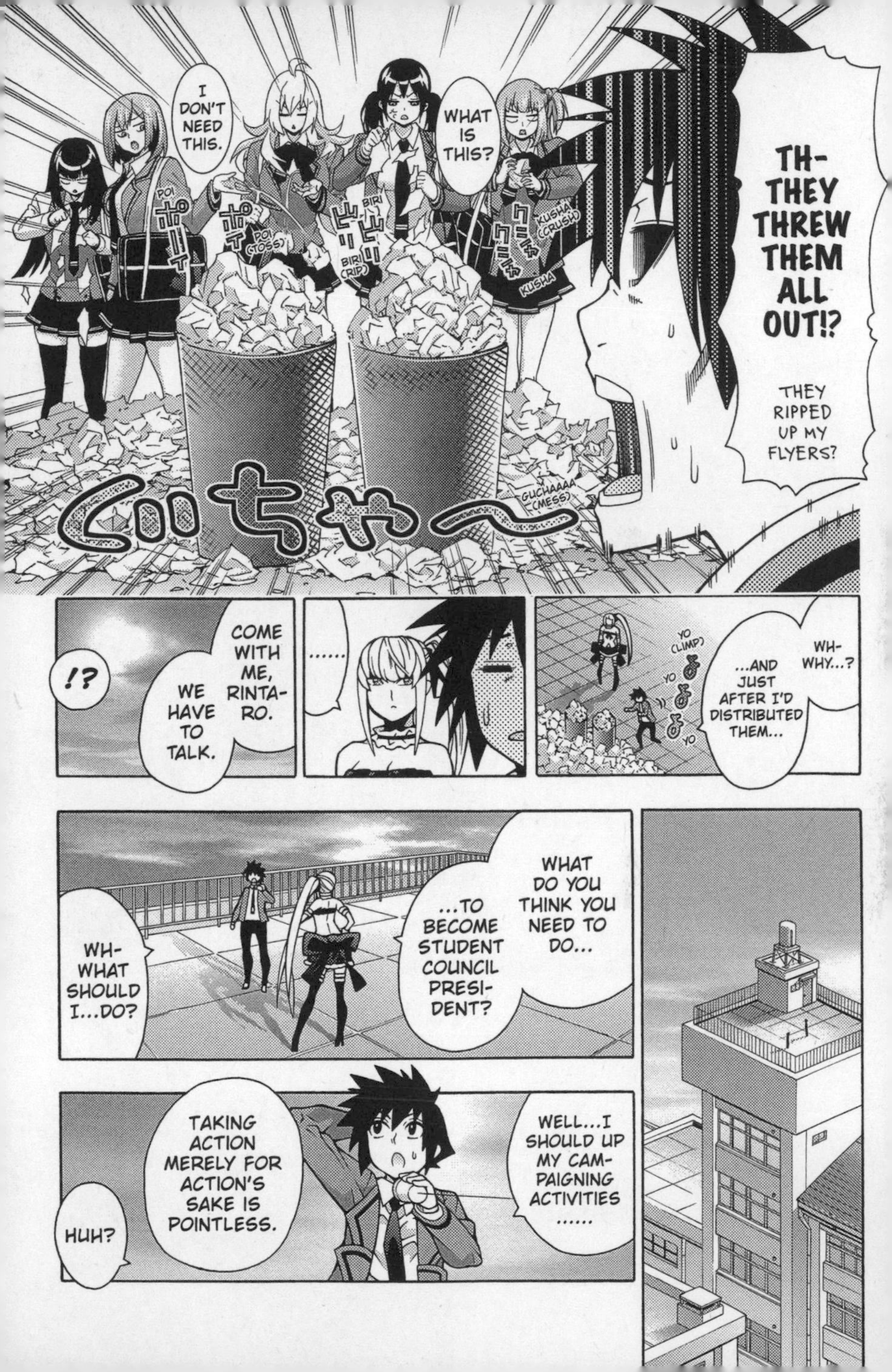
TH-THEY THREW THEM ALL OUT!?
THEY RIPPED UP MY FLYERS?
KUSHA (CRUSH)
KUSHA
WHAT IS THIS?
BIRI
BIRI (RIP)
I DON'T NEED THIS.
POI (TOSS)
POI
GUCHAAAA (MESS)
WH-WHY...?
...AND JUST AFTER I'D DISTRIBUTED THEM...
YO (LIMP)
YO
YO
......
COME WITH ME, RINTA-RO.
WE HAVE TO TALK.
!?
WHAT DO YOU THINK YOU NEED TO DO...
...TO BECOME STUDENT COUNCIL PRESI-DENT?
WH-WHAT SHOULD I...DO?
WELL...I SHOULD UP MY CAM-PAIGNING ACTIVITIES......
TAKING ACTION MERELY FOR ACTION'S SAKE IS POINTLESS.
HUH?

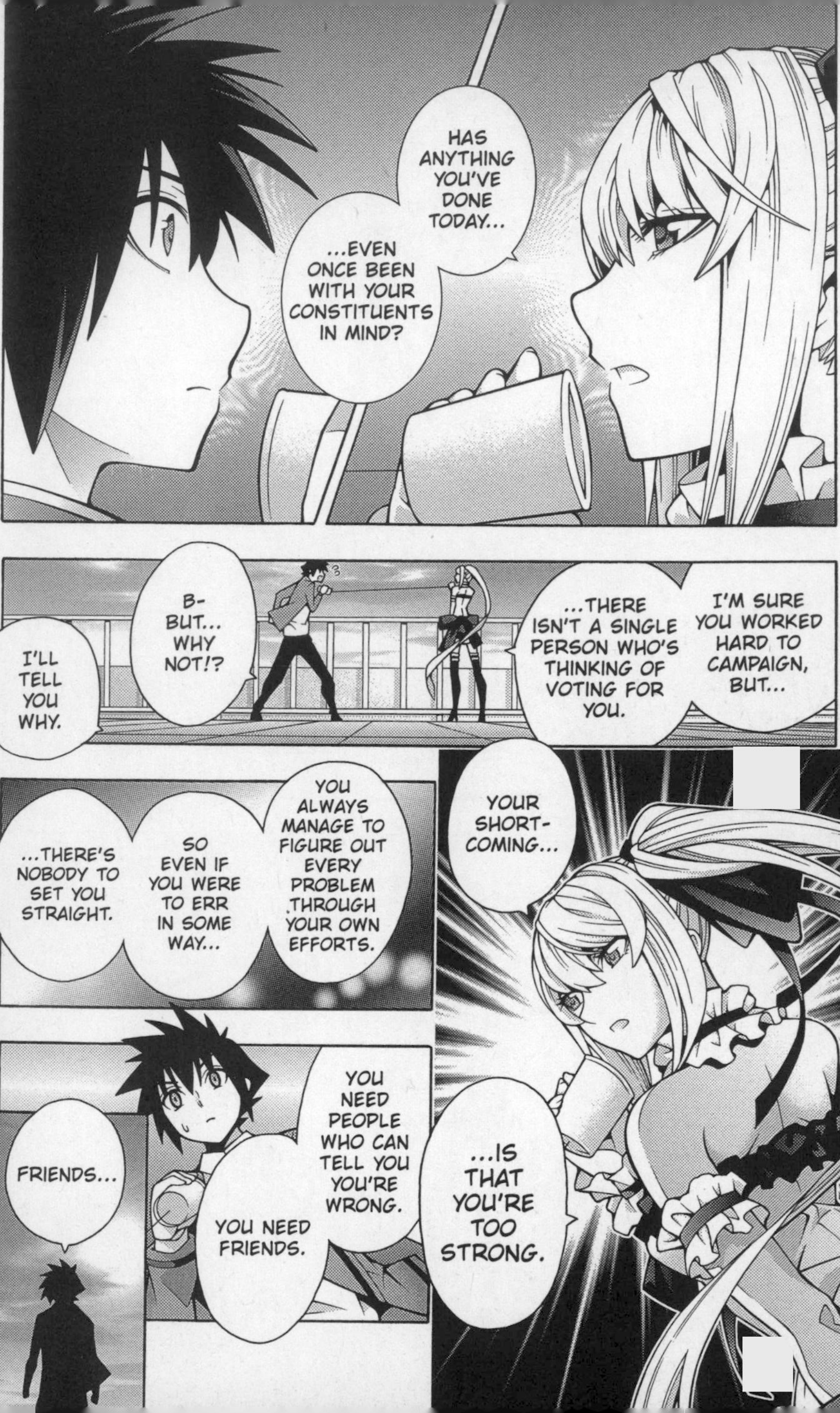
HAS ANYTHING YOU'VE DONE TODAY...
...EVEN ONCE BEEN WITH YOUR CONSTITUENTS IN MIND?
I'M SURE YOU WORKED HARD TO CAMPAIGN, BUT...
...THERE ISN'T A SINGLE PERSON WHO'S THINKING OF VOTING FOR YOU.
B-BUT... WHY NOT!?
I'LL TELL YOU WHY.
YOUR SHORT-COMING...
...IS THAT YOU'RE TOO STRONG.
YOU ALWAYS MANAGE TO FIGURE OUT EVERY PROBLEM THROUGH YOUR OWN EFFORTS.
SO EVEN IF YOU WERE TO ERR IN SOME WAY...
...THERE'S NOBODY TO SET YOU STRAIGHT.
YOU NEED PEOPLE WHO CAN TELL YOU YOU'RE WRONG.
YOU NEED FRIENDS.
FRIENDS...

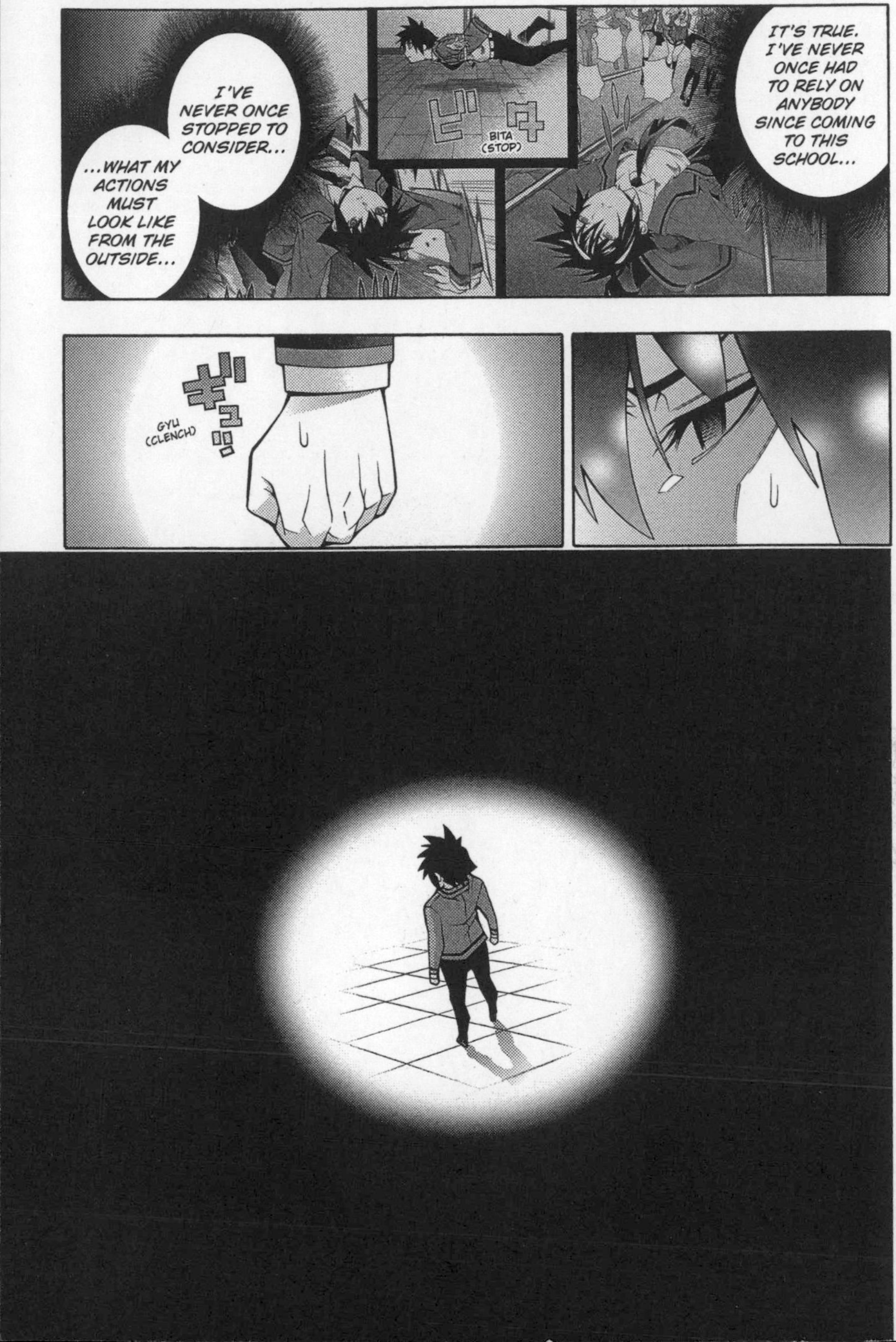
IT'S TRUE. I'VE NEVER ONCE HAD TO RELY ON ANYBODY SINCE COMING TO THIS SCHOOL...
BITA (STOP)
I'VE NEVER ONCE STOPPED TO CONSIDER...
...WHAT MY ACTIONS MUST LOOK LIKE FROM THE OUTSIDE...
GYU (CLENCH)

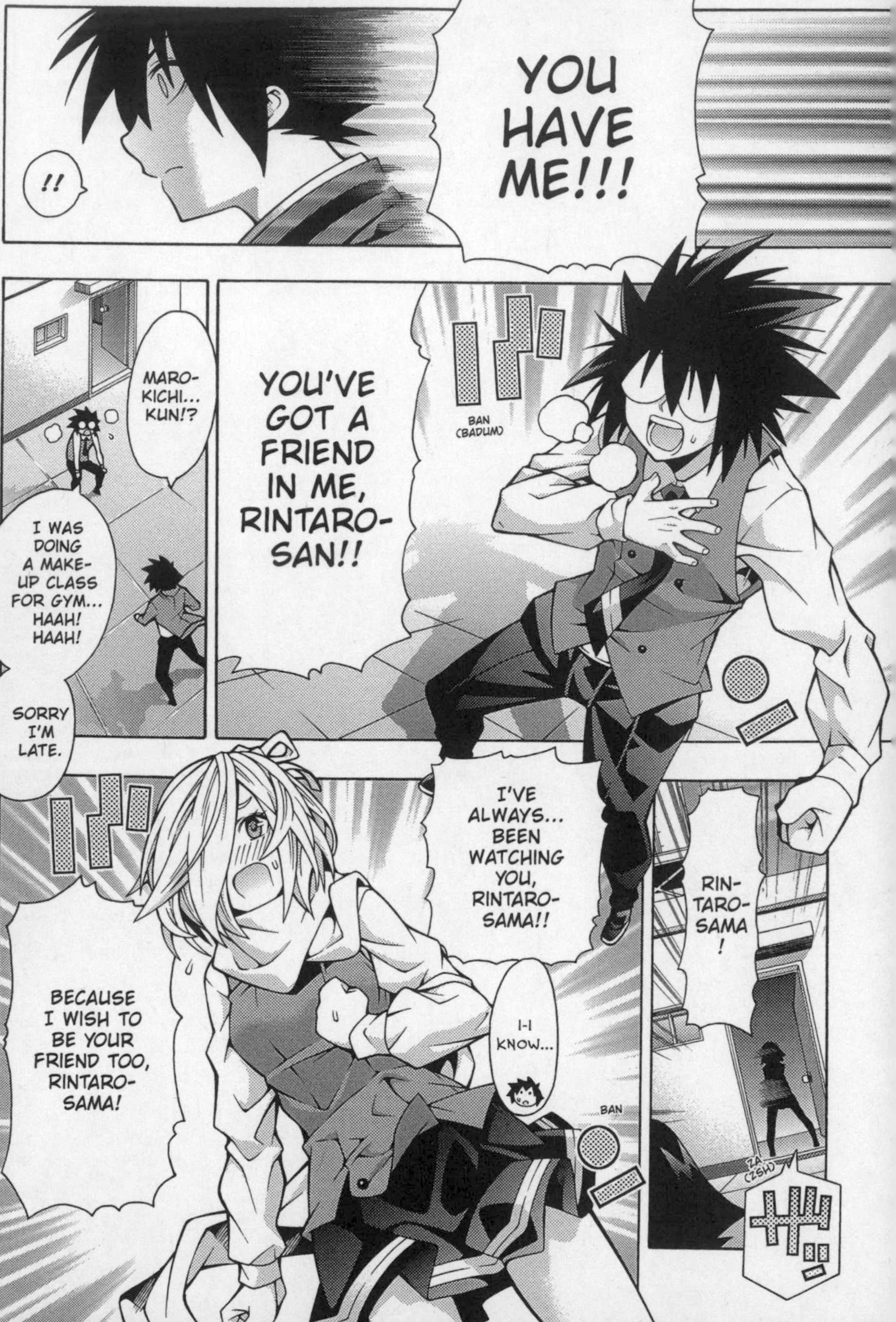
YOU HAVE ME!!!
!!
YOU'VE GOT A FRIEND IN ME, RINTARO-SAN!!
BAN (BADUM)
MARO-KICHI... KUN!?
I WAS DOING A MAKE-UP CLASS FOR GYM... HAAH! HAAH!
SORRY I'M LATE.
RIN-TARO-SAMA!
ZA (ZSH)
I'VE ALWAYS... BEEN WATCHING YOU, RINTARO-SAMA!!
BECAUSE I WISH TO BE YOUR FRIEND TOO, RINTARO-SAMA!
I-I KNOW...
BAN

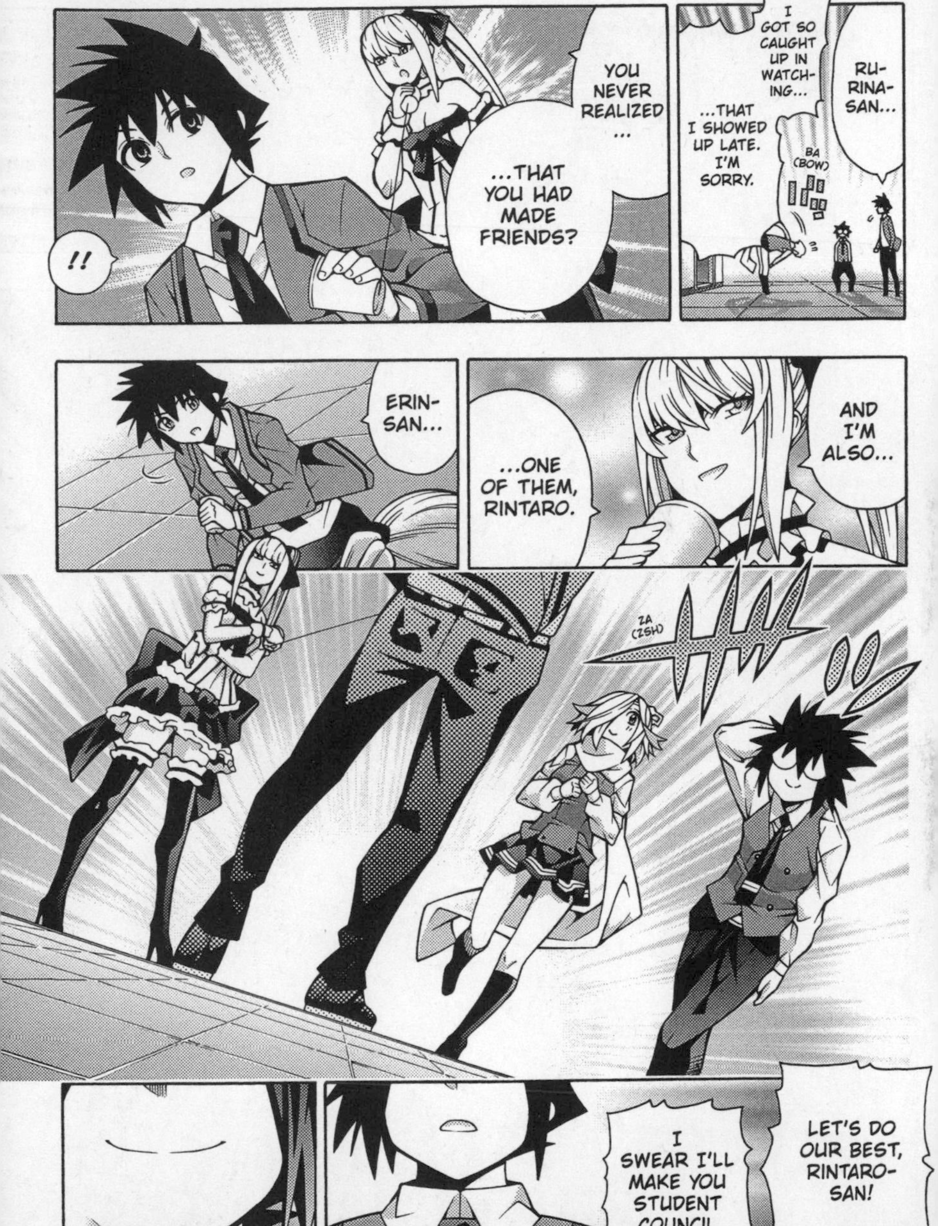
RU-RINA-SAN...
I GOT SO CAUGHT UP IN WATCH-ING...
...THAT I SHOWED UP LATE. I'M SORRY.
BA (BOW)
YOU NEVER REALIZED...
...THAT YOU HAD MADE FRIENDS?
!!
AND I'M ALSO...
...ONE OF THEM, RINTARO.
ERIN-SAN...
ZA (ZSH)
LET'S DO OUR BEST, RINTARO-SAN!
I SWEAR I'LL MAKE YOU STUDENT COUNCIL PRESIDENT.

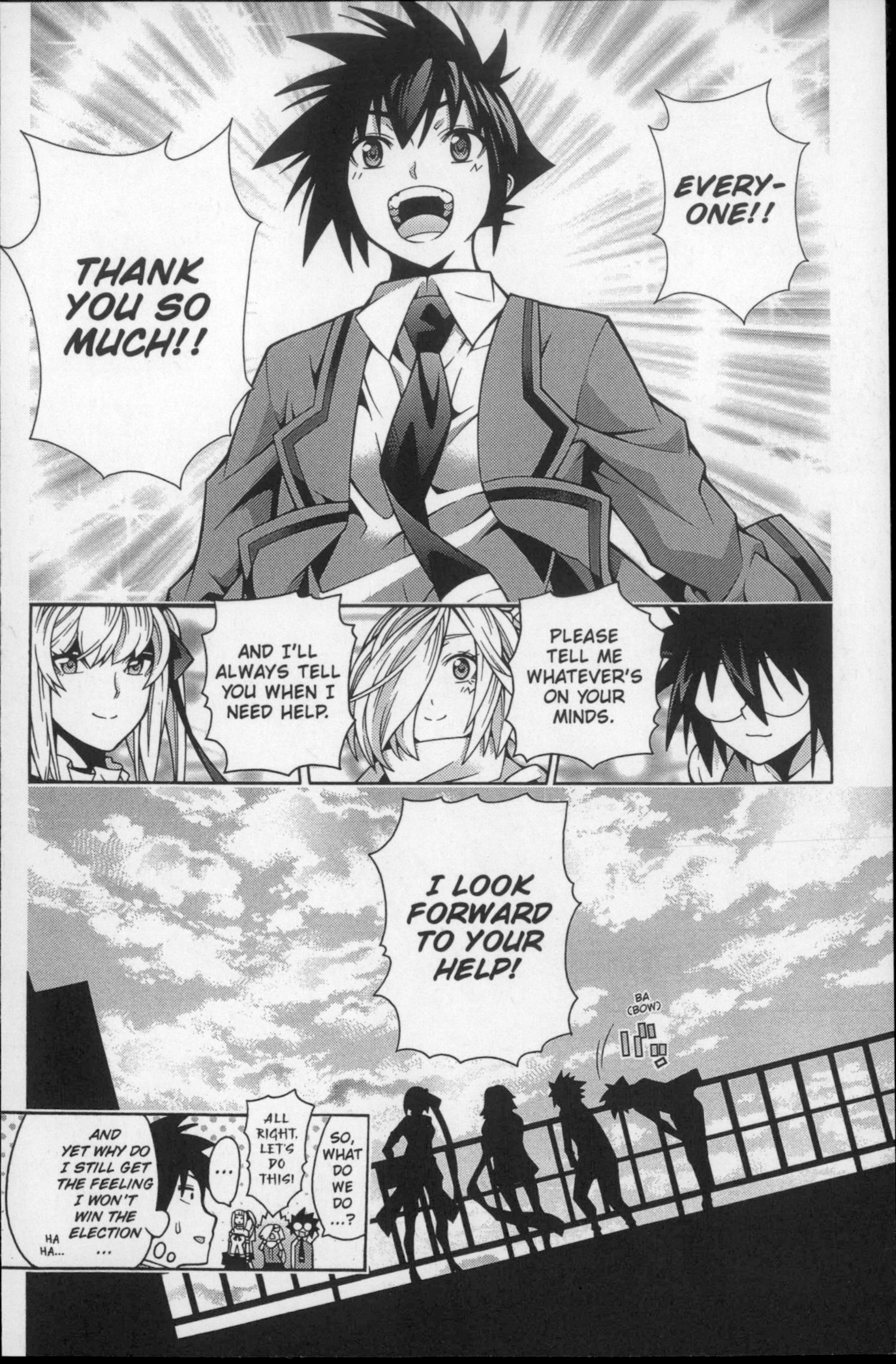
EVERY-ONE!!
THANK YOU SO MUCH!!
PLEASE TELL ME WHATEVER'S ON YOUR MINDS.
AND I'LL ALWAYS TELL YOU WHEN I NEED HELP.
I LOOK FORWARD TO YOUR HELP!
BA (BOW)
SO, WHAT DO WE DO ...?
ALL RIGHT. LET'S DO THIS!
...
AND YET WHY DO I STILL GET THE FEELING I WON'T WIN THE ELECTION ...
HA HA...

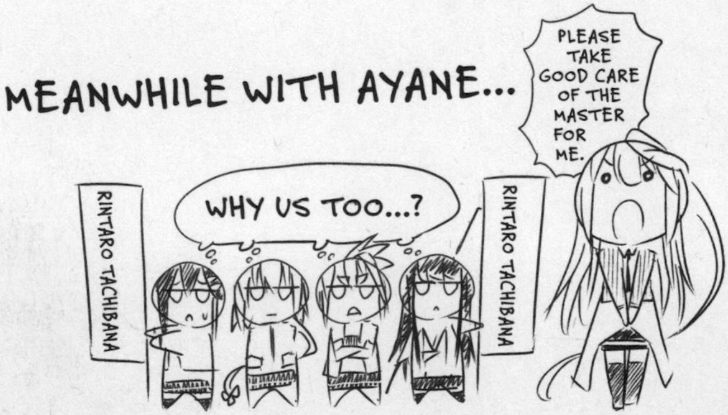
MEANWHILE WITH AYANE...
PLEASE TAKE GOOD CARE OF THE MASTER FOR ME.
RINTARO TACHIBANA
WHY US TOO...?
RINTARO TACHIBANA

Dragons Rioting

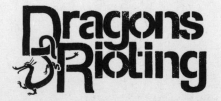

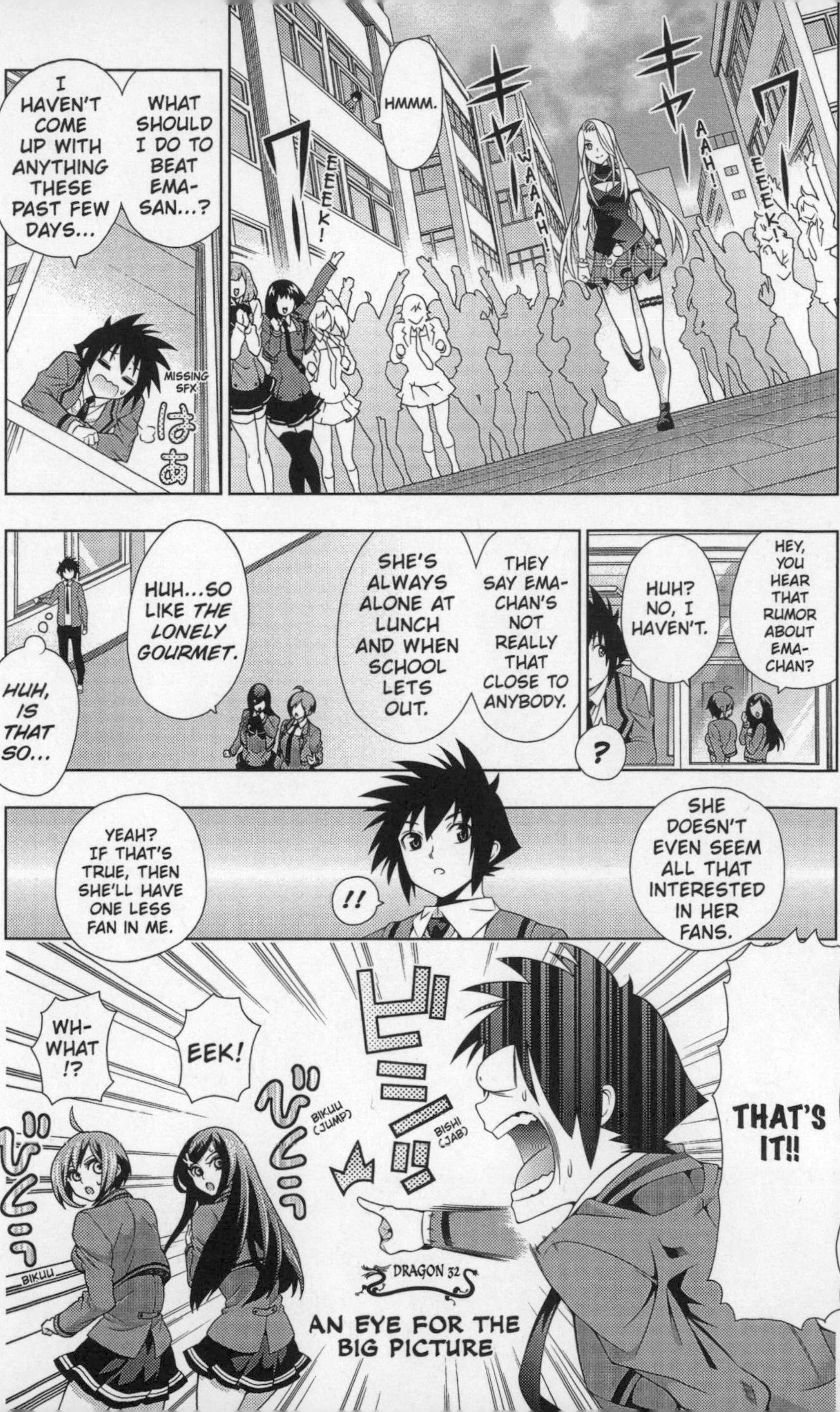
EEEEK!
AAAH!
WAAAH!
EEEEK!
HMMM.
WHAT SHOULD I DO TO BEAT EMA-SAN...?
I HAVEN'T COME UP WITH ANYTHING THESE PAST FEW DAYS...
MISSING SFX
はぁ
HEY, YOU HEAR THAT RUMOR ABOUT EMA-CHAN?
HUH? NO, I HAVEN'T.
?
THEY SAY EMA-CHAN'S NOT REALLY THAT CLOSE TO ANYBODY.
SHE'S ALWAYS ALONE AT LUNCH AND WHEN SCHOOL LETS OUT.
HUH...SO LIKE *THE LONELY GOURMET*.
HUH, IS THAT SO...
SHE DOESN'T EVEN SEEM ALL THAT INTERESTED IN HER FANS.
!!
YEAH? IF THAT'S TRUE, THEN SHE'LL HAVE ONE LESS FAN IN ME.
THAT'S IT!!
BISHI (JAB)
EEK!
BIKUU (JUMP)
WH-WHAT!?
BIKUU
DRAGON 32
AN EYE FOR THE BIG PICTURE

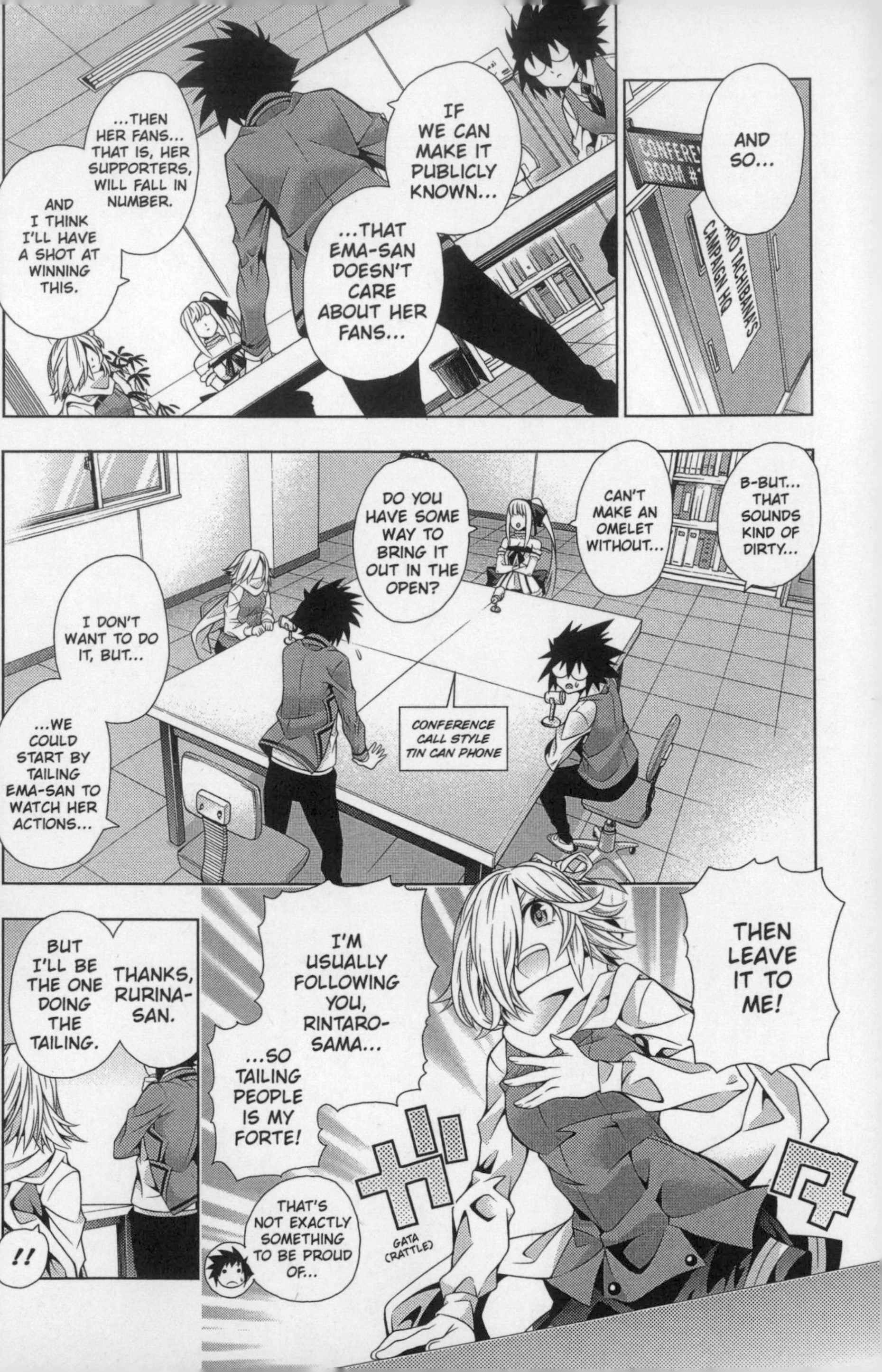
AND SO...
IF WE CAN MAKE IT PUBLICLY KNOWN...
...THAT EMA-SAN DOESN'T CARE ABOUT HER FANS...
...THEN HER FANS... THAT IS, HER SUPPORTERS, WILL FALL IN NUMBER.
AND I THINK I'LL HAVE A SHOT AT WINNING THIS.
B-BUT... THAT SOUNDS KIND OF DIRTY...
CAN'T MAKE AN OMELET WITHOUT...
DO YOU HAVE SOME WAY TO BRING IT OUT IN THE OPEN?
CONFERENCE CALL STYLE TIN CAN PHONE
I DON'T WANT TO DO IT, BUT...
...WE COULD START BY TAILING EMA-SAN TO WATCH HER ACTIONS...
THEN LEAVE IT TO ME!
I'M USUALLY FOLLOWING YOU, RINTARO-SAMA...
...SO TAILING PEOPLE IS MY FORTE!
GATA (RATTLE)
THAT'S NOT EXACTLY SOMETHING TO BE PROUD OF...
THANKS, RURINA-SAN.
BUT I'LL BE THE ONE DOING THE TAILING.
!!

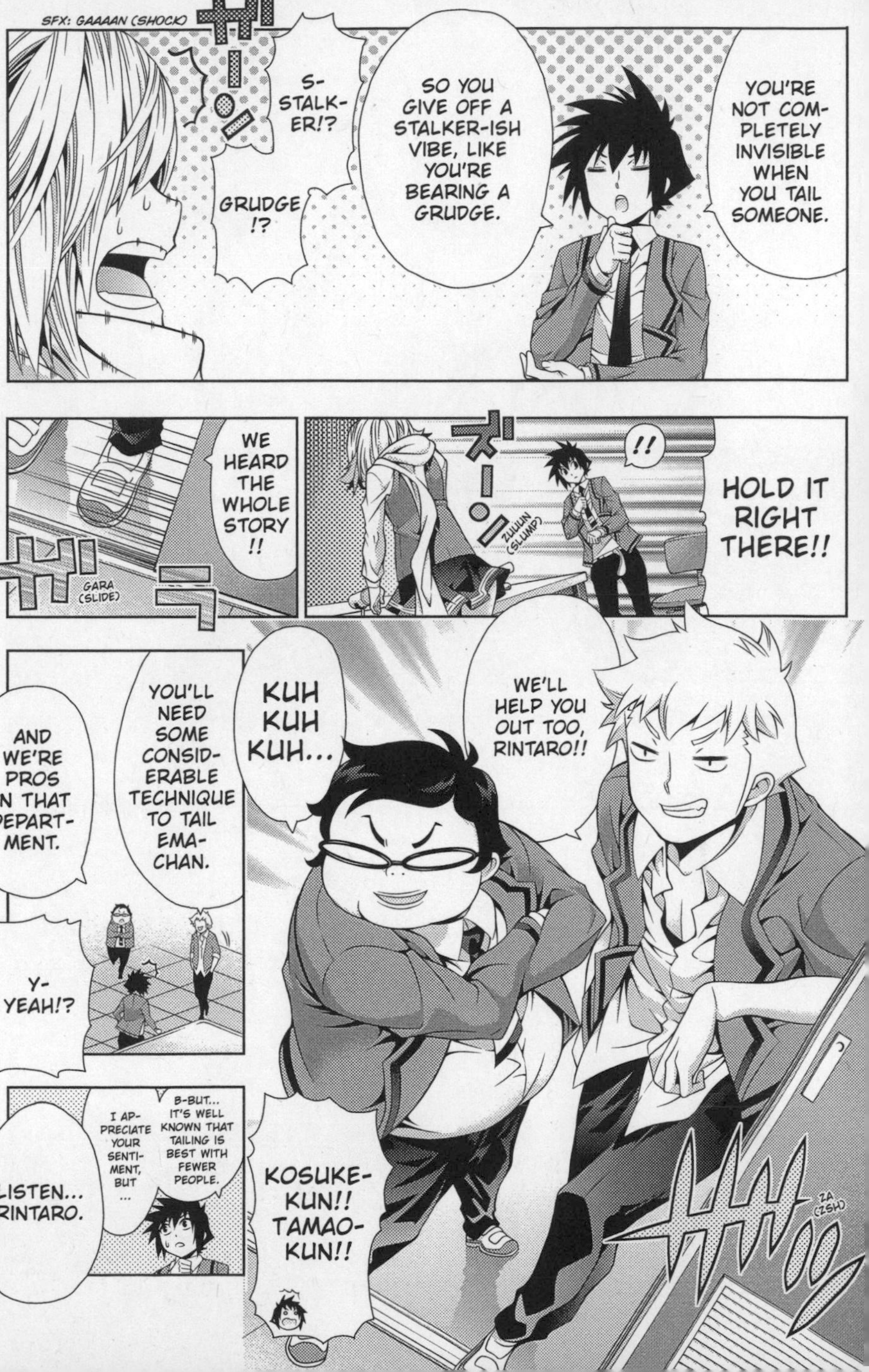
YOU'RE NOT COMPLETELY INVISIBLE WHEN YOU TAIL SOMEONE.
SO YOU GIVE OFF A STALKER-ISH VIBE, LIKE YOU'RE BEARING A GRUDGE.
S-STALKER!?
GRUDGE!?
SFX: GAAAAN (SHOCK)
HOLD IT RIGHT THERE!!
!!
ZUUUN (SLUMP)
WE HEARD THE WHOLE STORY!!
GARA (SLIDE)
WE'LL HELP YOU OUT TOO, RINTARO!!
KUH KUH KUH...
YOU'LL NEED SOME CONSIDERABLE TECHNIQUE TO TAIL EMA-CHAN.
AND WE'RE PROS IN THAT DEPARTMENT.
Y-YEAH!?
ZA (ZSH)
KOSUKE-KUN!! TAMAO-KUN!!
B-BUT... IT'S WELL KNOWN THAT TAILING IS BEST WITH FEWER PEOPLE.
I APPRECIATE YOUR SENTIMENT, BUT ...
LISTEN... RINTARO.

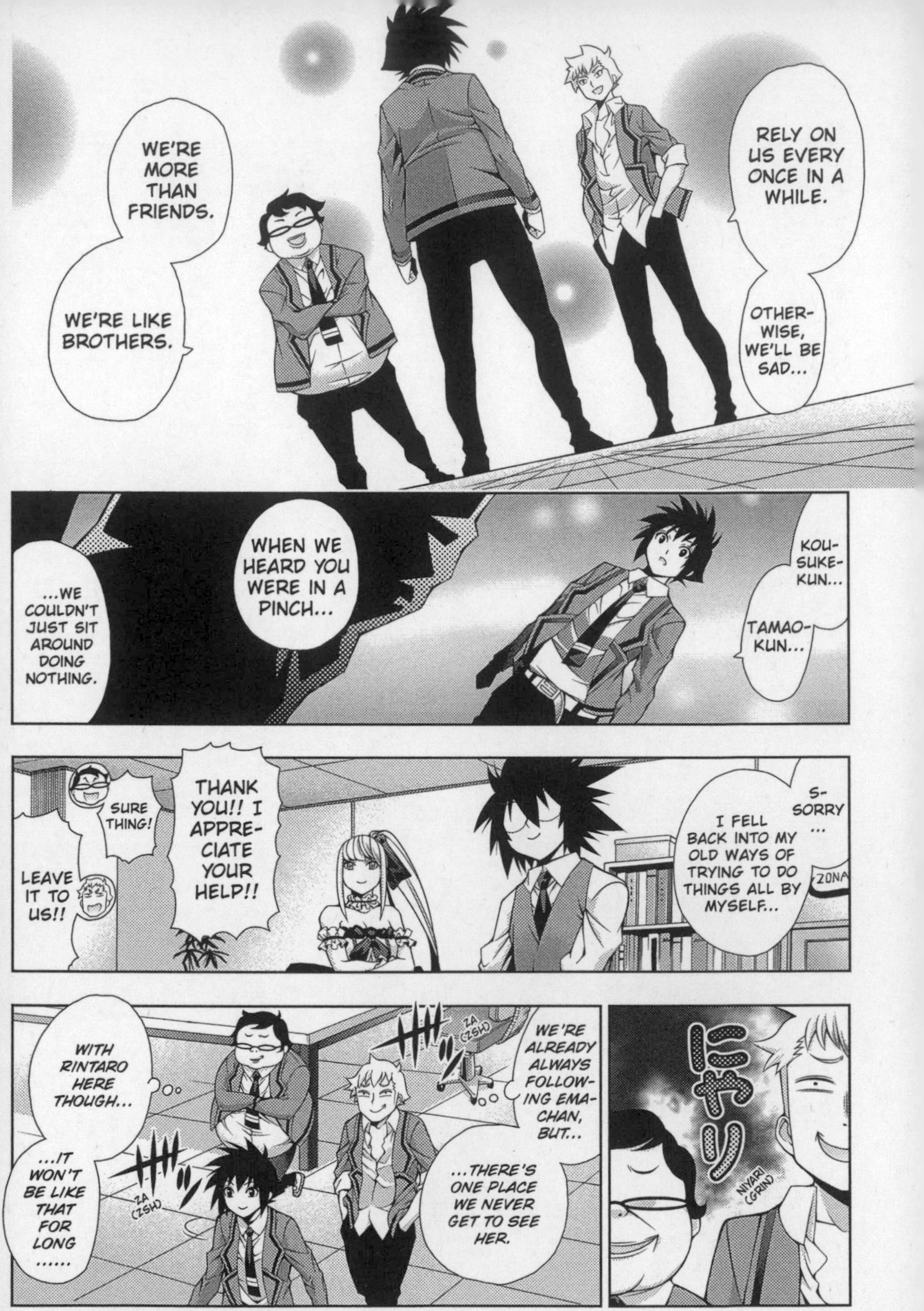
RELY ON US EVERY ONCE IN A WHILE.
OTHERWISE, WE'LL BE SAD...
WE'RE MORE THAN FRIENDS.
WE'RE LIKE BROTHERS.
KOUSUKE-KUN...
TAMAO-KUN...
WHEN WE HEARD YOU WERE IN A PINCH...
...WE COULDN'T JUST SIT AROUND DOING NOTHING.
S-SORRY...
I FELL BACK INTO MY OLD WAYS OF TRYING TO DO THINGS ALL BY MYSELF...
ZONA
THANK YOU!! I APPRECIATE YOUR HELP!!
SURE THING!
LEAVE IT TO US!!
にやり
NIYARI (GRIN)
ZA (ZSH)
WE'RE ALREADY ALWAYS FOLLOWING EMA-CHAN, BUT...
...THERE'S ONE PLACE WE NEVER GET TO SEE HER.
WITH RINTARO HERE THOUGH...
...IT WON'T BE LIKE THAT FOR LONG......
ZA (ZSH)

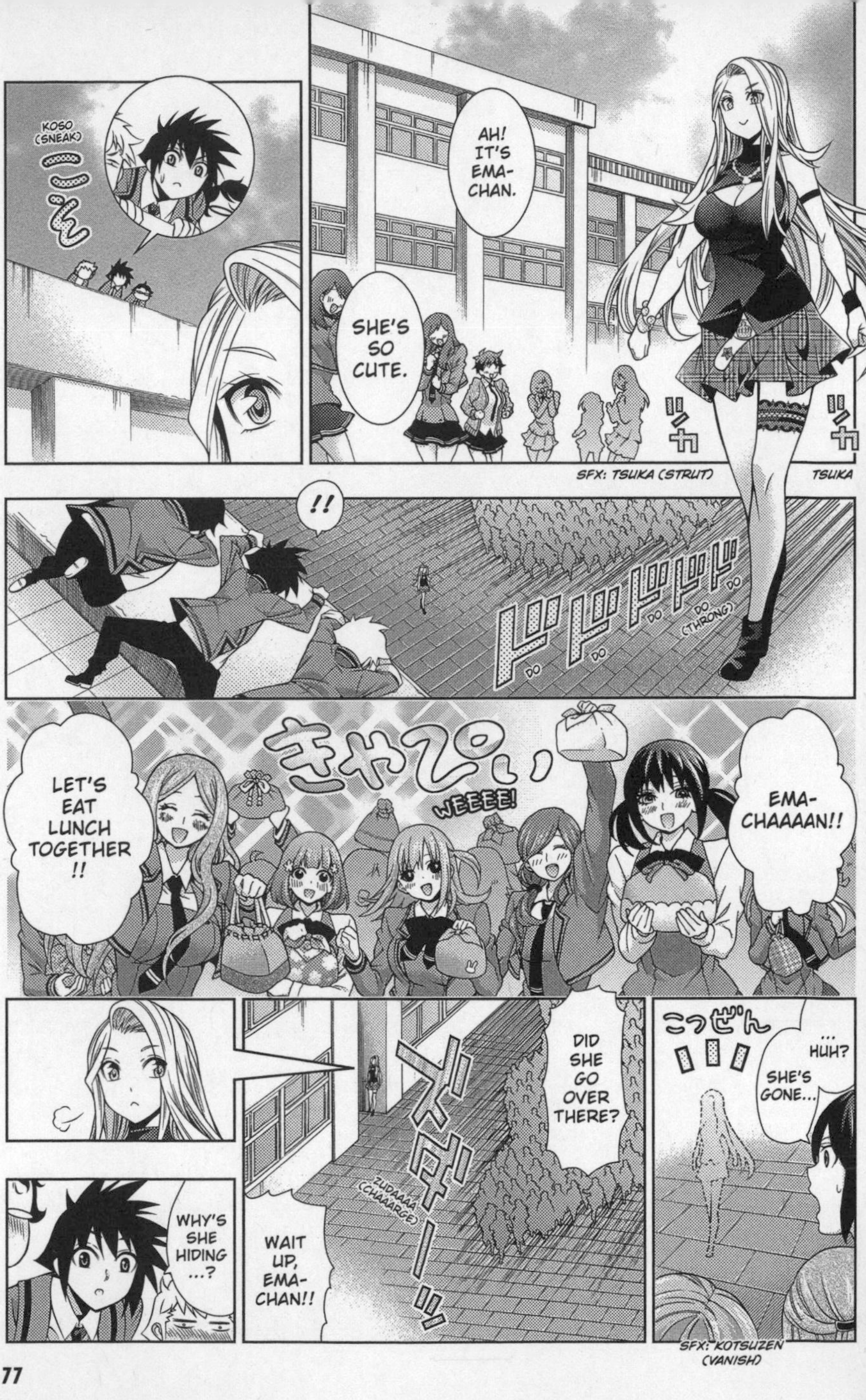

AH! IT'S EMA-CHAN.
SHE'S SO CUTE.
SFX: TSUKA (STRUT)
TSUKA
KOSO (SNEAK)
!!
DO DO DO DO DO (THRONG)
EMA-CHAAAAN!!
WEEEE!
LET'S EAT LUNCH TOGETHER!!
... HUH?
SHE'S GONE...
SFX: KOTSUZEN (VANISH)
DID SHE GO OVER THERE?
ZUDAAAA (CHAAARGE)
WAIT UP, EMA-CHAN!!
WHY'S SHE HIDING ...?

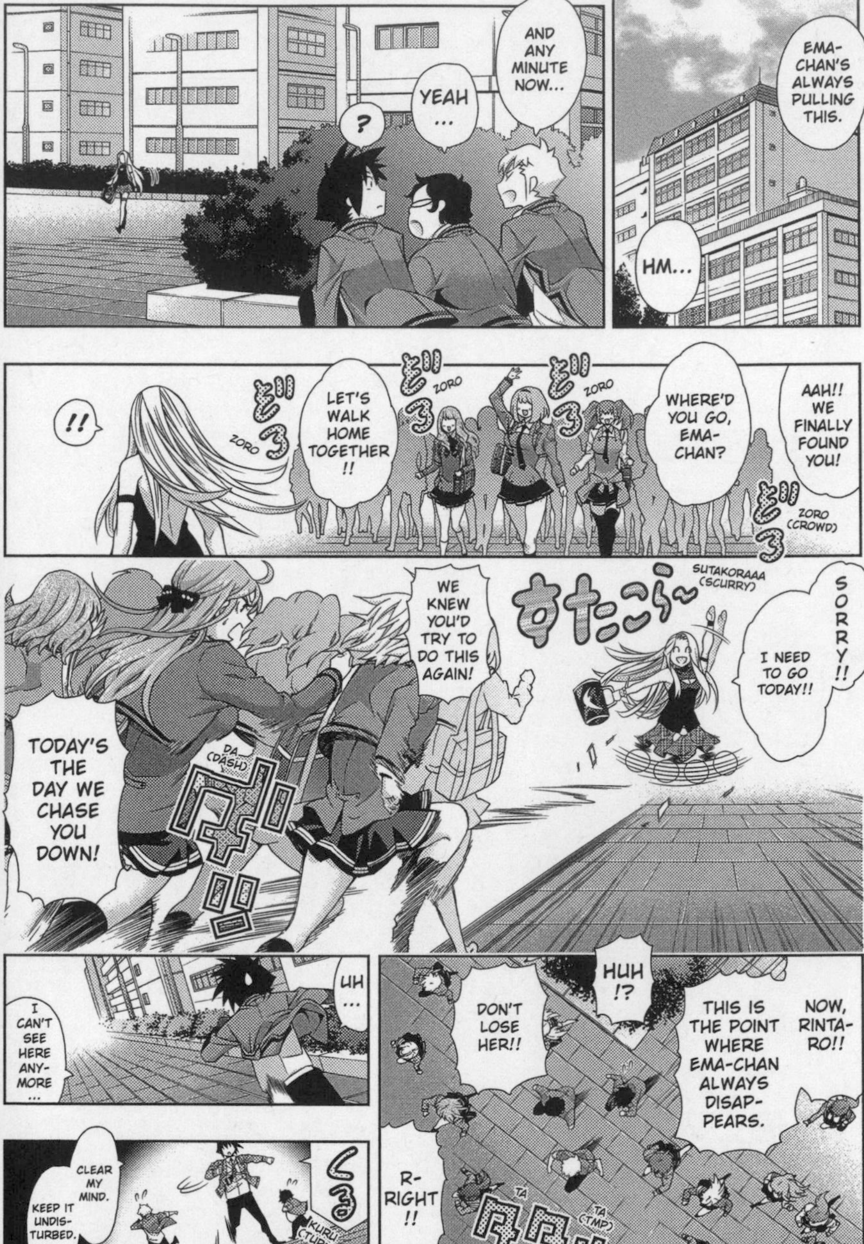
EMA-CHAN'S ALWAYS PULLING THIS.
HM...
AND ANY MINUTE NOW...
YEAH...
?
AAH!! WE FINALLY FOUND YOU!
ZORO (CROWD)
WHERE'D YOU GO, EMA-CHAN?
ZORO
ZORO
LET'S WALK HOME TOGETHER!!
ZORO
!!
SORRY!! I NEED TO GO TODAY!!
SUTAKORAAA (SCURRY)
WE KNEW YOU'D TRY TO DO THIS AGAIN!
TODAY'S THE DAY WE CHASE YOU DOWN!
DA (DASH)
NOW, RINTARO!!
THIS IS THE POINT WHERE EMA-CHAN ALWAYS DISAPPEARS.
HUH!?
DON'T LOSE HER!!
R-RIGHT!!
TA
TA (TMP)
UH...
I CAN'T SEE HERE ANYMORE...
CLEAR MY MIND. KEEP IT UNDISTURBED.
KURU (TURN)

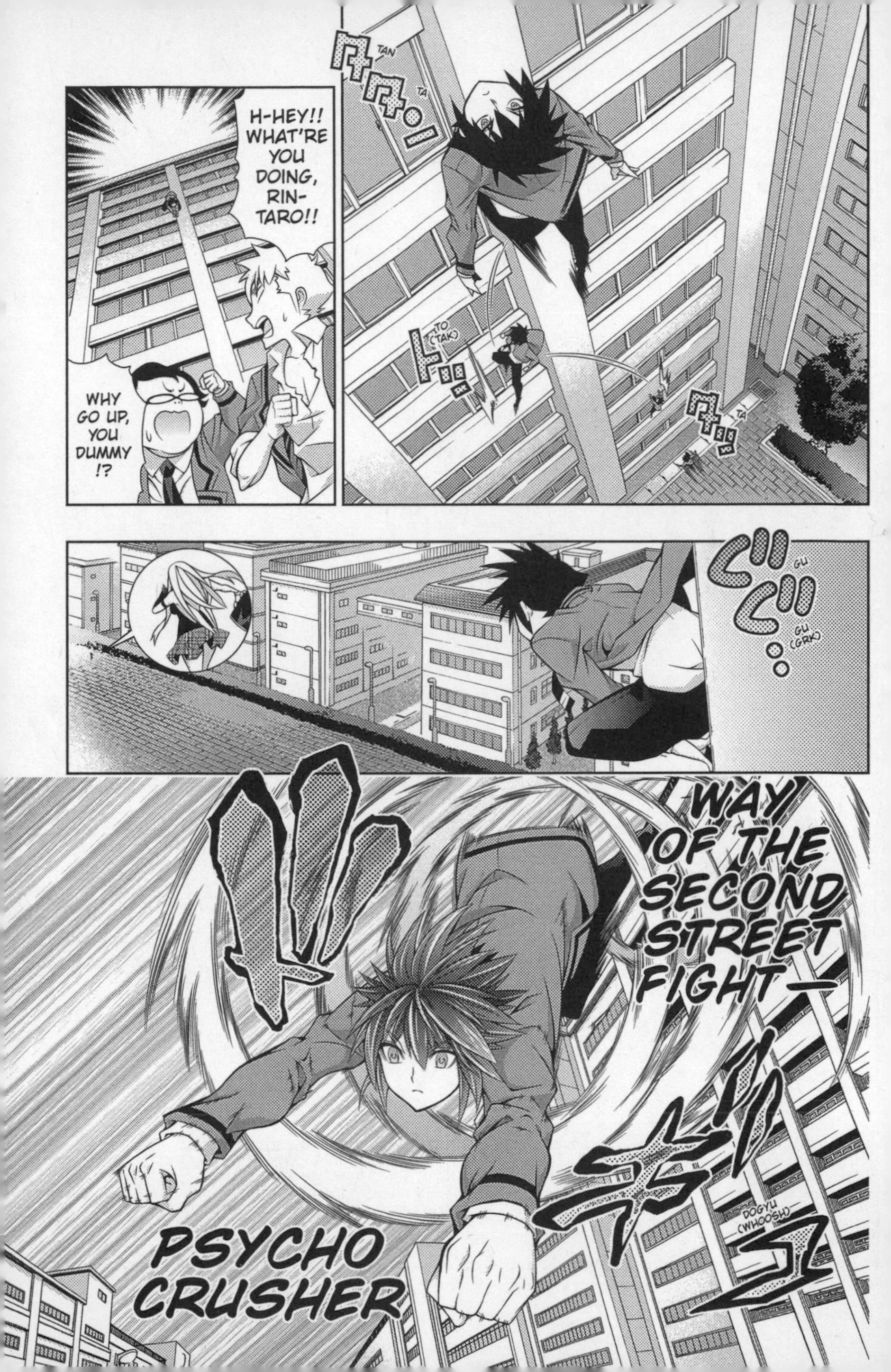
TAN
TA
TO (TAK)
TA
H-HEY!! WHAT'RE YOU DOING, RIN-TARO!!
WHY GO UP, YOU DUMMY !?
GU
GU (GRK)
WAY OF THE SECOND STREET FIGHT—
DOGYU (WHOOSH)
PSYCHO CRUSHER

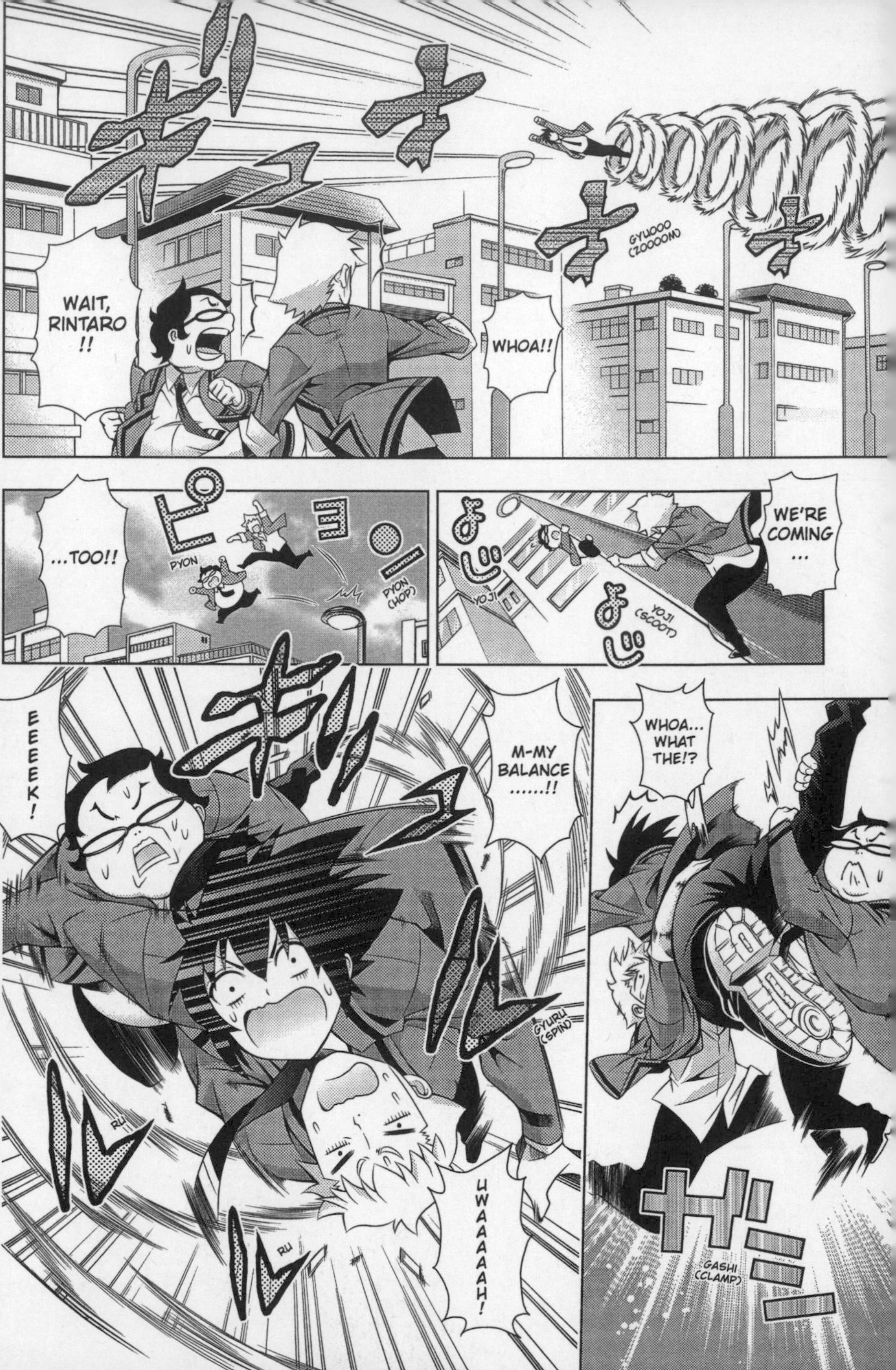
GYUOOO (ZOOOOM)
WHOA!!
WAIT, RINTARO!!
WE'RE COMING...
YOJI (SCOOT)
YOJI
PYON (HOP)
PYON
...TOO!!
WHOA... WHAT THE!?
GASHI (CLAMP)
M-MY BALANCE......!!
EEEEEK!
GYURU (SPIN)
RU
RU
UWAAAAAAH!

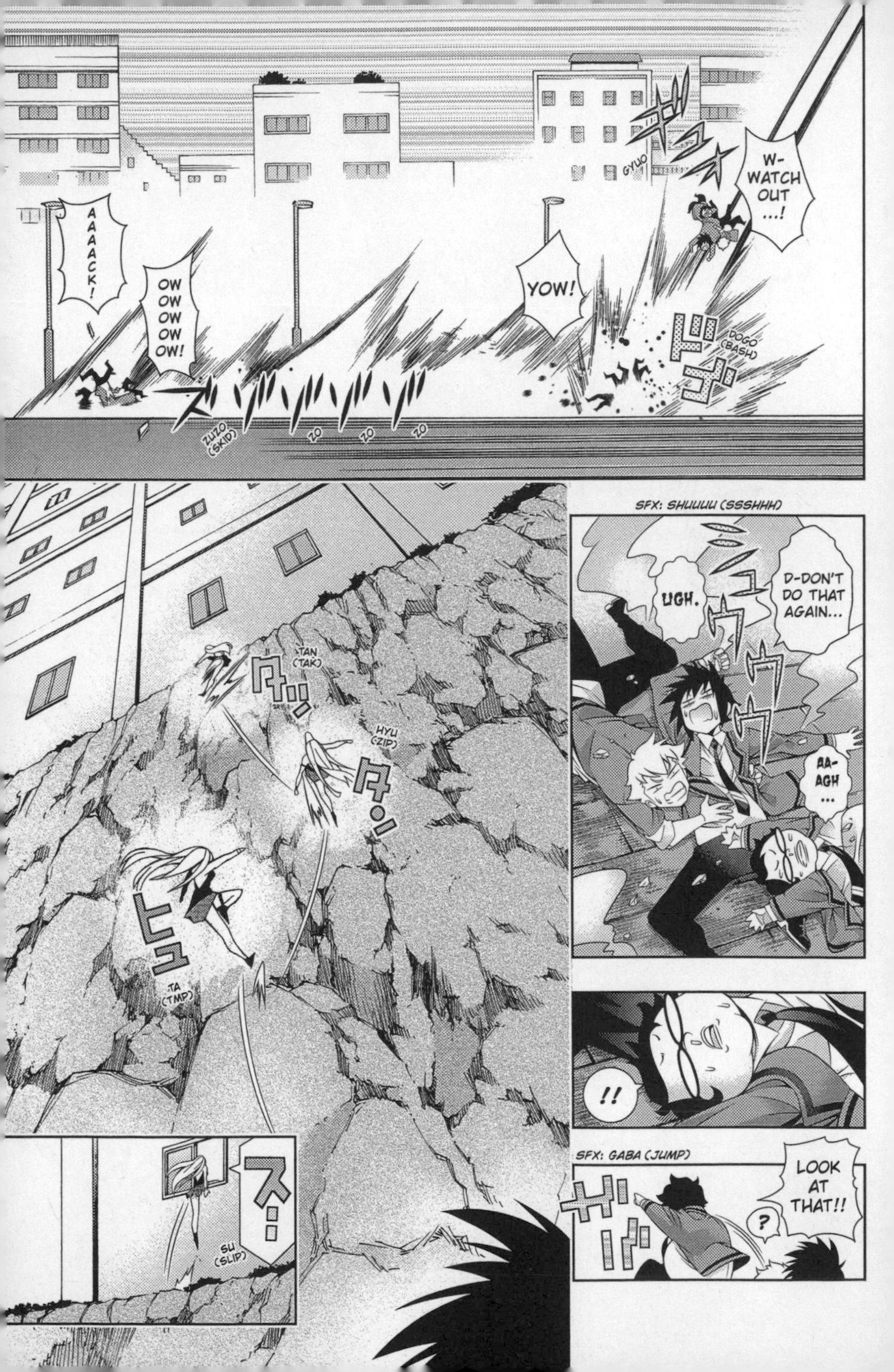
W-WATCH OUT...!
GYUO
YOW!
DOGO (BASH)
OW OW OW OW OW!
AAAACK!
ZUZO (SKID)
ZO
ZO
ZO
SFX: SHUUUU (SSSHHH)
D-DON'T DO THAT AGAIN...
UGH.
AA-AGH...
!!
SFX: GABA (JUMP)
LOOK AT THAT!!
?
TAN (TAK)
HYU (ZIP)
TA (TMP)
SU (SLIP)

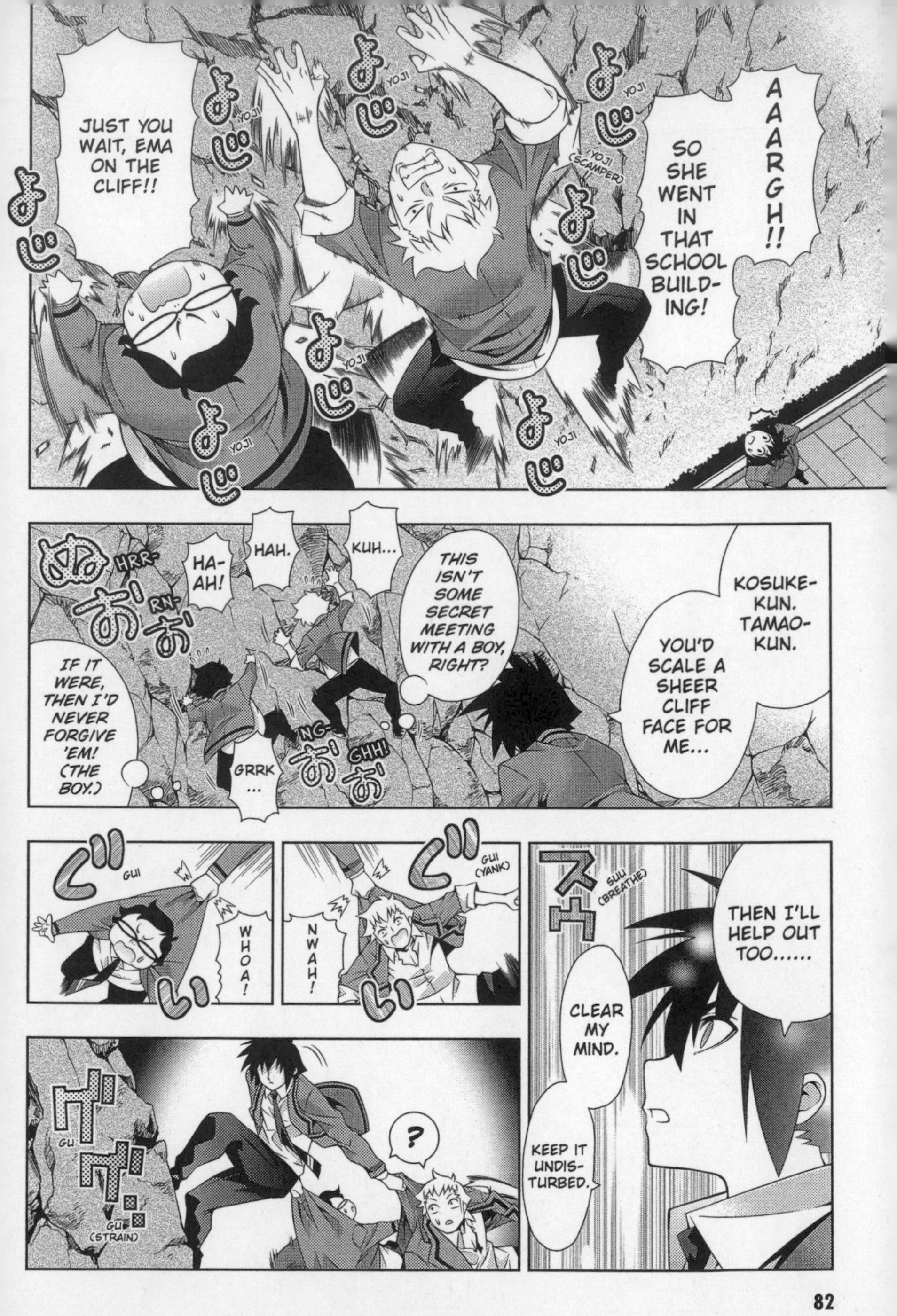

AAARGH!!
SO SHE WENT IN THAT SCHOOL BUILDING!
YOJI
YOJI (SCAMPER)
YOJI
YOJI
YOJI
YOJI
JUST YOU WAIT, EMA ON THE CLIFF!!
KOSUKE-KUN. TAMAO-KUN.
YOU'D SCALE A SHEER CLIFF FACE FOR ME...
THIS ISN'T SOME SECRET MEETING WITH A BOY, RIGHT?
KUH...
HAH.
HA-AH!
HRR-RN-
NG-GHH!
GRRK...
IF IT WERE, THEN I'D NEVER FORGIVE 'EM! (THE BOY.)
SUU (BREATHE)
THEN I'LL HELP OUT TOO......
CLEAR MY MIND.
KEEP IT UNDISTURBED.
GUI (YANK)
NWAH!
GUI
WHOA!
?
GU
GU (STRAIN)

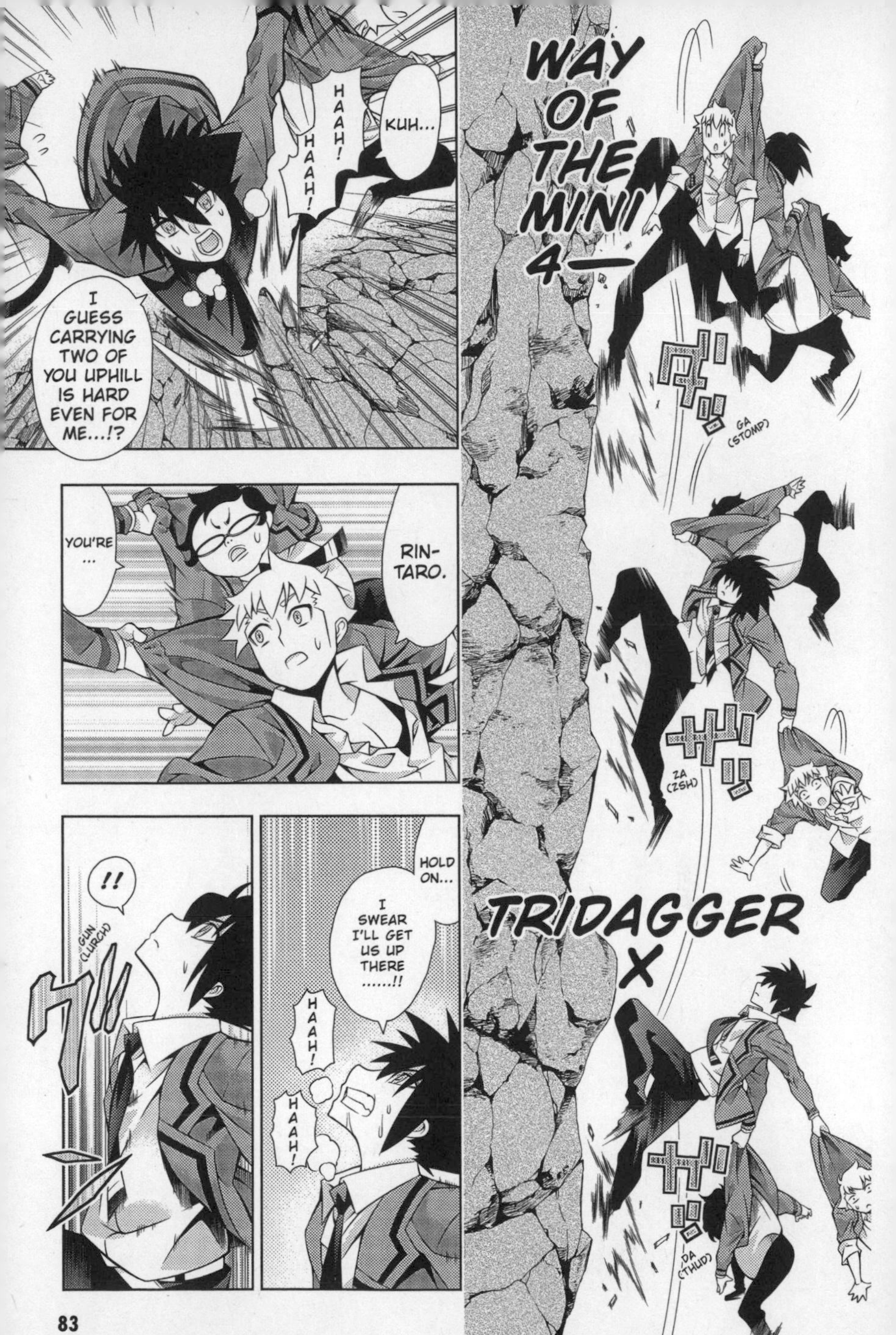
WAY OF THE MINI 4—
GA (STOMP)
ZA (ZSH)
TRIDAGGER X
DA (THUD)
KUH...
HAAAH! HAAAH!
I GUESS CARRYING TWO OF YOU UPHILL IS HARD EVEN FOR ME...!?
RIN-TARO.
YOU'RE ...
HOLD ON...
I SWEAR I'LL GET US UP THERE ......!!
HAAAH! HAAAH!
!!
GUN (CLUTCH)

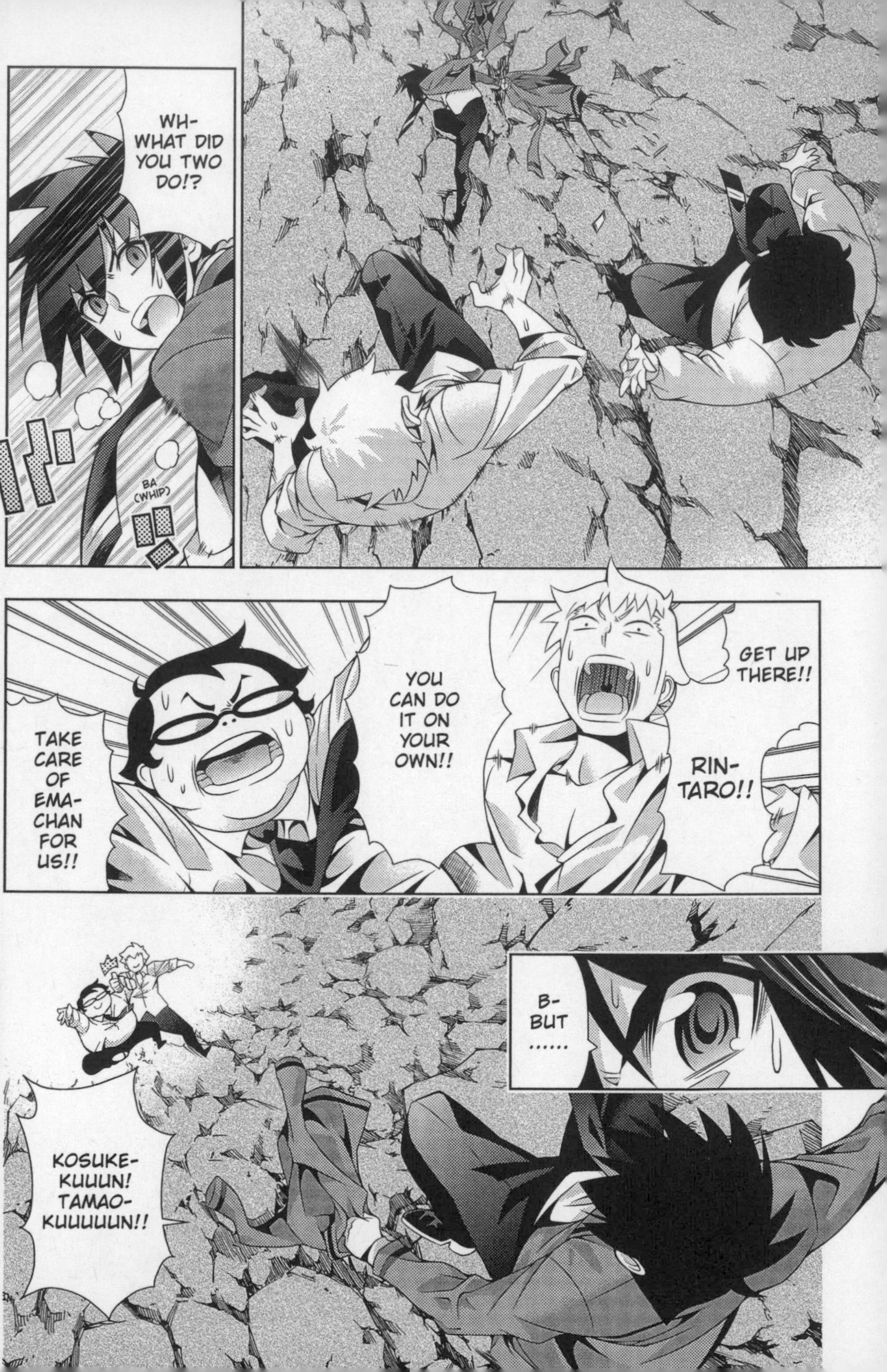
WH-WHAT DID YOU TWO DO!?
BA (WHIP)
GET UP THERE!!
RIN-TARO!!
YOU CAN DO IT ON YOUR OWN!!
TAKE CARE OF EMA-CHAN FOR US!!
B-BUT ......
KOSUKE-KUUUN! TAMAO-KUUUUUN!!

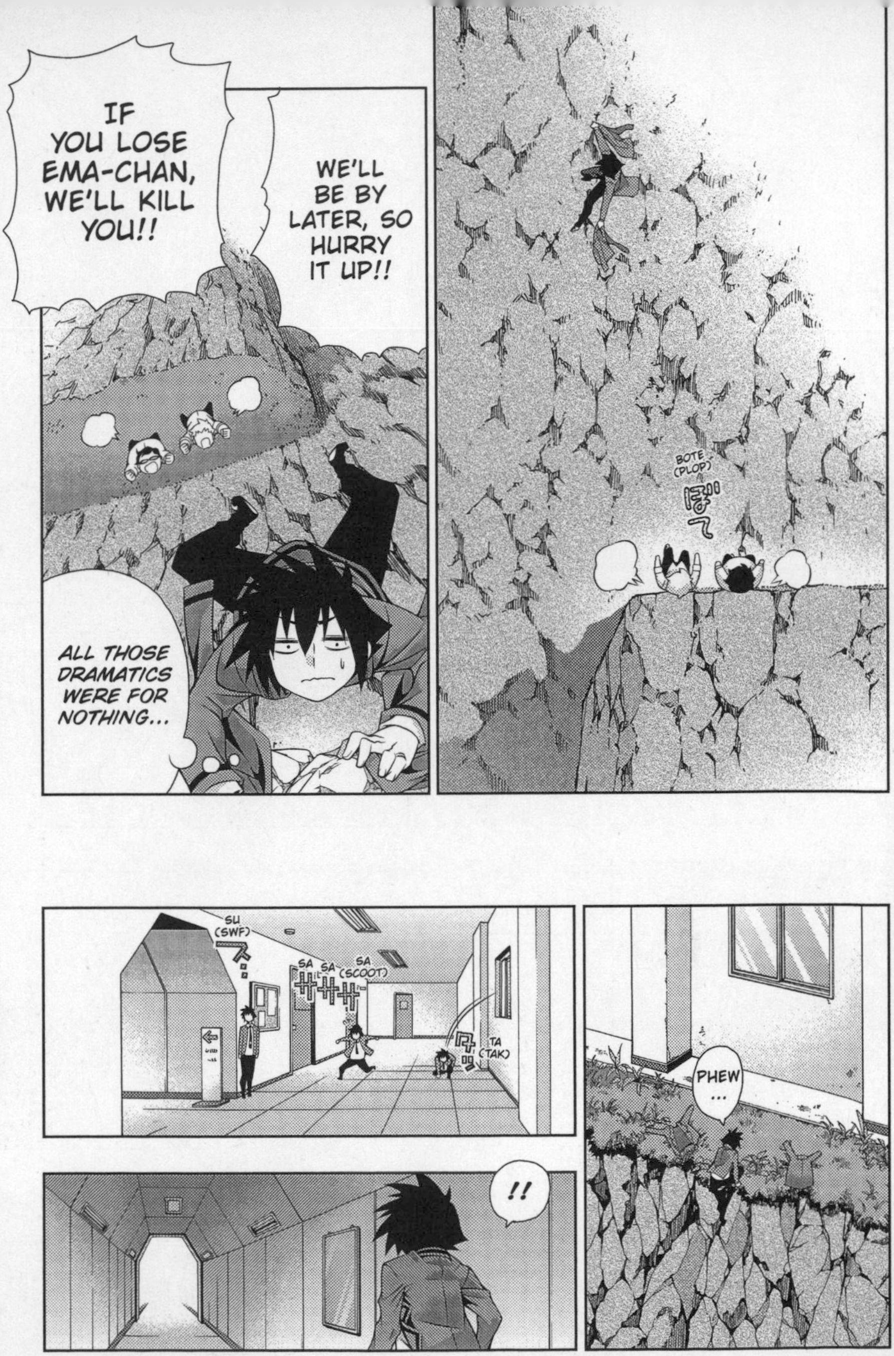

BOTE (PLOP)
ぼて
WE'LL BE BY LATER, SO HURRY IT UP!!
IF YOU LOSE EMA-CHAN, WE'LL KILL YOU!!
ALL THOSE DRAMATICS WERE FOR NOTHING...
PHEW...
SU (SWF)
SA SA SA (SCOOT)
TA (TAK)
!!

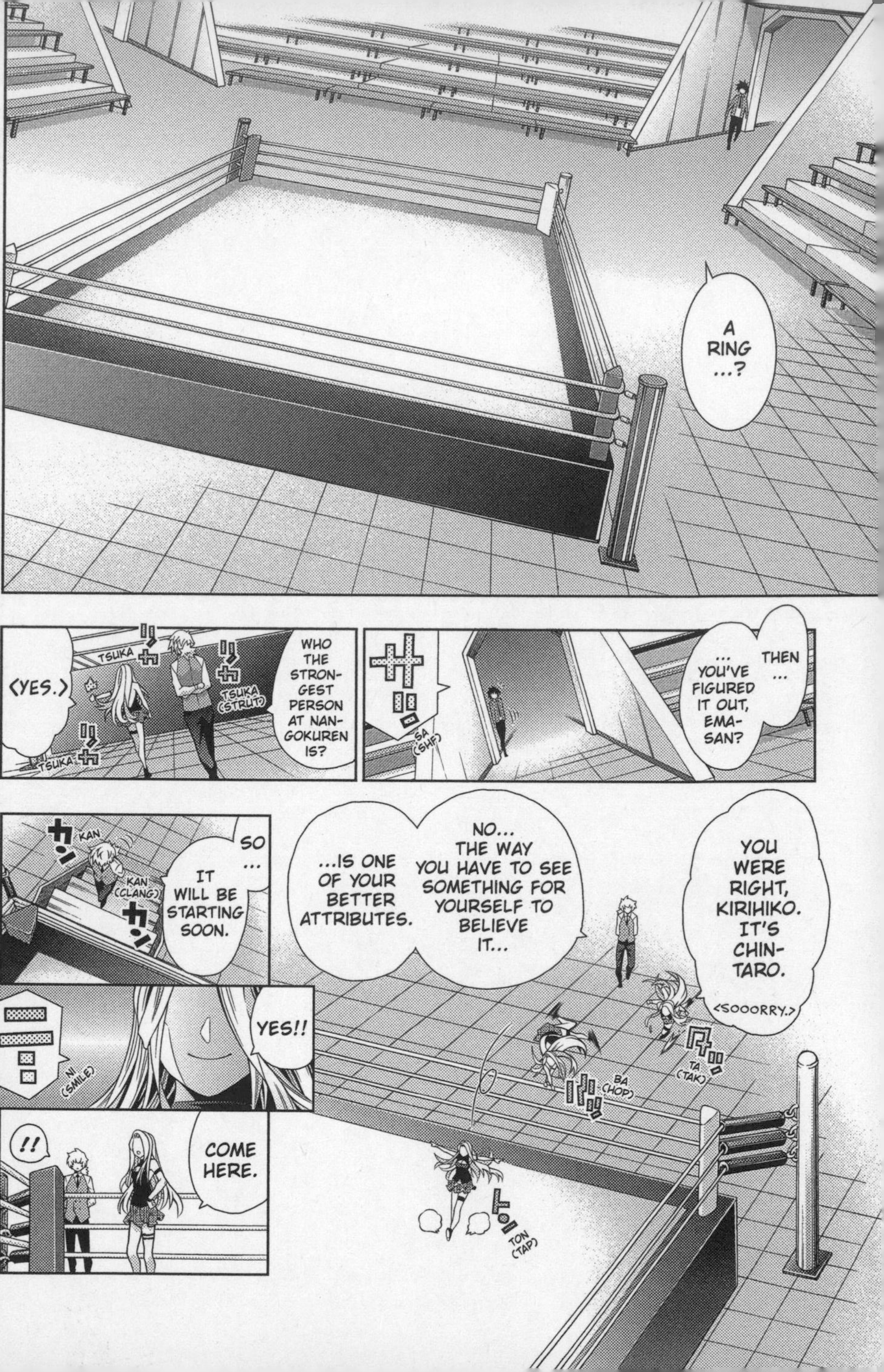
A RING ...?
THEN ...
... YOU'VE FIGURED IT OUT, EMA-SAN?
SA (SHF)
WHO THE STRONG-EST PERSON AT NAN-GOKUREN IS?
TSUKA
TSUKA (STRUT)
<YES.>
TSUKA
YOU WERE RIGHT, KIRIHIKO. IT'S CHIN-TARO.
<SOOORRY.>
TA (TAK)
NO... THE WAY YOU HAVE TO SEE SOMETHING FOR YOURSELF TO BELIEVE IT...
...IS ONE OF YOUR BETTER ATTRIBUTES.
KAN
KAN (CLANG)
SO ... IT WILL BE STARTING SOON.
YES!!
NI (SMILE)
BA (HOP)
!!
COME HERE.
TON (TAP)

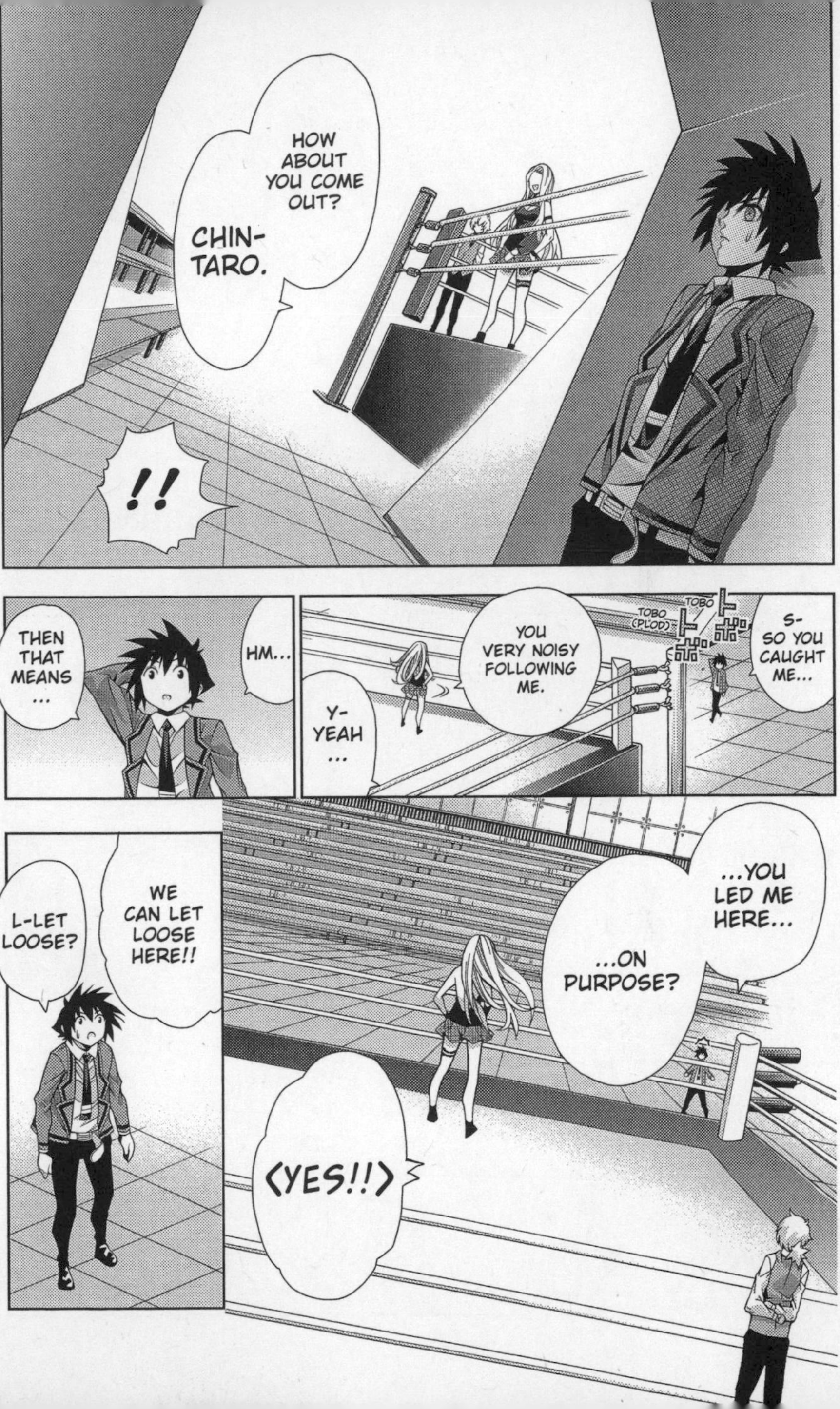
HOW ABOUT YOU COME OUT?
CHIN-TARO.
!!
S- SO YOU CAUGHT ME...
TOBO
TOBO (PLOD)
YOU VERY NOISY FOLLOWING ME.
Y-YEAH...
HM...
THEN THAT MEANS...
...YOU LED ME HERE...
...ON PURPOSE?
⟨YES!!⟩
WE CAN LET LOOSE HERE!!
L-LET LOOSE?

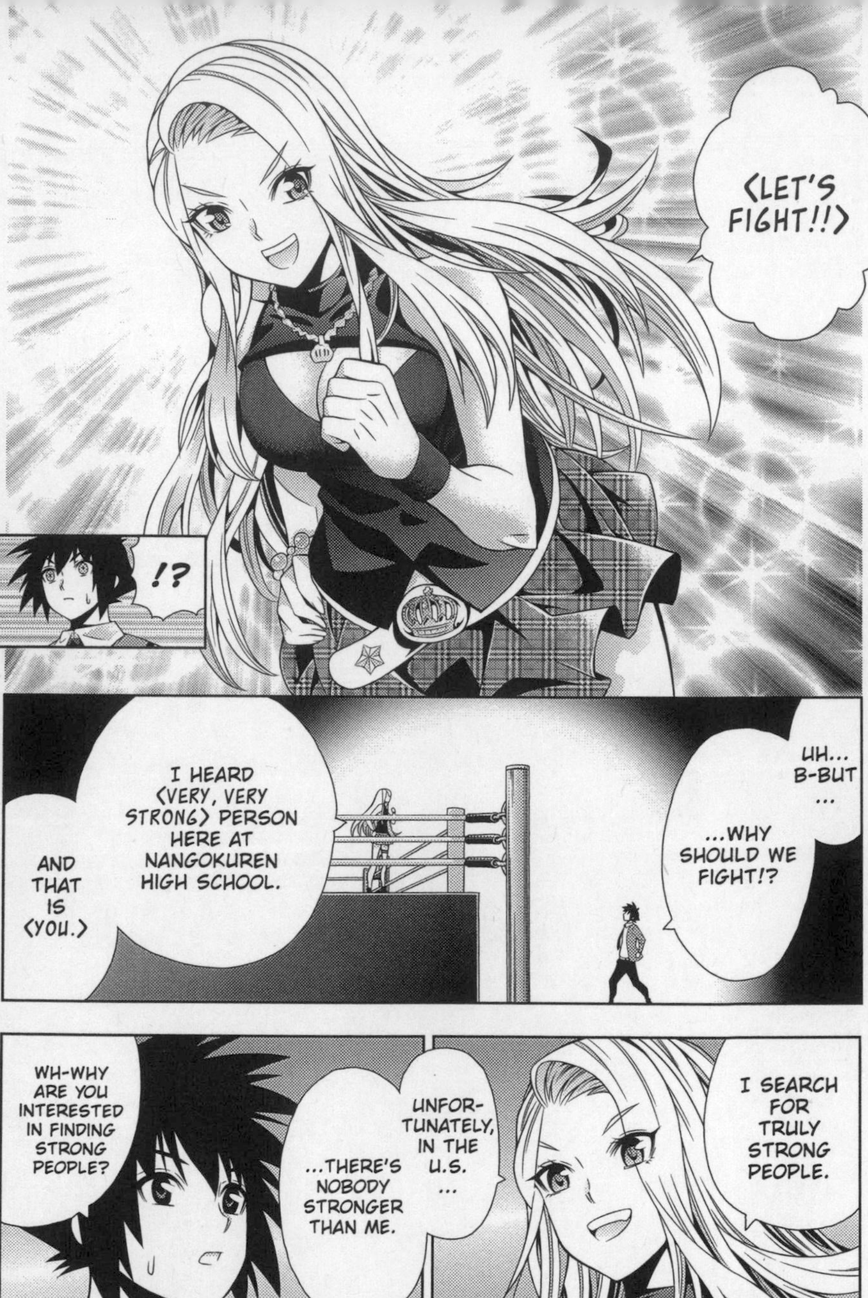

<LET'S FIGHT!!>
!?
UH... B-BUT ...
...WHY SHOULD WE FIGHT!?
I HEARD <VERY, VERY STRONG> PERSON HERE AT NANGOKUREN HIGH SCHOOL.
AND THAT IS <YOU.>
I SEARCH FOR TRULY STRONG PEOPLE.
UNFORTUNATELY, IN THE U.S. ...
...THERE'S NOBODY STRONGER THAN ME.
WH-WHY ARE YOU INTERESTED IN FINDING STRONG PEOPLE?

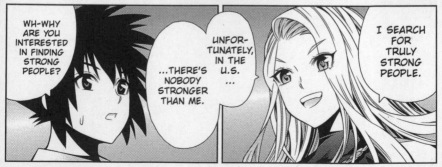

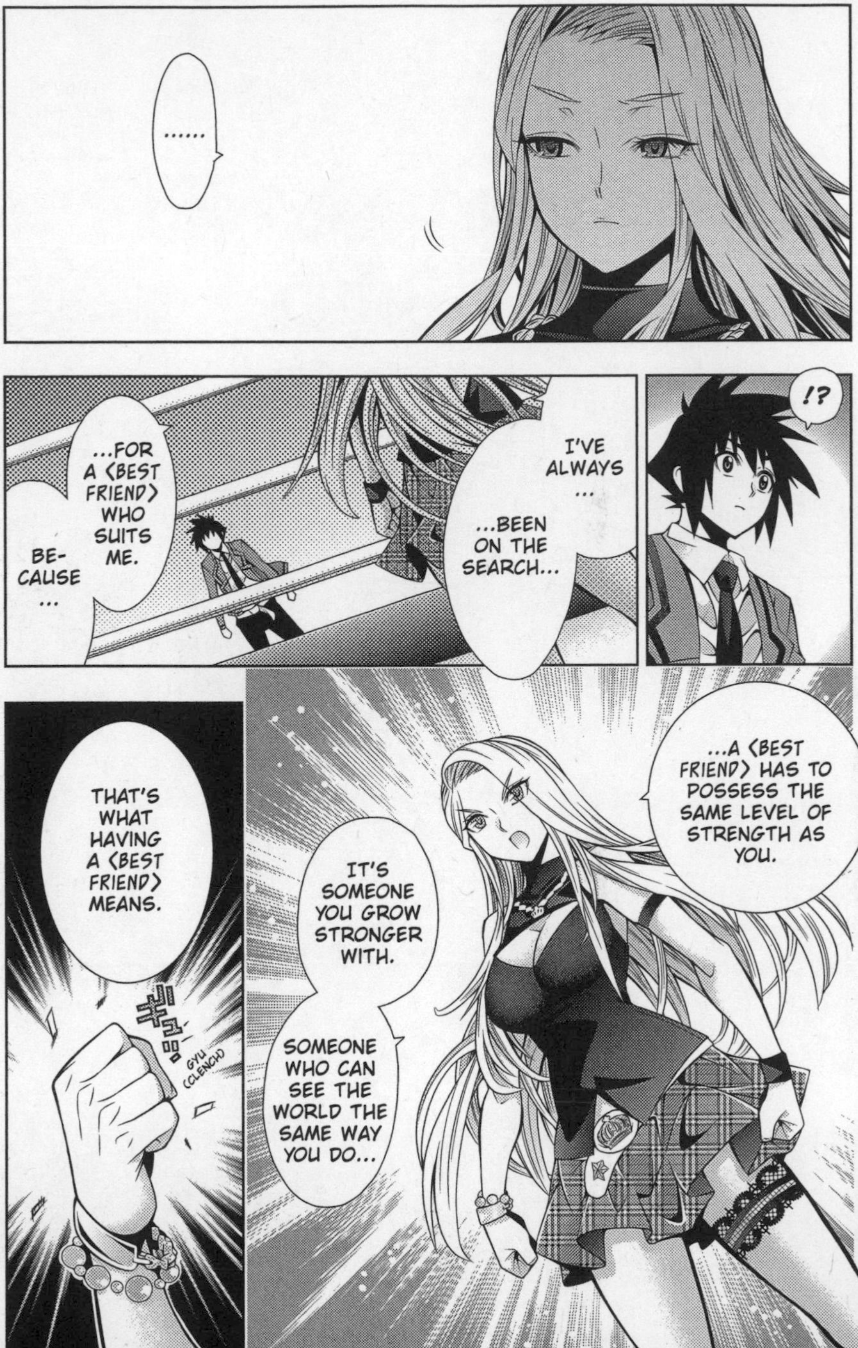
......
!?
I'VE ALWAYS ...
...BEEN ON THE SEARCH...
...FOR A 〈BEST FRIEND〉 WHO SUITS ME.
BE-CAUSE ...
...A 〈BEST FRIEND〉 HAS TO POSSESS THE SAME LEVEL OF STRENGTH AS YOU.
IT'S SOMEONE YOU GROW STRONGER WITH.
SOMEONE WHO CAN SEE THE WORLD THE SAME WAY YOU DO...
THAT'S WHAT HAVING A 〈BEST FRIEND〉 MEANS.
GYU (CLENCH)

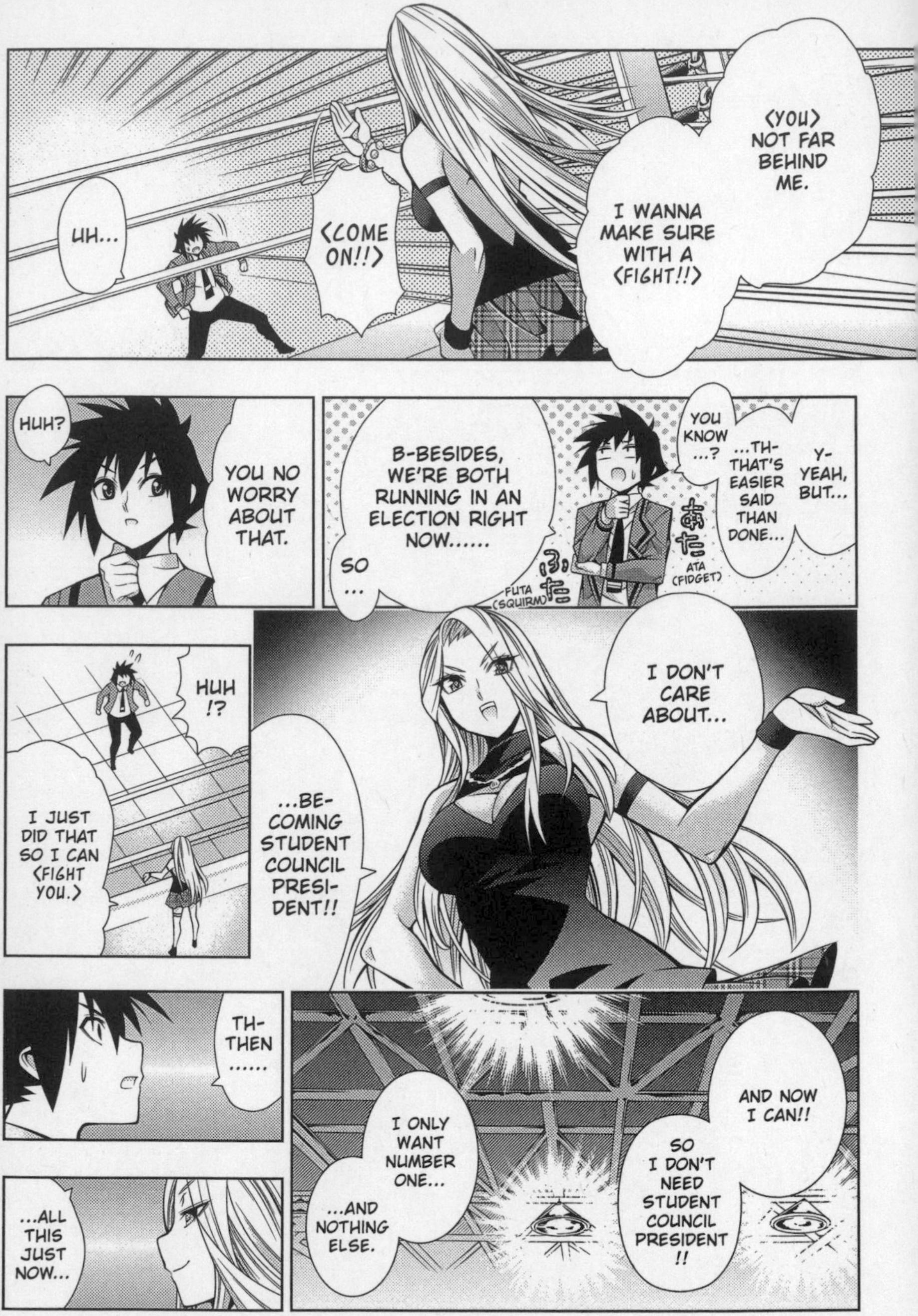
<YOU> NOT FAR BEHIND ME.
I WANNA MAKE SURE WITH A <FIGHT!!>
<COME ON!!>
UH...
Y-YEAH, BUT...
...TH-THAT'S EASIER SAID THAN DONE...
YOU KNOW...?
あた
ATA (FIDGET)
ふた
FUTA (SQUIRM)
B-BESIDES, WE'RE BOTH RUNNING IN AN ELECTION RIGHT NOW......
SO...
YOU NO WORRY ABOUT THAT.
HUH?
I DON'T CARE ABOUT...
...BE-COMING STUDENT COUNCIL PRESI-DENT!!
HUH!?
I JUST DID THAT SO I CAN <FIGHT YOU.>
AND NOW I CAN!!
SO I DON'T NEED STUDENT COUNCIL PRESIDENT!!
I ONLY WANT NUMBER ONE...
...AND NOTHING ELSE.
TH-THEN......
...ALL THIS JUST NOW...

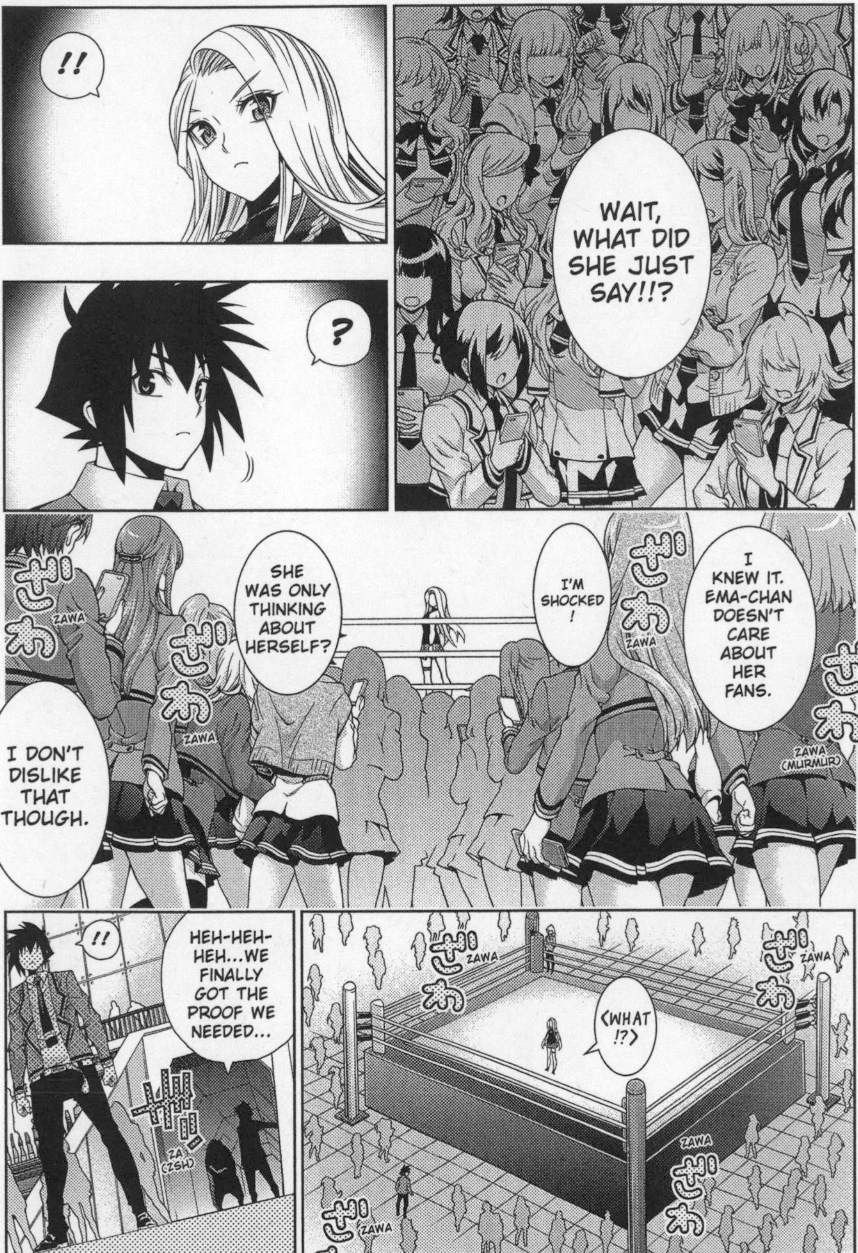
WAIT, WHAT DID SHE JUST SAY!!?
!!
?
ZAWA (MURMUR)
I KNEW IT. EMA-CHAN DOESN'T CARE ABOUT HER FANS.
ZAWA
I'M SHOCKED!
SHE WAS ONLY THINKING ABOUT HERSELF?
ZAWA
ZAWA
I DON'T DISLIKE THAT THOUGH.
ZAWA
ZAWA
<WHAT!?>
ZAWA
ZAWA
HEH-HEH-HEH...WE FINALLY GOT THE PROOF WE NEEDED...
!!
ZA (ZSH)

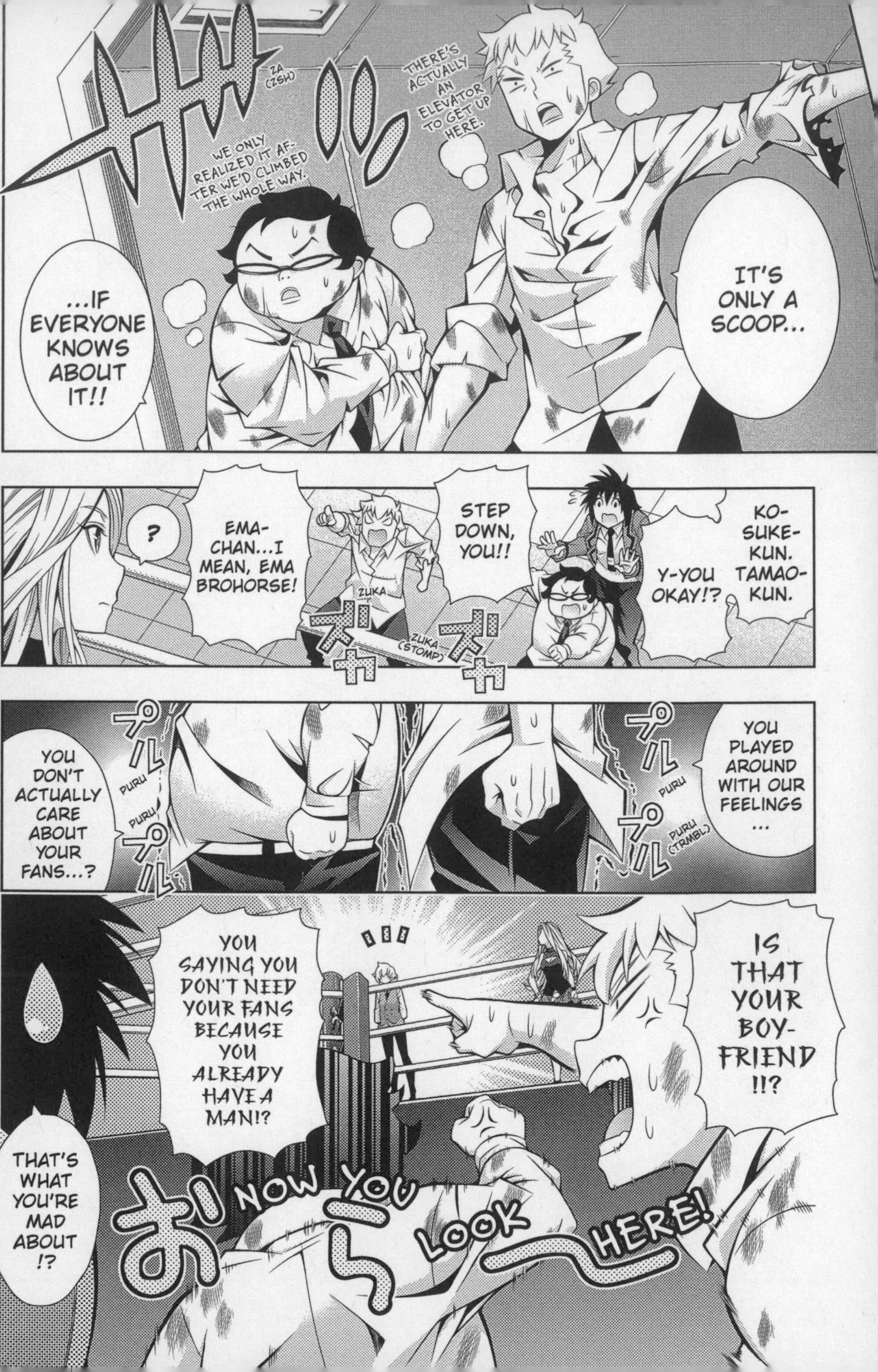
IT'S ONLY A SCOOP...
THERE'S ACTUALLY AN ELEVATOR TO GET UP HERE.
WE ONLY REALIZED IT AFTER WE'D CLIMBED THE WHOLE WAY.
ZA (ZSH)
...IF EVERYONE KNOWS ABOUT IT!!
KO-SUKE-KUN. TAMAO-KUN.
Y-YOU OKAY!?
STEP DOWN, YOU!!
ZUKA
ZUKA (STOMP)
EMA-CHAN...I MEAN, EMA BROHORSE!
?
YOU PLAYED AROUND WITH OUR FEELINGS ...
PURU
PURU (TRMBL)
PURU
PURU
YOU DON'T ACTUALLY CARE ABOUT YOUR FANS...?
IS THAT YOUR BOY-FRIEND!!?
YOU SAYING YOU DON'T NEED YOUR FANS BECAUSE YOU ALREADY HAVE A MAN!?
NOW YOU LOOK HERE!
THAT'S WHAT YOU'RE MAD ABOUT!?

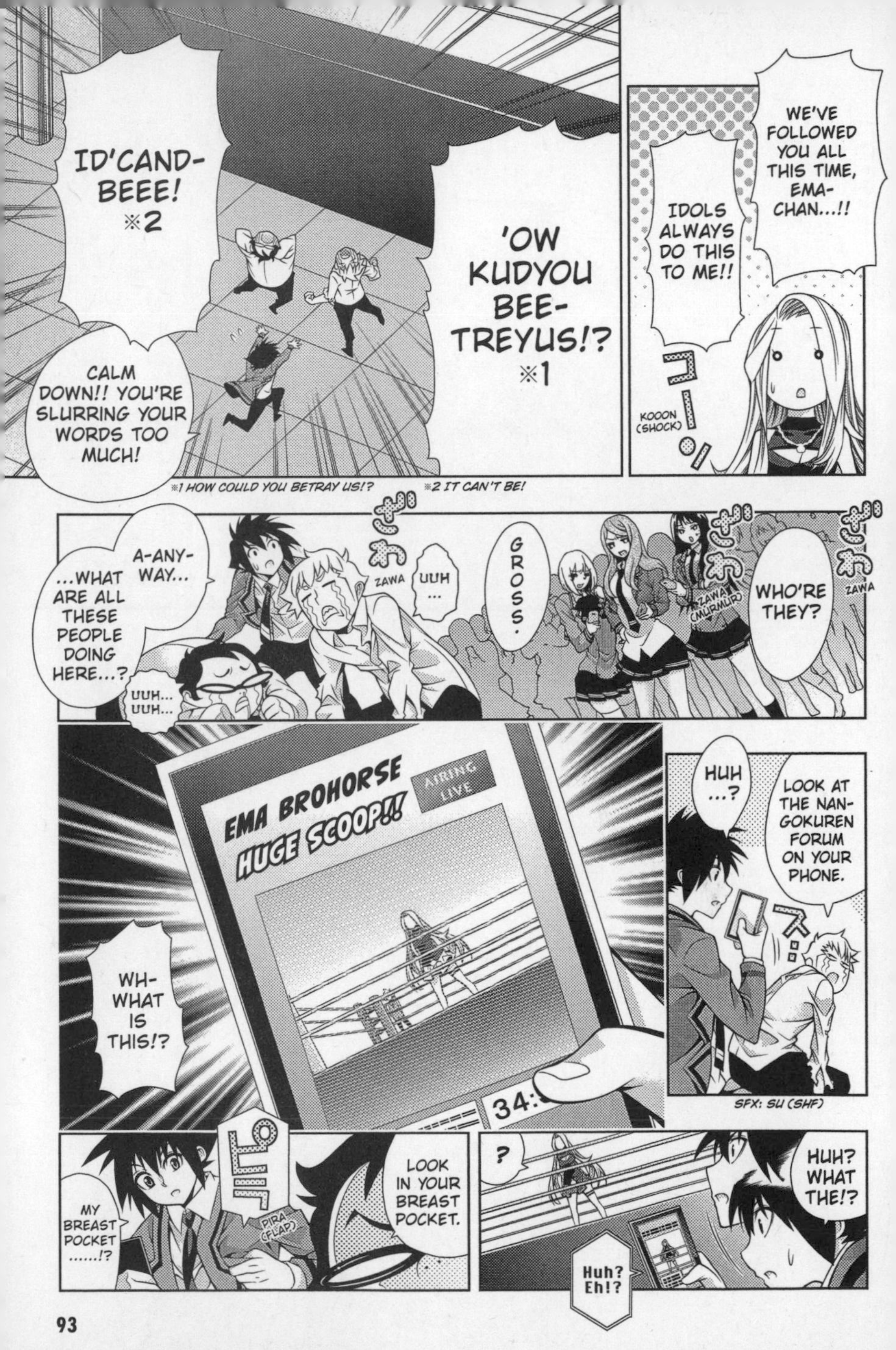
WE'VE FOLLOWED YOU ALL THIS TIME, EMA-CHAN...!!
IDOLS ALWAYS DO THIS TO ME!!
KOOON (SHOCK)
'OW KUDYOU BEE-TREYUS!? ※1
ID'CAND-BEEE! ※2
CALM DOWN!! YOU'RE SLURRING YOUR WORDS TOO MUCH!
※1 HOW COULD YOU BETRAY US!?
※2 IT CAN'T BE!
ZAWA
WHO'RE THEY?
ZAWA (MURMUR)
GROSS.
UUH ...
ZAWA
A-ANYWAY...
...WHAT ARE ALL THESE PEOPLE DOING HERE...?
UUH... UUH...
LOOK AT THE NAN-GOKUREN FORUM ON YOUR PHONE.
HUH ...?
SFX: SU (SHF)
EMA BROHORSE
HUGE SCOOP!!
AIRING LIVE
34:
WH-WHAT IS THIS!?
HUH? WHAT THE!?
?
Huh? Eh!?
LOOK IN YOUR BREAST POCKET.
PIRA (FLAP)
MY BREAST POCKET ......!?

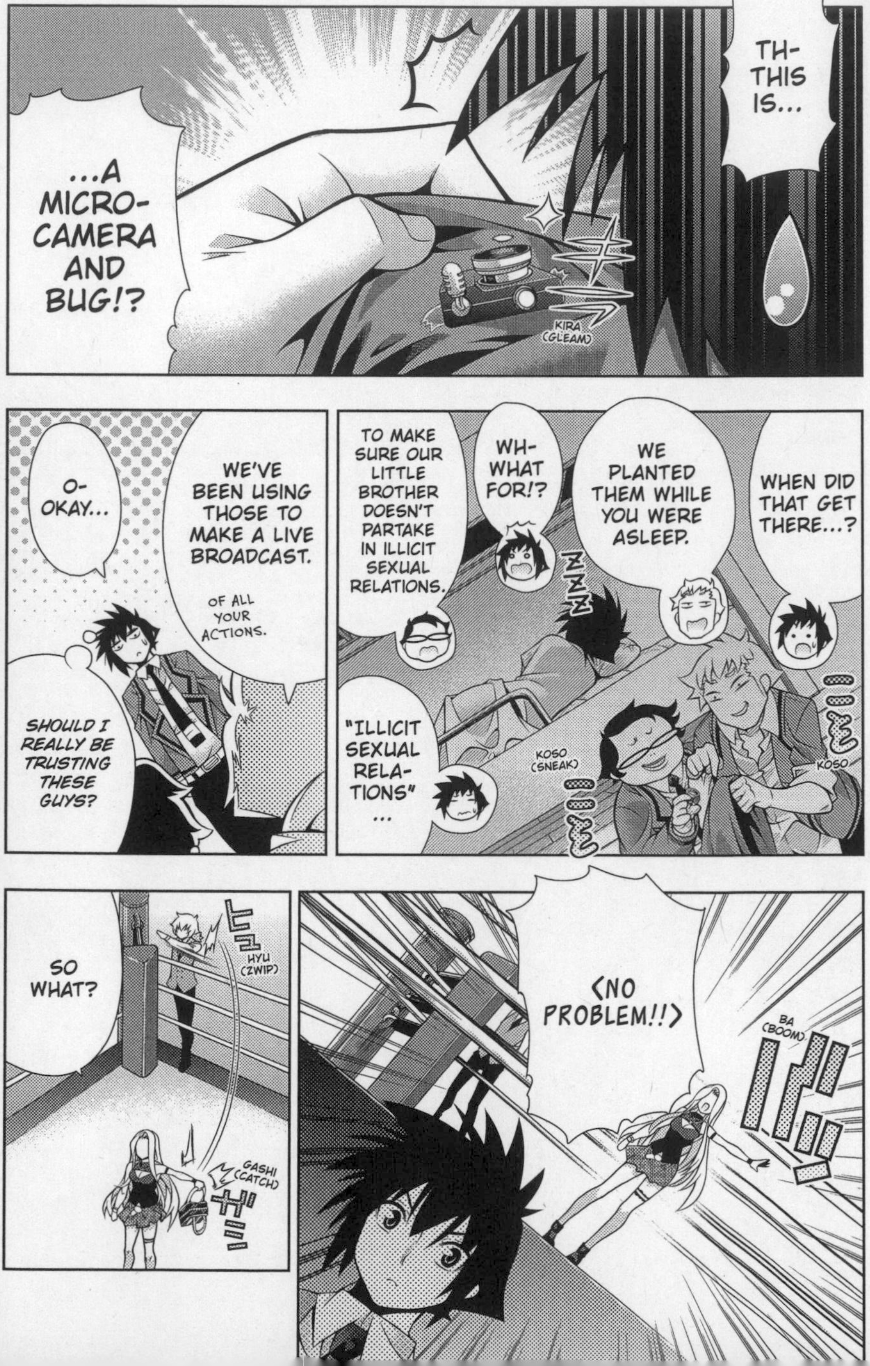
TH-THIS IS...
...A MICRO-CAMERA AND BUG!?
KIRA (GLEAM)
WHEN DID THAT GET THERE...?
WE PLANTED THEM WHILE YOU WERE ASLEEP.
WH-WHAT FOR!?
TO MAKE SURE OUR LITTLE BROTHER DOESN'T PARTAKE IN ILLICIT SEXUAL RELATIONS.
KOSO
KOSO (SNEAK)
"ILLICIT SEXUAL RELA-TIONS" ...
WE'VE BEEN USING THOSE TO MAKE A LIVE BROADCAST.
OF ALL YOUR ACTIONS.
O-OKAY...
SHOULD I REALLY BE TRUSTING THESE GUYS?
‹NO PROBLEM!!›
BA (BOOM)
HYU (ZWIP)
SO WHAT?
GASHI (CATCH)

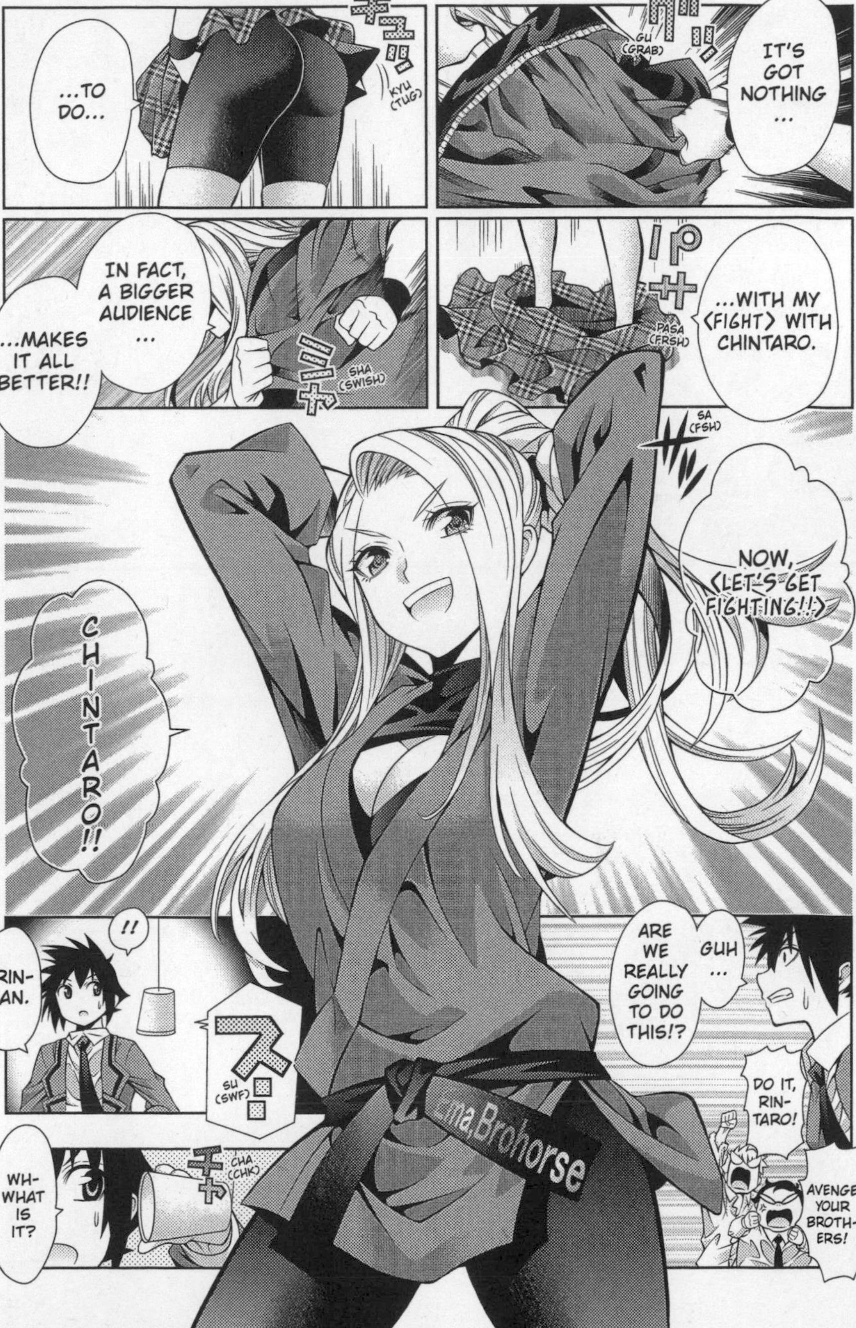
IT'S GOT NOTHING ...
GU (GRAB)
...TO DO...
KYU (TUG)
...WITH MY 〈FIGHT〉 WITH CHINTARO.
PASA (FRSH)
IN FACT, A BIGGER AUDIENCE ...
...MAKES IT ALL BETTER!!
SHA (SWISH)
SA (FSH)
NOW, 〈LET'S GET FIGHTING!!〉
CHINTARO!!
GUH ...
ARE WE REALLY GOING TO DO THIS!?
DO IT, RINTARO!
AVENGE YOUR BROTHERS!
!!
ERIN-SAN.
SU (SWF)
ma,Brohorse
CHA (CHK)
WH-WHAT IS IT?

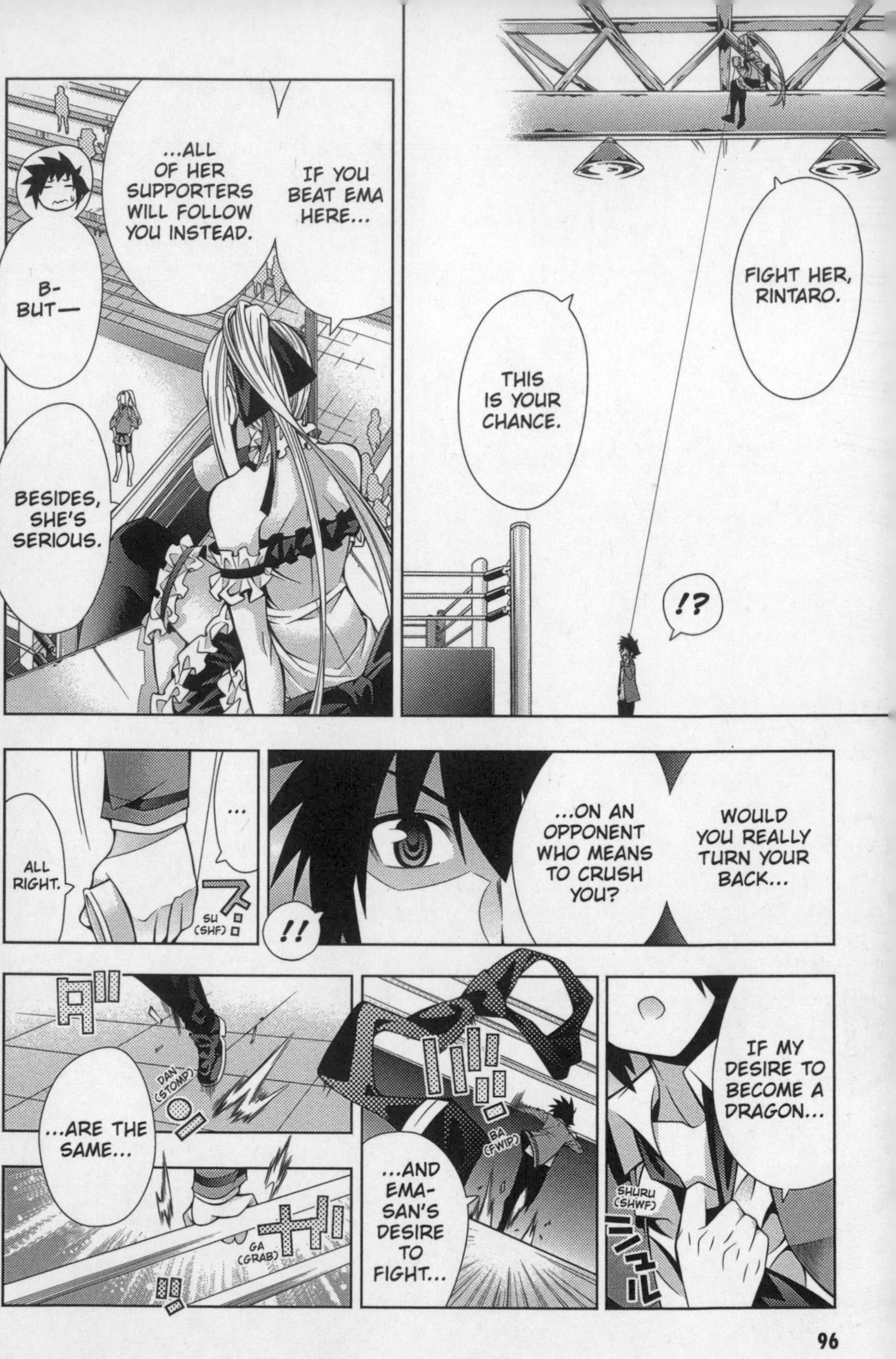
FIGHT HER, RINTARO.
THIS IS YOUR CHANCE.
!?
IF YOU BEAT EMA HERE...
...ALL OF HER SUPPORTERS WILL FOLLOW YOU INSTEAD.
B-BUT—
BESIDES, SHE'S SERIOUS.
WOULD YOU REALLY TURN YOUR BACK...
...ON AN OPPONENT WHO MEANS TO CRUSH YOU?
!!
...
ALL RIGHT.
SU (SHF)
IF MY DESIRE TO BECOME A DRAGON...
SHURU (SHWF)
BA (FWIP)
...AND EMA-SAN'S DESIRE TO FIGHT...
DAN (STOMP)
...ARE THE SAME...
GA (GRAB)

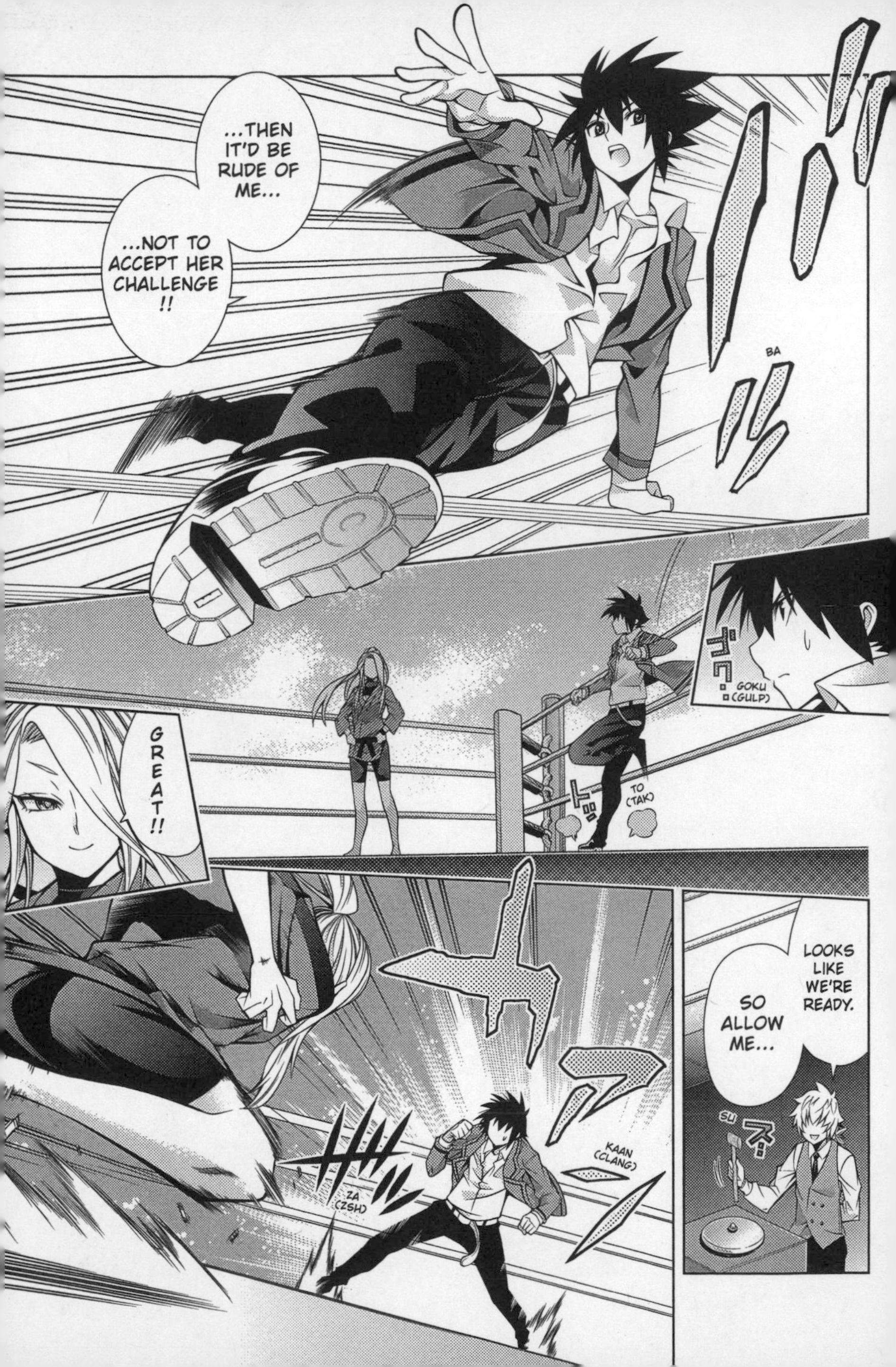
...THEN IT'D BE RUDE OF ME...
...NOT TO ACCEPT HER CHALLENGE !!
BA
GOKU (GULP)
TO (TAK)
GREAT!!
LOOKS LIKE WE'RE READY.
SO ALLOW ME...
SU
KAAN (CLANG)
ZA (ZSH)

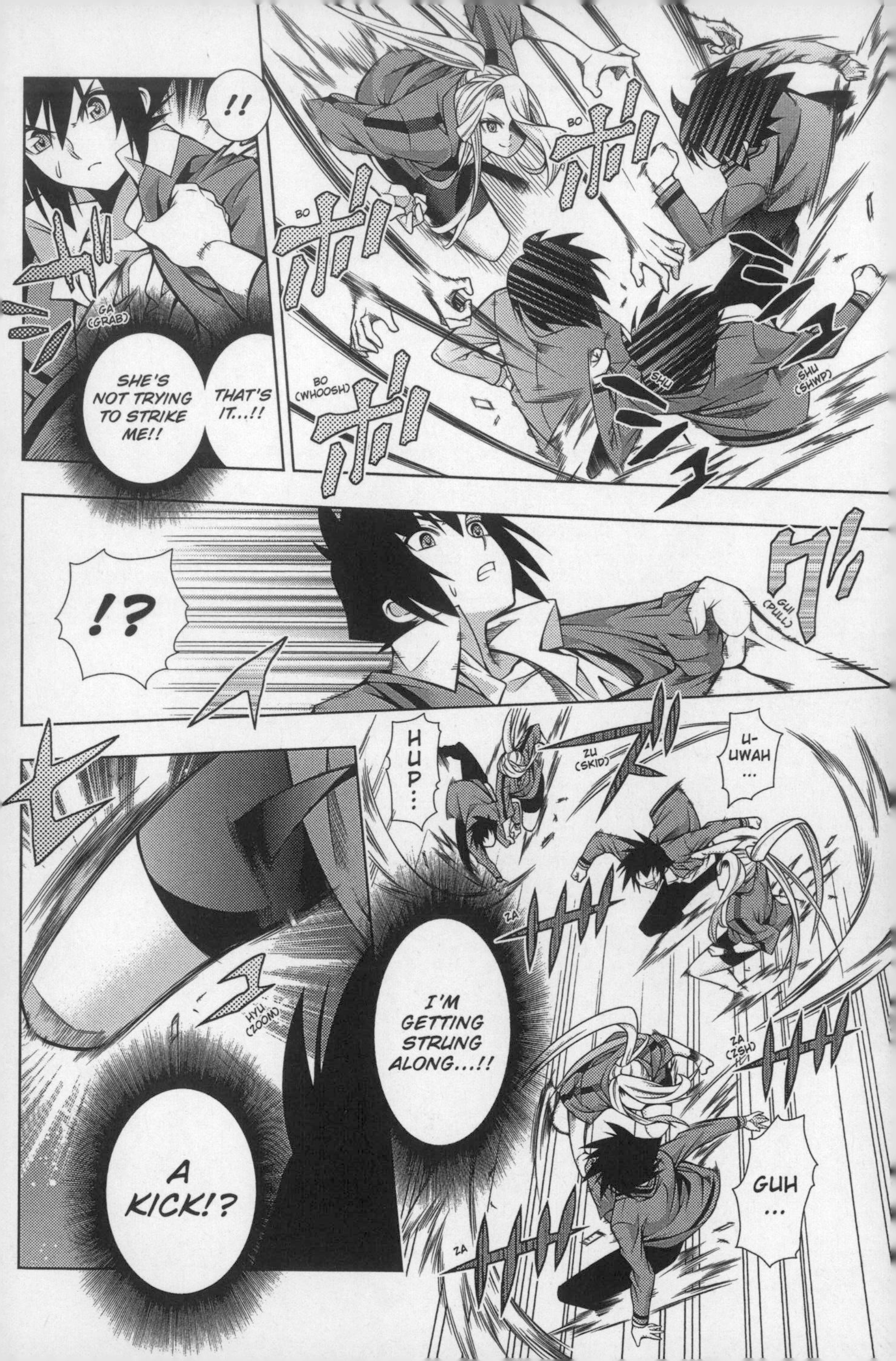
BO
BO
BO (WHOOSH)
SHU
SHU (SHWP)
!!
GA (GRAB)
THAT'S IT...!!
SHE'S NOT TRYING TO STRIKE ME!!
GUI (PULL)
!?
U-UWAH...
ZU (SKID)
HUP...
ZA
ZA (ZSH)
GUH...
ZA
I'M GETTING STRUNG ALONG...!!
HYU (ZOOM)
A KICK!?

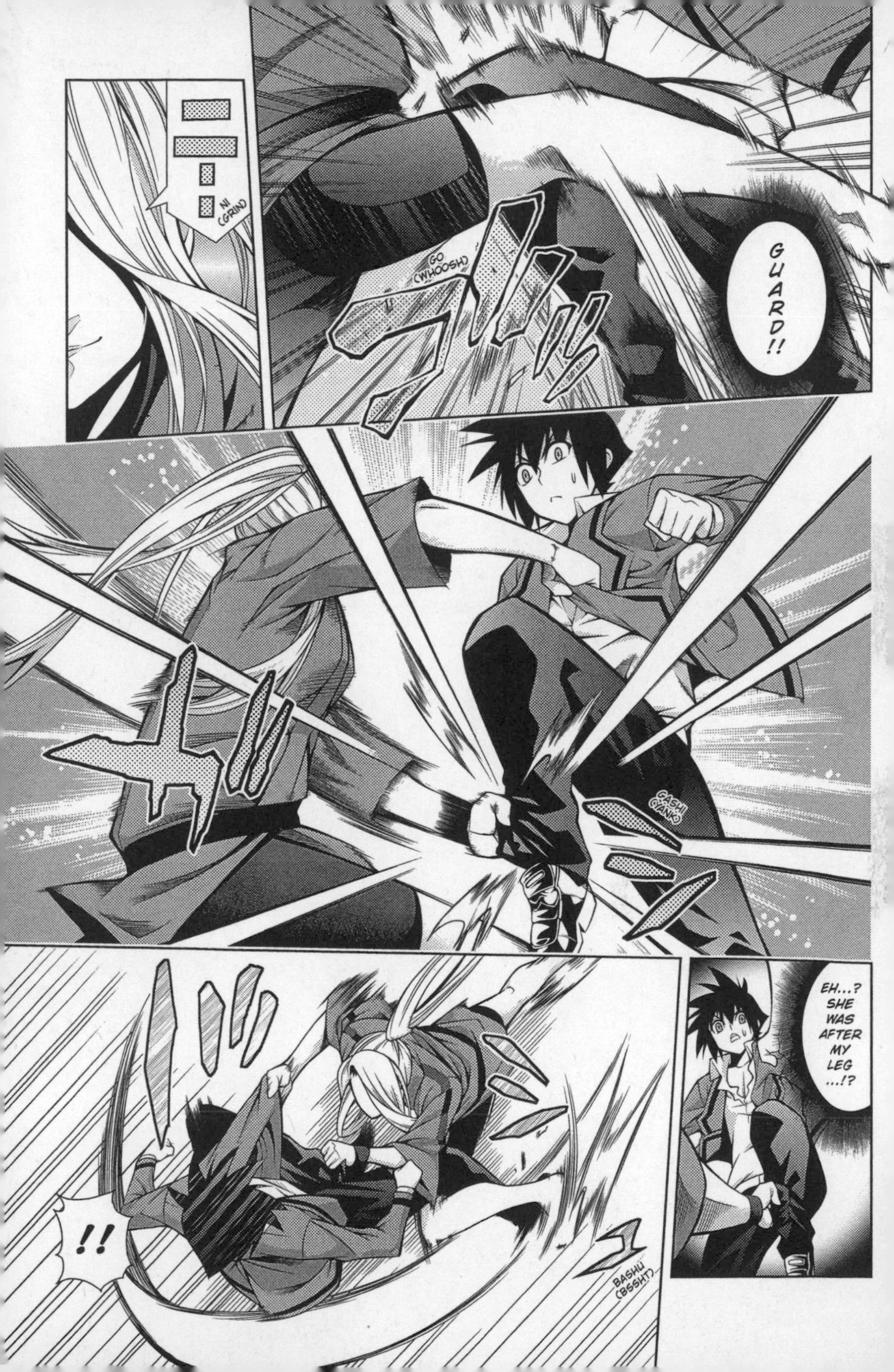
GUARD!!
GO (WHOOSH)
NI (GRIN)
GASHI (YANK)
EH...? SHE WAS AFTER MY LEG ...!?
!!
BASHU (BSSHT)

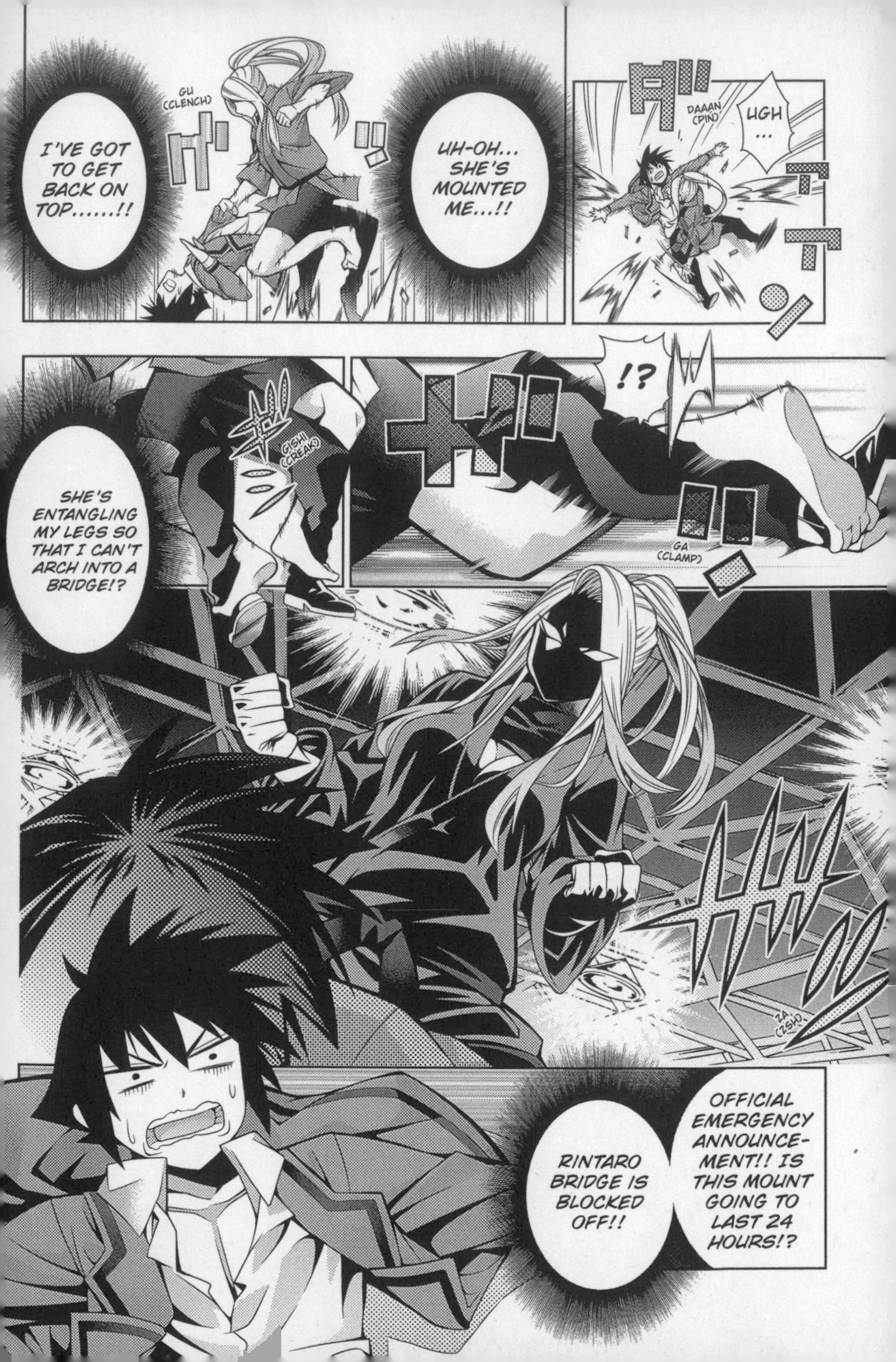
DAAAN (PIN)
UGH ...
UH-OH... SHE'S MOUNTED ME...!!
GU (CLENCH)
I'VE GOT TO GET BACK ON TOP......!!
!?
GA (CLAMP)
GISHI (CREAK)
SHE'S ENTANGLING MY LEGS SO THAT I CAN'T ARCH INTO A BRIDGE!?
ZA (ZSH)
OFFICIAL EMERGENCY ANNOUNCE-MENT!! IS THIS MOUNT GOING TO LAST 24 HOURS!?
RINTARO BRIDGE IS BLOCKED OFF!!

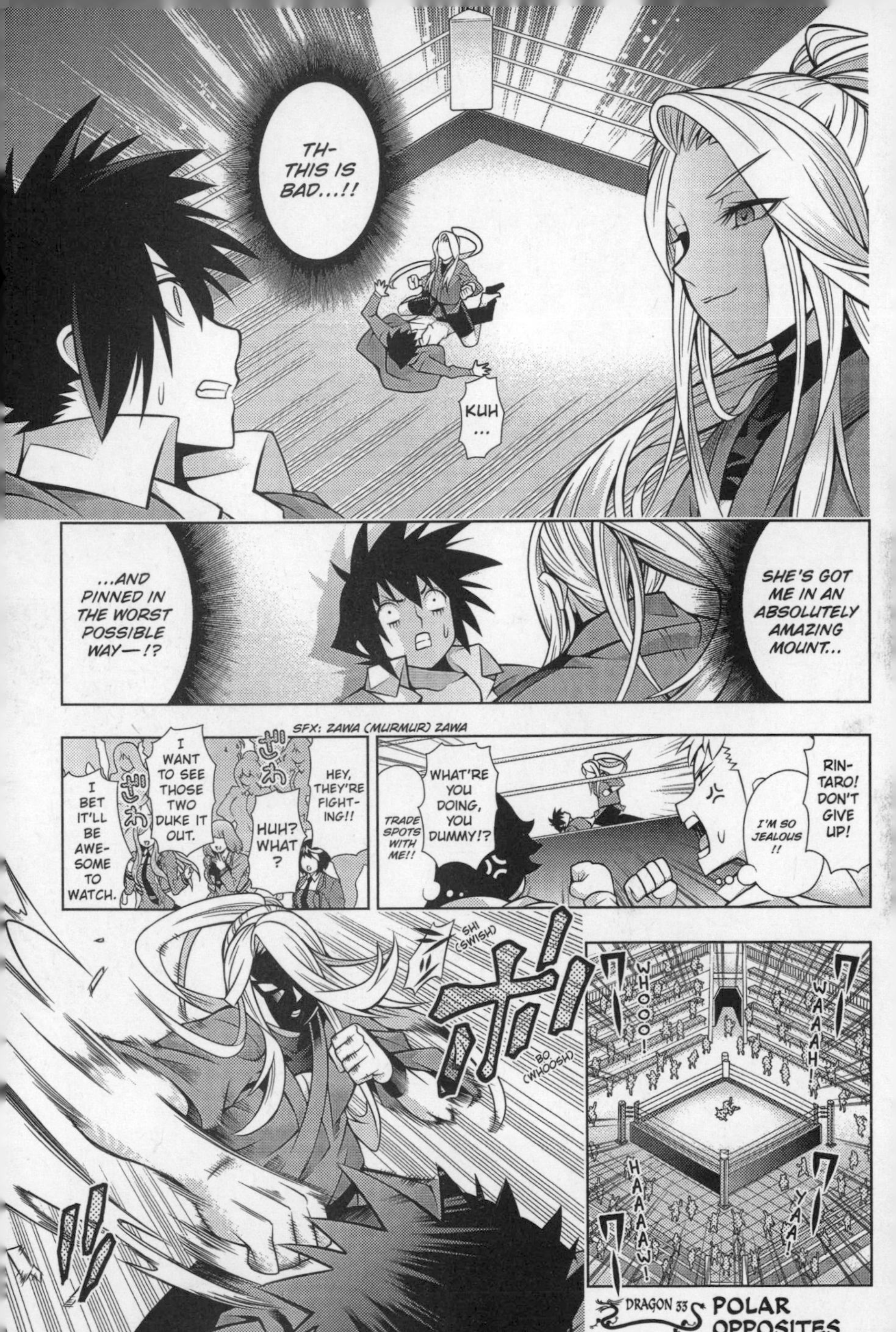
TH- THIS IS BAD...!!
KUH ...
SHE'S GOT ME IN AN ABSOLUTELY AMAZING MOUNT...
...AND PINNED IN THE WORST POSSIBLE WAY—!?
SFX: ZAWA (MURMUR) ZAWA
RIN-TARO! DON'T GIVE UP!
I'M SO JEALOUS!!
WHAT'RE YOU DOING, YOU DUMMY!?
TRADE SPOTS WITH ME!!
HEY, THEY'RE FIGHT-ING!!
HUH? WHAT?
I WANT TO SEE THOSE TWO DUKE IT OUT.
I BET IT'LL BE AWE-SOME TO WATCH.
WAAAAH!!
WHOOO!
YAA!
HAAAAW!
SHI (SWISH)
BO (WHOOSH)

DRAGON 33 **POLAR OPPOSITES**

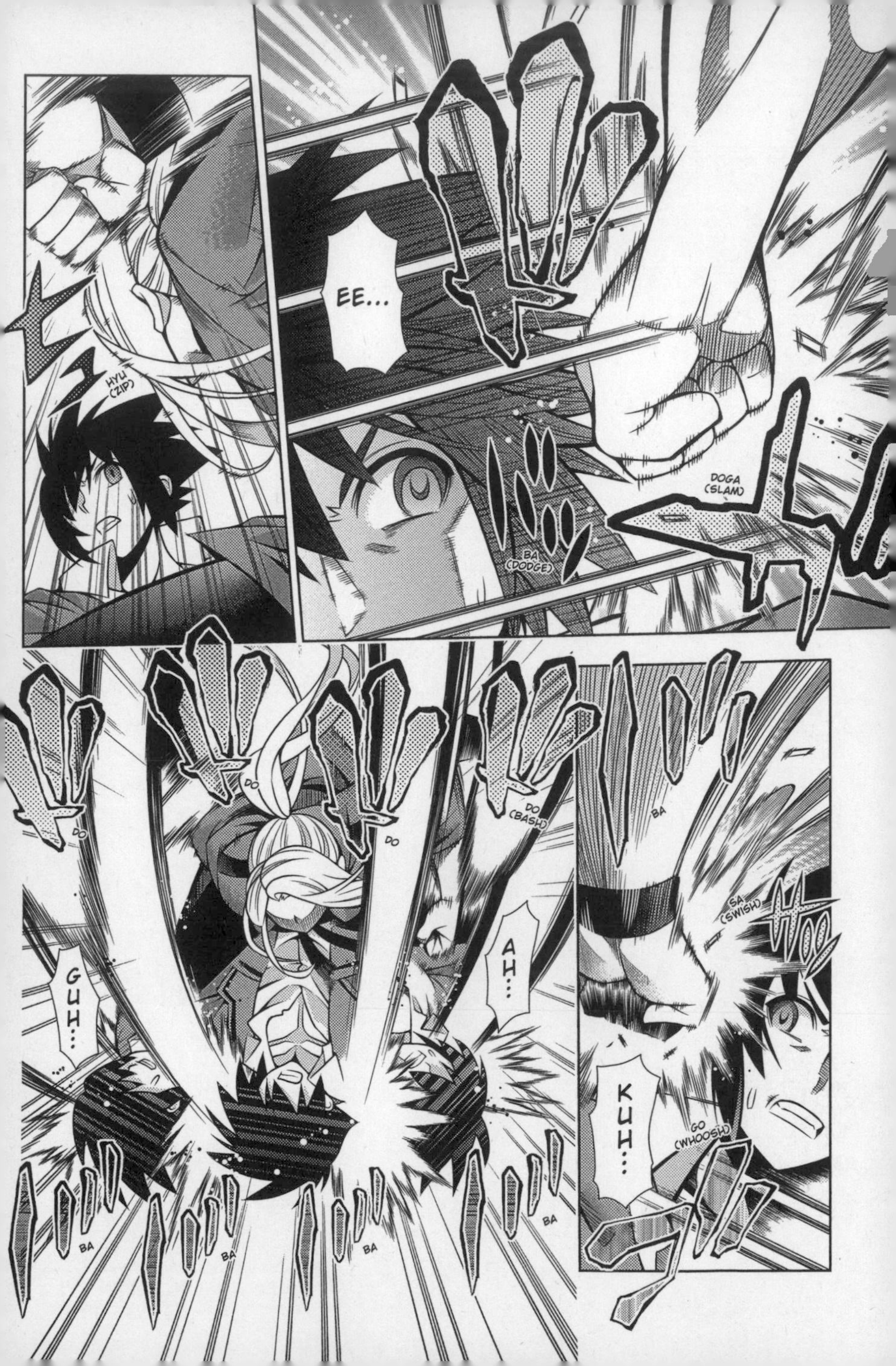
EE...
DOGA (SLAM)
BA (DODGE)
HYU (ZIP)
BA
SA (SWISH)
KUH...
GO (WHOOSH)
DO (BASH)
DO
AH...
DO
DO
GUH...
BA
BA
BA
BA

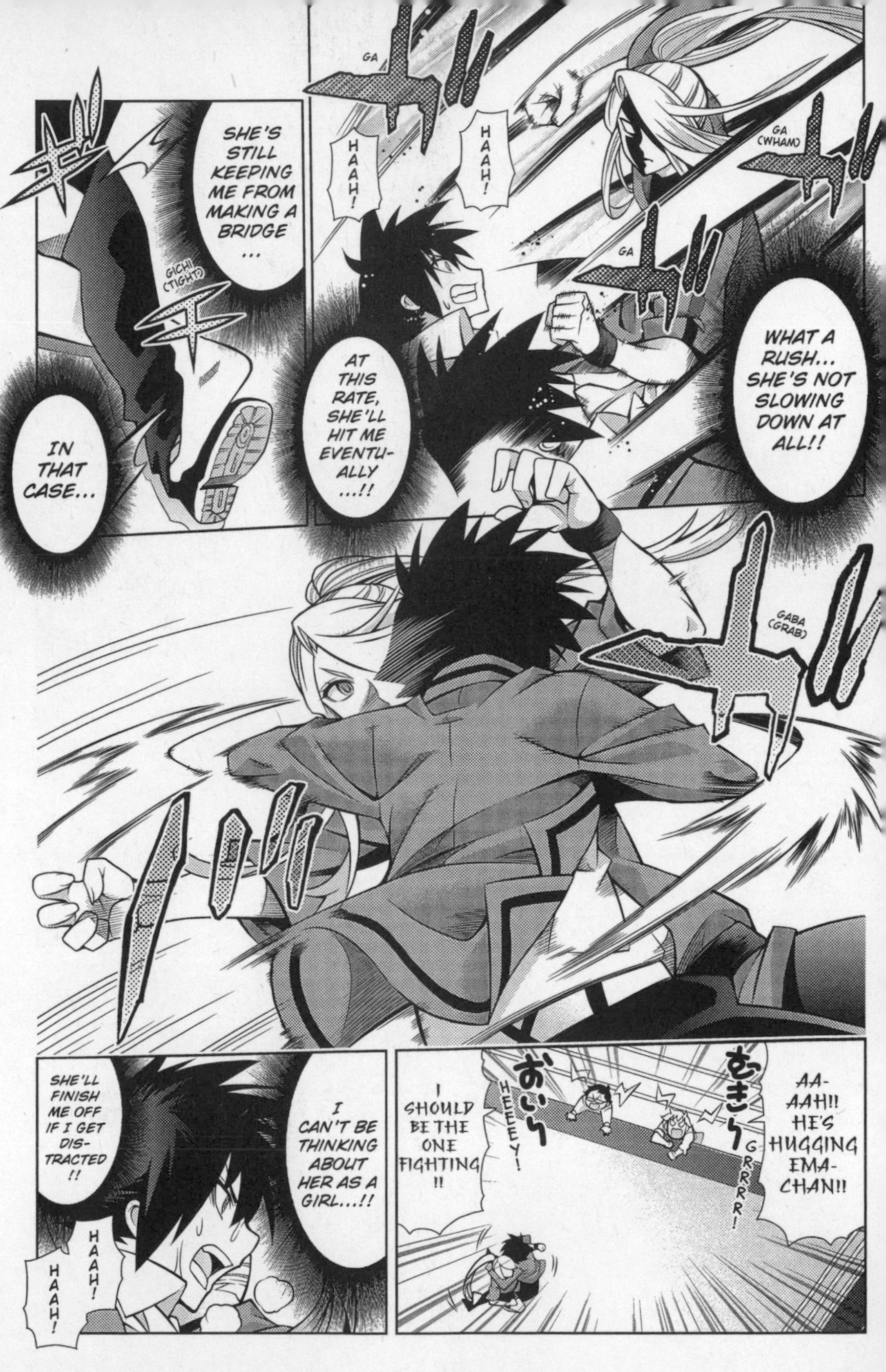
GA
GA (WHAM)
HAAH!
HAAH!
GA
WHAT A RUSH... SHE'S NOT SLOWING DOWN AT ALL!!
AT THIS RATE, SHE'LL HIT ME EVENTU-ALLY ...!!
SHE'S STILL KEEPING ME FROM MAKING A BRIDGE ...
GICHI (TIGHT)
IN THAT CASE...
GABA (GRAB)
AA-AAH!! HE'S HUGGING EMA-CHAN!!
むき～
GRRRR!
おい～
HEEEY!
I SHOULD BE THE ONE FIGHTING !!
I CAN'T BE THINKING ABOUT HER AS A GIRL...!!
SHE'LL FINISH ME OFF IF I GET DIS-TRACTED !!
HAAH!
HAAH!

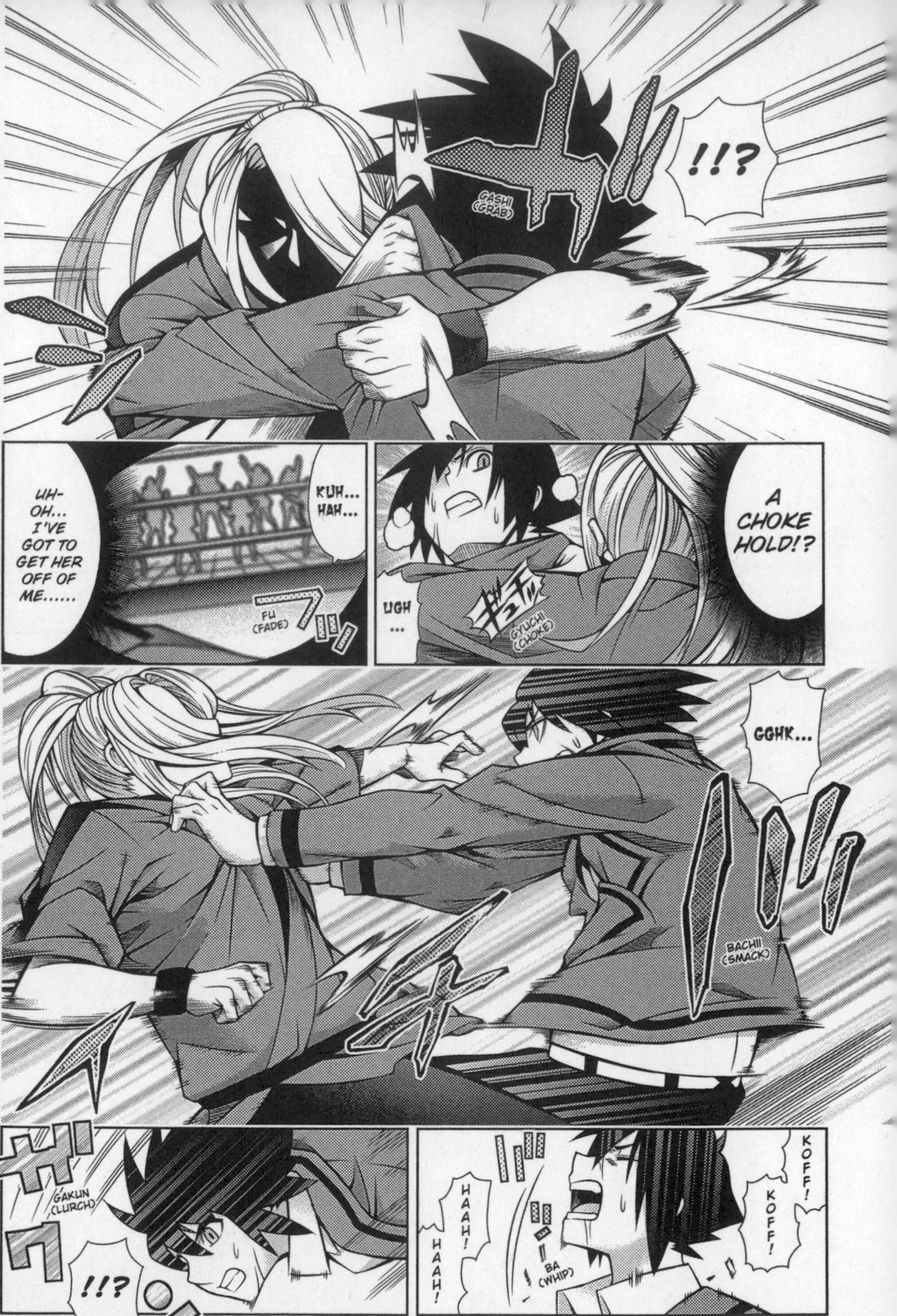
!!?
GASHI (GRAB)
A CHOKE HOLD!?
UGH ...
GYUCHI (CHOKE)
KUH... HAH...
UH-OH... I'VE GOT TO GET HER OFF OF ME......
FU (FADE)
GGHK...
BACHII (SMACK)
KOFF! KOFF!
HAAH! HAAH!
BA (WHIP)
GAKUN (CLURCH)
!!?

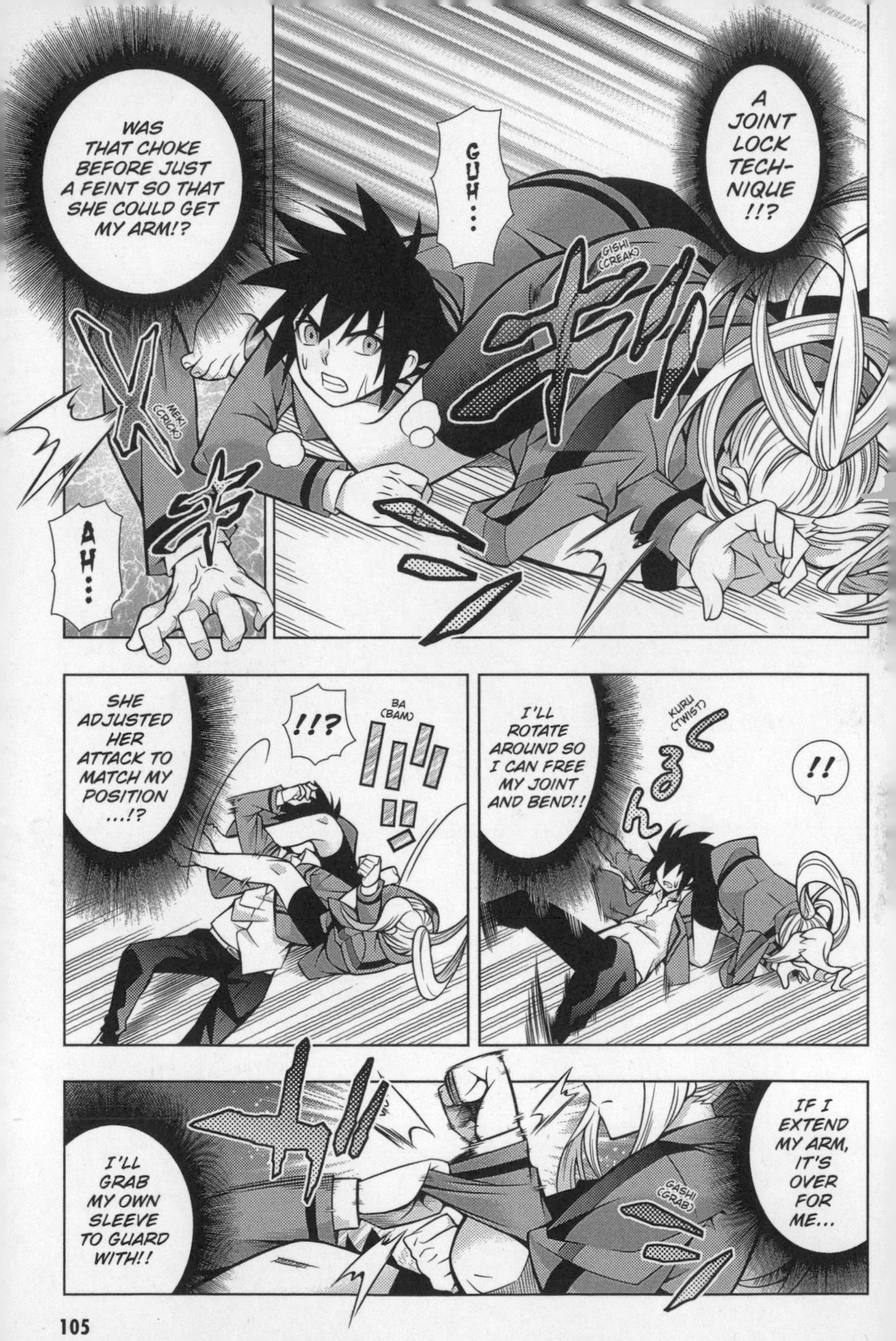
A JOINT LOCK TECHNIQUE!!?
GISHI (CREAK)
GUH...
WAS THAT CHOKE BEFORE JUST A FEINT SO THAT SHE COULD GET MY ARM!?
MEKI (CRICK)
AH...
KURU (TWIST)
!!
I'LL ROTATE AROUND SO I CAN FREE MY JOINT AND BEND!!
BA (BAM)
!!?
SHE ADJUSTED HER ATTACK TO MATCH MY POSITION ...!?
IF I EXTEND MY ARM, IT'S OVER FOR ME...
GASHI (GRAB)
I'LL GRAB MY OWN SLEEVE TO GUARD WITH!!

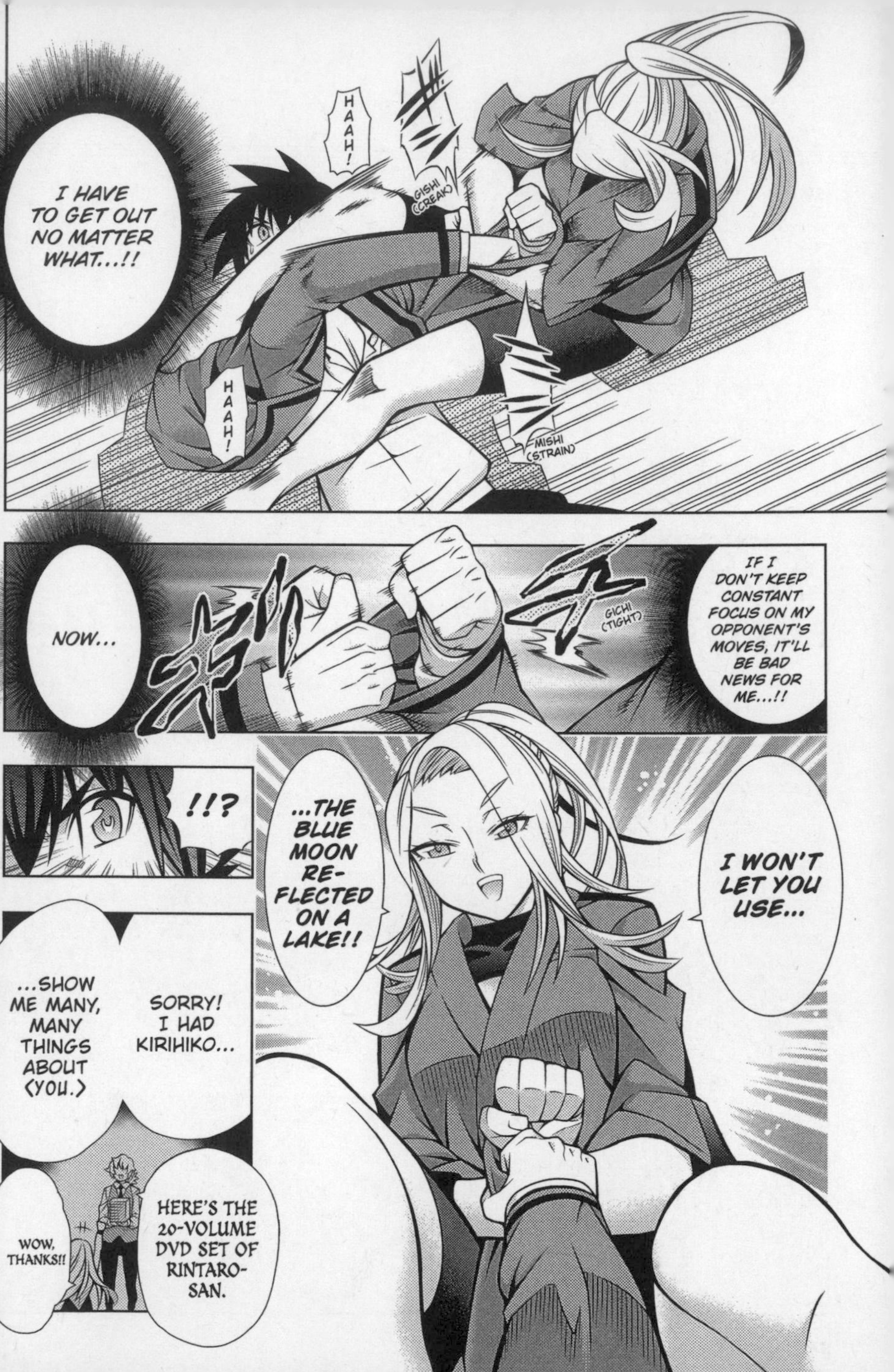
HAAH!
GISHI (CREAK)
I HAVE TO GET OUT NO MATTER WHAT...!!
HAAH!
MISHI (STRAIN)
IF I DON'T KEEP CONSTANT FOCUS ON MY OPPONENT'S MOVES, IT'LL BE BAD NEWS FOR ME...!!
GICHI (TIGHT)
NOW...
I WON'T LET YOU USE...
...THE BLUE MOON RE-FLECTED ON A LAKE!!
!!?
SORRY! I HAD KIRIHIKO...
...SHOW ME MANY, MANY THINGS ABOUT <YOU.>
HERE'S THE 20-VOLUME DVD SET OF RINTARO-SAN.
WOW, THANKS!!

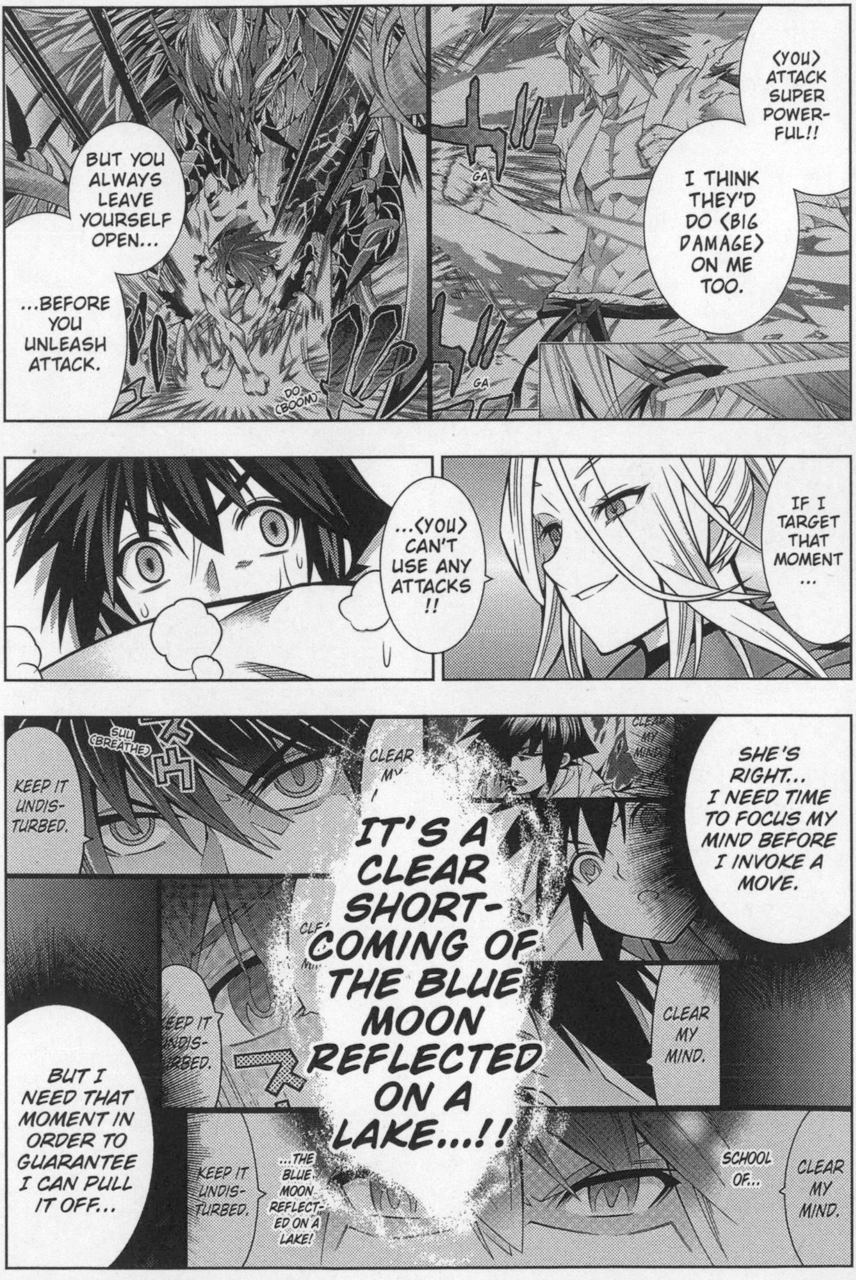

<YOU> ATTACK SUPER POWER-FUL!!
I THINK THEY'D DO <BIG DAMAGE> ON ME TOO.
GA
GA
BUT YOU ALWAYS LEAVE YOURSELF OPEN...
...BEFORE YOU UNLEASH ATTACK.
DO (BOOM)
IF I TARGET THAT MOMENT ...
...<YOU> CAN'T USE ANY ATTACKS !!
SHE'S RIGHT... I NEED TIME TO FOCUS MY MIND BEFORE I INVOKE A MOVE.
SUU (BREATHE)
CLEAR MY
KEEP IT UNDIS-TURBED.
IT'S A CLEAR SHORT-COMING OF THE BLUE MOON REFLECTED ON A LAKE...!!
CLEAR MY MIND.
BUT I NEED THAT MOMENT IN ORDER TO GUARANTEE I CAN PULL IT OFF...
CLEAR MY MIND.
SCHOOL OF...
...THE BLUE MOON REFLECT-ED ON A LAKE!
KEEP IT UNDIS-TURBED.

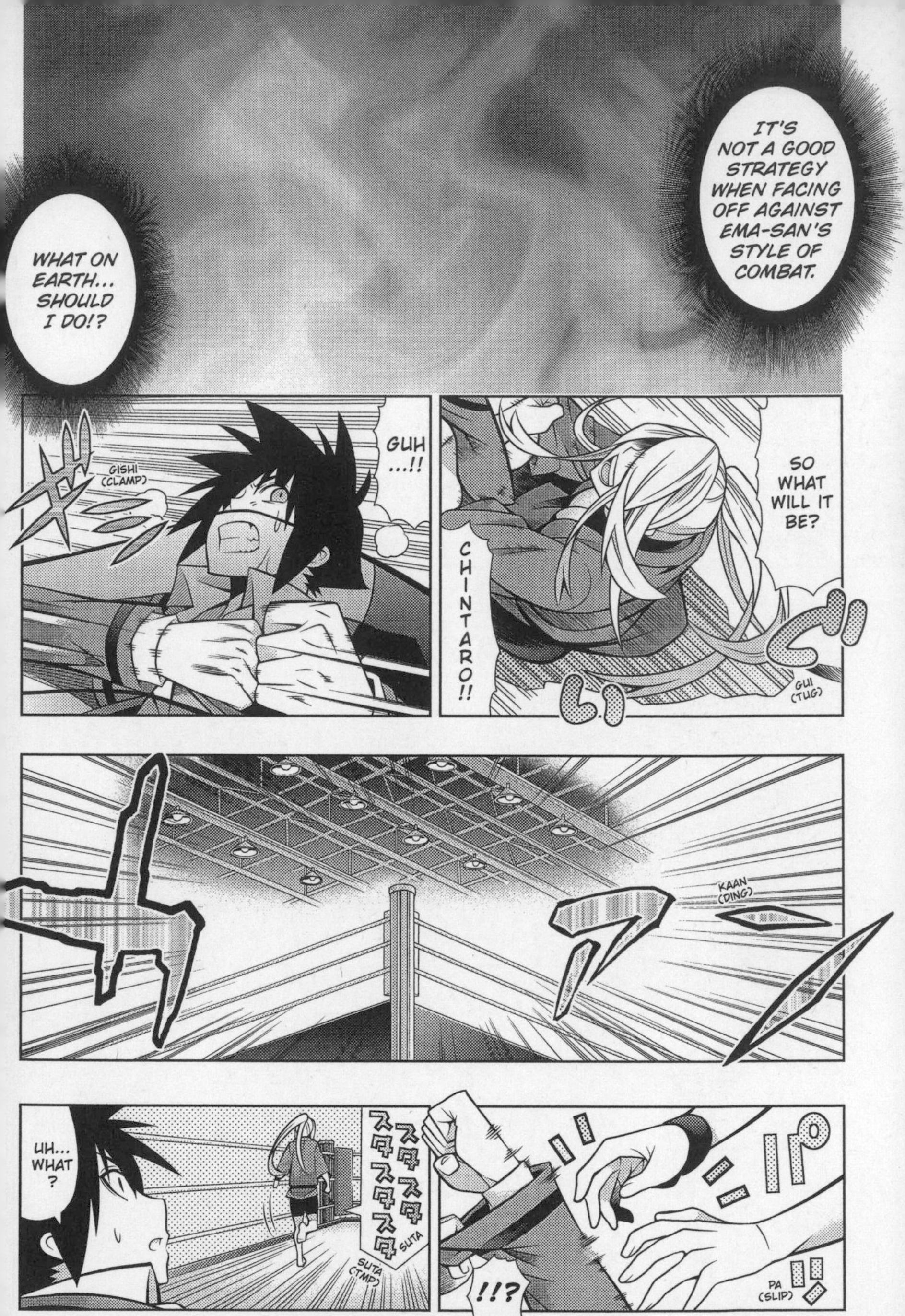

IT'S NOT A GOOD STRATEGY WHEN FACING OFF AGAINST EMA-SAN'S STYLE OF COMBAT.
WHAT ON EARTH... SHOULD I DO!?
SO WHAT WILL IT BE?
CHINTARO!!
GUI (TUG)
GUH ...!!
GISHI (CLAMP)
KAAN (DING)
PA (SLIP)
!!?
SUTA
SUTA (TMP)
UH... WHAT?

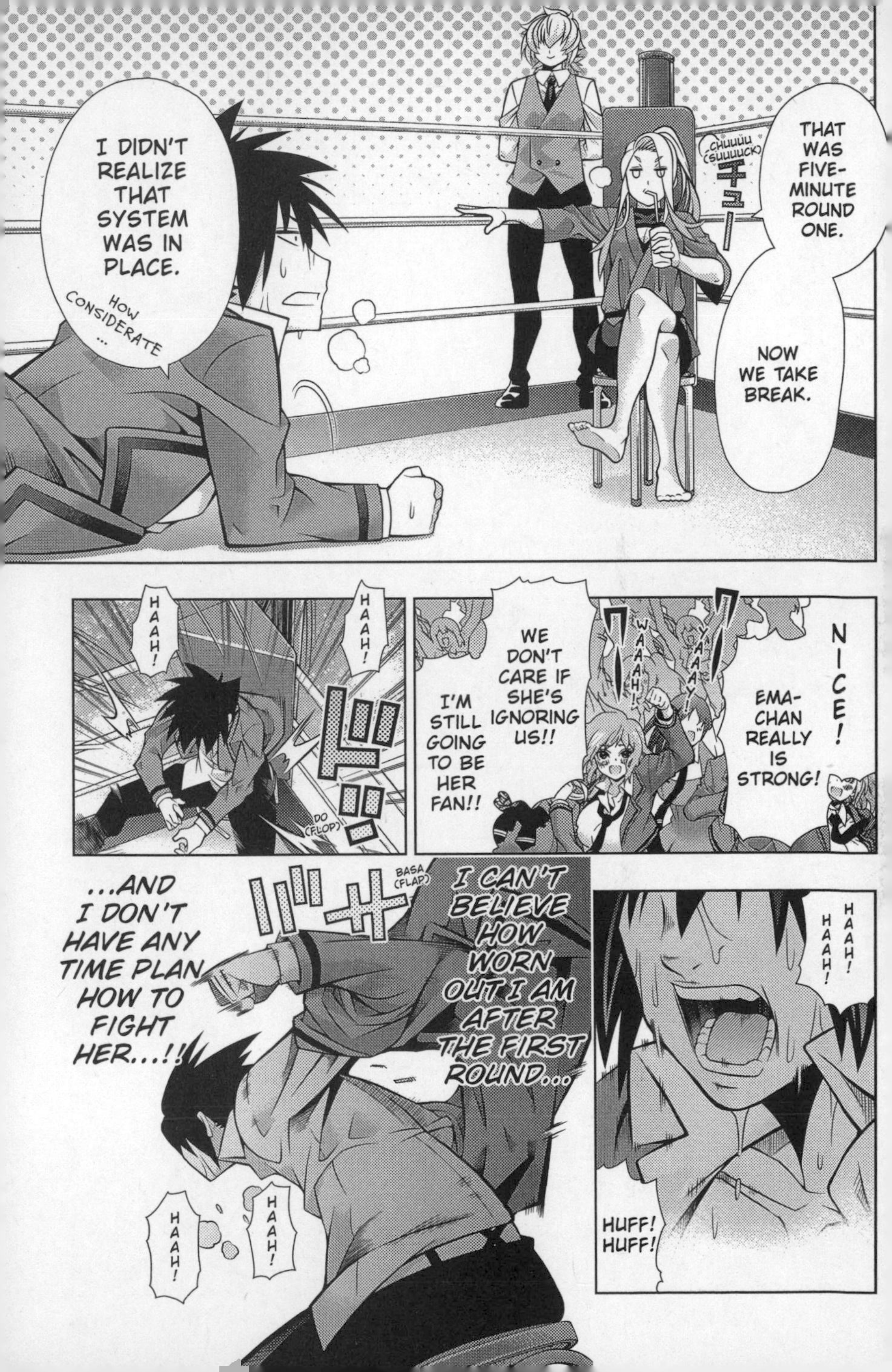
THAT WAS FIVE-MINUTE ROUND ONE.
NOW WE TAKE BREAK.
CHUUUUU (SUUUUUCK)
チュー
I DIDN'T REALIZE THAT SYSTEM WAS IN PLACE.
HOW CONSIDERATE ...
NICE!
EMA-CHAN REALLY IS STRONG!
YAAAAY!
WAAAAH!
WE DON'T CARE IF SHE'S IGNORING US!!
I'M STILL GOING TO BE HER FAN!!
HAAAH!
HAAAH!
DO (FLOP)
HAAAH!
HAAAH!
HUFF! HUFF!
I CAN'T BELIEVE HOW WORN OUT I AM AFTER THE FIRST ROUND...
BASA (FLAP)
...AND I DON'T HAVE ANY TIME PLAN HOW TO FIGHT HER...!!
HAAAH!
HAAAH!

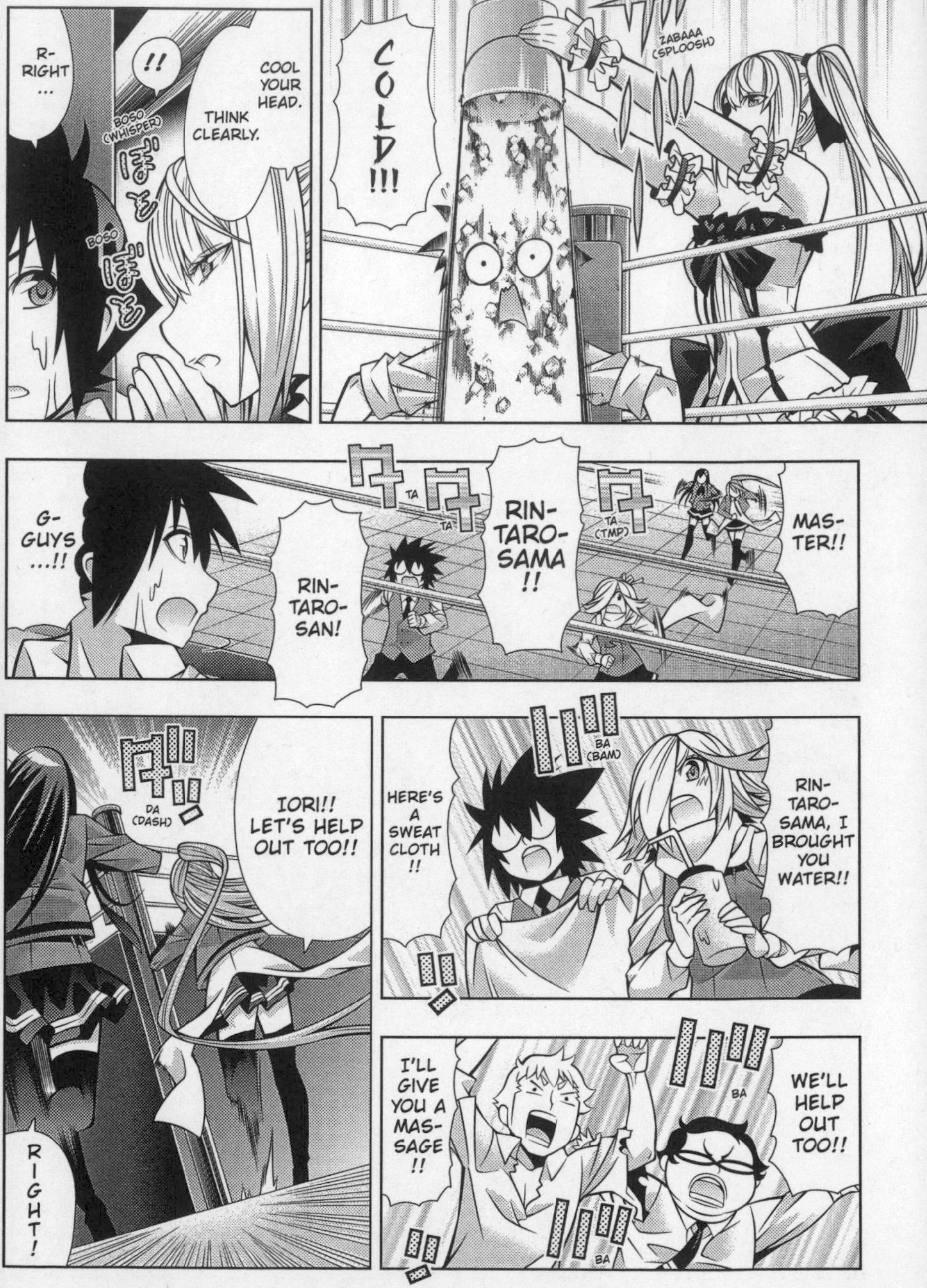
ZABAAA (SPLOOSH)
COLD!!!
COOL YOUR HEAD.
THINK CLEARLY.
!!
BOSO (WHISPER)
BOSO
R-RIGHT...
MASTER!!
TA (TMP)
RIN-TARO-SAMA!!
TA
TA
RIN-TARO-SAN!
G-GUYS...!!
RIN-TARO-SAMA, I BROUGHT YOU WATER!!
BA (BAM)
HERE'S A SWEAT CLOTH!!
WE'LL HELP OUT TOO!!
BA
I'LL GIVE YOU A MAS-SAGE!!
BA
IORI!! LET'S HELP OUT TOO!!
DA (DASH)
RIGHT!

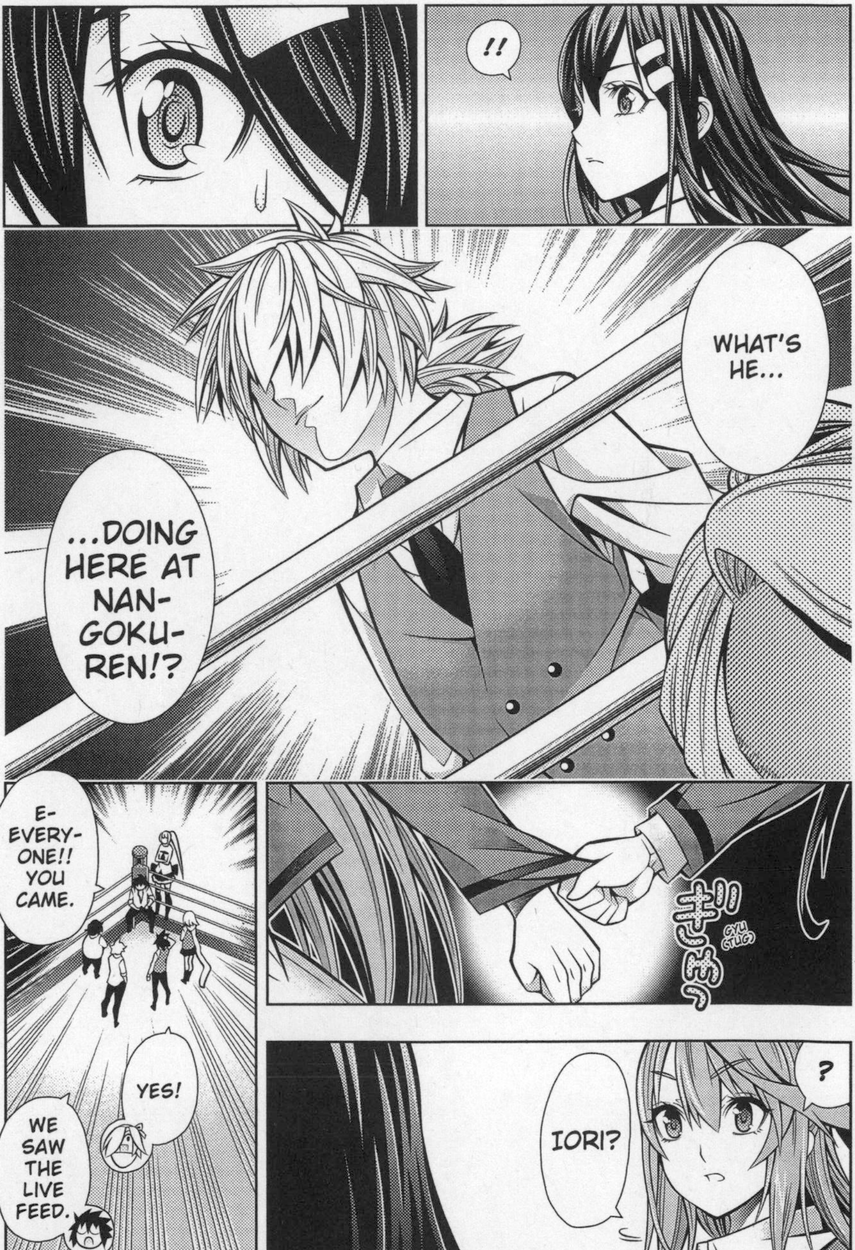
!!
WHAT'S HE...
...DOING HERE AT NAN-GOKU-REN!?
ぎゅっ
GYU (TUG)
?
IORI?
E-EVERYONE!! YOU CAME.
YES!
WE SAW THE LIVE FEED.

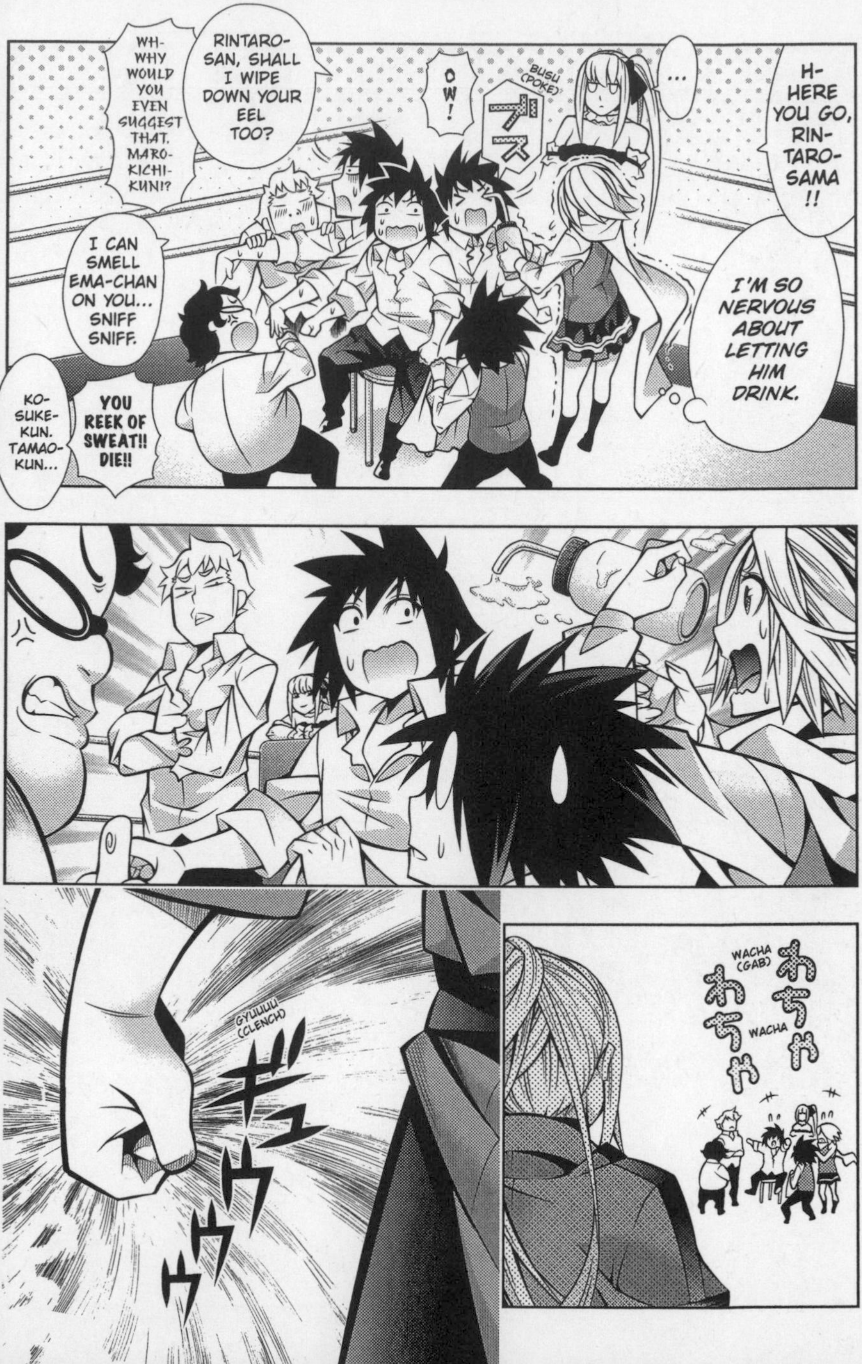
H-HERE YOU GO, RIN-TARO-SAMA!!
I'M SO NERVOUS ABOUT LETTING HIM DRINK.
...
BUSU (POKE)
ブス
OW!
RINTARO-SAN, SHALL I WIPE DOWN YOUR EEL TOO?
WH-WHY WOULD YOU EVEN SUGGEST THAT, MARO-KICHI-KUN!?
I CAN SMELL EMA-CHAN ON YOU... SNIFF SNIFF.
YOU REEK OF SWEAT!! DIE!!
KO-SUKE-KUN. TAMAO-KUN...
WACHA (GAB)
わちゃ
WACHA
わちゃ
GYUUUU (CLENCH)
ギュウウウ

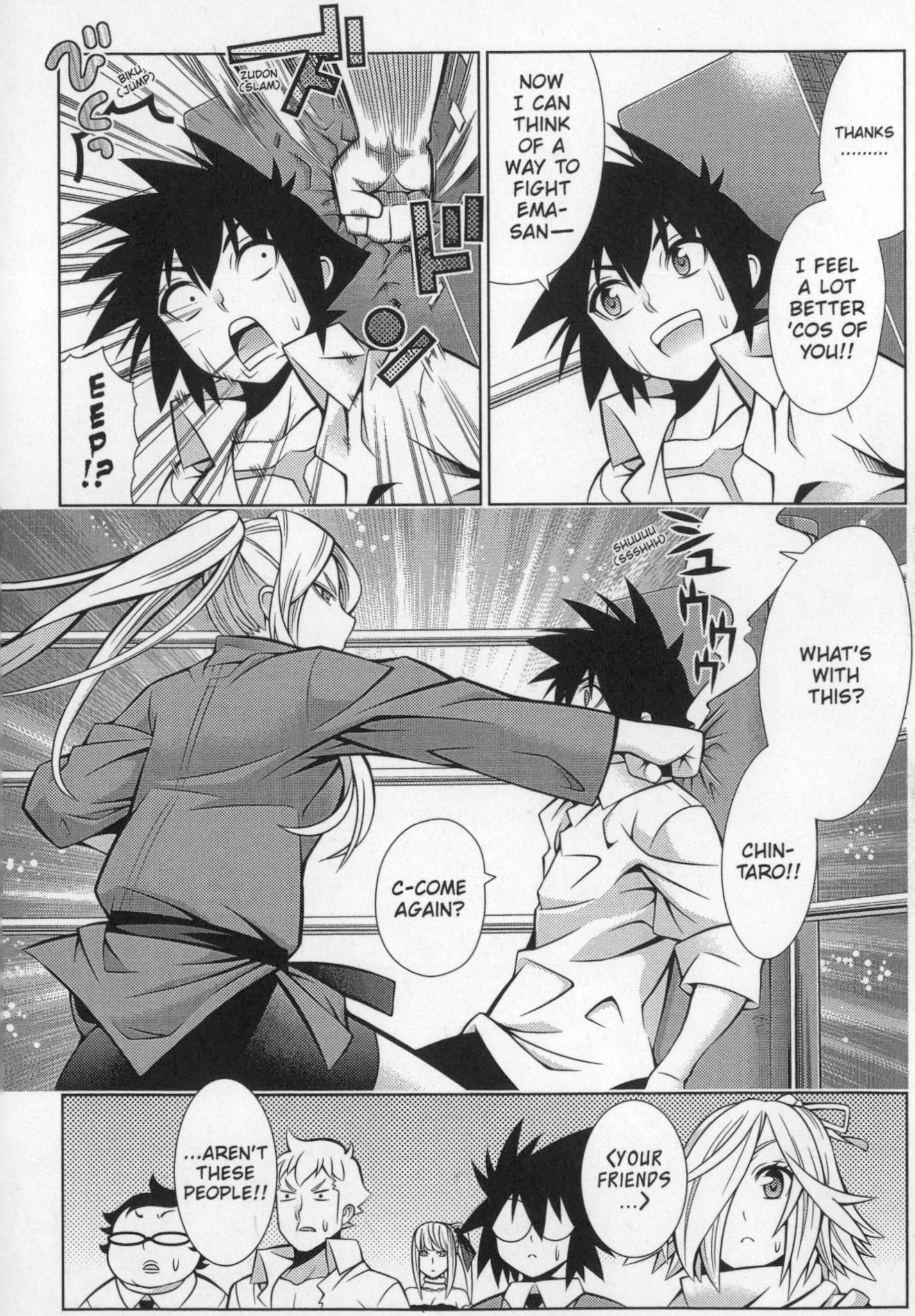
THANKS ....
I FEEL A LOT BETTER 'COS OF YOU!!
NOW I CAN THINK OF A WAY TO FIGHT EMA-SAN—
ZUDON (SLAM)
BIKU (JUMP)
EEP!?
SHUUUU (SSSHHH)
WHAT'S WITH THIS?
CHIN-TARO!!
C-COME AGAIN?
<YOUR FRIENDS ...>
...AREN'T THESE PEOPLE!!

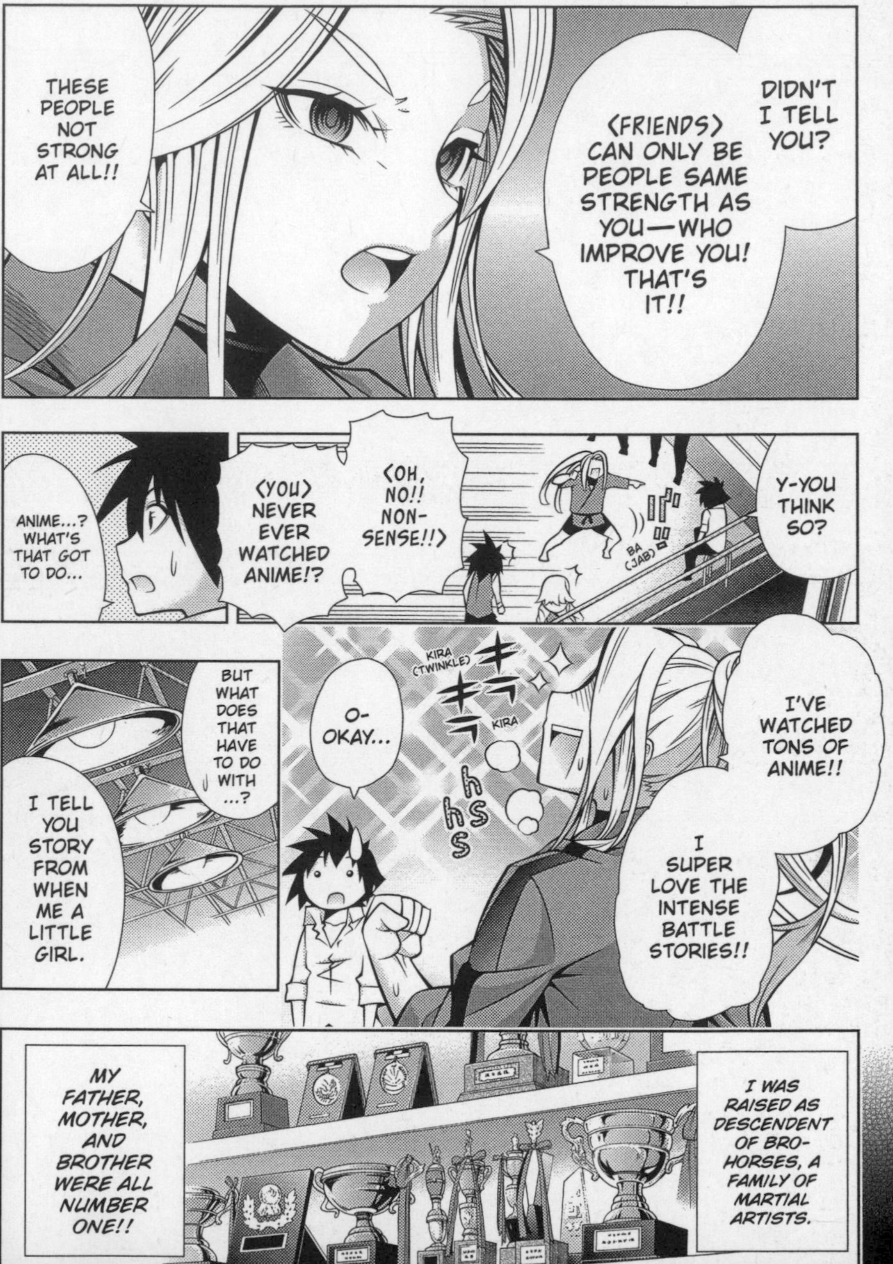

DIDN'T I TELL YOU?
〈FRIENDS〉 CAN ONLY BE PEOPLE SAME STRENGTH AS YOU—WHO IMPROVE YOU! THAT'S IT!!
THESE PEOPLE NOT STRONG AT ALL!!
Y-YOU THINK SO?
BA (JAB)
〈OH, NO!! NON-SENSE!!〉
〈YOU〉 NEVER EVER WATCHED ANIME!?
ANIME...? WHAT'S THAT GOT TO DO...
I'VE WATCHED TONS OF ANIME!!
KIRA (TWINKLE)
KIRA
O-OKAY...
I SUPER LOVE THE INTENSE BATTLE STORIES!!
BUT WHAT DOES THAT HAVE TO DO WITH ...?
I TELL YOU STORY FROM WHEN ME A LITTLE GIRL.
I WAS RAISED AS DESCENDENT OF BRO-HORSES, A FAMILY OF MARTIAL ARTISTS.
MY FATHER, MOTHER, AND BROTHER WERE ALL NUMBER ONE!!

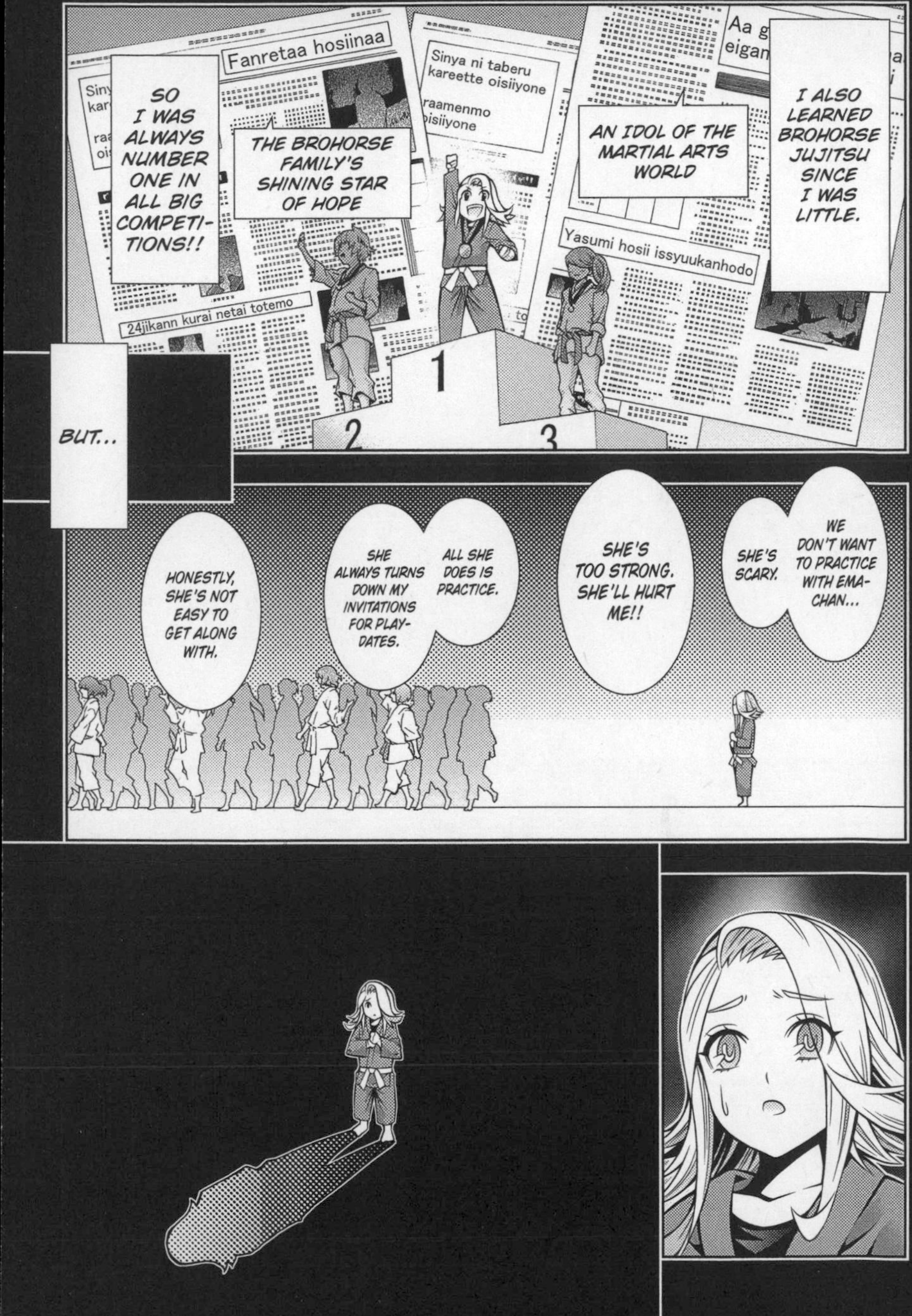
I ALSO LEARNED BROHORSE JUJITSU SINCE I WAS LITTLE.
AN IDOL OF THE MARTIAL ARTS WORLD
Sinya ni taberu kareette oisiiyone raamenmo oisiiyone
THE BROHORSE FAMILY'S SHINING STAR OF HOPE
Fanretaa hosiinaa
SO I WAS ALWAYS NUMBER ONE IN ALL BIG COMPETI-TIONS!!
Yasumi hosii issyuukanhodo
24jikann kurai netai totemo
BUT...
WE DON'T WANT TO PRACTICE WITH EMA-CHAN...
SHE'S SCARY.
SHE'S TOO STRONG. SHE'LL HURT ME!!
ALL SHE DOES IS PRACTICE.
SHE ALWAYS TURNS DOWN MY INVITATIONS FOR PLAY-DATES.
HONESTLY, SHE'S NOT EASY TO GET ALONG WITH.

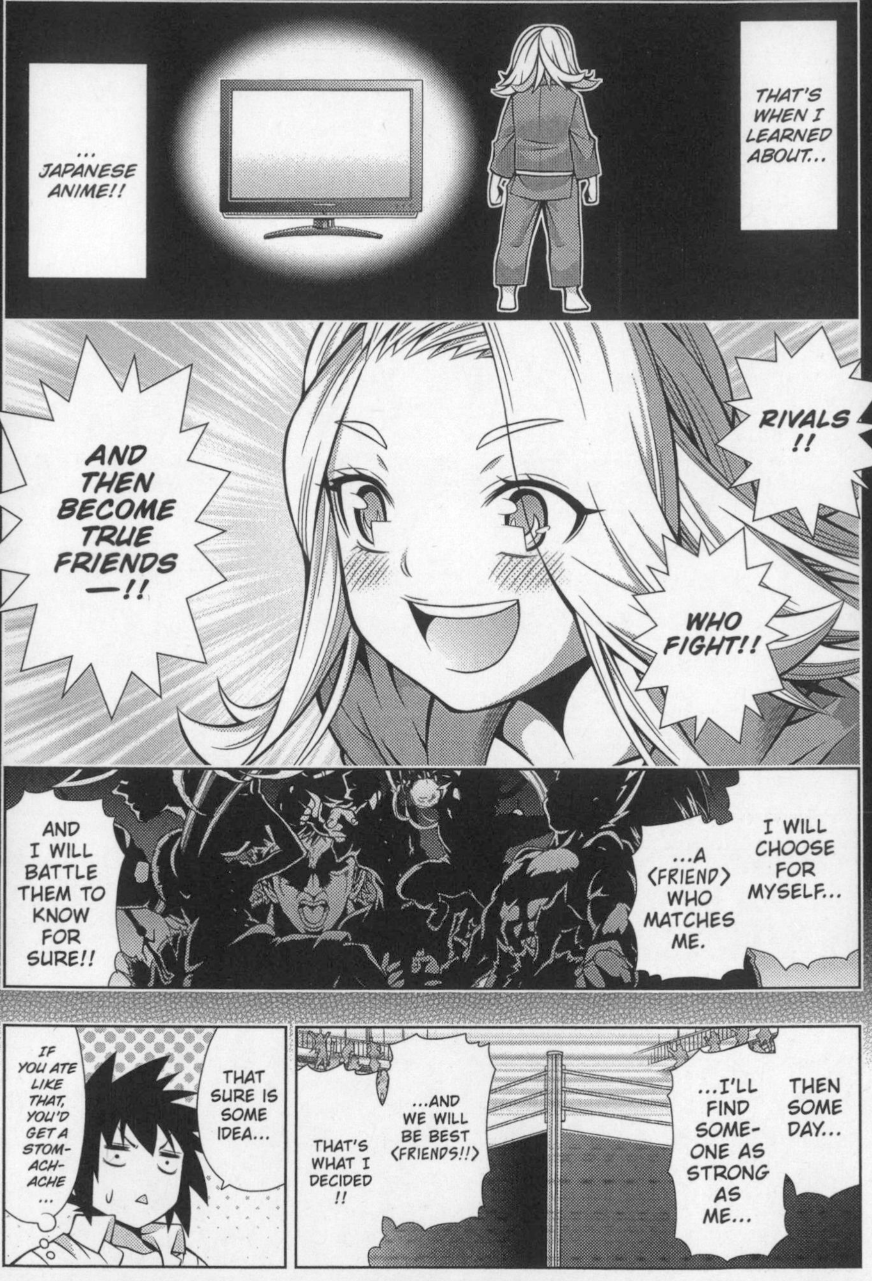
THAT'S WHEN I LEARNED ABOUT...
...JAPANESE ANIME!!
RIVALS!!
WHO FIGHT!!
AND THEN BECOME TRUE FRIENDS—!!
I WILL CHOOSE FOR MYSELF...
...A ⟨FRIEND⟩ WHO MATCHES ME.
AND I WILL BATTLE THEM TO KNOW FOR SURE!!
THEN SOME DAY...
...I'LL FIND SOME-ONE AS STRONG AS ME...
...AND WE WILL BE BEST ⟨FRIENDS!!⟩
THAT'S WHAT I DECIDED!!
THAT SURE IS SOME IDEA...
IF YOU ATE LIKE THAT, YOU'D GET A STOMACH-ACHE...

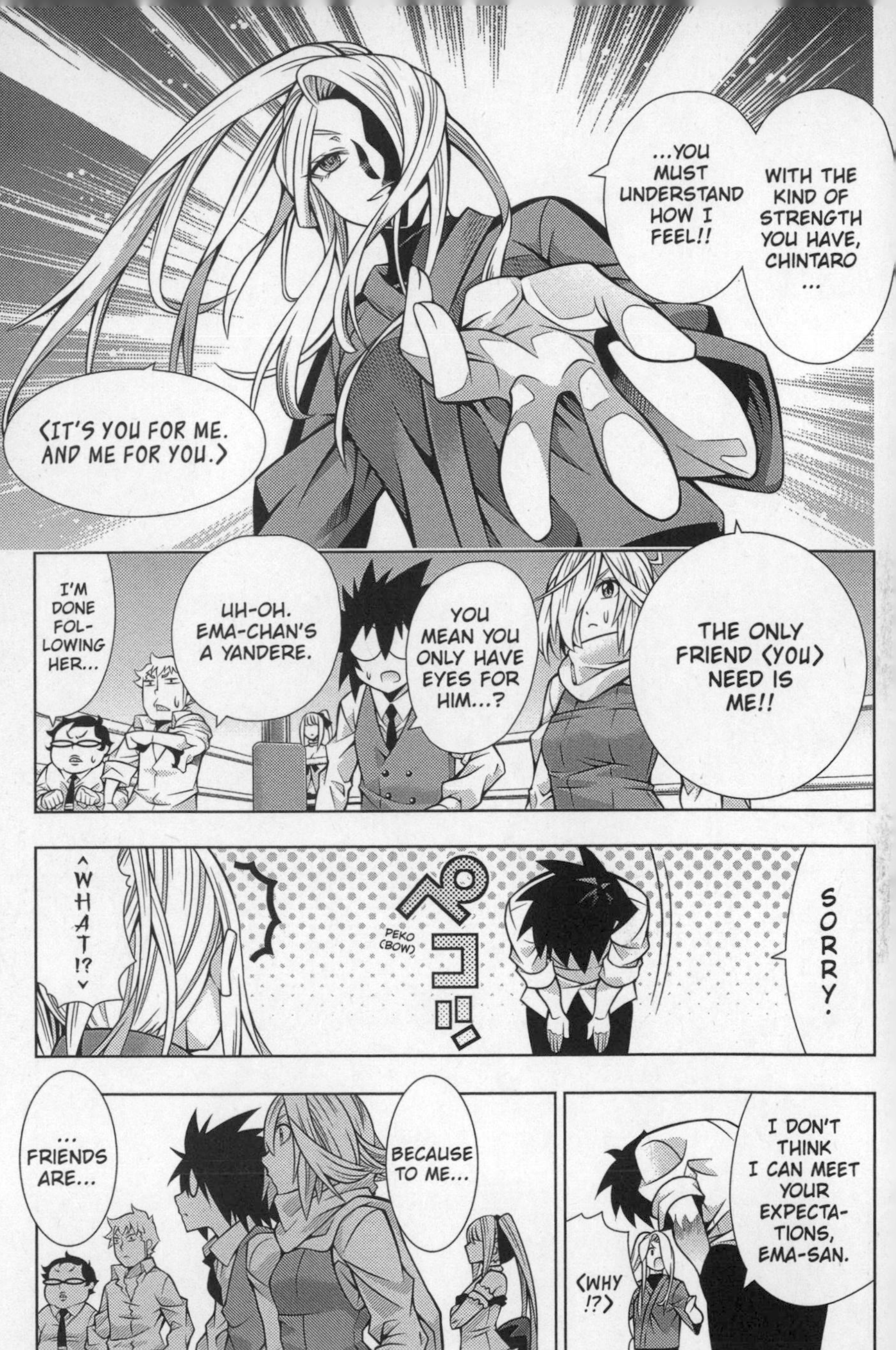
WITH THE KIND OF STRENGTH YOU HAVE, CHINTARO ...
...YOU MUST UNDERSTAND HOW I FEEL!!
<IT'S YOU FOR ME. AND ME FOR YOU.>
THE ONLY FRIEND <YOU> NEED IS ME!!
YOU MEAN YOU ONLY HAVE EYES FOR HIM...?
UH-OH. EMA-CHAN'S A YANDERE.
I'M DONE FOL-LOWING HER...
SORRY.
PEKO (BOW)
<WHAT!?>
I DON'T THINK I CAN MEET YOUR EXPECTA-TIONS, EMA-SAN.
<WHY !?>
BECAUSE TO ME...
... FRIENDS ARE...

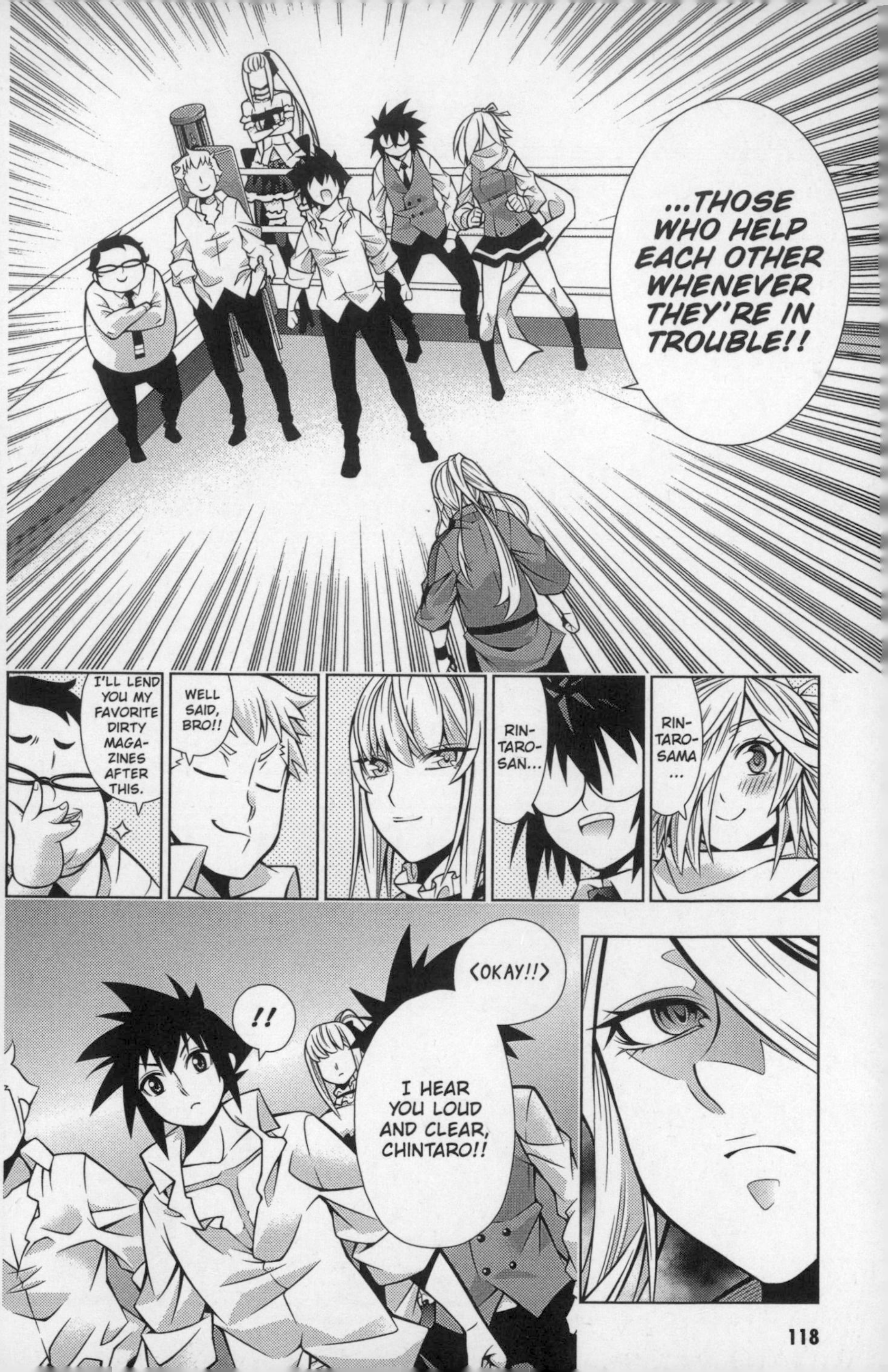
...THOSE WHO HELP EACH OTHER WHENEVER THEY'RE IN TROUBLE!!
RIN-TARO-SAMA ...
RIN-TARO-SAN...
WELL SAID, BRO!!
I'LL LEND YOU MY FAVORITE DIRTY MAGA-ZINES AFTER THIS.
<OKAY!!>
!!
I HEAR YOU LOUD AND CLEAR, CHINTARO!!

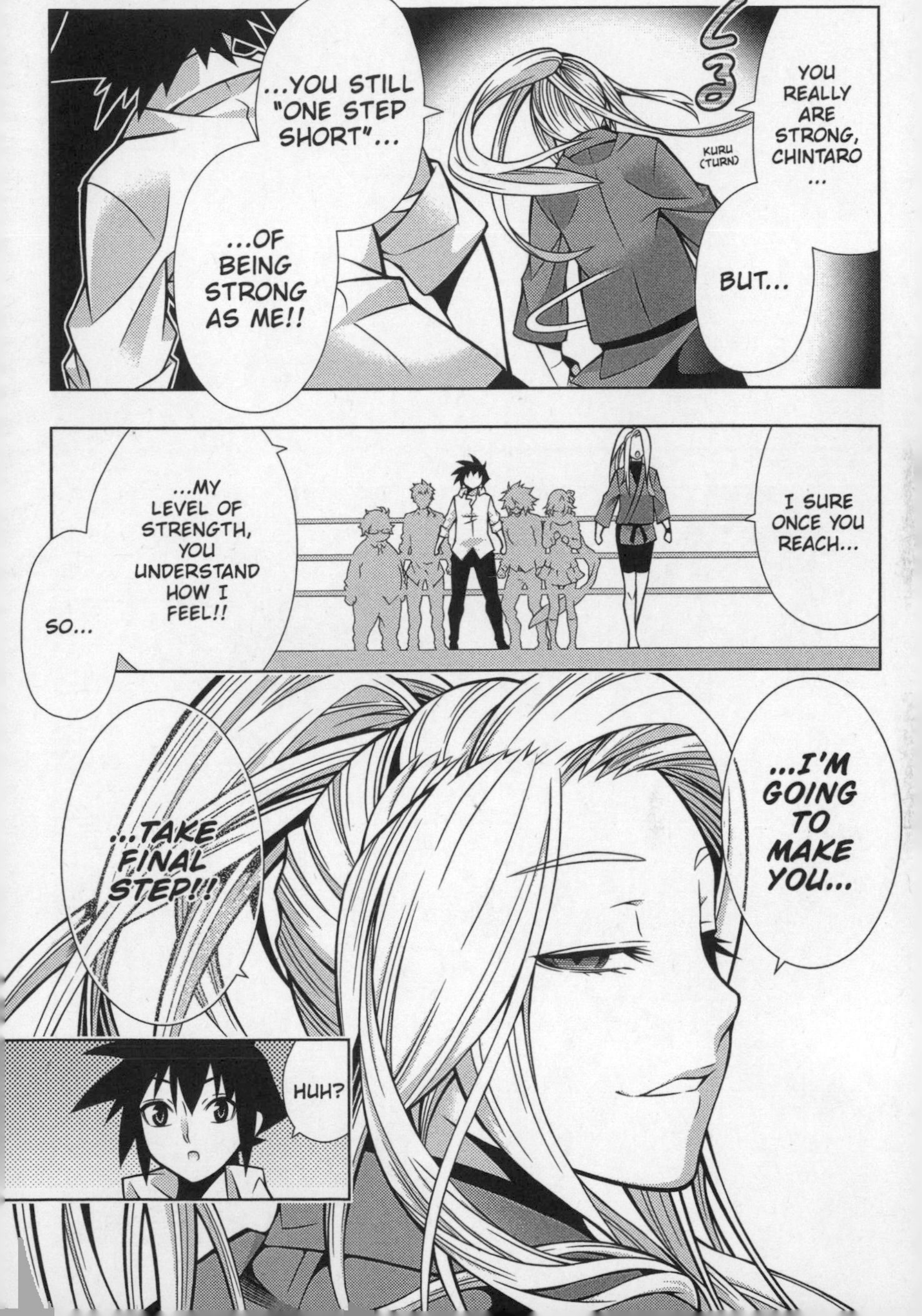
くる
KURU (TURN)
YOU REALLY ARE STRONG, CHINTARO ...
BUT...
...YOU STILL "ONE STEP SHORT"...
...OF BEING STRONG AS ME!!
I SURE ONCE YOU REACH...
...MY LEVEL OF STRENGTH, YOU UNDERSTAND HOW I FEEL!!
SO...
...I'M GOING TO MAKE YOU...
...TAKE FINAL STEP!!
HUH?

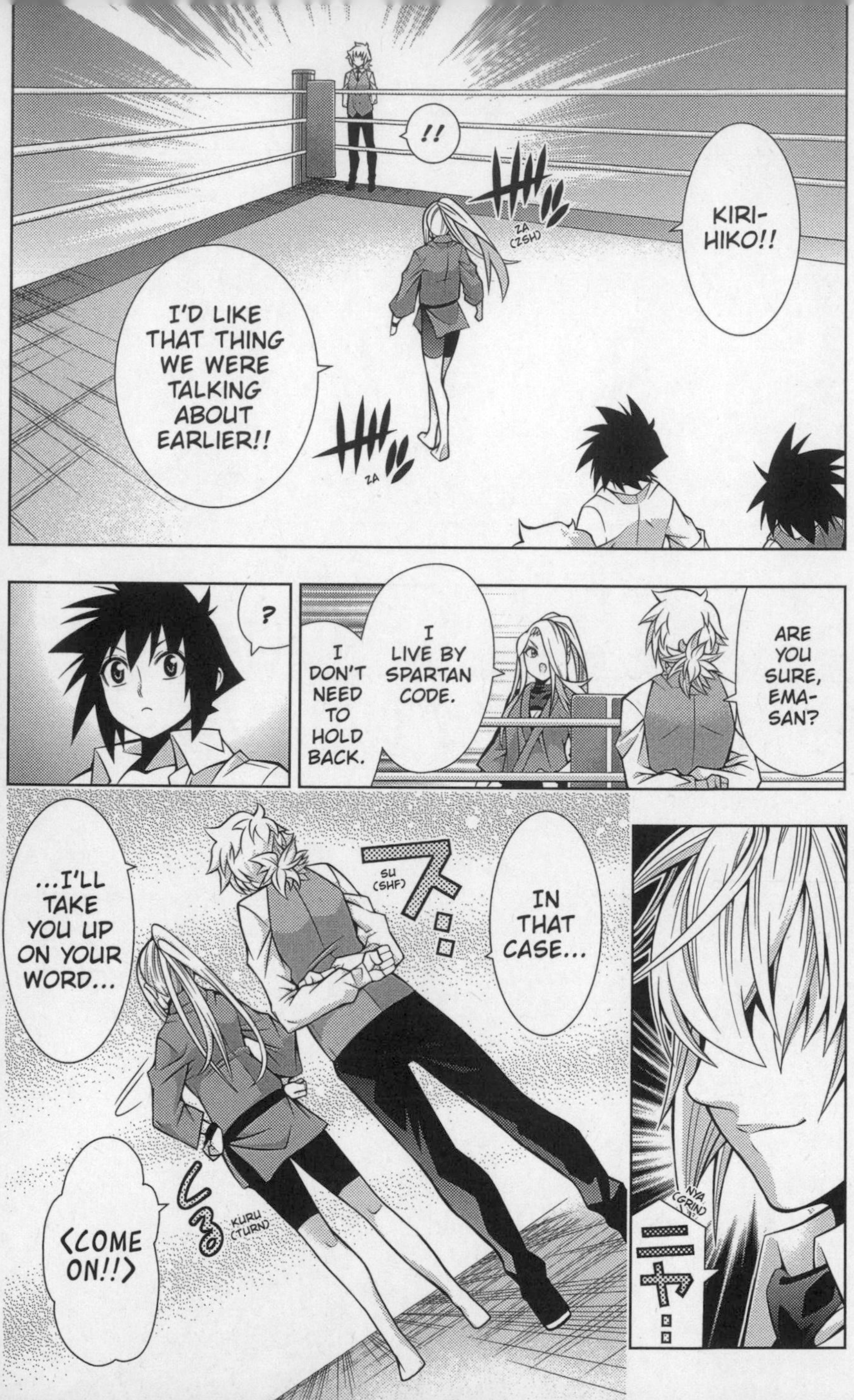
!!
ZA (ZSH)
KIRI-HIKO!!
I'D LIKE THAT THING WE WERE TALKING ABOUT EARLIER!!
ZA
ARE YOU SURE, EMA-SAN?
I LIVE BY SPARTAN CODE.
I DON'T NEED TO HOLD BACK.
?
NYA (GRIND)
IN THAT CASE...
SU (SHF)
...I'LL TAKE YOU UP ON YOUR WORD...
KURU (TURN)
<COME ON!!>

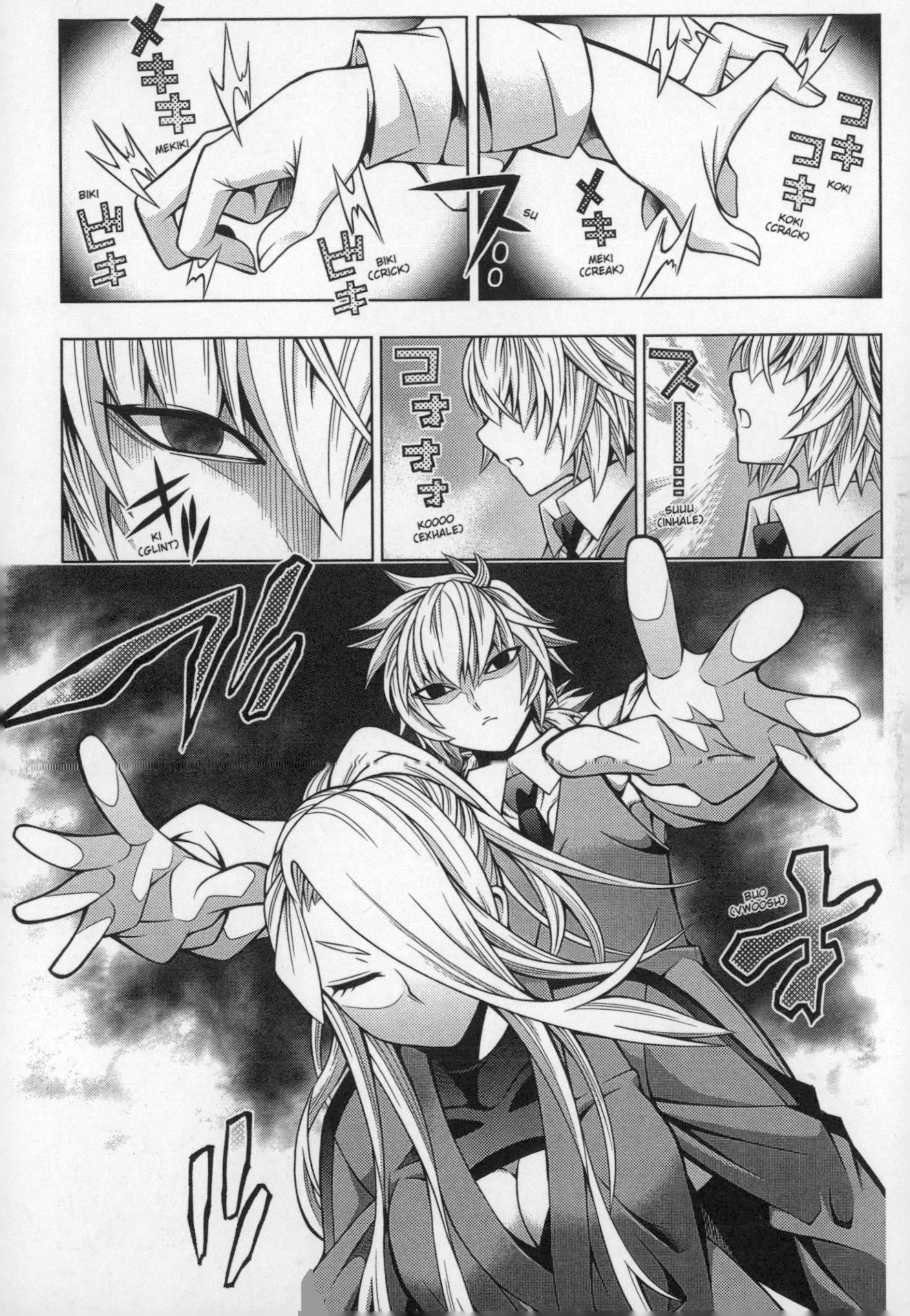
KOKI
KOKI (CRACK)
MEKI (CREAK)
SU
MEKIKI
BIKI
BIKI (CRICK)
SUUU (INHALE)
KOOOO (EXHALE)
KI (GLINT)
BUO (VWOOSH)

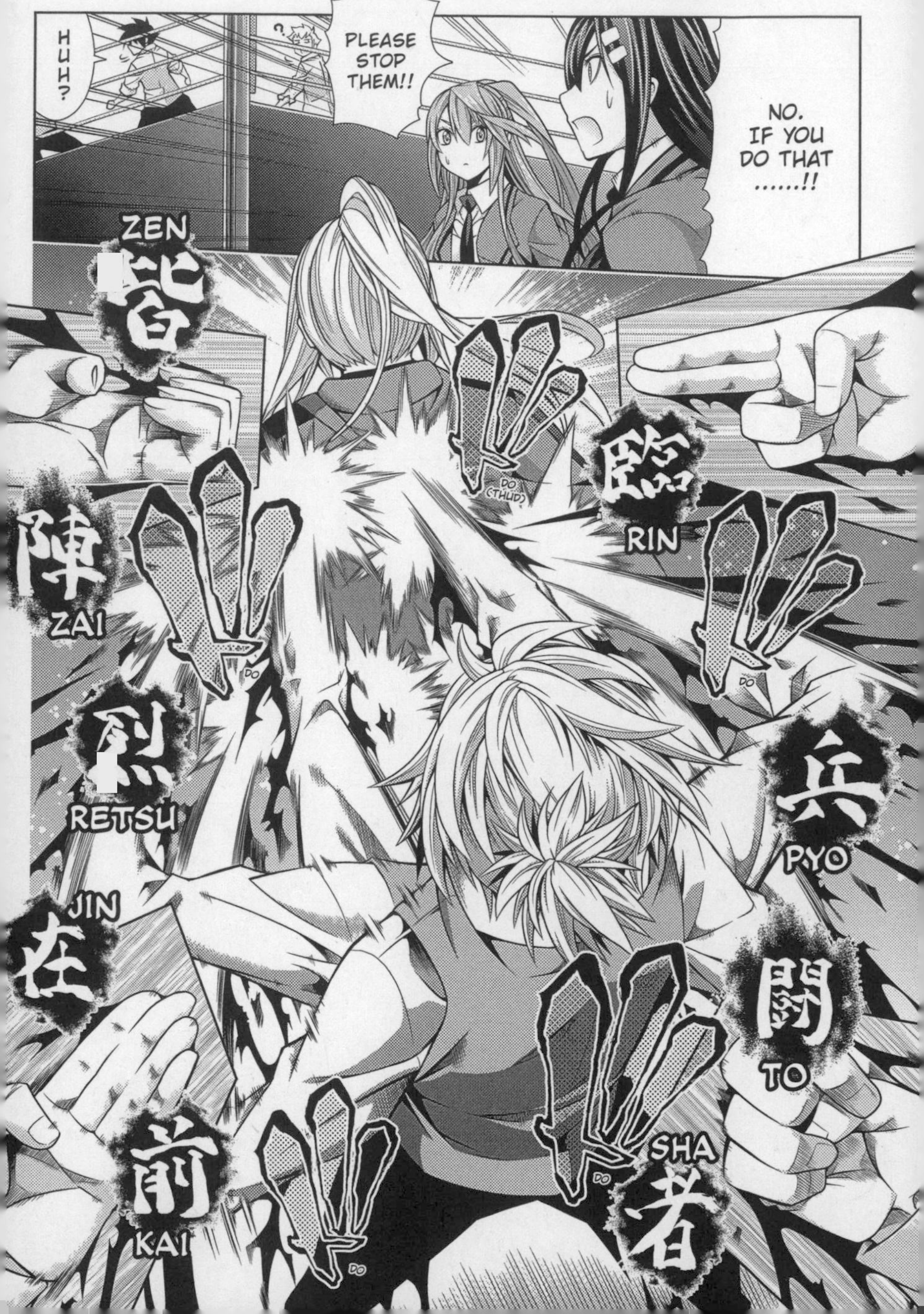
NO. IF YOU DO THAT ......!!
PLEASE STOP THEM!!
HUH?
臨
RIN
DO (THUD)
皆
ZEN
DO
陣
ZAI
DO
兵
PYO
烈
RETSU
闘
TO
JIN
在
DO
SHA
者
前
KAI
DO

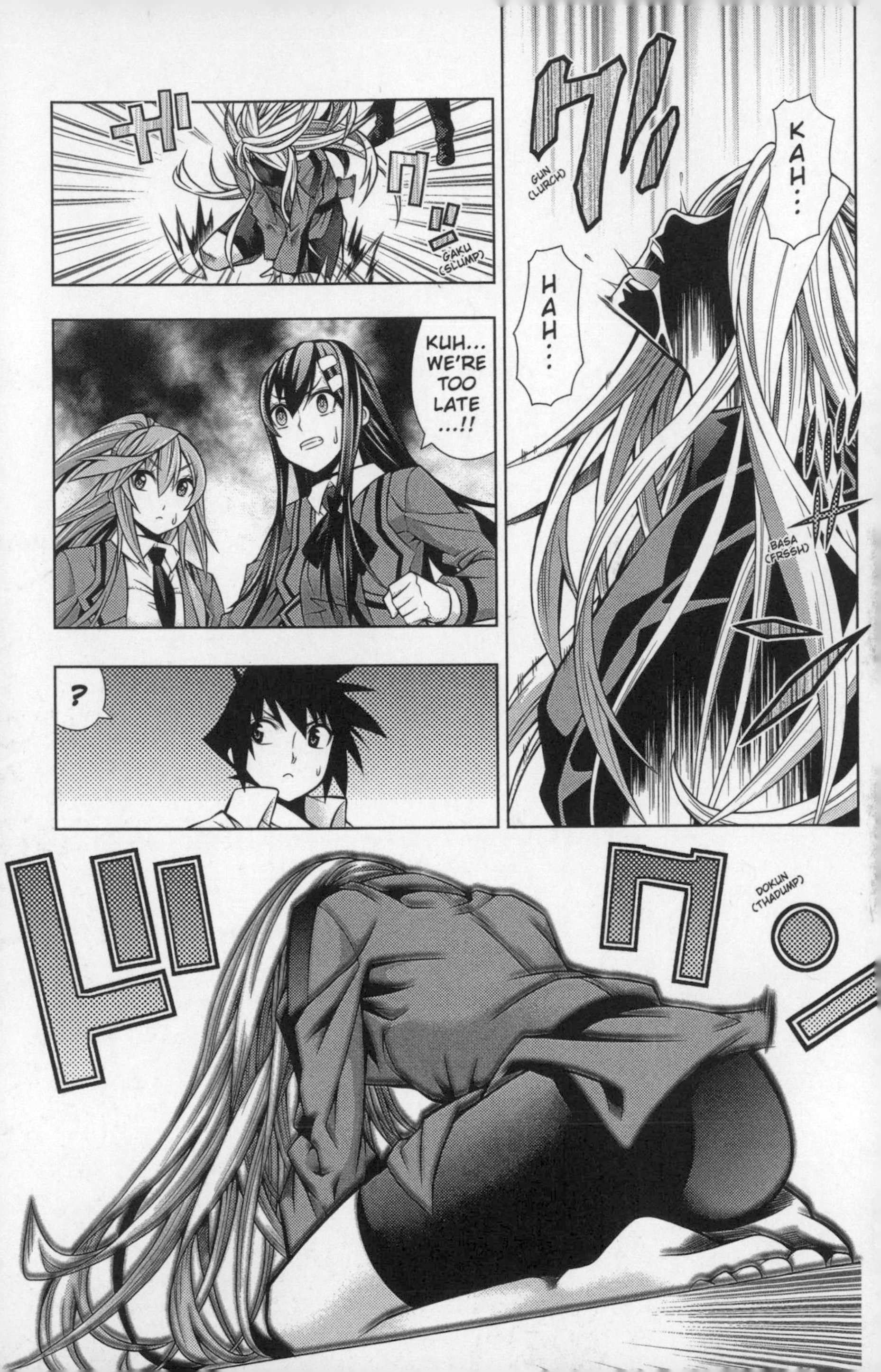
KAH...
GUN (LURCH)
HAH...
BASA (FRSSH)
GAKU (SLUMP)
KUH... WE'RE TOO LATE ...!!
?
DOKUN (THADUMP)

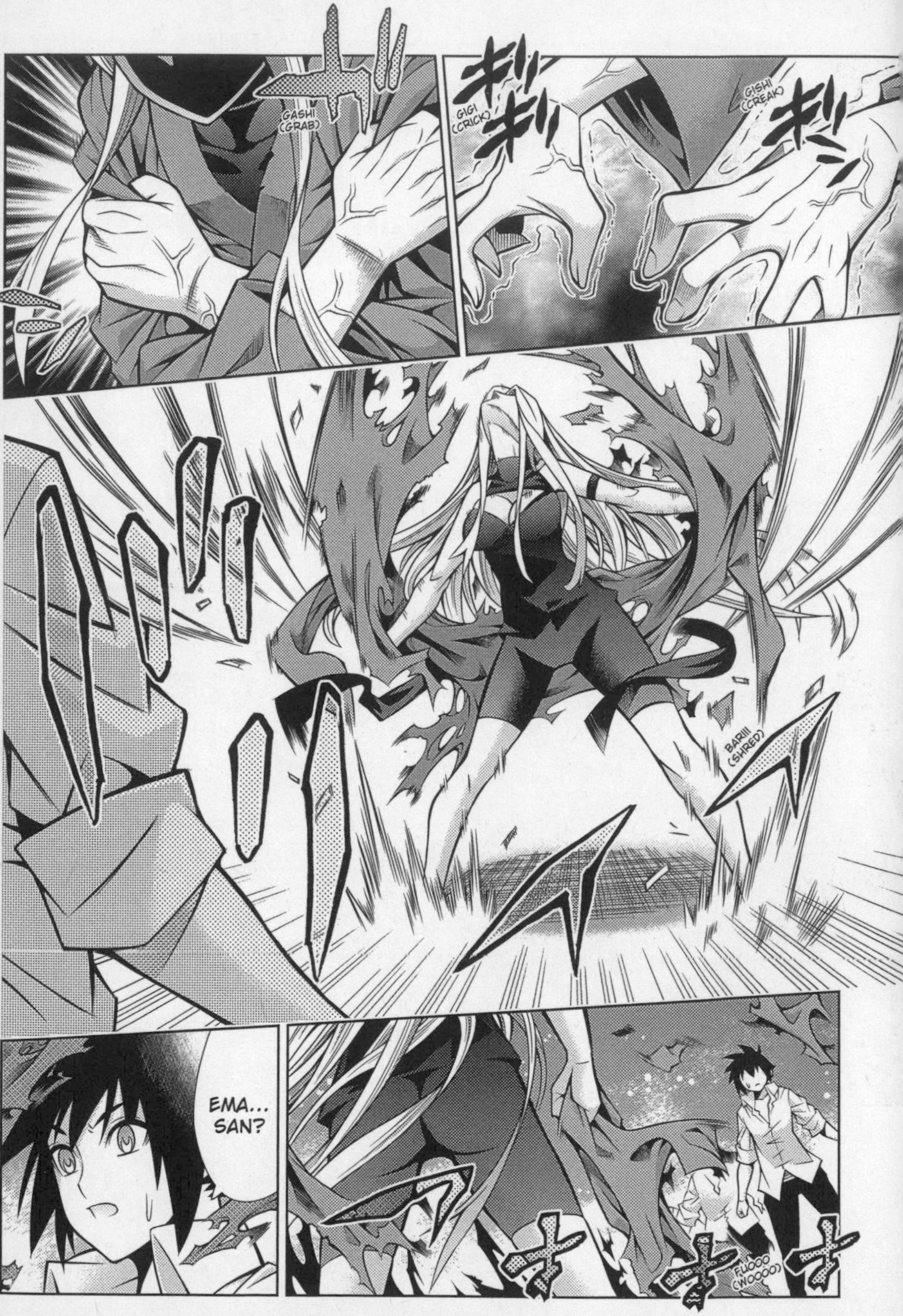
GISHI (CREAK)
GIGI (CRICK)
GASHI (GRAB)
BARIII (SHRED)
FUOOO (WOOOO)
EMA... SAN?

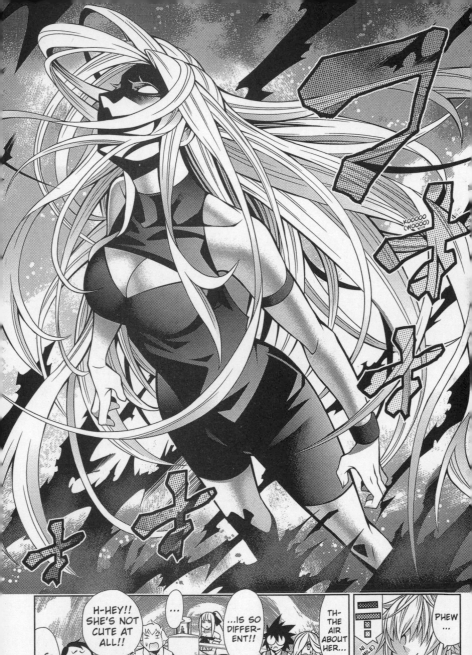

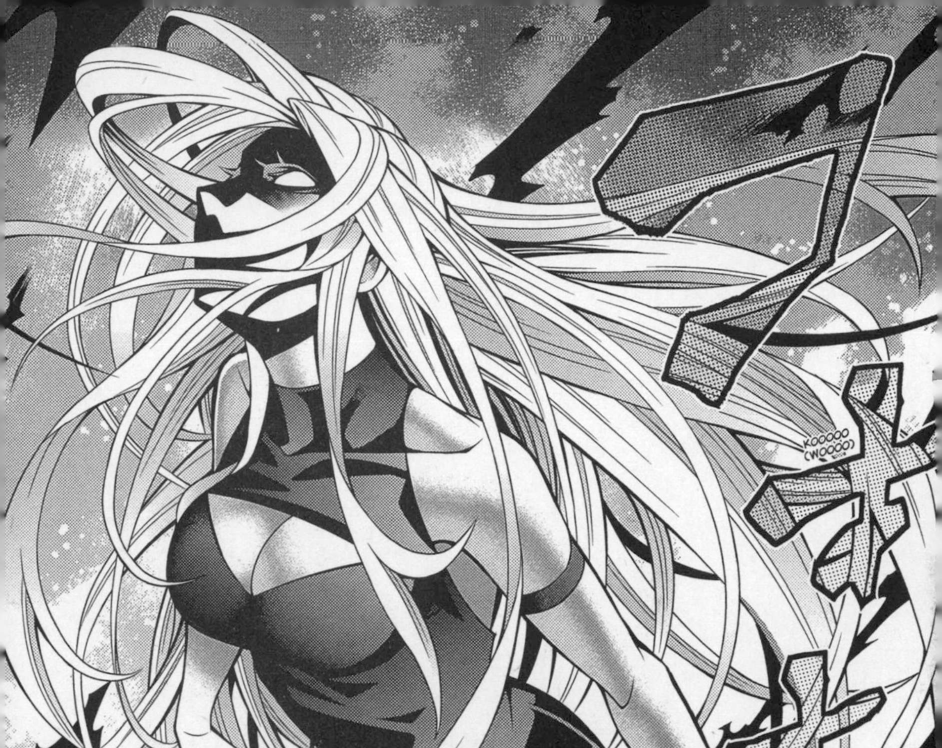
KOOOOO
(WOOOO)
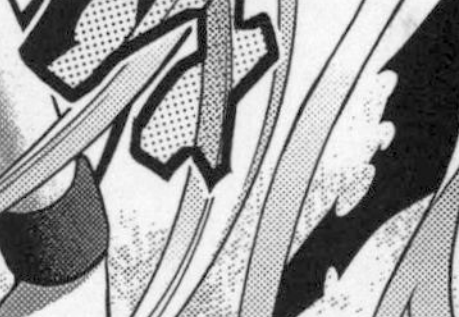
PHEW...
NI (SMILE)
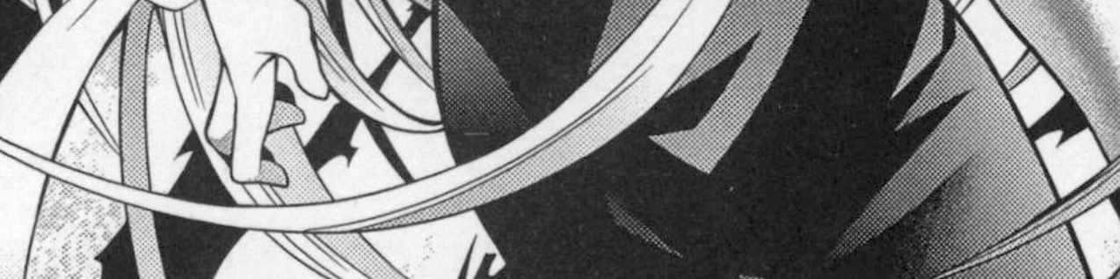
TH-THE AIR ABOUT HER...
...IS SO DIFFERENT!!
...
H-HEY!! SHE'S NOT CUTE AT ALL!!
S-SCARY.

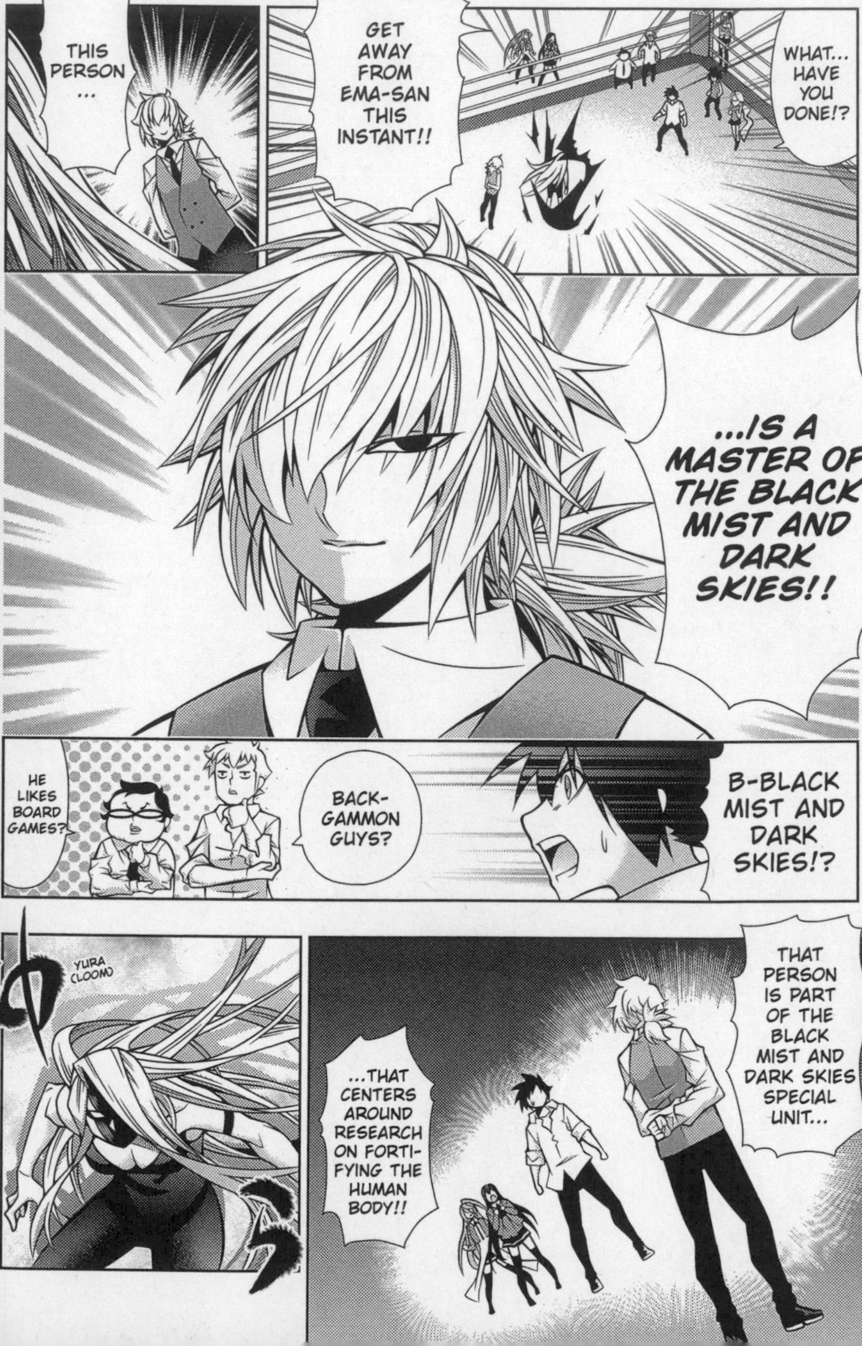
WHAT... HAVE YOU DONE!?
GET AWAY FROM EMA-SAN THIS INSTANT!!
THIS PERSON ...
...IS A MASTER OF THE BLACK MIST AND DARK SKIES!!
B-BLACK MIST AND DARK SKIES!?
BACK-GAMMON GUYS?
HE LIKES BOARD GAMES?
THAT PERSON IS PART OF THE BLACK MIST AND DARK SKIES SPECIAL UNIT...
...THAT CENTERS AROUND RESEARCH ON FORTI-FYING THE HUMAN BODY!!
YURA (LOOM)

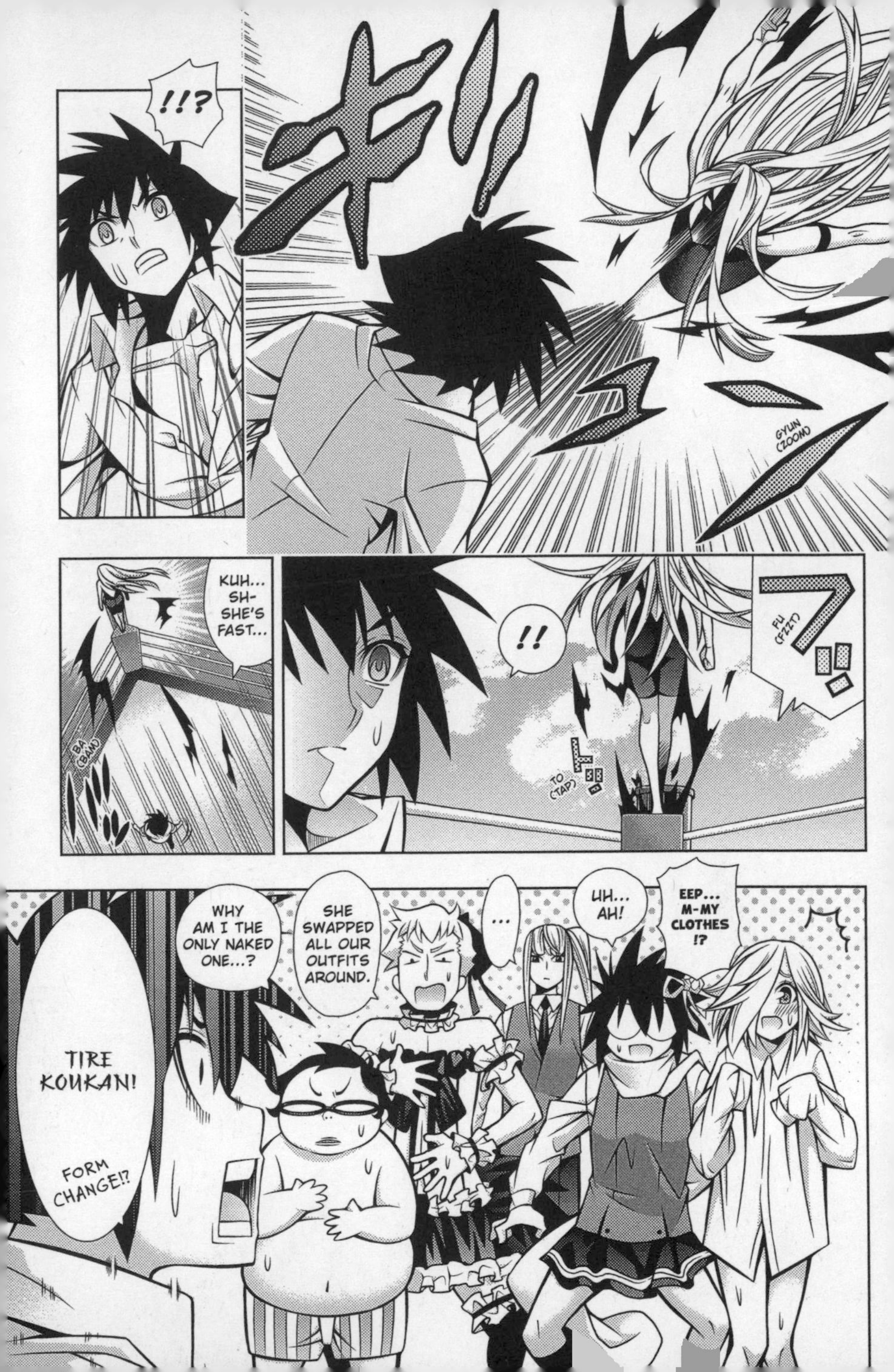
GYUN (ZOOM)
!!?
FU (FZZT)
!!
TO (TAP)
KUH... SH-SHE'S FAST...
BA (BAM)
EEP... M-MY CLOTHES !?
UH... AH!
...
SHE SWAPPED ALL OUR OUTFITS AROUND.
WHY AM I THE ONLY NAKED ONE...?
TIRE KOUKAN!
FORM CHANGE!?

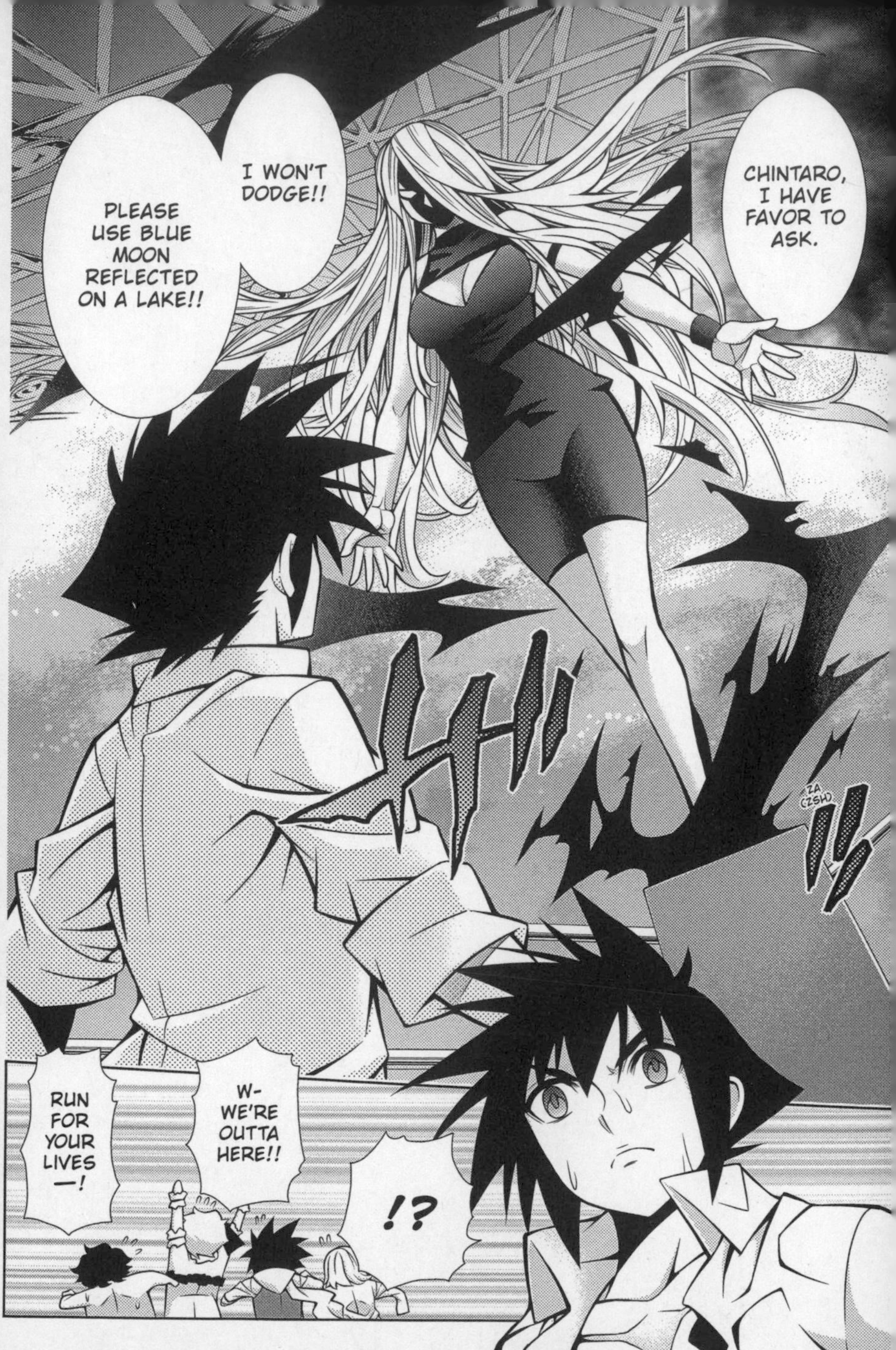
CHINTARO, I HAVE FAVOR TO ASK.
I WON'T DODGE!!
PLEASE USE BLUE MOON REFLECTED ON A LAKE!!
ZA (ZSH)
W-WE'RE OUTTA HERE!!
RUN FOR YOUR LIVES—!
!?

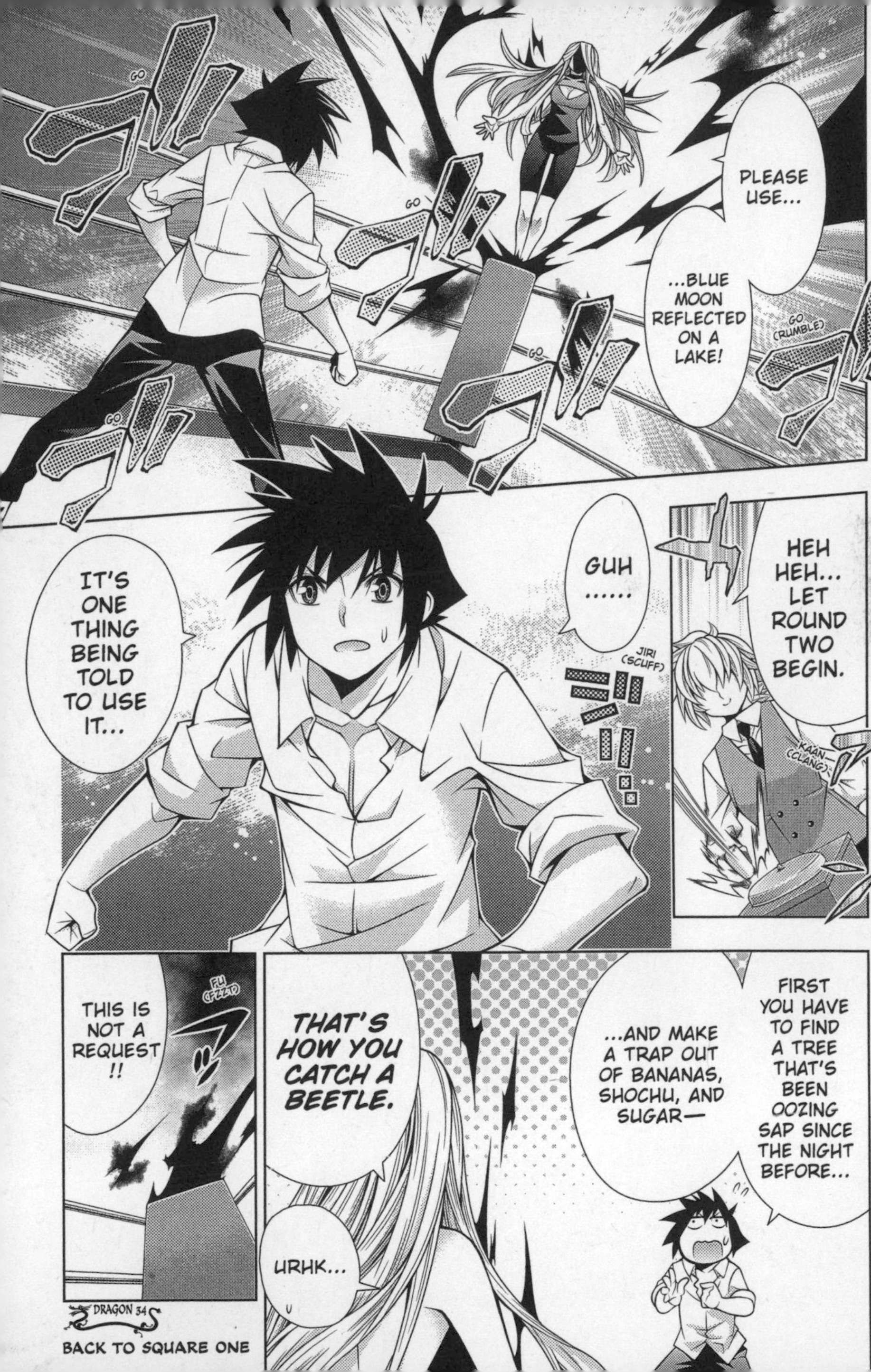
GO
GO
PLEASE USE...
...BLUE MOON REFLECTED ON A LAKE!
GO (RUMBLE)
GO
GO
HEH HEH... LET ROUND TWO BEGIN.
KAAN (CLANG)
GUH ......
JIRI (SCUFF)
IT'S ONE THING BEING TOLD TO USE IT...
FIRST YOU HAVE TO FIND A TREE THAT'S BEEN OOZING SAP SINCE THE NIGHT BEFORE...
...AND MAKE A TRAP OUT OF BANANAS, SHOCHU, AND SUGAR—
THAT'S HOW YOU CATCH A BEETLE.
URHK...
FU (FZZZT)
THIS IS NOT A REQUEST !!

DRAGON 34

BACK TO SQUARE ONE

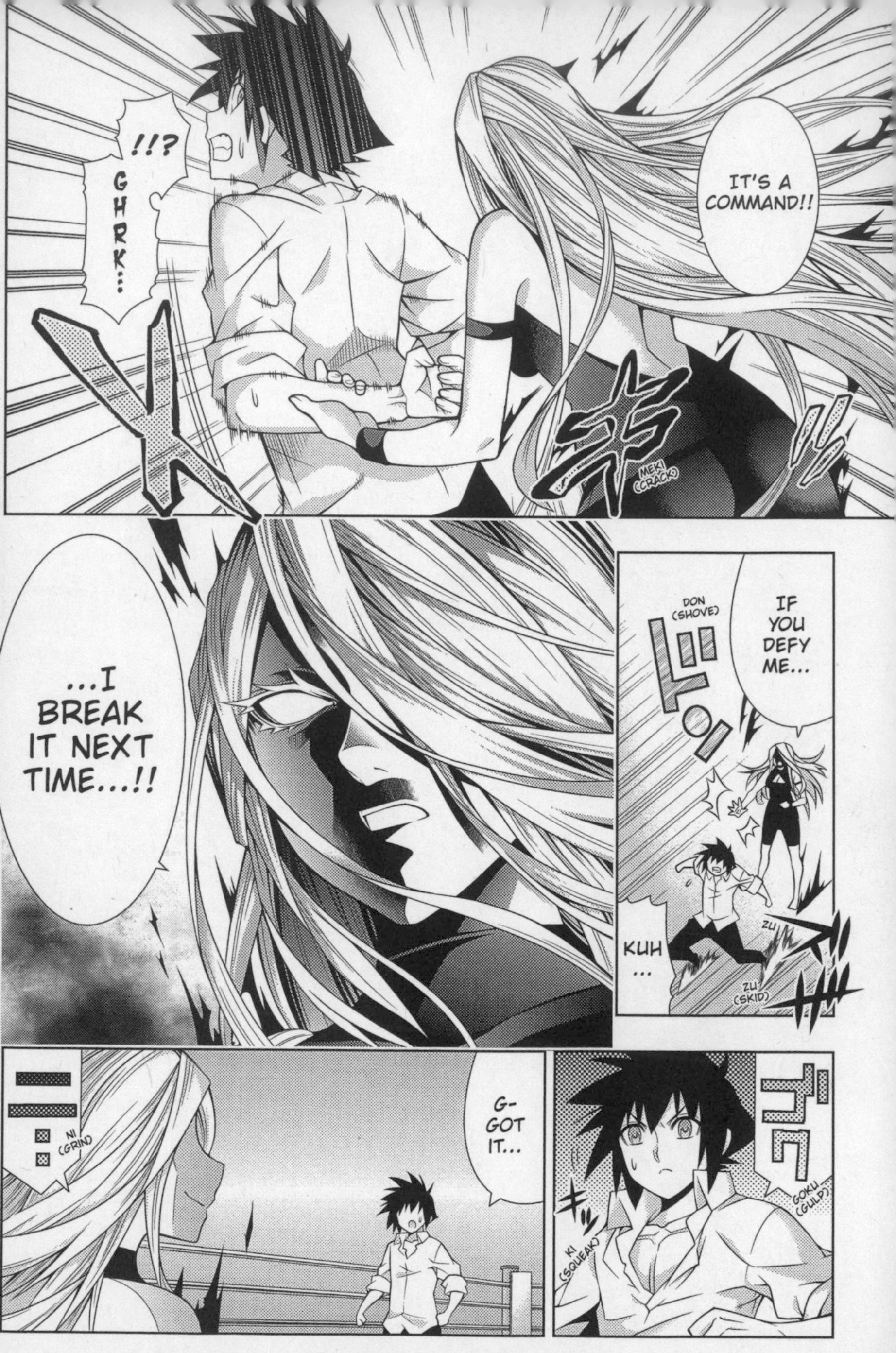
IT'S A COMMAND!!
MEKI (CRACK)
!!? GHRK...
IF YOU DEFY ME...
DON (SHOVE)
KUH...
ZU
ZU (SKID)
...I BREAK IT NEXT TIME...!!
GOKU (GULP)
KI (SQUEAK)
G-GOT IT...
NI (GRIN)

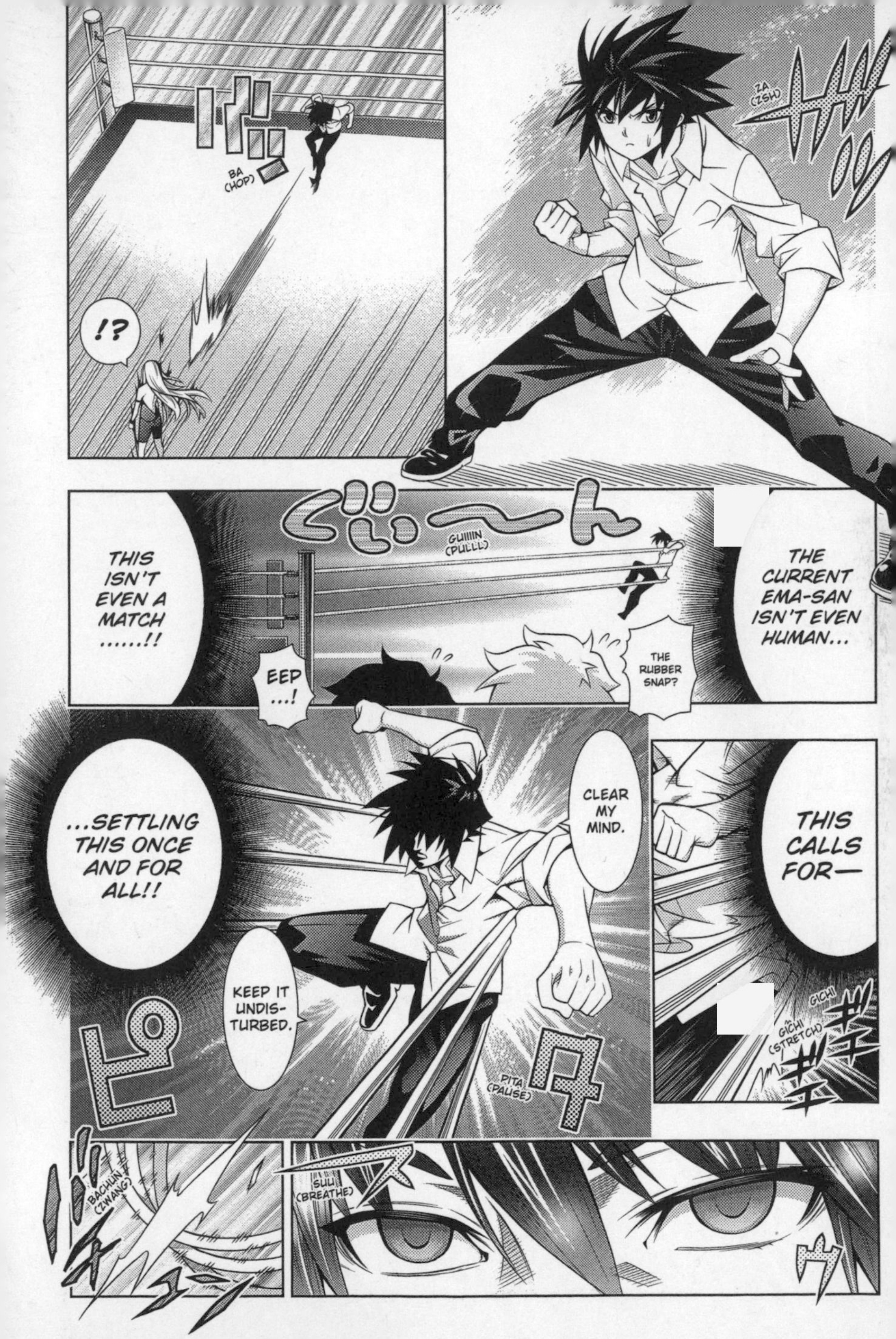
ZA (ZSH)
BA (HOP)
!?
THE CURRENT EMA-SAN ISN'T EVEN HUMAN...
THE RUBBER SNAP?
GUIIIN (PULLL)
EEP ...!
THIS ISN'T EVEN A MATCH......!!
THIS CALLS FOR—
GICHI GICHI (STRETCH)
CLEAR MY MIND.
...SETTLING THIS ONCE AND FOR ALL!!
PITA (PAUSE)
KEEP IT UNDIS-TURBED.
SUU (BREATHE)
BACHUN (ZWANG)

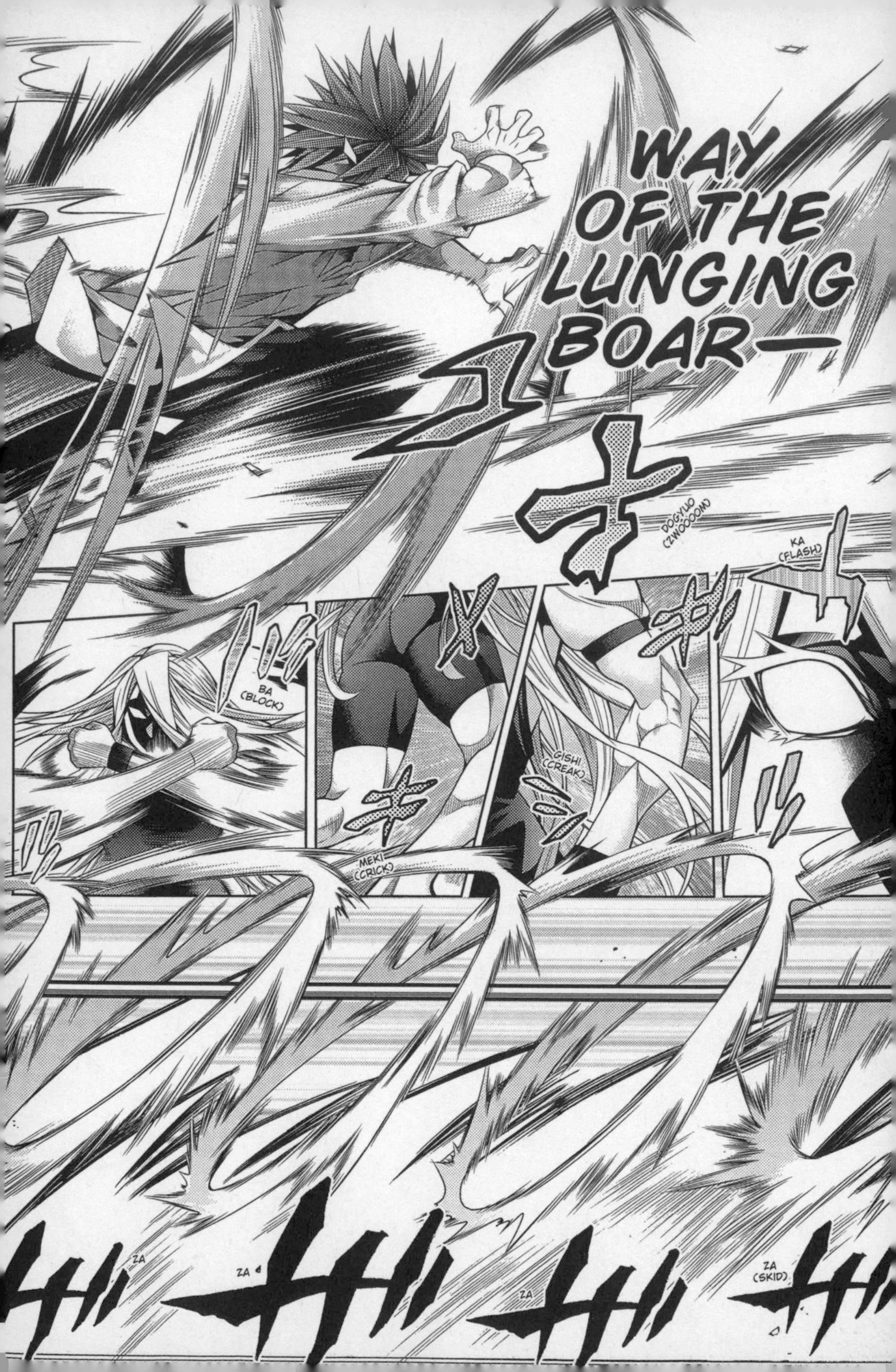
WAY OF THE LUNGING BOAR—
DOGYUO (ZWOOOOM)
KA (FLASH)
GISHI (CREAK)
MEKI (CRICK)
BA (BLOCK)
ZA (SKID)
ZA
ZA
ZA

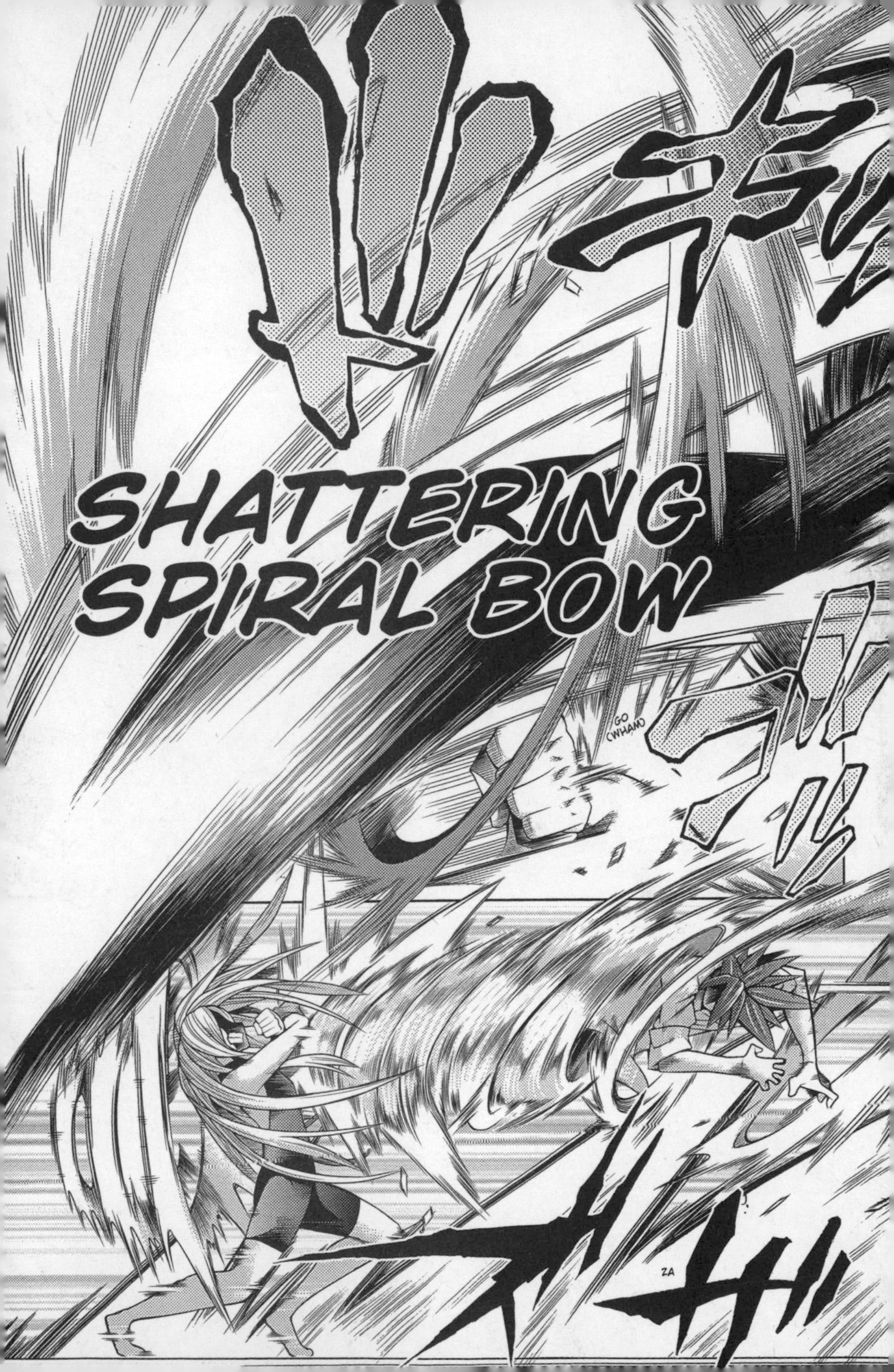
SHATTERING
SPIRAL BOW
GO
(WHAM)
ZA

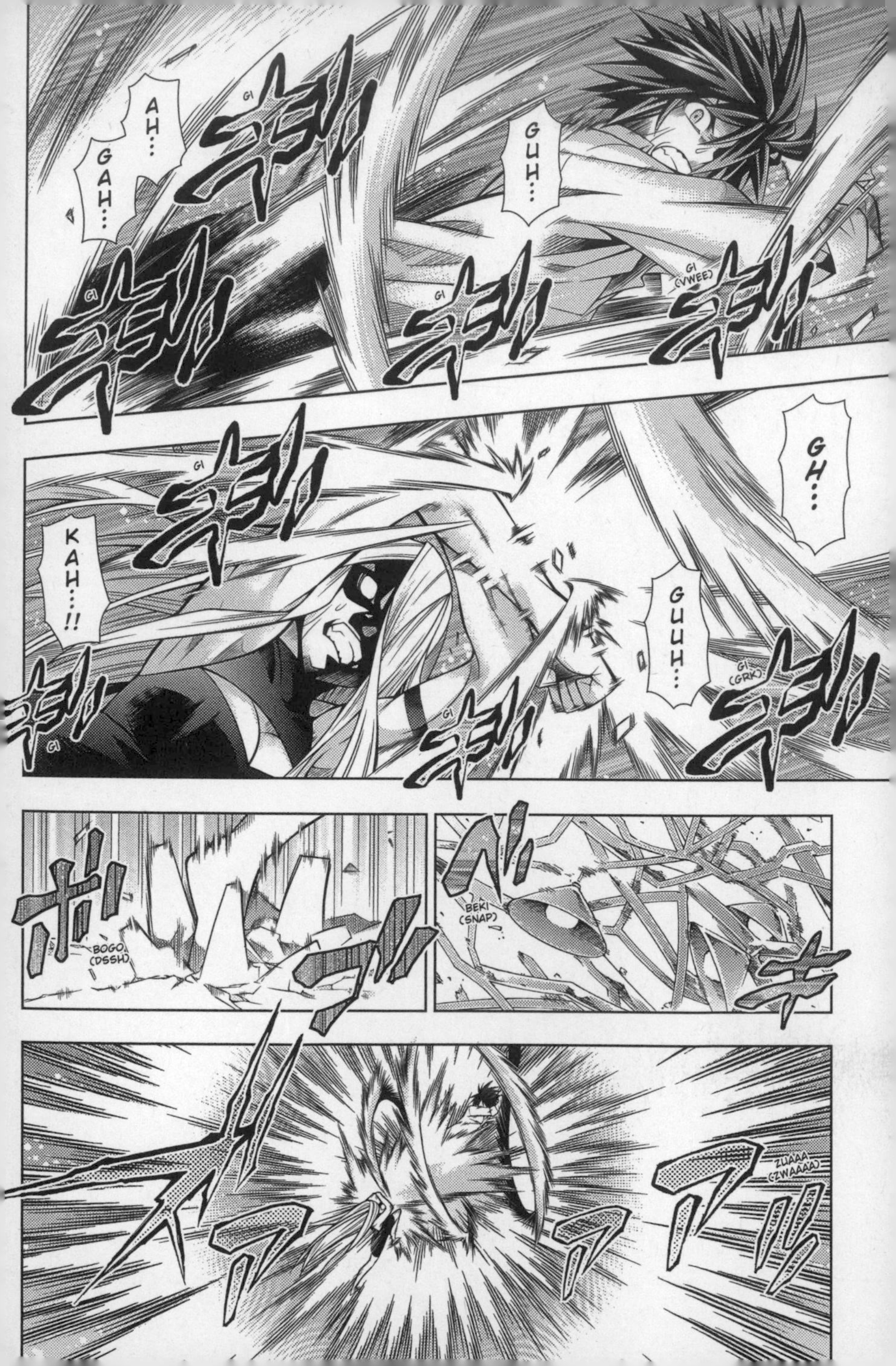
GUH...
AH... GAH...
GI
GI (VWEE)
GI
GI
GH...
GUUH...
GI (GRK)
GI
KAH...!!
GI
GI
BEKI (SNAP)
BOGO (DSSH)
ZUAAA (ZWAAAA)

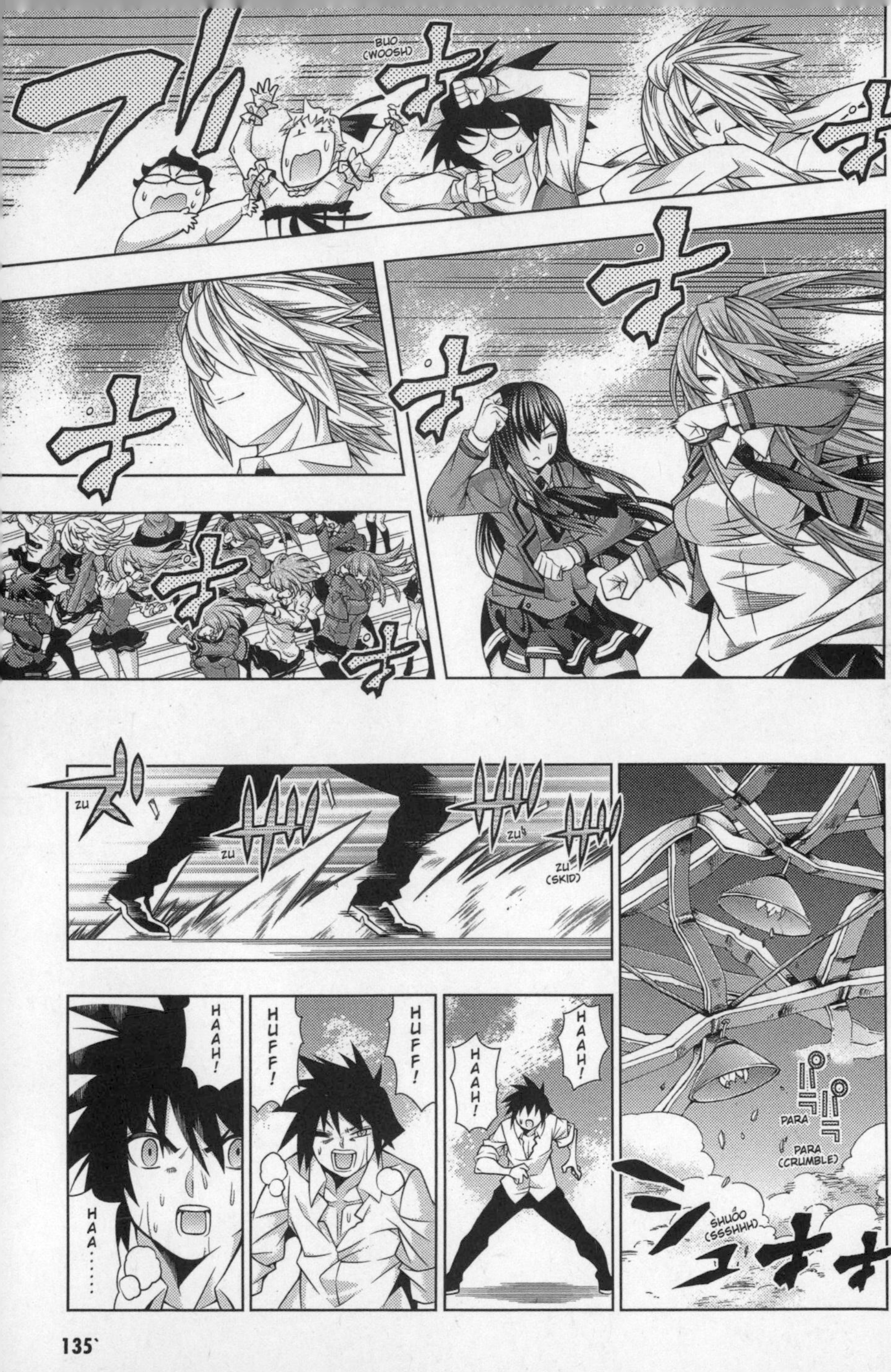
BUO
(WOOSH)
PARA
PARA
(CRUMBLE)
SHUOO
(SSSHHH)
ZU
(SKID)
ZU
ZU
ZU
HAAH!
HAAH!
HUFF!
HUFF!
HAAH!
HAA......

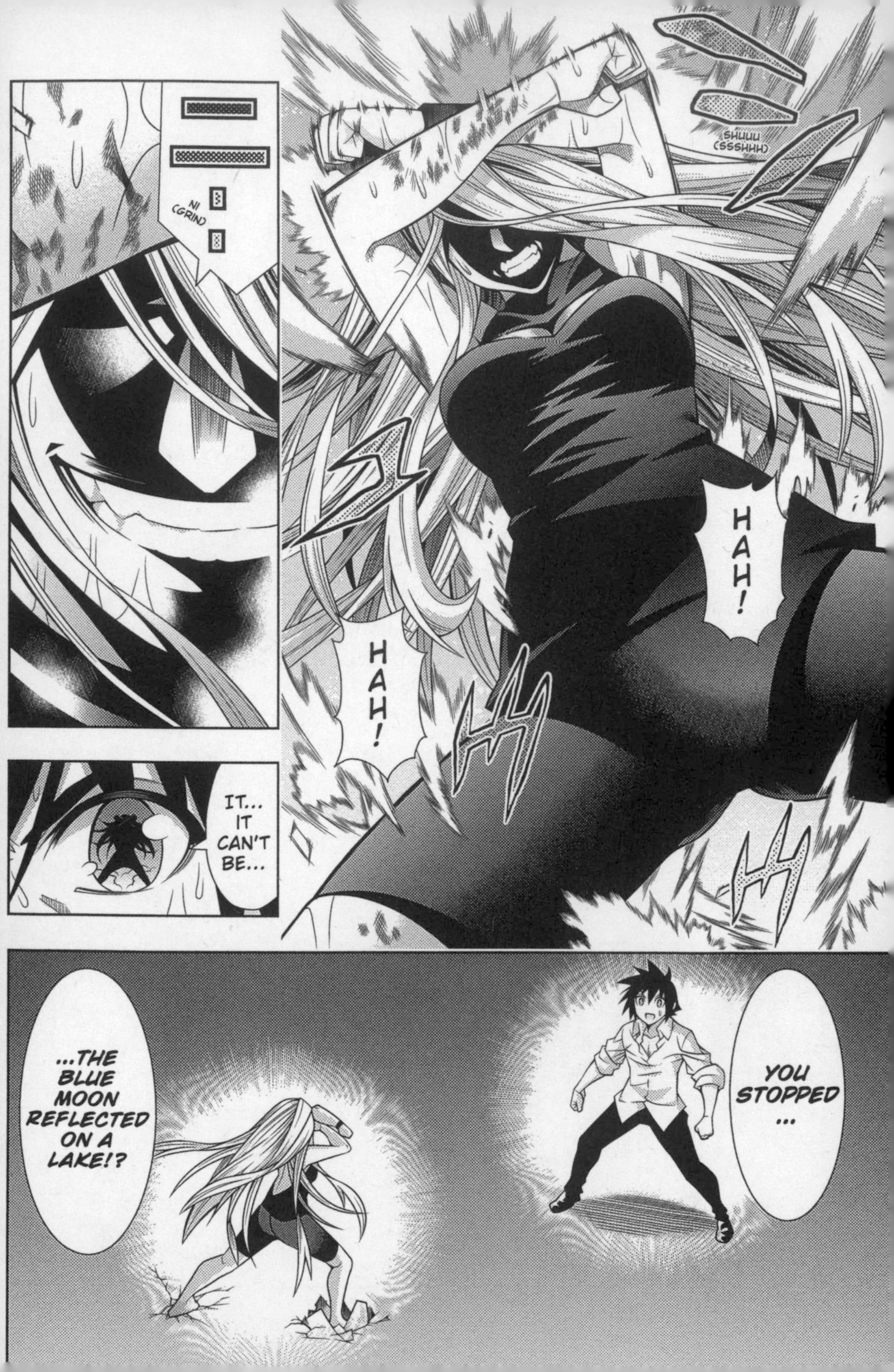
SHUUU
(SSSHHH)
HAH!
HAH!
NI
(GRIN)
IT... IT CAN'T BE...
YOU STOPPED ...
...THE BLUE MOON REFLECTED ON A LAKE!?

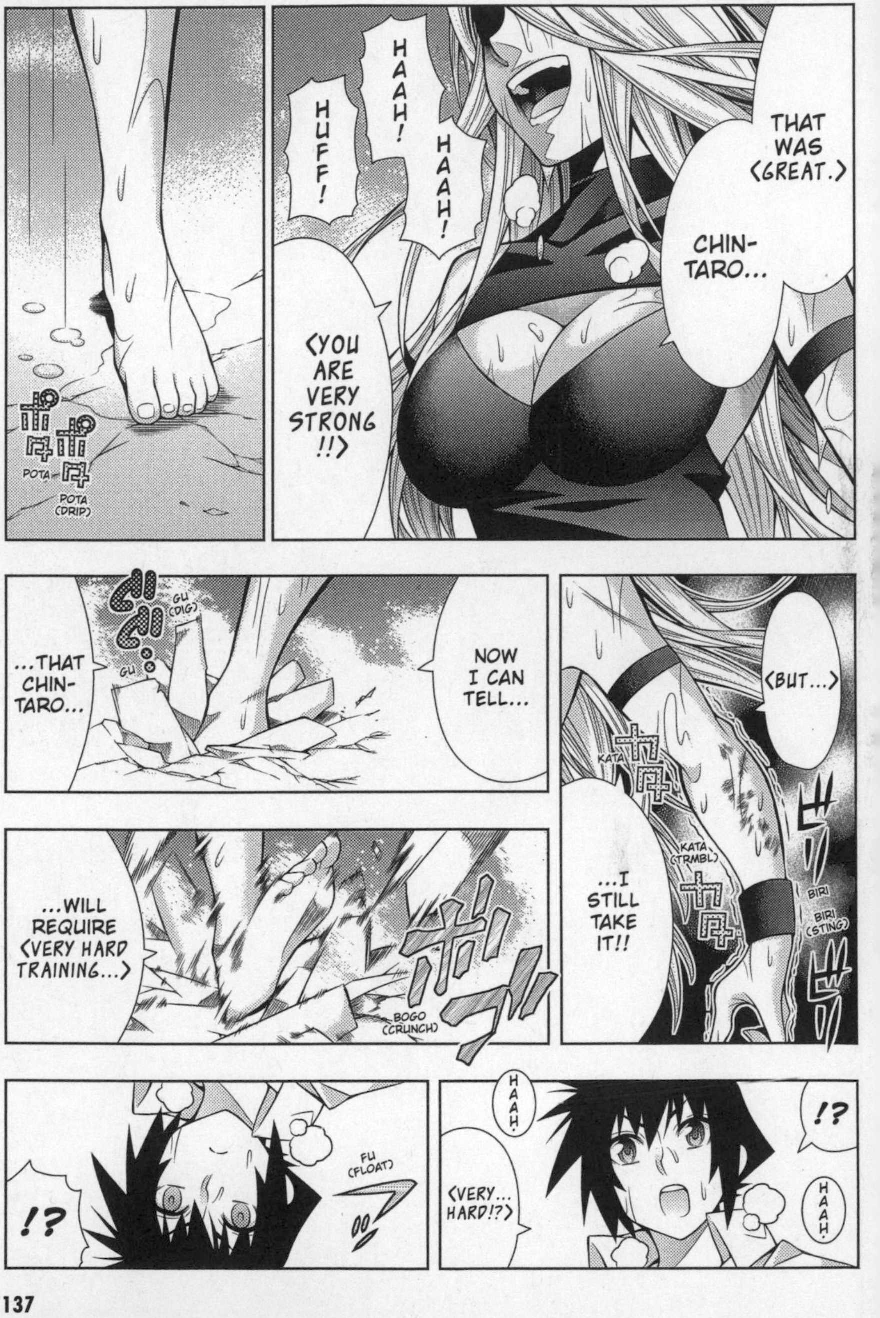
THAT WAS <GREAT.>
CHIN-TARO...
HAAAH!
HAAAH!
HUFF!
<YOU ARE VERY STRONG!!>
POTA
POTA (DRIP)
<BUT...>
KATA
KATA (TRMBL)
...I STILL TAKE IT!!
BIRI
BIRI (STING)
NOW I CAN TELL...
GU (DIG)
GU
...THAT CHIN-TARO...
BOGO (CRUNCH)
...WILL REQUIRE <VERY HARD TRAINING...>
!?
HAAAH.
HAAAH.
<VERY... HARD!?>
FU (FLOAT)
!?

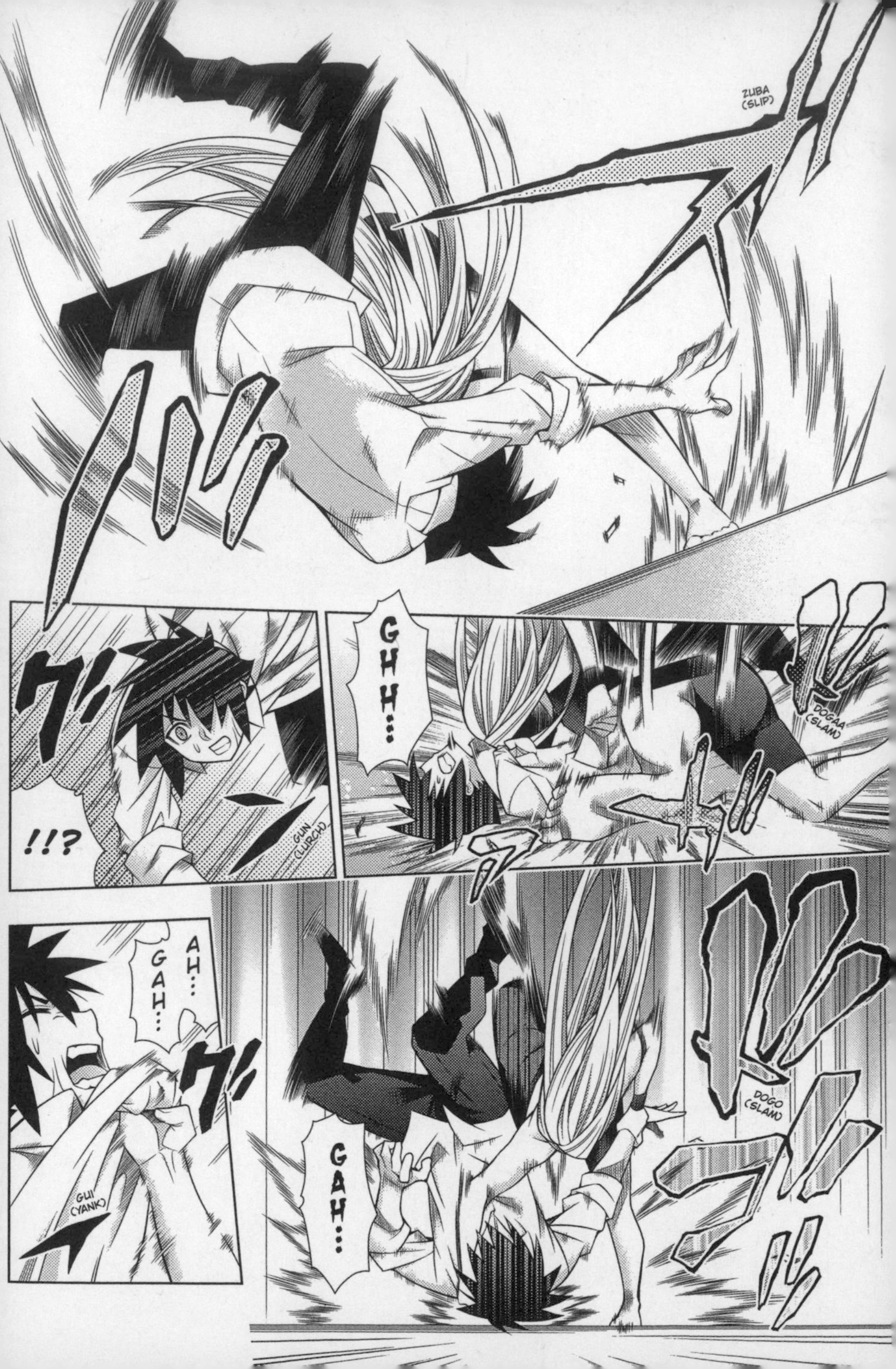
ZUBA (SLIP)
GHH...
DOGAA (SLAM)
!!?
GUIN (LURCH)
DOGO (SLAM)
GAH...
AH... GAH...
GUI (YANK)

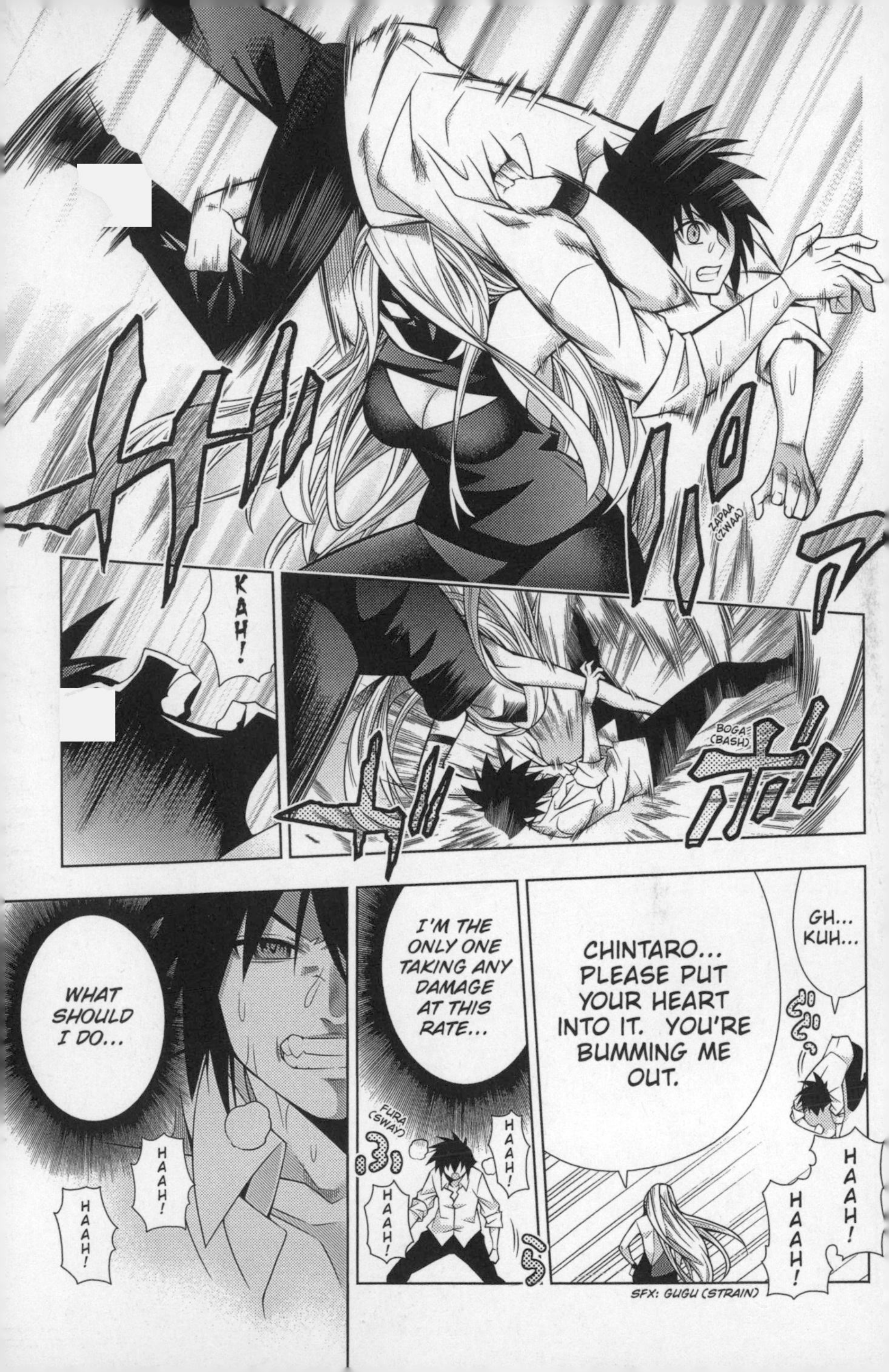
ZAPAA (ZWAA)
BOGA (BASH)
KAH!
GH... KUH...
CHINTARO... PLEASE PUT YOUR HEART INTO IT. YOU'RE BUMMING ME OUT.
HAAAH!
HAAAH!
I'M THE ONLY ONE TAKING ANY DAMAGE AT THIS RATE...
FURA (SWAY)
HAAAH!
HAAAH!
WHAT SHOULD I DO...
HAAAH!
HAAAH!
SFX: GUGU (STRAIN)

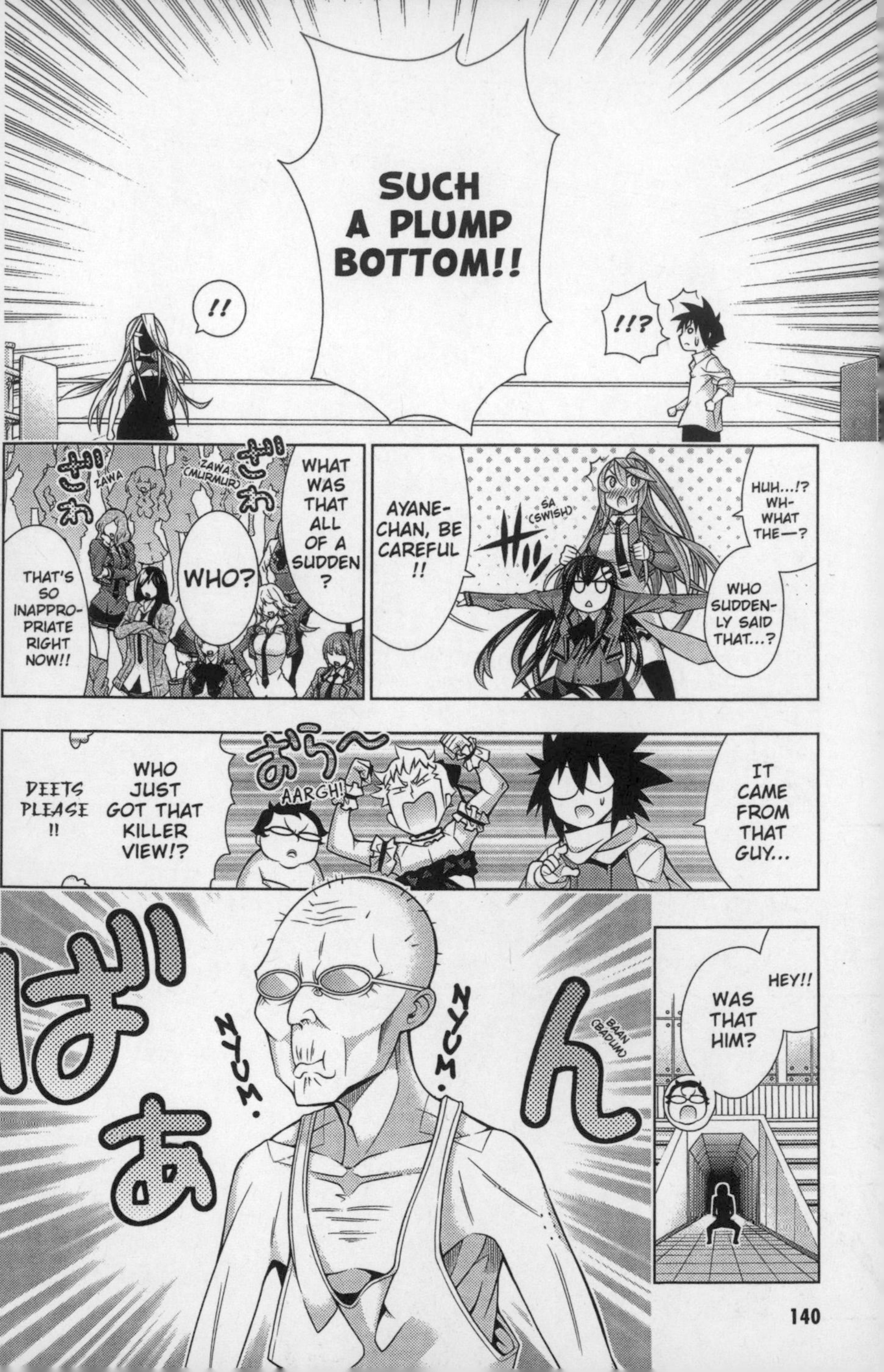
SUCH A PLUMP BOTTOM!!
!!?
!!
HUH...!? WH-WHAT THE—?
WHO SUDDENLY SAID THAT...?
SA (SWISH)
AYANE-CHAN, BE CAREFUL!!
WHAT WAS THAT ALL OF A SUDDEN?
ZAWA (MURMUR)
ZAWA
WHO?
THAT'S SO INAPPROPRIATE RIGHT NOW!!
IT CAME FROM THAT GUY...
AARGH!
WHO JUST GOT THAT KILLER VIEW!?
DEETS PLEASE!!
HEY!!
WAS THAT HIM?
BAAN (BADUM)
NYUM.
NYUM.

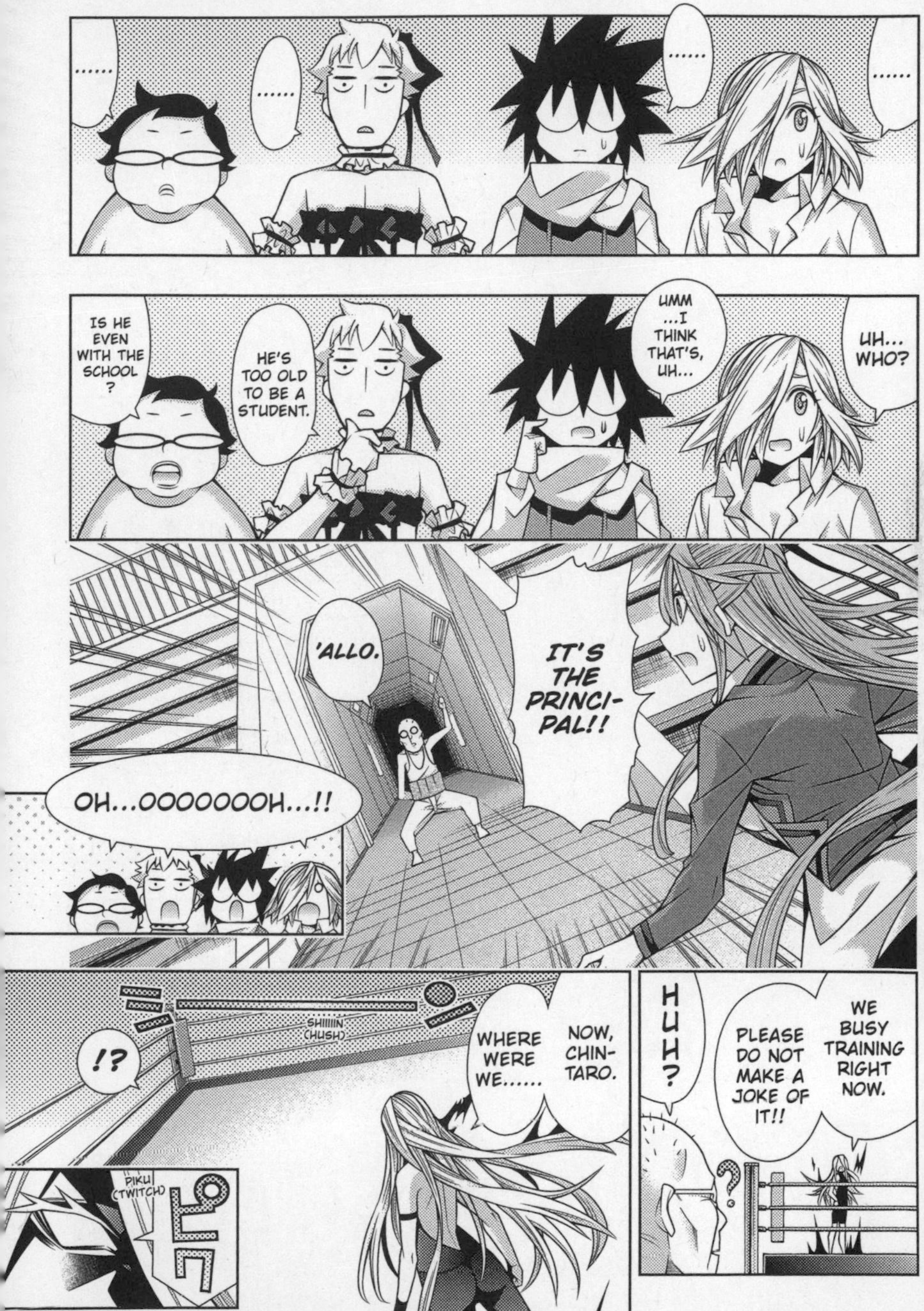
......
......
......
......
UH... WHO?
UMM ...I THINK THAT'S, UH...
HE'S TOO OLD TO BE A STUDENT.
IS HE EVEN WITH THE SCHOOL ?
IT'S THE PRINCI-PAL!!
'ALLO.
OH...OOOOOOOH...!!
WE BUSY TRAINING RIGHT NOW.
PLEASE DO NOT MAKE A JOKE OF IT!!
HUH?
NOW, CHIN-TARO.
WHERE WERE WE......
SHIIIIN (HUSH)
!?
PIKU (TWITCH)

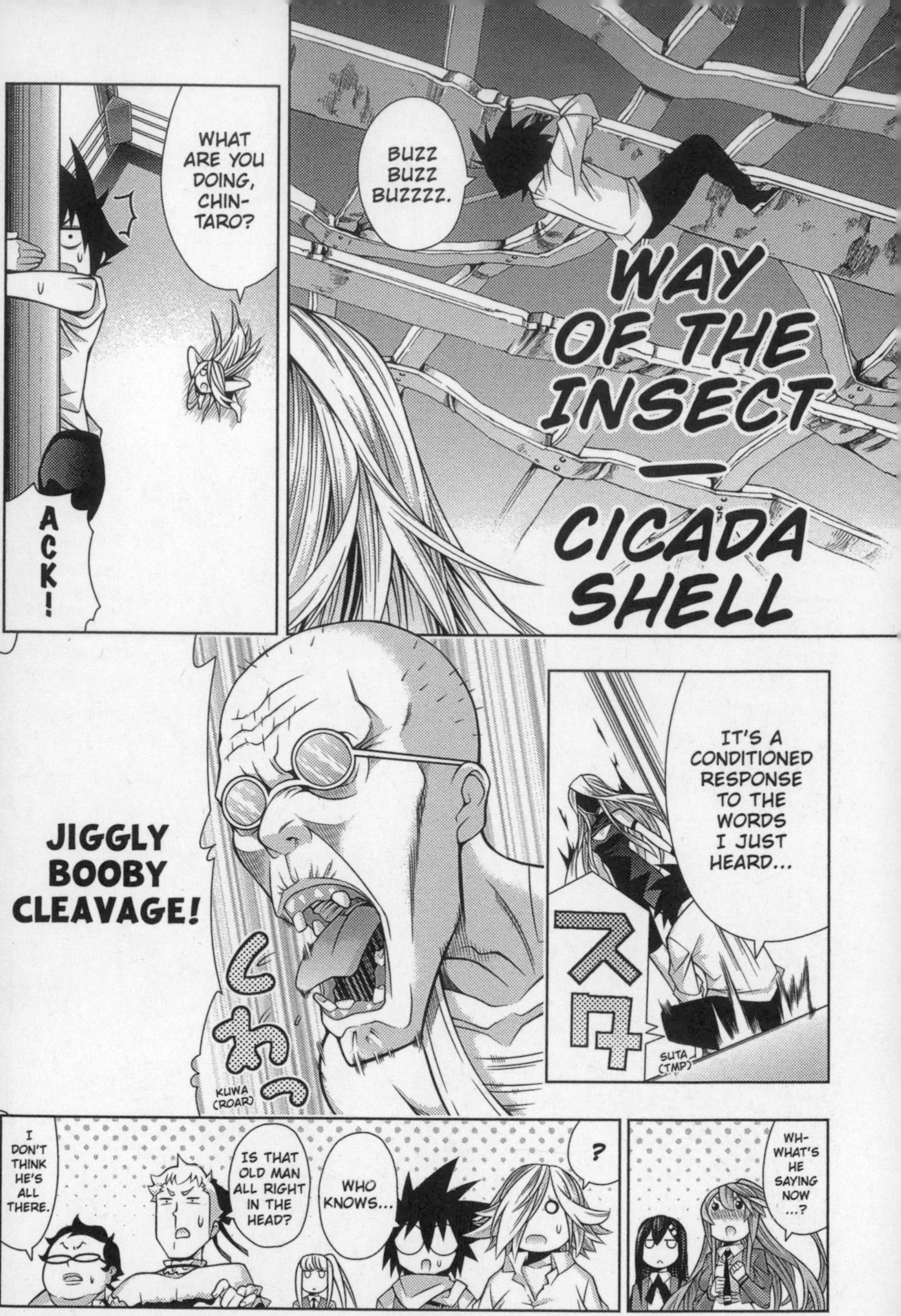
BUZZ BUZZ BUZZZZ.
WAY OF THE INSECT — CICADA SHELL
WHAT ARE YOU DOING, CHIN-TARO?
ACK!
IT'S A CONDITIONED RESPONSE TO THE WORDS I JUST HEARD...
SUTA (TMP)
JIGGLY BOOBY CLEAVAGE!
KUWA (ROAR)
WH-WHAT'S HE SAYING NOW ...?
?
WHO KNOWS...
IS THAT OLD MAN ALL RIGHT IN THE HEAD?
I DON'T THINK HE'S ALL THERE.

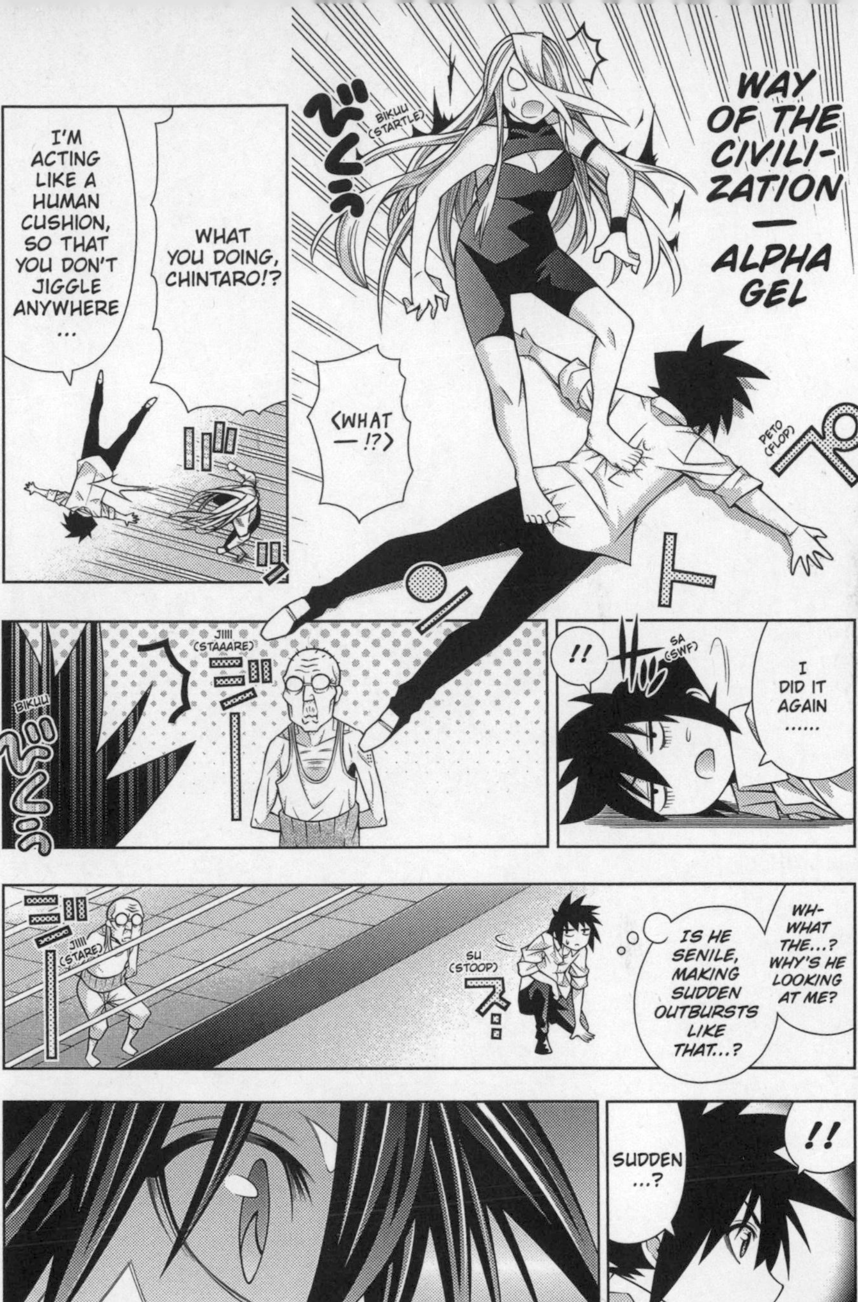
WAY OF THE CIVILIZATION — ALPHA GEL
BIKUU (STARTLE)
<WHAT —!?>
PETO (FLOP)
WHAT YOU DOING, CHINTARO!?
I'M ACTING LIKE A HUMAN CUSHION, SO THAT YOU DON'T JIGGLE ANYWHERE ...
I DID IT AGAIN ......
SA (SWF)
!!
JIIII (STAAARE)
BIKUU
WH-WHAT THE...? WHY'S HE LOOKING AT ME?
IS HE SENILE, MAKING SUDDEN OUTBURSTS LIKE THAT...?
SU (STOOP)
JIIII (STARE)
!!
SUDDEN ...?

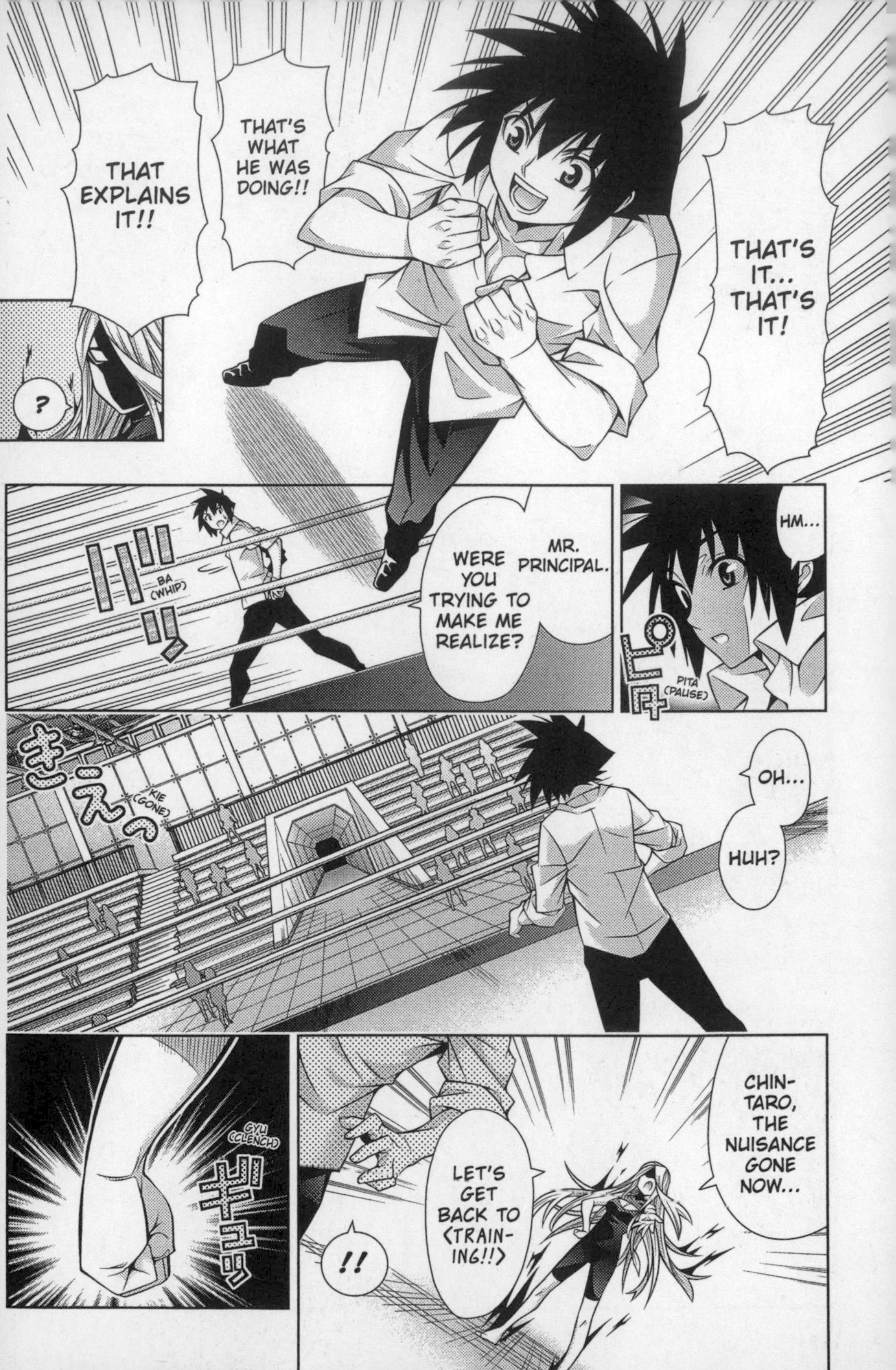
THAT'S IT... THAT'S IT!
THAT'S WHAT HE WAS DOING!!
THAT EXPLAINS IT!!
?
HM...
PITA (PAUSE)
MR. PRINCIPAL.
WERE YOU TRYING TO MAKE ME REALIZE?
BA (WHIP)
OH...
HUH?
KIE (GONE)
CHIN-TARO, THE NUISANCE GONE NOW...
LET'S GET BACK TO <TRAIN-ING!!>
!!
GYU (CLENCH)

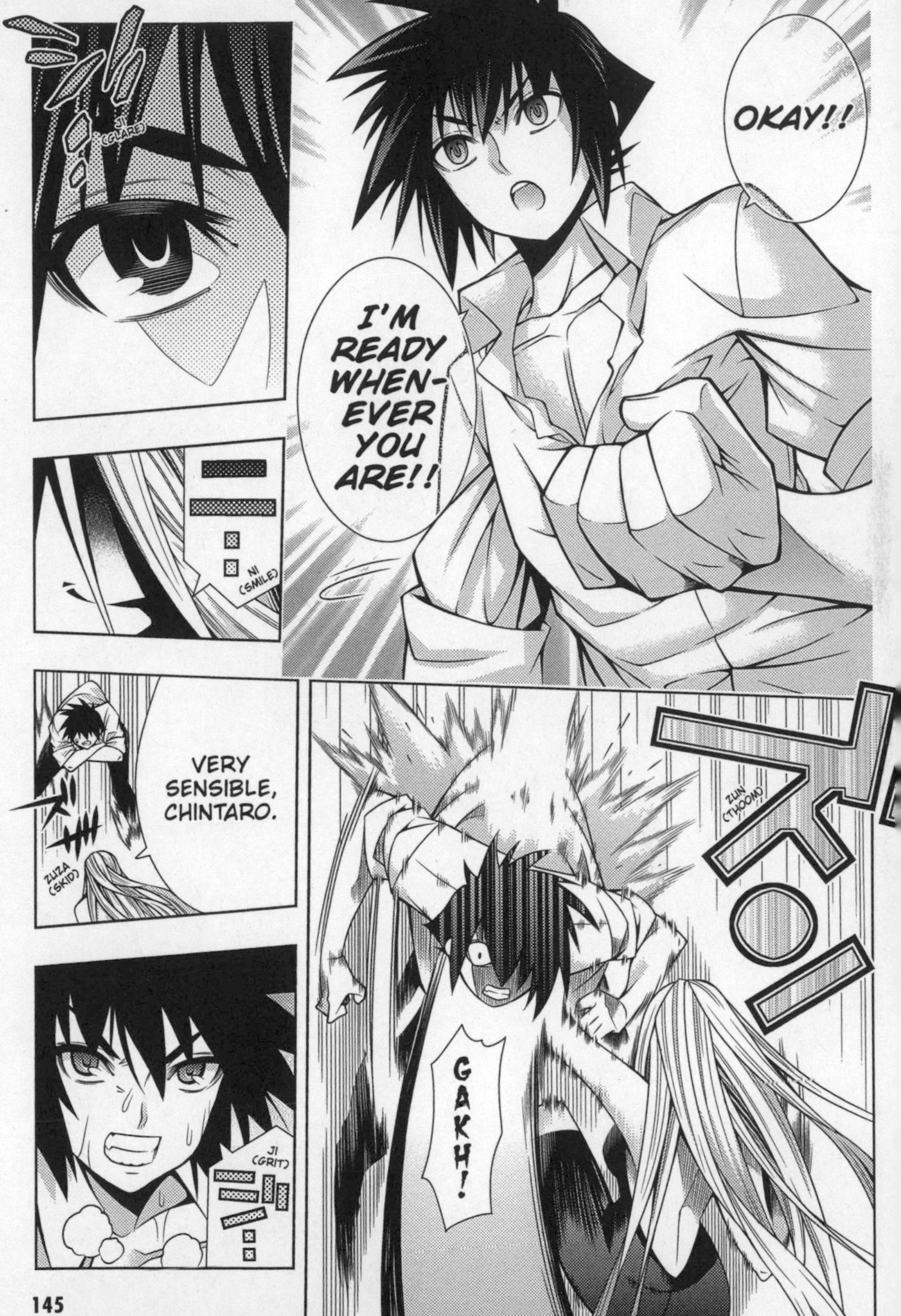
OKAY!!
I'M READY WHENEVER YOU ARE!!
JI (GLARE)
NI (SMILE)
ZUN (THOOM)
GAKH!
VERY SENSIBLE, CHINTARO.
ZUZA (SKID)
JI (GRIT)

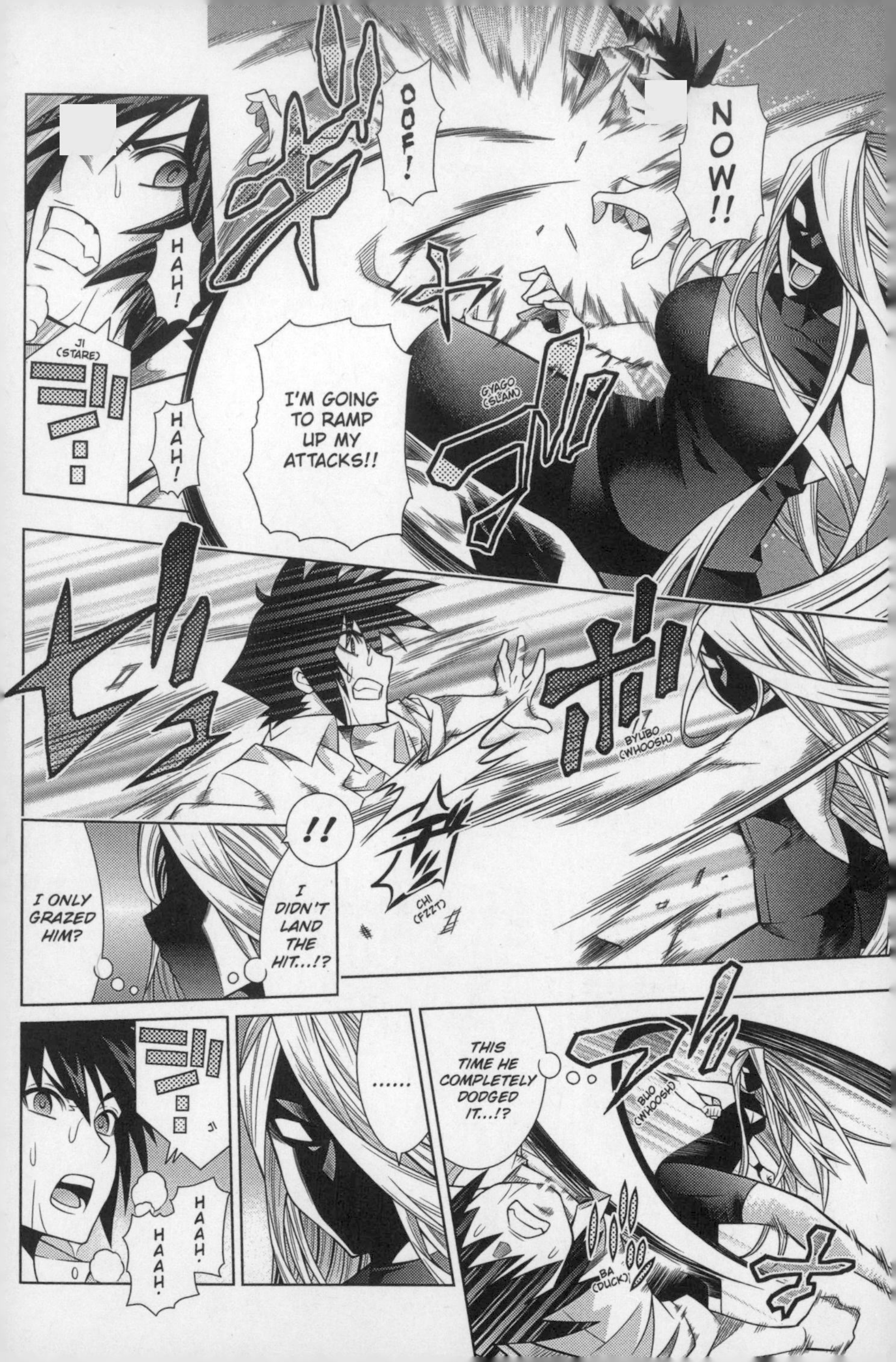
NOW!!
OOF!
GYAGO (SLAM)
I'M GOING TO RAMP UP MY ATTACKS!!
HAH!
HAH!
JI (STARE)
BYUBO (WHOOSH)
!!
CHI (FZZZT)
I DIDN'T LAND THE HIT...!?
I ONLY GRAZED HIM?
BUO (WHOOSH)
THIS TIME HE COMPLETELY DODGED IT...!?
BA (DUCK)
......
JI
HAAH.
HAAH.

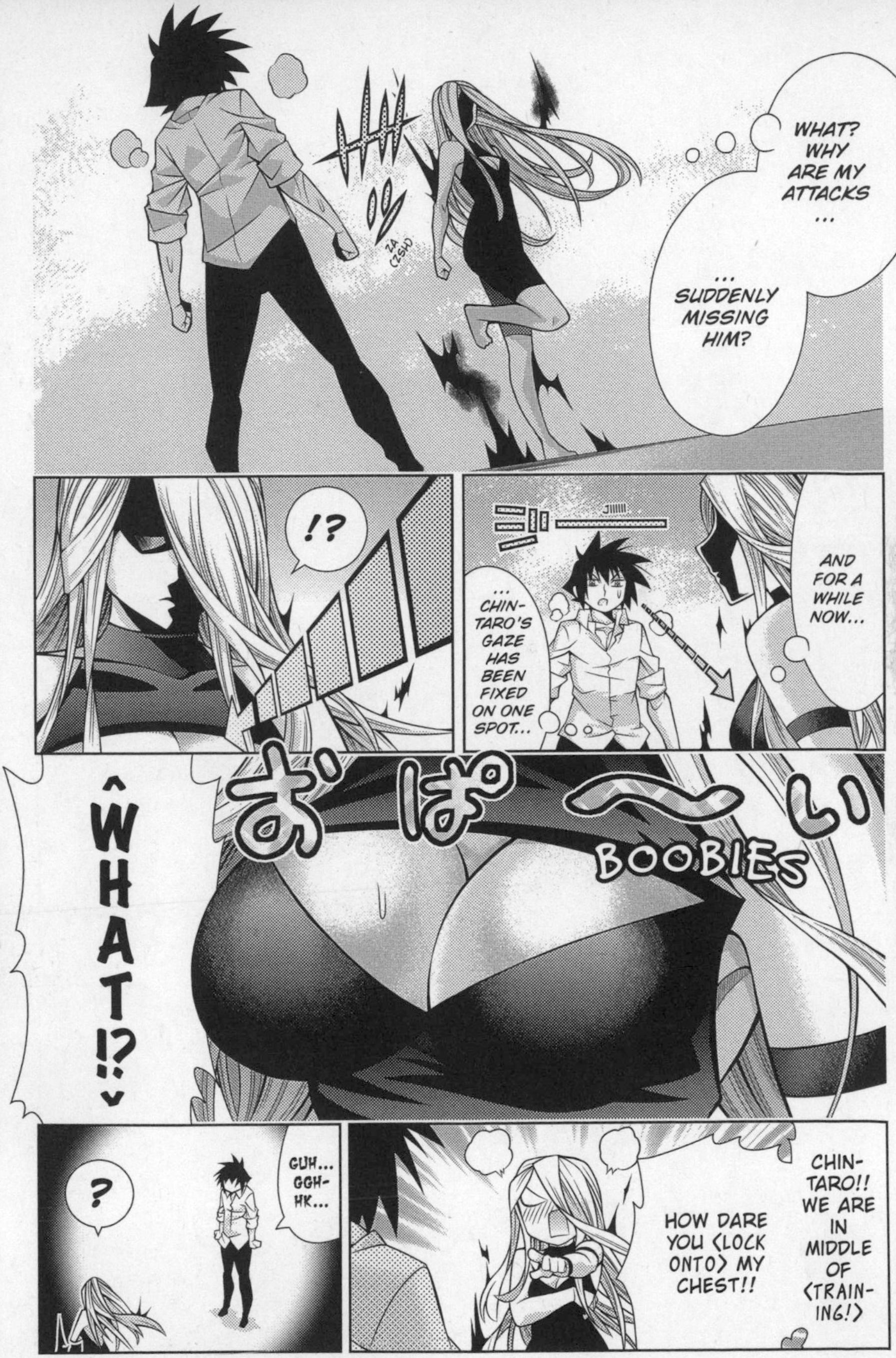
WHAT? WHY ARE MY ATTACKS ...
... SUDDENLY MISSING HIM?
ZA (ZSH)
AND FOR A WHILE NOW...
... CHINTARO'S GAZE HAS BEEN FIXED ON ONE SPOT...
JIIIII
!?
BOOBIES
WHAT!?
CHINTARO!! WE ARE IN MIDDLE OF <TRAINING!>
HOW DARE YOU <LOCK ONTO> MY CHEST!!
GUH... GGHHK...
?

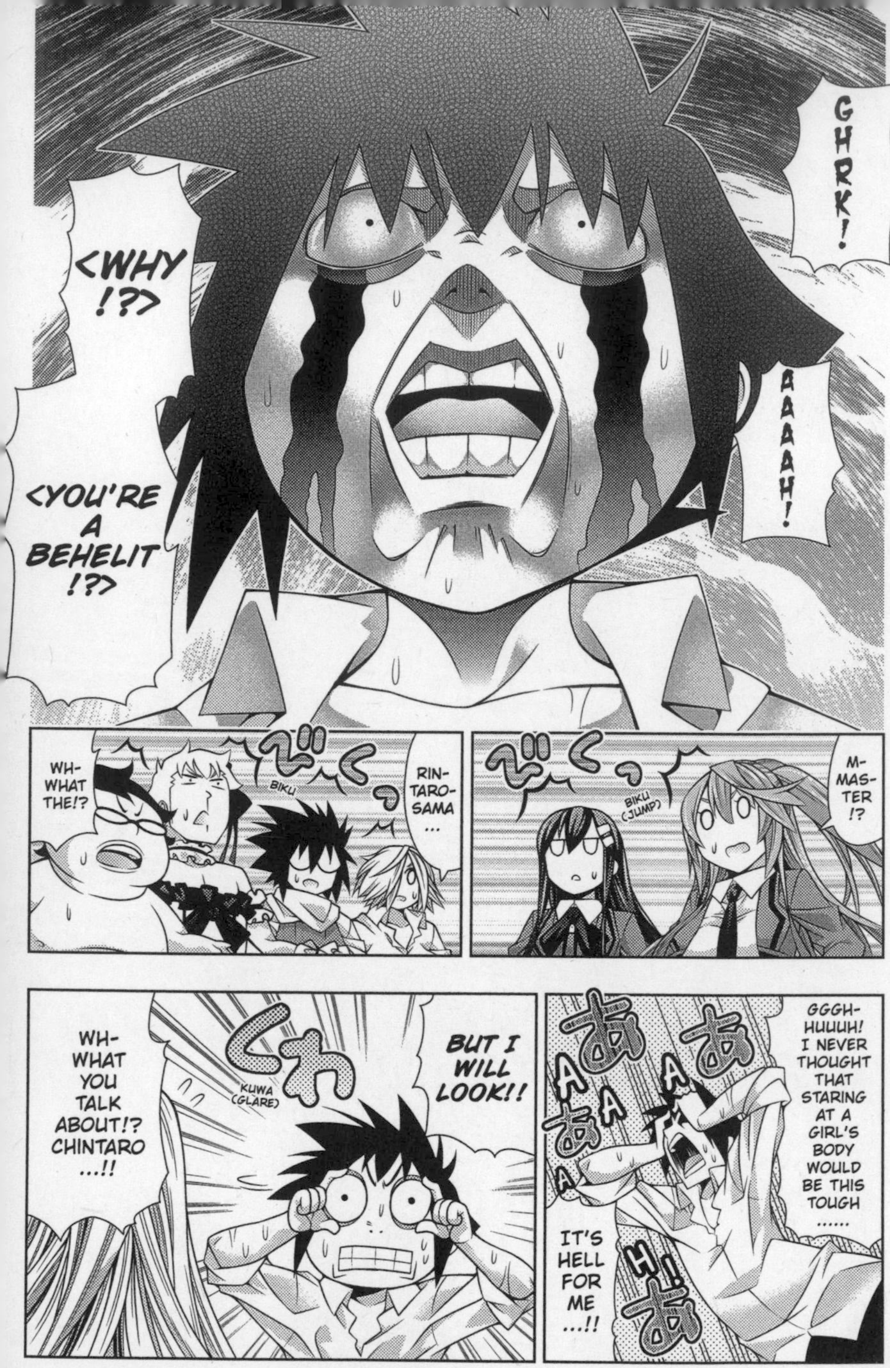
GHRK!
<WHY!?>
AAAAAH!
<YOU'RE A BEHELIT!?>
M-MASTER!?
びくっ
BIKU (JUMP)
RIN-TARO-SAMA...
びくっ
BIKU
WH-WHAT THE!?
GGGH-HUUUH! I NEVER THOUGHT THAT STARING AT A GIRL'S BODY WOULD BE THIS TOUGH......
ああ
A A A A
IT'S HELL FOR ME...!!
H!
お
BUT I WILL LOOK!!
くわ
KUWA (GLARE)
WH-WHAT YOU TALK ABOUT!? CHINTARO...!!

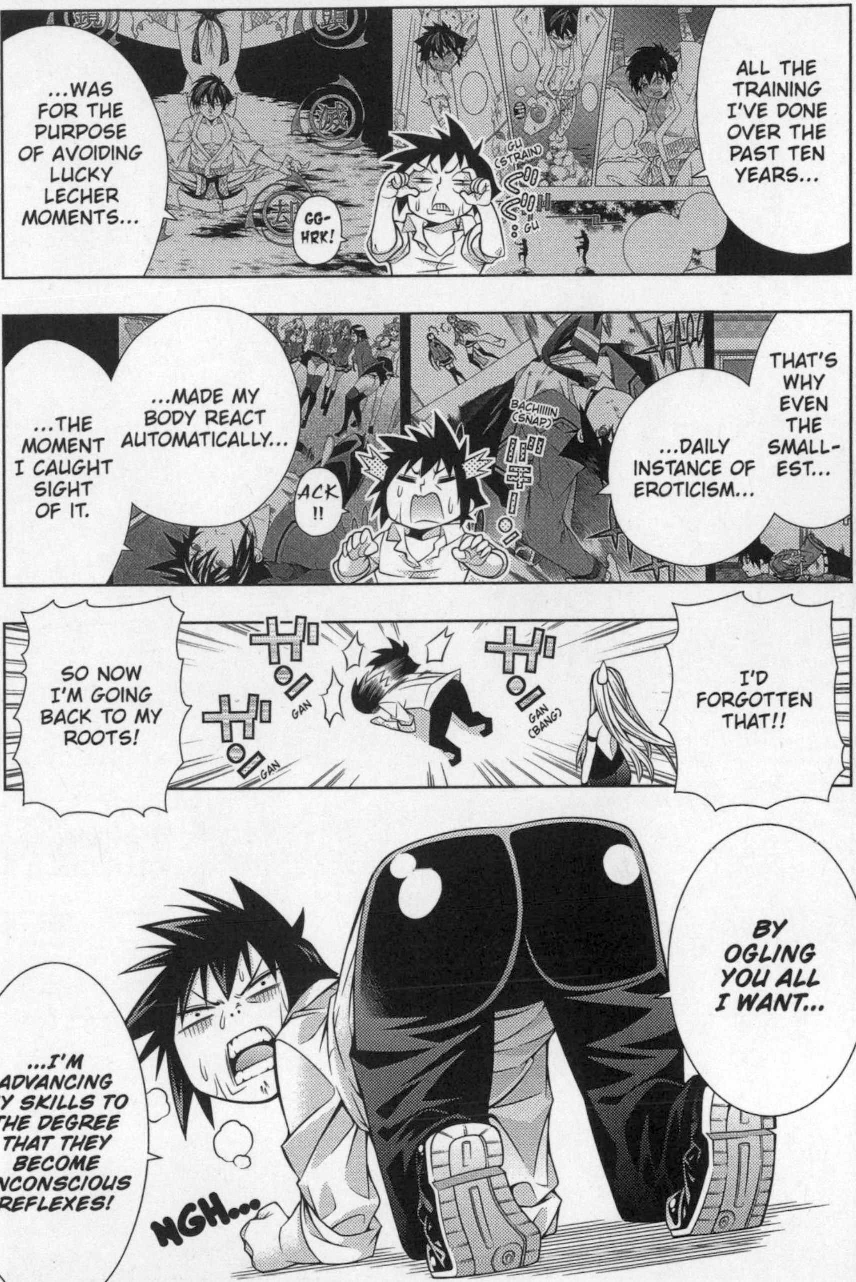
ALL THE TRAINING I'VE DONE OVER THE PAST TEN YEARS...
GU (STRAIN)
GU
GG-HRK!
...WAS FOR THE PURPOSE OF AVOIDING LUCKY LECHER MOMENTS...
THAT'S WHY EVEN THE SMALLEST...
...DAILY INSTANCE OF EROTICISM...
BACHIIIIN (SNAP)
ACK!!
...MADE MY BODY REACT AUTOMATICALLY...
...THE MOMENT I CAUGHT SIGHT OF IT.
I'D FORGOTTEN THAT!!
GAN (BANG)
GAN
GAN
SO NOW I'M GOING BACK TO MY ROOTS!
BY OGLING YOU ALL I WANT...
...I'M ADVANCING MY SKILLS TO THE DEGREE THAT THEY BECOME UNCONSCIOUS REFLEXES!
NGH...

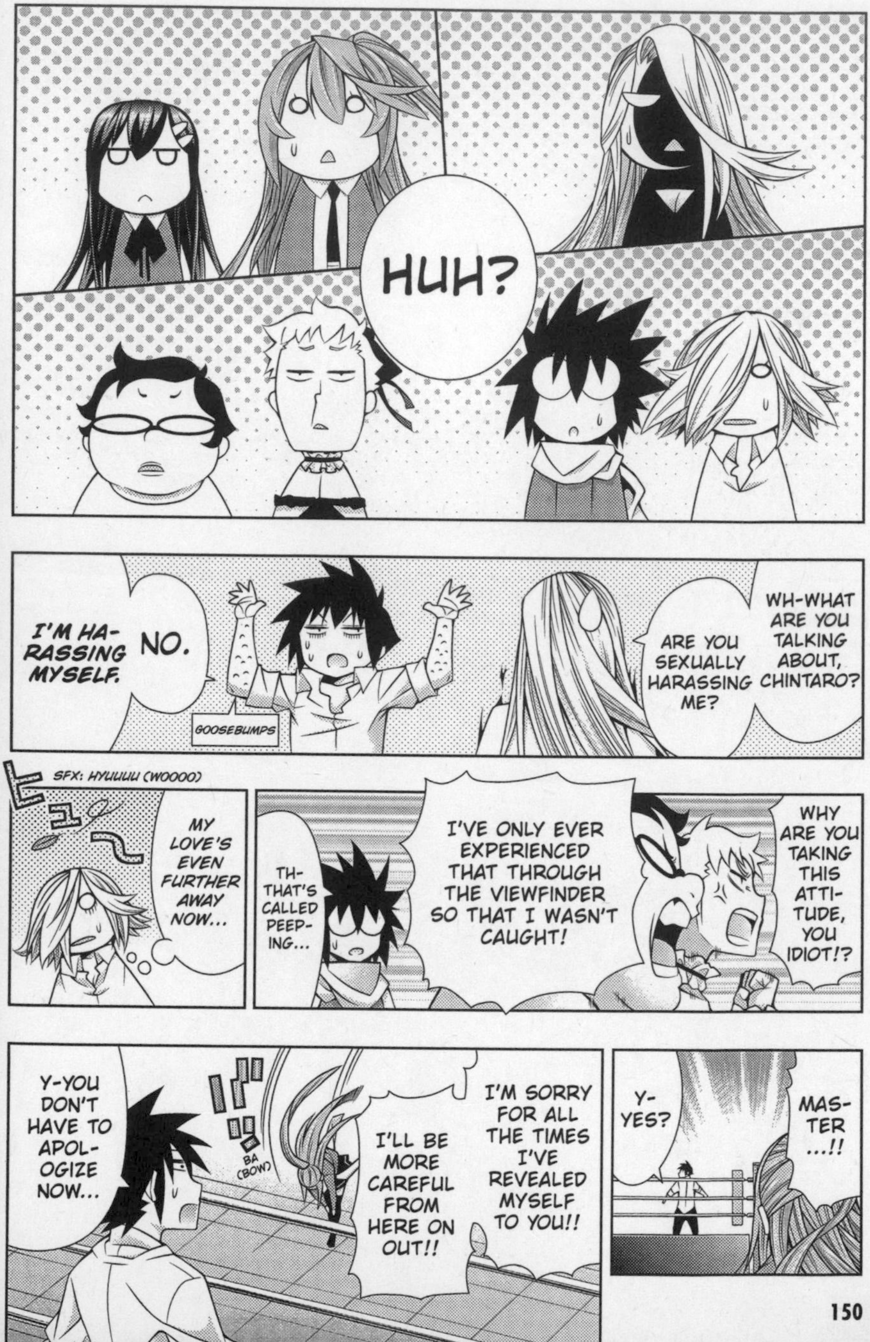
HUH?
WH-WHAT ARE YOU TALKING ABOUT, CHINTARO?
ARE YOU SEXUALLY HARASSING ME?
NO.
I'M HARASSING MYSELF.
GOOSEBUMPS
WHY ARE YOU TAKING THIS ATTITUDE, YOU IDIOT!?
I'VE ONLY EVER EXPERIENCED THAT THROUGH THE VIEWFINDER SO THAT I WASN'T CAUGHT!
TH-THAT'S CALLED PEEPING...
SFX: HYUUUU (WOOOO)
MY LOVE'S EVEN FURTHER AWAY NOW...
MASTER...!!
Y-YES?
I'M SORRY FOR ALL THE TIMES I'VE REVEALED MYSELF TO YOU!!
I'LL BE MORE CAREFUL FROM HERE ON OUT!!
BA (BOW)
Y-YOU DON'T HAVE TO APOLOGIZE NOW...

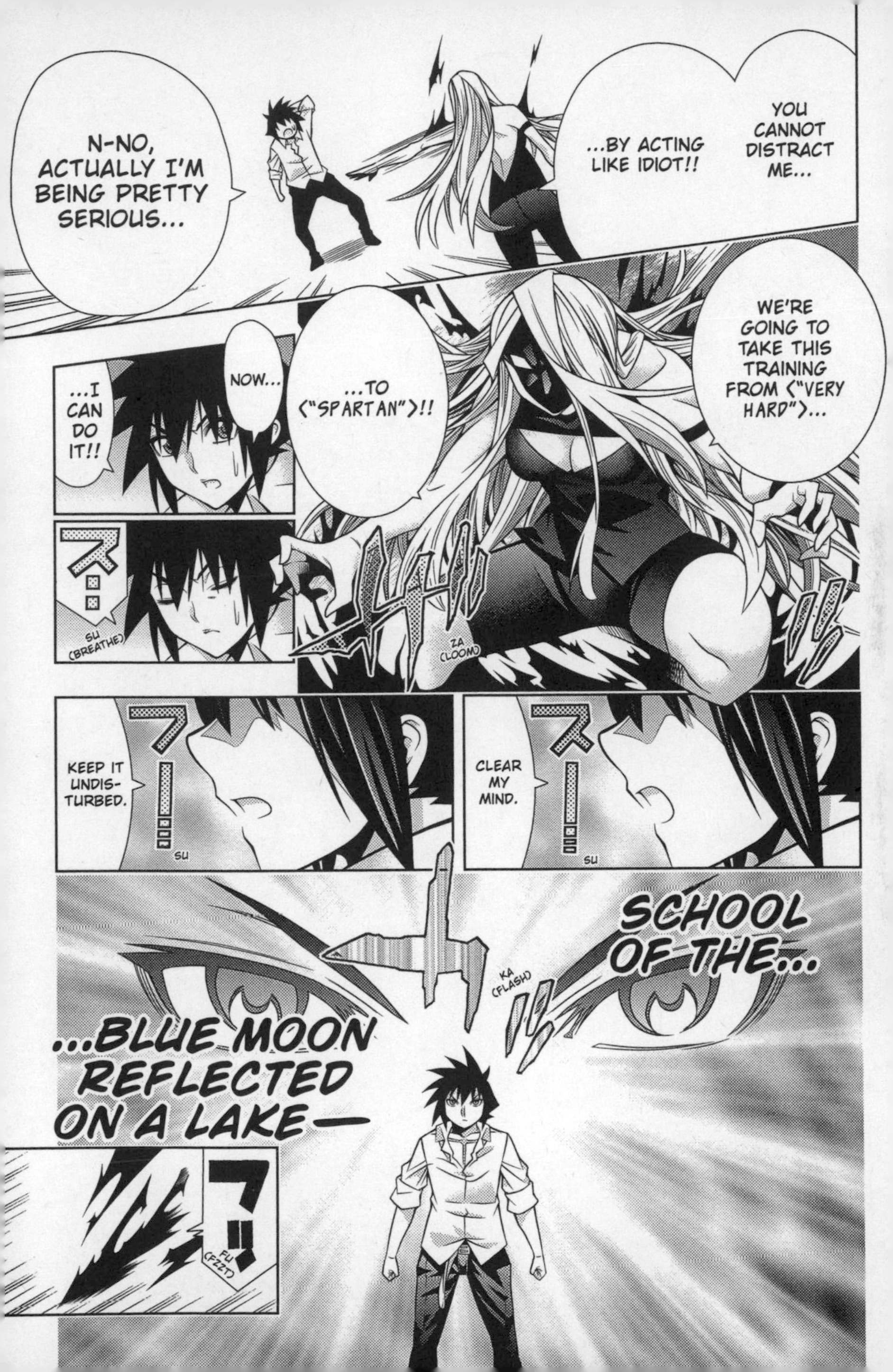
YOU CANNOT DISTRACT ME...
...BY ACTING LIKE IDIOT!!
N-NO, ACTUALLY I'M BEING PRETTY SERIOUS...
WE'RE GOING TO TAKE THIS TRAINING FROM 〈"VERY HARD"〉...
...TO 〈"SPARTAN"〉!!
ZA (LOOM)
NOW...
...I CAN DO IT!!
SU (BREATHE)
CLEAR MY MIND.
SU
KEEP IT UNDIS-TURBED.
SU
SCHOOL OF THE...
KA (FLASH)
...BLUE MOON REFLECTED ON A LAKE—
FU (FZZT)

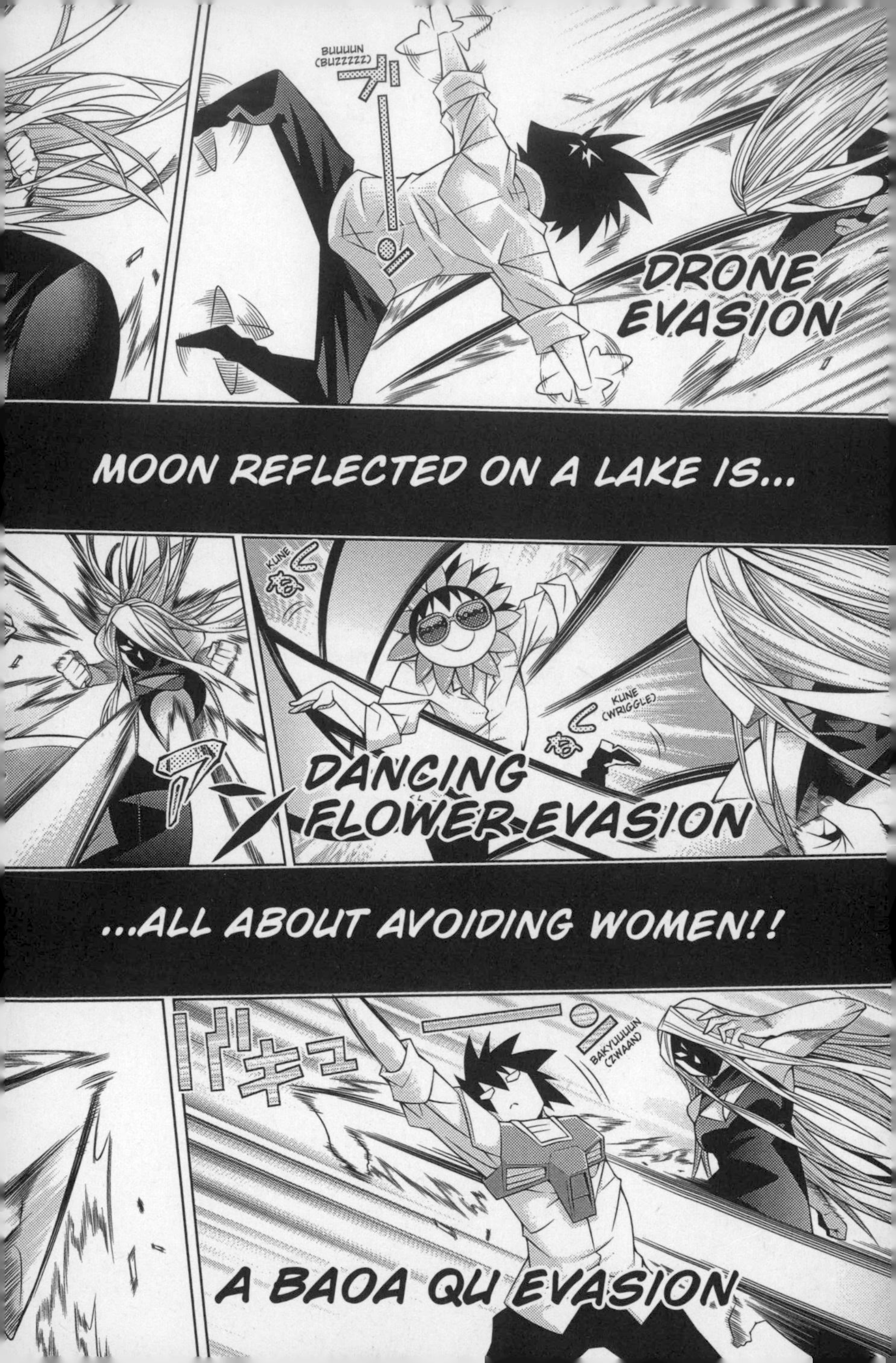
BUUUUUN (BUZZZZZ)
DRONE EVASION
MOON REFLECTED ON A LAKE IS...
KUNE
KUNE (WRIGGLE)
DANCING FLOWER EVASION
...ALL ABOUT AVOIDING WOMEN!!
BAKYUUUUUN (ZWAAN)
A BAOA QU EVASION

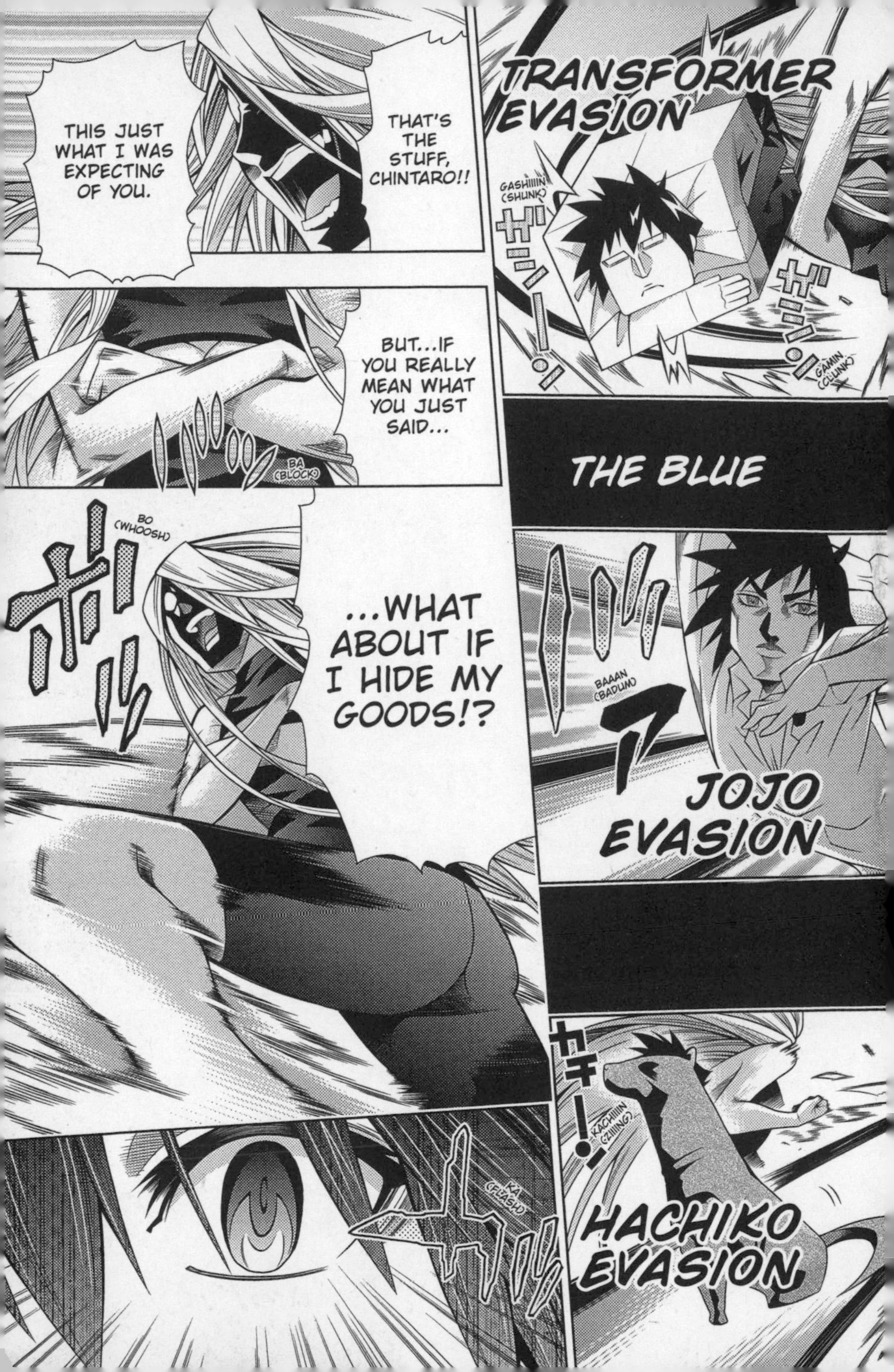
TRANSFORMER EVASION
GASHIIIIN (SHUNK)
GAMIN (CLUNK)
THE BLUE
BAAAN (BADUM)
JOJO EVASION
KACHIIIIN (ZIIING)
HACHIKO EVASION
THAT'S THE STUFF, CHINTARO!!
THIS JUST WHAT I WAS EXPECTING OF YOU.
BUT...IF YOU REALLY MEAN WHAT YOU JUST SAID...
BA (BLOCK)
...WHAT ABOUT IF I HIDE MY GOODS!?
BO (WHOOSH)
KA (FLASH)

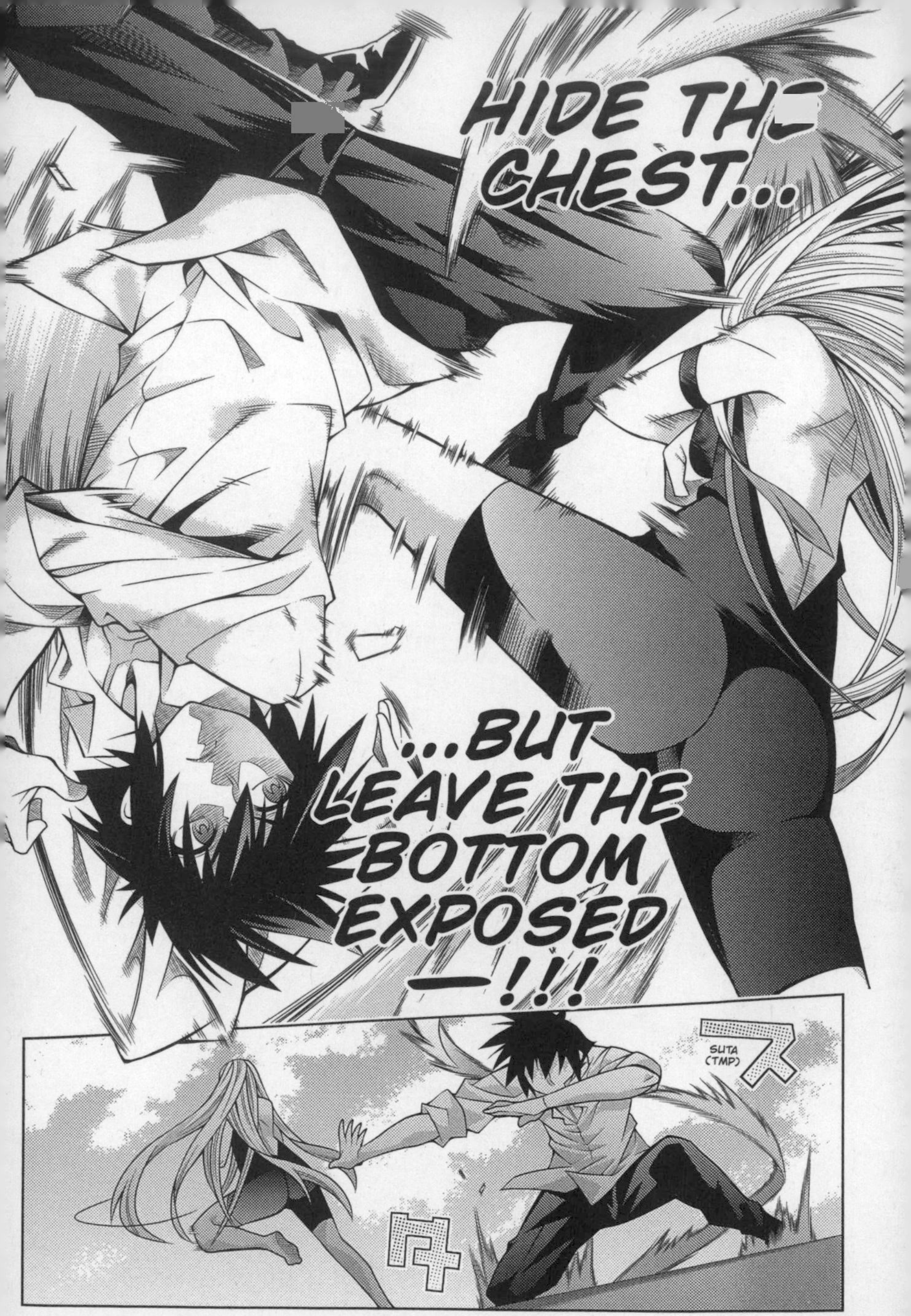
HIDE THE CHEST...
...BUT LEAVE THE BOTTOM EXPOSED —!!!
SUTA (TMP)

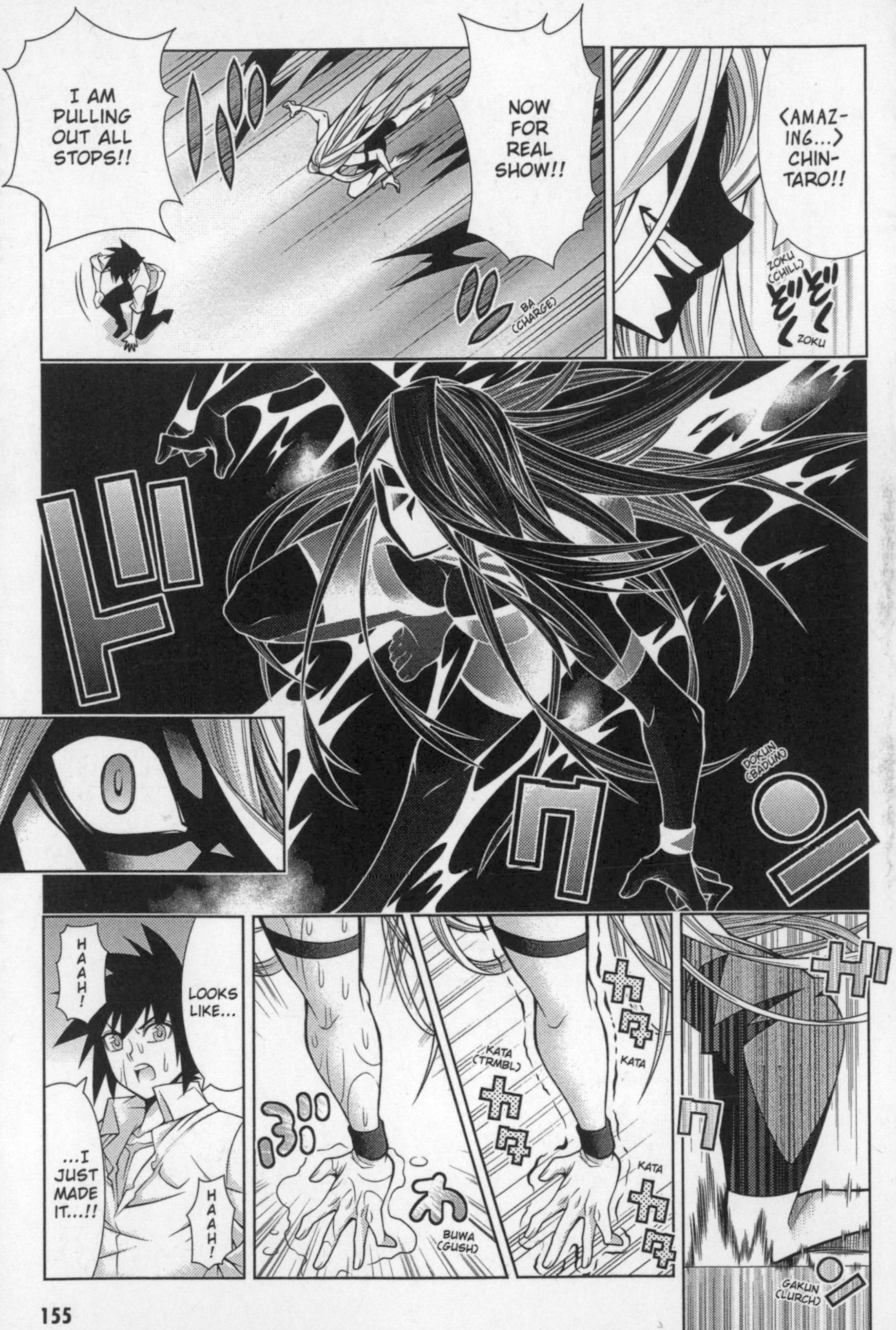
<AMAZ-ING...> CHIN-TARO!!
ZOKU (CHILL)
ZOKU
NOW FOR REAL SHOW!!
BA (CHARGE)
I AM PULLING OUT ALL STOPS!!
DOKUN (BADUM)
GAKUN (LURCH)
KATA (TRMBL)
KATA
KATA
BUWA (GUSH)
LOOKS LIKE...
HAAH!
...I JUST MADE IT...!!
HAAH!

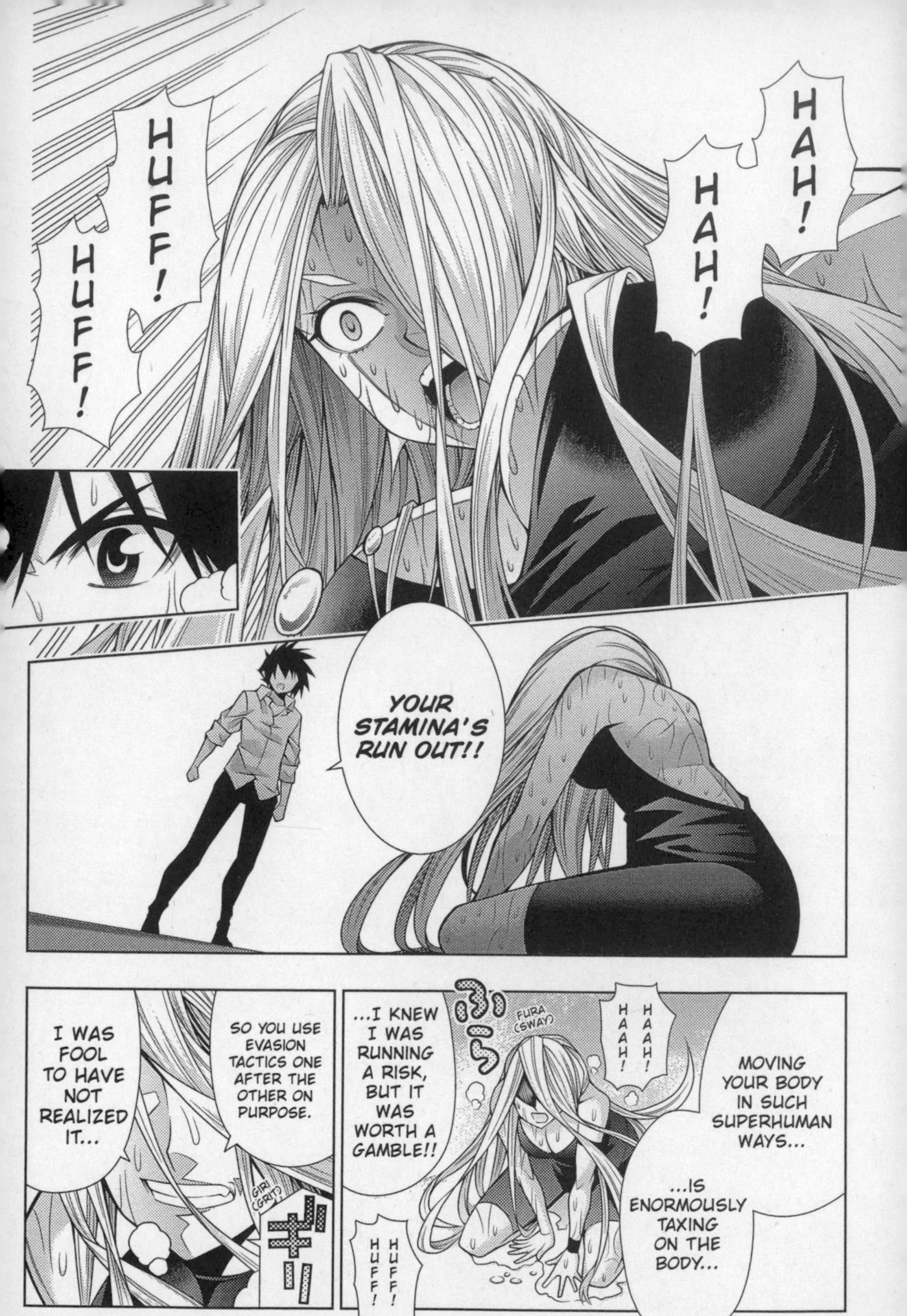

HAH! HAH!
HUFF! HUFF!
YOUR STAMINA'S RUN OUT!!
MOVING YOUR BODY IN SUCH SUPERHUMAN WAYS...
...IS ENORMOUSLY TAXING ON THE BODY...
HAAH! HAAH!
ふら
FURA (SWAY)
...I KNEW I WAS RUNNING A RISK, BUT IT WAS WORTH A GAMBLE!!
HUFF! HUFF!
SO YOU USE EVASION TACTICS ONE AFTER THE OTHER ON PURPOSE.
I WAS FOOL TO HAVE NOT REALIZED IT...
ギリ
GIRI (GRIT)

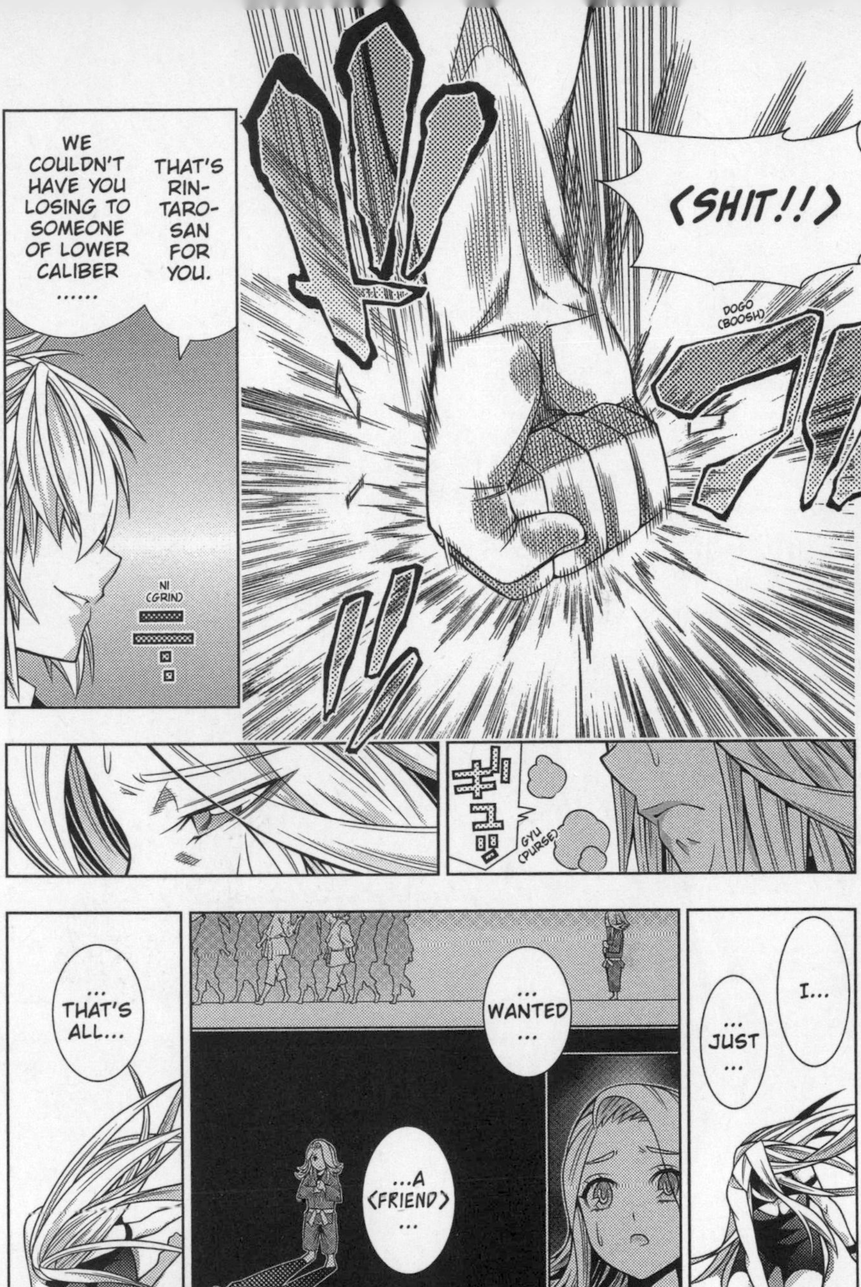
<SHIT!!>
DOGO (BOOSH)
THAT'S RIN-TARO-SAN FOR YOU.
WE COULDN'T HAVE YOU LOSING TO SOMEONE OF LOWER CALIBER ......
NI (GRIN)
GYU (PURSE)
I...
...JUST...
...WANTED...
...A <FRIEND>...
...THAT'S ALL...

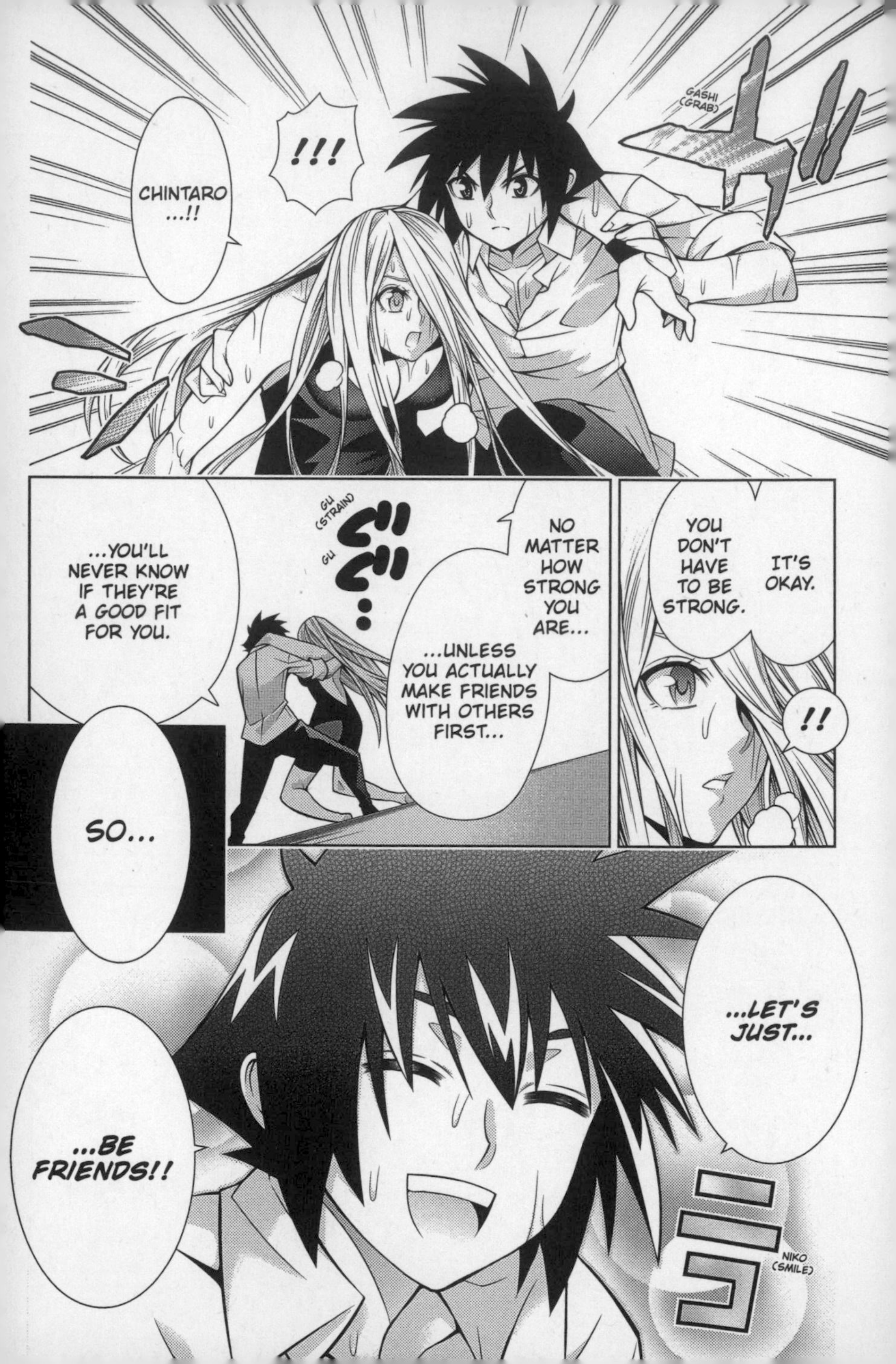
GASHI (GRAB)
!!!
CHINTARO ...!!
IT'S OKAY.
YOU DON'T HAVE TO BE STRONG.
!!
NO MATTER HOW STRONG YOU ARE...
GU (STRAIN)
GU
...UNLESS YOU ACTUALLY MAKE FRIENDS WITH OTHERS FIRST...
...YOU'LL NEVER KNOW IF THEY'RE A GOOD FIT FOR YOU.
SO...
...LET'S JUST...
NIKO (SMILE)
...BE FRIENDS!!

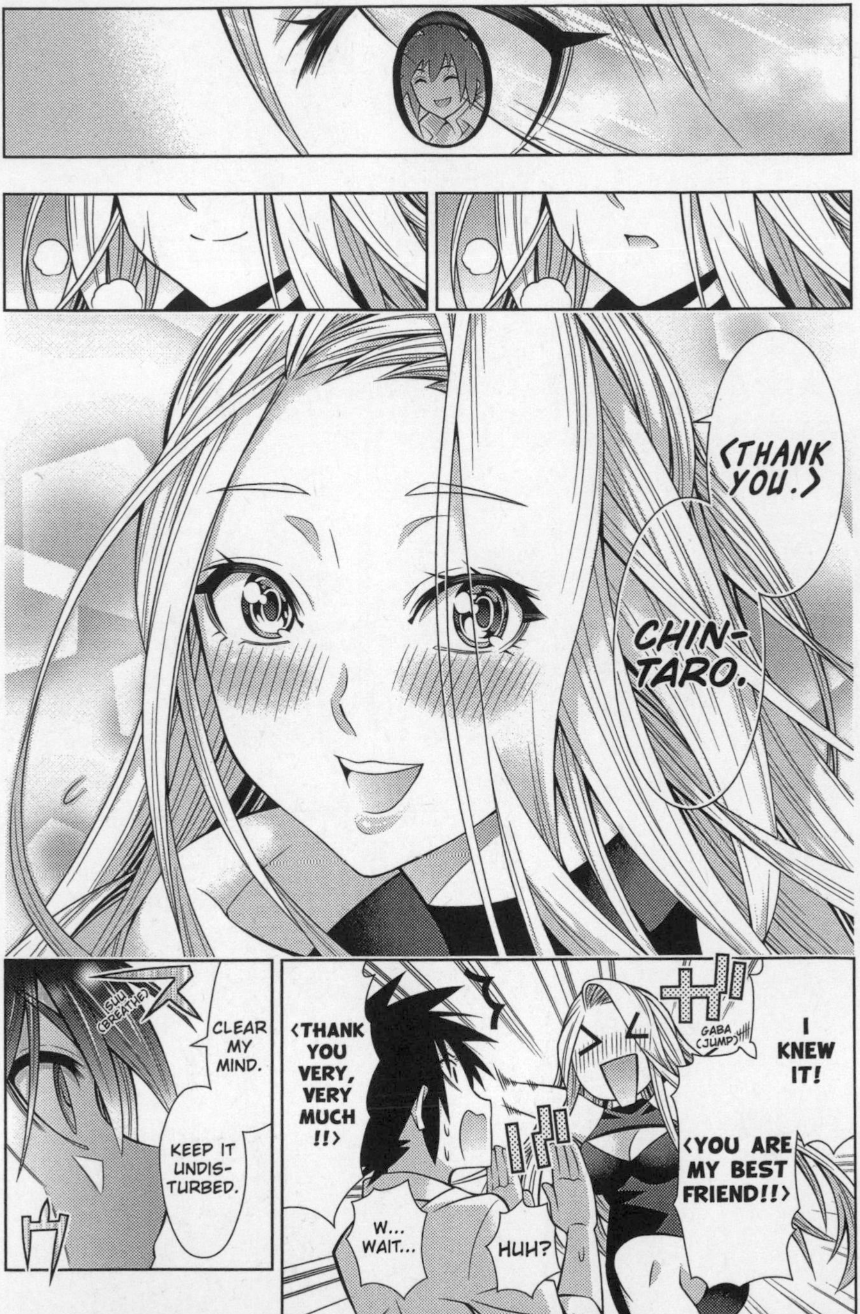
<THANK YOU.>
CHIN-TARO.
I KNEW IT!
GABA (JUMP)
<YOU ARE MY BEST FRIEND!!>
<THANK YOU VERY, VERY MUCH!!>
HUH?
W... WAIT...
SUU (BREATHE)
CLEAR MY MIND.
KEEP IT UNDIS-TURBED.

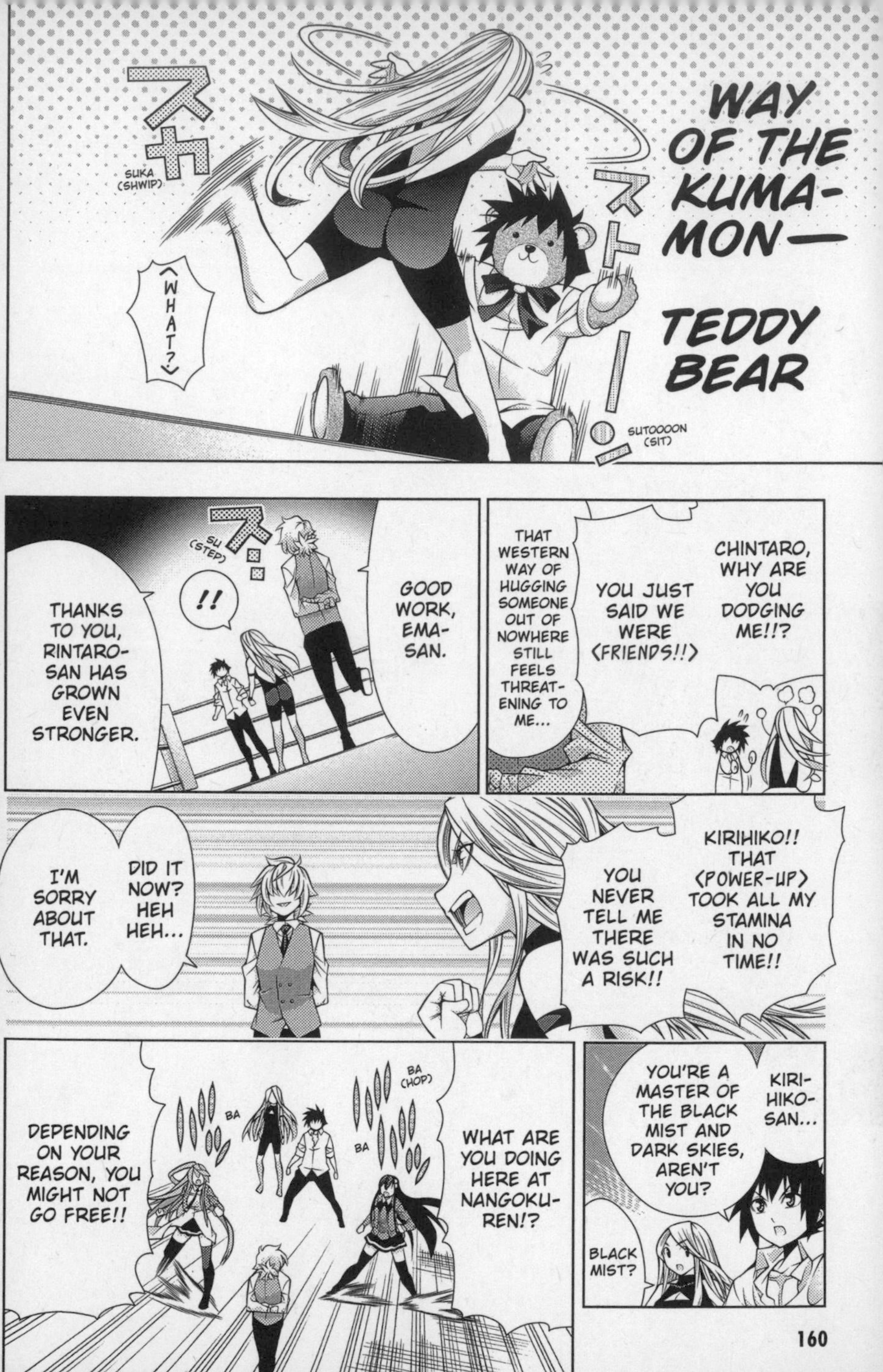
WAY OF THE KUMA-MON—
TEDDY BEAR
SUTOOOON (SIT)
SUKA (SHWIP)
〈WHAT?〉
CHINTARO, WHY ARE YOU DODGING ME!!?
YOU JUST SAID WE WERE 〈FRIENDS!!〉
THAT WESTERN WAY OF HUGGING SOMEONE OUT OF NOWHERE STILL FEELS THREAT-ENING TO ME...
GOOD WORK, EMA-SAN.
SU (STEP)
!!
THANKS TO YOU, RINTARO-SAN HAS GROWN EVEN STRONGER.
KIRIHIKO!! THAT 〈POWER-UP〉 TOOK ALL MY STAMINA IN NO TIME!!
YOU NEVER TELL ME THERE WAS SUCH A RISK!!
DID IT NOW? HEH HEH...
I'M SORRY ABOUT THAT.
KIRI-HIKO-SAN...
YOU'RE A MASTER OF THE BLACK MIST AND DARK SKIES, AREN'T YOU?
BLACK MIST?
BA (HOP)
WHAT ARE YOU DOING HERE AT NANGOKU-REN!?
BA
BA
DEPENDING ON YOUR REASON, YOU MIGHT NOT GO FREE!!

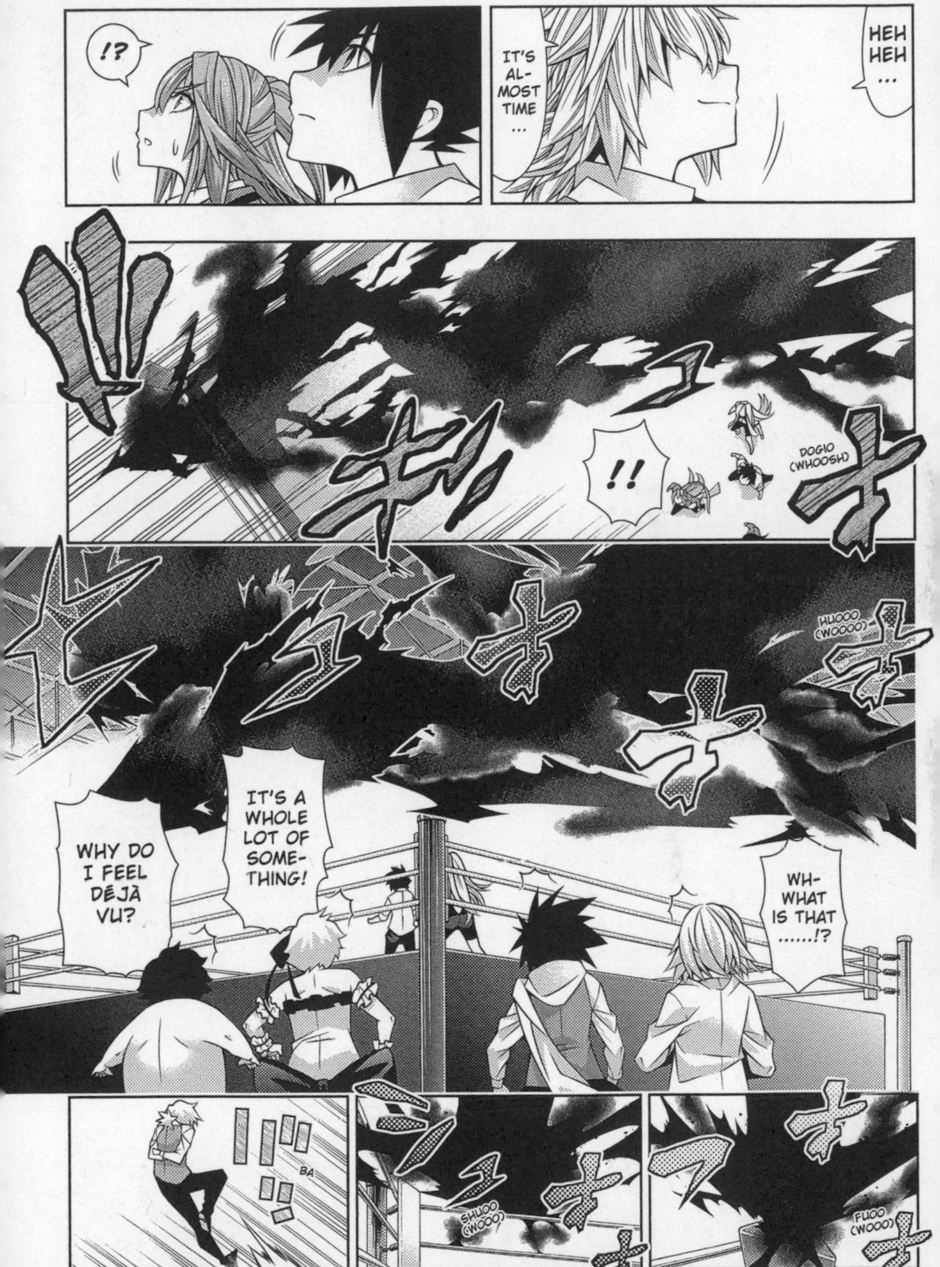
HEH HEH ...
IT'S AL-MOST TIME ...
!?
DOGIO (WHOOSH)
!!
HUOOO (WOOOO)
WH-WHAT IS THAT ......!?
IT'S A WHOLE LOT OF SOME-THING!
WHY DO I FEEL DÉJÀ VU?
FUOO (WOOO)
SHUOO (WOOO)
BA

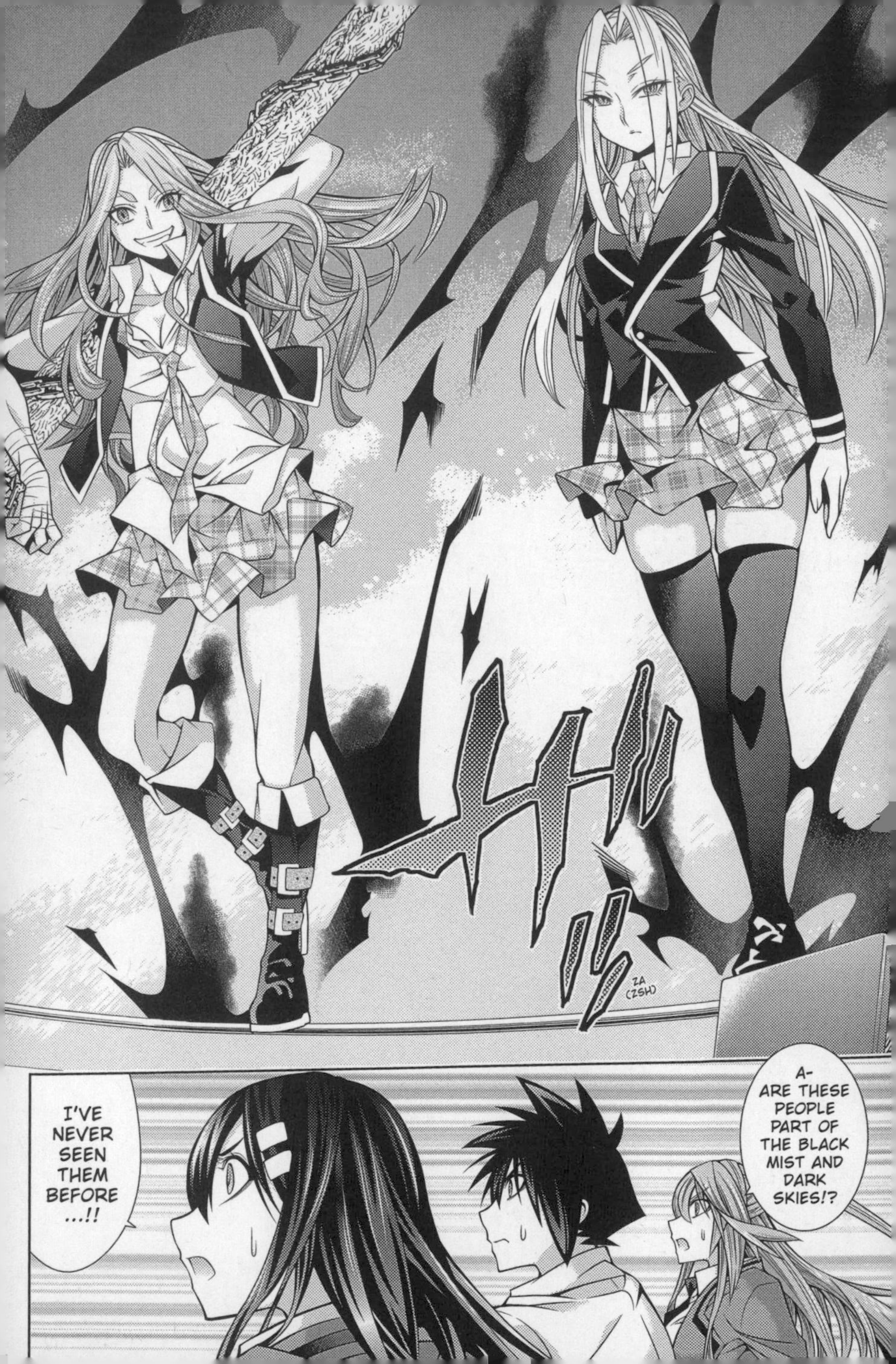
ZA (ZSH)
A- ARE THESE PEOPLE PART OF THE BLACK MIST AND DARK SKIES!?
I'VE NEVER SEEN THEM BEFORE ...!!

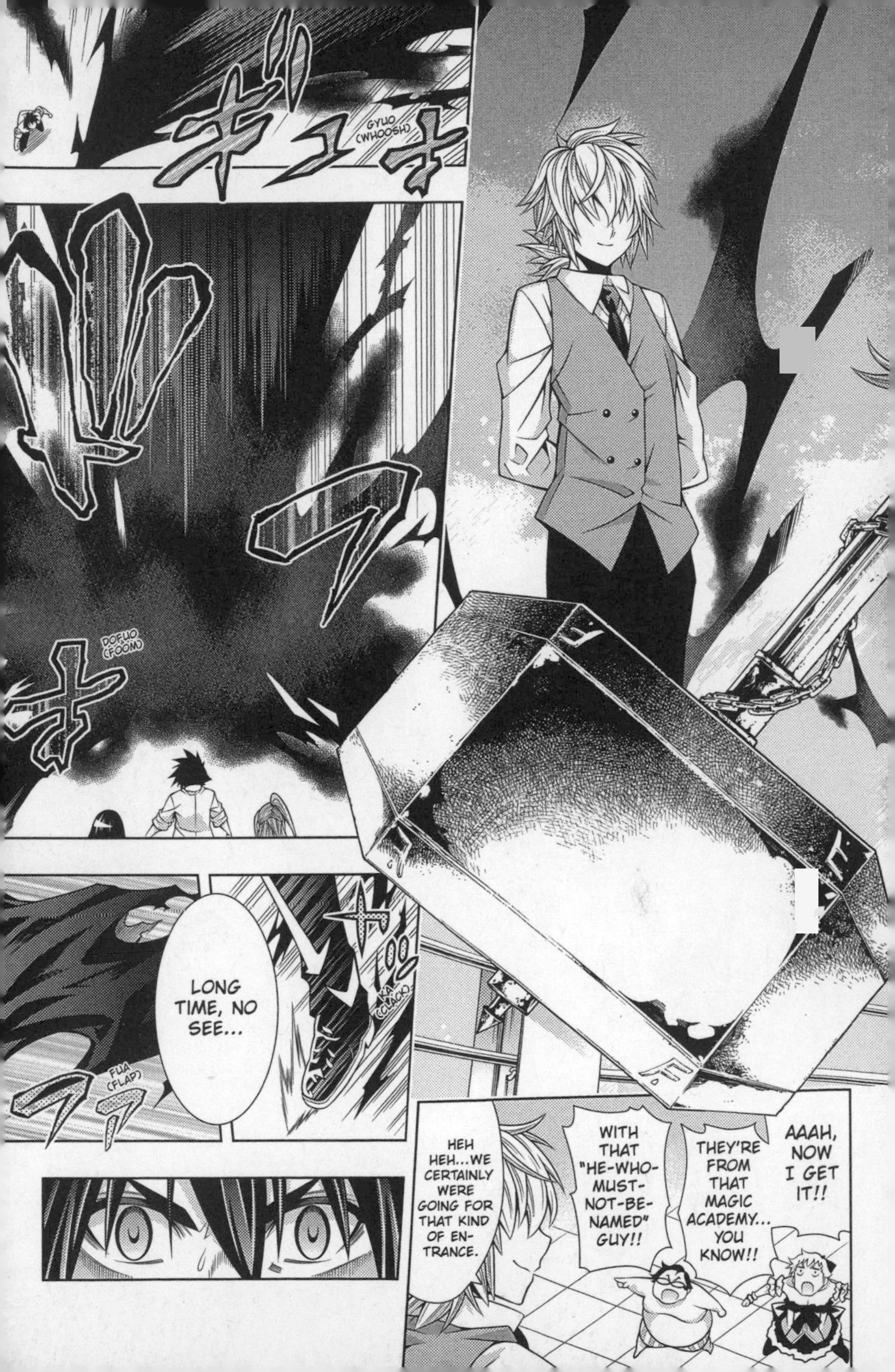
GYUO (WHOOSH)
DOFUO (FOOM)
KA (CLACK)
LONG TIME, NO SEE...
FUA (FLAP)
AAAH, NOW I GET IT!!
THEY'RE FROM THAT MAGIC ACADEMY... YOU KNOW!!
WITH THAT "HE-WHO-MUST-NOT-BE-NAMED" GUY!!
HEH HEH...WE CERTAINLY WERE GOING FOR THAT KIND OF EN-TRANCE.

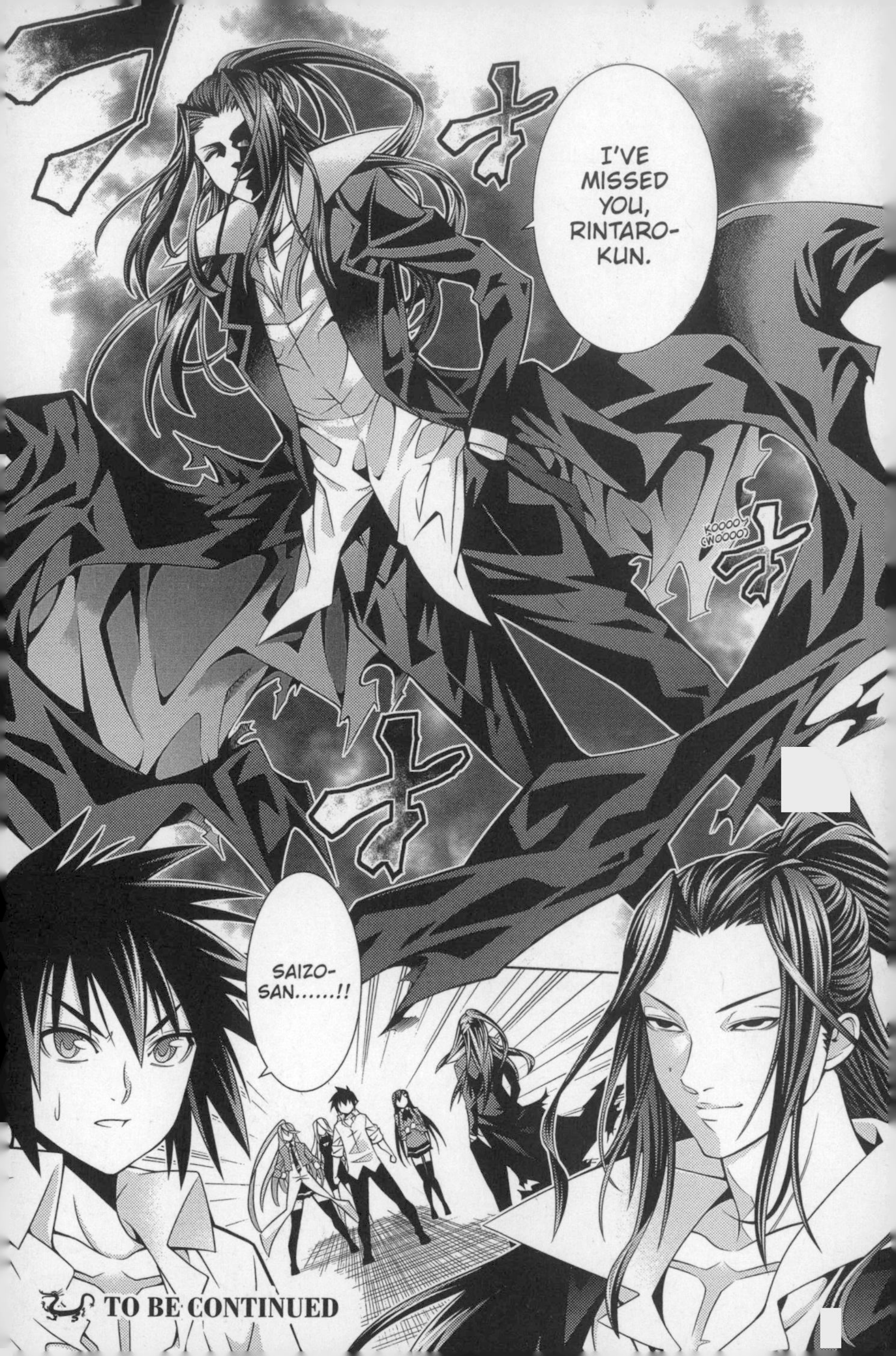
I'VE MISSED YOU, RINTARO-KUN.
KOOOO (WOOOO)
SAIZO-SAN......!!

TO BE CONTINUED

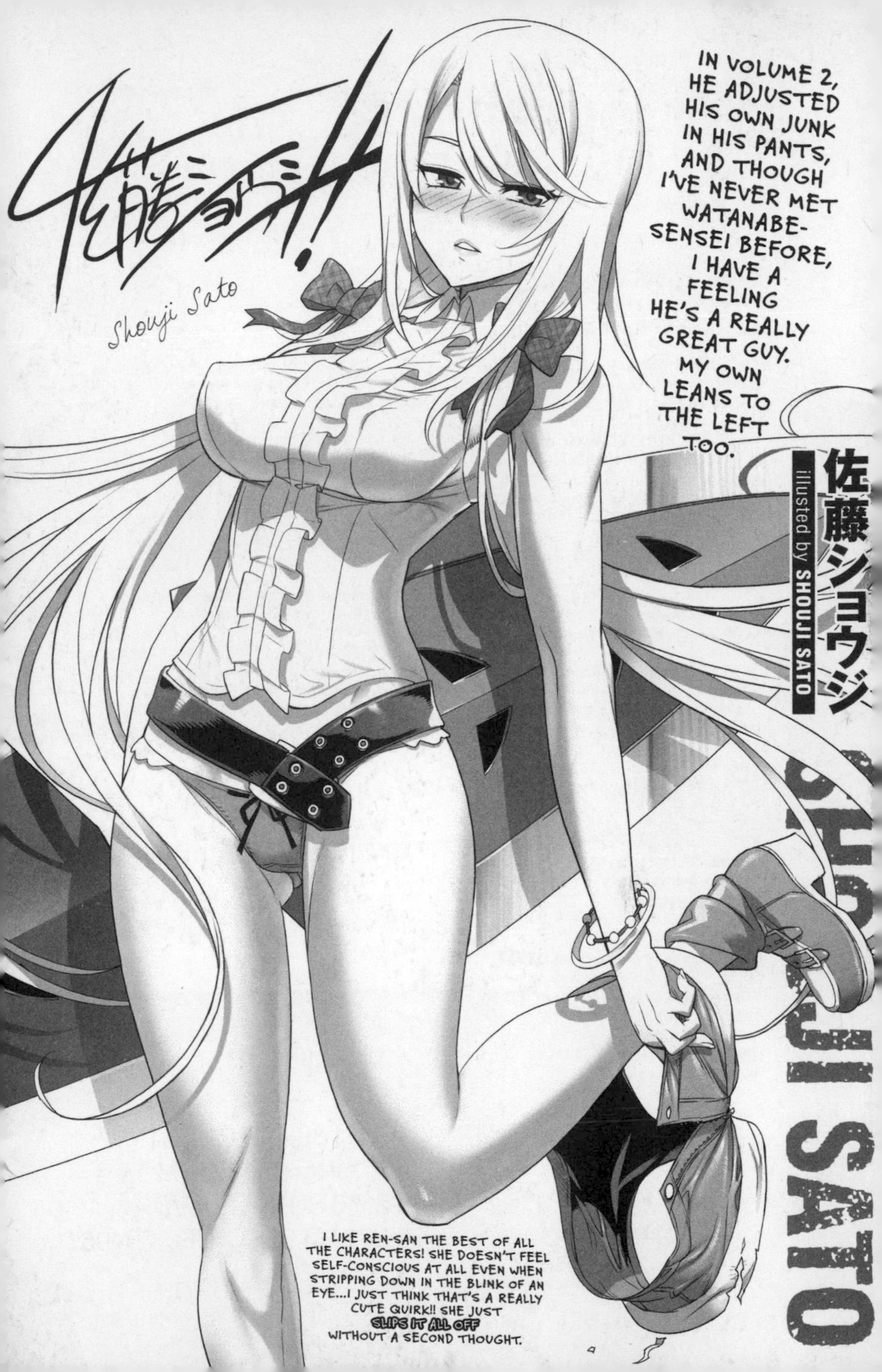
佐藤ショウジ!
Shouji Sato
IN VOLUME 2, HE ADJUSTED HIS OWN JUNK IN HIS PANTS, AND THOUGH I'VE NEVER MET WATANABE-SENSEI BEFORE, I HAVE A FEELING HE'S A REALLY GREAT GUY. MY OWN LEANS TO THE LEFT TOO.
illusted by 佐藤ショウジ SHOUJI SATO
SHOUJI SATO
I LIKE REN-SAN THE BEST OF ALL THE CHARACTERS! SHE DOESN'T FEEL SELF-CONSCIOUS AT ALL EVEN WHEN STRIPPING DOWN IN THE BLINK OF AN EYE...I JUST THINK THAT'S A REALLY CUTE QUIRK!! SHE JUST SLIPS IT ALL OFF WITHOUT A SECOND THOUGHT.

DRAGONS RIOTING ⑦

TSUYOSHI WATANABE

Translation: Christine Dashiell

Lettering: Anthony Quintessenza

This book is a work of fiction. Names, characters, places, and incidents are the product of the author's imagination or are used fictitiously. Any resemblance to actual events, locales, or persons, living or dead, is coincidental.

DRAGONS RIOTING Volume 7
© TSUYOSHI WATANABE 2016
First published in Japan in 2016 by KADOKAWA CORPORATION, Tokyo.
English translation rights arranged with KADOKAWA CORPORATION, Tokyo, through TUTTLE-MORI AGENCY, INC., Tokyo.

English translation © 2017 by Yen Press, LLC

Yen Press
1290 Avenue of the Americas
New York, NY 10104

Visit us at yenpress.com
facebook.com/yenpress
twitter.com/yenpress
yenpress.tumblr.com
instagram.com/yenpress

First Yen Press Edition: June

Yen Press is an imprint of Yen Press, LLC.
The Yen Press name and logo are trademarks of Yen Press, LLC.

The publisher is not responsible for websites (or their content) that are not owned by the publisher.

Library of Congress Control Number: 2015952605

ISBNs: 978-0-316-47090-2 (paperback)
       978-0-316-47093-3 (ebook)

10 9 8 7 6 5 4 3 2

BVG

Printed in the United States of America